W9-BGL-392

A Persistent Revolution

History, Nationalism, and Politics
in Mexico since 1968

RANDAL SHEPPARD

University of New Mexico Press | Albuquerque

© 2016 by the University of New Mexico Press
All rights reserved. Published 2016
Printed in the United States of America
21   20   19   18   17   16   1   2   3   4   5   6

Library of Congress Cataloging-in-Publication Data

Names: Sheppard, Randal, 1981– author.
Title: A persistent revolution : history, nationalism, and
politics in Mexico since 1968 / Randal Sheppard.

Description: Albuquerque : University of New Mexico
Press, 2016. | Includes bibliographical references and
index.

Identifiers: LCCN 2015028438 | ISBN 9780826356819
(cloth : alk. paper) | ISBN 9780826356826 (electronic)

Subjects: LCSH: Nationalism—Mexico—History. |
Mexico—History—1946– | Mexico—Politics and
government—1970–1988. | Mexico—Politics and
government—1988–2000. | Mexico—
Politics and government—2000–

Classification: LCC F1226.S515 2016 | DDC
972/.08/35—dc23
LC record available at http://lccn.loc.gov/2015028438

Cover photograph courtesy of the author
Composed in Saboon and Syntax

CONTENTS

Figures

Map

This book is the product of a long journey that began when, as an undergraduate, I plucked up the courage to visit the office of Barry Carr at La Trobe University in Melbourne, Australia, to discuss my interest in Mexican history and politics. Barry proved to be a more knowledgeable, patient, supportive, and generous guide than I ever could have hoped for. His suggestions, advice, and friendship during the preparation of this book have been invaluable and I cannot do justice here to his impact on my formation as a historian of Mexico other than simply to offer my gratitude.

I also had the great fortune to study under the guidance of Claudia Haake in the La Trobe History Program. Claudia demonstrated unflagging dedication to encouraging and advising me in my work and, possibly excepting me, Claudia has spent more time and energy than anyone poring over and commenting on the chapters of this book with precision and humor. Claudia has also always been a font of wisdom when it came to conference papers, journal articles, and lecturing, as well as great company when we have met up in various parts of the world. Without both Barry and Claudia, this book would certainly not have been possible and the only way I can begin to repay them for their continuing support is to dedicate this book to both of them.

The research in this book was made possible by an Australian Postgraduate Award scholarship and a La Trobe University Research Travel Grant. I would like to thank everyone in the La Trobe History Program who supported me in my teaching and research activities, including (but not limited to) Richard Broome, Roland Burke, Philip Bull, Ian Coller, Diane Kirkby, Tim Minchin, and Ingrid Sykes. A further thanks to David Harris for reading through my work and giving feedback, as well as everyone who participated in the history seminars in which I had the opportunity to present and discuss my research. I must also make a special mention of the crack administration team during my time there, Udani Gunawardena and Anita Allen.

The seminars and other activities of the Institute of Latin American Studies (ILAS) at La Trobe University provided me opportunities to present my research and receive feedback as well as benefit from the work of a wide range of international scholars. I therefore acknowledge the dedicated team of people, including Barry Carr, Stephen Niblo, and Ralph Newmark, who have kept ILAS going. I would also like to especially thank Isabel Moutinho from the Spanish Program.

At the University of Cologne, I want to thank above all my colleagues Aribert Reimann and Elena Díaz-Silva for their support, advice, and friendship as I prepared this book. My gratitude also to everyone at the Instituto de Historia Ibérica y Latinoamericana (IHILA) in Cologne for providing opportunities to engage with scholars on Latin American topics. In particular, my thanks to Barbara Potthast.

I am furthermore exceedingly grateful to Víctor Macías-González for the thoughtful engagement, detailed suggestions, and new perspectives he offered for this book, as well as for his general enthusiasm and encouragement. A big thank you, also, to Linda Hall for her comments and suggestions on this manuscript. For their rigorous and critical engagement with the research that led to this book, I also thank Jeff Browitt, Kevin Middlebrook, and Mauricio Tenorio-Trillo.

Thank you also to everyone in Mexico who helped me with my research and life in general in Mexico City during my year there and subsequent trips researching this book. In particular, my gratitude to the tireless staff at the Biblioteca and Hemeroteca Nacional who obliged my requests for newspapers based on a nationalist commemorative rather than more conventional standards of chronology. I also owe a debt of gratitude to Melbourne-based Victor del Rio for the time and effort he put into organizing my time as an International Observer during the 2012 Mexican presidential elections, as well as for all the conversations about Mexican politics.

A very big thank you to Clark Whitehorn and everybody at the University of New Mexico Press for all their hard work, enthusiasm, and patience. These include Jessica Knauss, Elizabeth Hadas, Katherine White, and Lisa Tremaine. Thank you also to the reviewers for their suggestions on how to improve the book.

I am much indebted to all my friends and family who have accompanied me in various ways as I have bounced between Australia, Mexico, the United States, Germany, and elsewhere in recent years. I won't name names in fear of leaving someone out, but I do want to offer an extra special thank you Damir Mitric and Michelle Carmody for the conversations, long lunches, and general mutual support that were intertwined with the experience of researching and writing this book.

Finally, thank you to my parents, without whose support none of this would have been possible.

CCE	Consejo Coordinador Empresarial (Business Coordinating Council)
CNC	Confederación Nacional Campesina (National Peasants' Confederation)
CNH	Consejo Nacional de Huelga (National Strike Council, 1968 student movement)
COCEI	Coalición Obrero Campesino Estudiantil del Istmo (Coalition of Workers, Peasants, and Students of the Isthmus)
Conaculta	Consejo Nacional para la Cultura y las Artes (National Council for Culture and the Arts)
Coparmex	Confederación Patronal de la República Mexicana (Mexican Employers' Association)
CNTE	Coordinadora Nacional de Trabajadores de la Educación (National Coordinator for Educational Workers)
CTM	Confederación de Trabajadores de México (Confederation of Mexican Workers)
CUD	Comité Único de Damnificados (Coordinating Committee of Earthquake Victims)
EZLN	Ejército Zapatista de Liberación Nacional (Zapatista Army of National Liberation)
FDN	Frente Democrático Nacional (National Democratic Front, 1988 electoral coalition behind Cuauhtémoc Cárdenas)
GATT	General Agreement on Trade and Tariffs
IMF	International Monetary Fund
INI	Instituto Nacional Indigenista (National Indigenous Institute)

IPN   Instituto Politécnico Nacional (National Polytechnic Institute)

NAFTA   North American Free Trade Agreement

PAN   Partido Acción Nacional (National Action Party)

PMS   Partido Mexicano Socialista (Mexican Socialist Party)

PMT   Partido Mexicano de los Trabajadores (Mexican Workers' Party)

PNR   Partido Nacional Revolucionario (National Revolutionary Party, forerunner to the PRI)

PRD   Partido de la Revolución Democrática (Party of the Democratic Revolution)

PRI   Partido Revolucionario Institucional (Institutional Revolutionary Party)

Procampo   Programa de Apoyos Directos al Campo (Program of Direct Assistance to the Countryside)

Procede   Programa de Certificación de Derechos Ejidales y Titulación de Solares Urbanos (Program for the Certification of Ejido Land Rights and the Titling of Urban House Lots)

Pronasol   Programa de Solidaridad Nacional (National Solidarity Program)

PRT   Partido Revolucionario de los Trabajadores (Revolutionary Workers' Party)

PSUM   Partido Socialista Unificado de México (Unified Socialist Party of Mexico)

Sedesol   Secretaría de Desarrollo Social (Secretariat of Social Development)

SEP   Secretaría de Educación Pública (Secretariat of Public Education)

SNTE   Sindicato Nacional de Trabajadores de la Educación (National Education Workers' Union)

SPP   Secretaría de Programación y Presupuesto (Secretariat of Programming and Budget)

UNAM   Universidad Nacional Autónoma de México (National Autonomous University of Mexico)

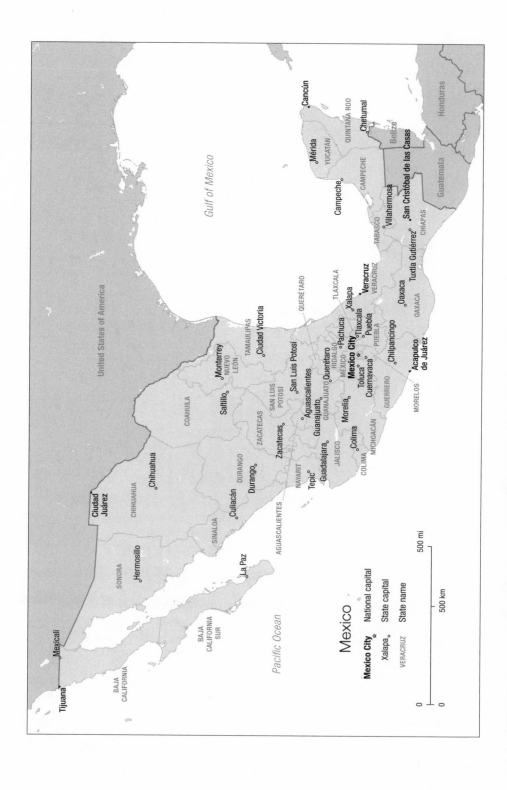

Mexico's National Epic

A t 1:00 a.m. on July 3, 2000, Mexican president-elect Vicente Fox Quesada of the conservative National Action Party (PAN) joined jubilant supporters at Mexico City's Angel of Independence monument to celebrate his election victory. The confirmation of Fox's victory hours before signified the end of over seventy years in power of the hegemonic state party formed in 1929 following the Mexican Revolution (1910–1920), called the Institutional Revolutionary Party (PRI) since 1946. There was thus a sense of historical drama as crowds gathered at the Angel of Independence chanting, "Yes, we could!" waving homemade signs supporting Fox. Those gathered also held aloft a coffin decorated with the PRI's logo and colors that were, not coincidentally, the red, white, and green of the national flag.[1] This coffin was intended to represent not only the electoral defeat of a political party, but also the symbolic death of a model that had ordered national political life in Mexico for most of the twentieth century.

The postrevolutionary Mexican state referred to throughout this book as the PRI state took its institutional shape during the 1930s and 1940s. A broadly corporatist system, the population was integrated into the state through group-based peasant, worker, and popular (which in practice meant the bureaucracy, professionals, and some teachers' organizations) sectoral organizations. The structure of this model is usually represented as pyramidal, with power flowing from the sectoral organizations through the PRI as a hegemonic state party to the powerful executive at the pyramid's peak.[2] In terms of its development model, the PRI state had traditionally played an active role in managing wage and price levels and encouraging national industrial development through mechanisms such as trade tariffs.

Following the 1982 debt crisis, successive administrations began to dismantle this political and economic model as they implemented neoliberal development policies designed to wind back the state's active role in the economy and society. However, the PRI state was built around more than a set of institutional arrangements and economic policies. A framework of historical myths and symbols promoted by the postrevolutionary state from the 1920s onward formed the basis of a revolutionary nationalism that had always been central to the postrevolutionary state's construction and routine functioning.

The great heroes of prerevolutionary, liberal nationalist frameworks were largely incorporated into revolutionary nationalism. However, postrevolutionary state- and nation-building elites adjusted their meanings. At least symbolically, revolutionary nationalism emphasized social justice by legitimizing certain social and material rights, including fair conditions for urban workers and land for peasants. National culture following the Revolution was also recast as "popular," inclusive, and distinctly Mexican. The institutions of the postrevolutionary state, including its corporatist sectoral organizations, complemented this symbolic framework as an idiom for political inclusion, the lack of which had been one of main the catalysts for the Mexican Revolution.

According to the historical narrative of revolutionary nationalism, Mexico's history had been driven forward by a series of great ruptures that propelled the nation into new, superior stages in its history. The three great ruptures of Mexico's national narrative were the independence struggle from 1810 to 1821, the liberal Reform of the mid-1850s to the late 1860s, and the Mexican Revolution, which began in 1910 and lasted until roughly 1920. This national narrative was progressive and teleological, legitimizing the Mexican state as the culmination of the historical struggles of past generations.

During the nineteenth and twentieth centuries, the ruptures that structured this narrative of the national epic were cast in bronze on and around the grand central stretch of the Paseo de la Reforma. Built during the nineteenth century to resemble the grand boulevards of Europe, this section of Reforma runs through the heart of the national capital from Mexico City's historic center to the Bosque de Chapultepec park.[3] Providing a comprehensible picture of Mexico's past and an end of history that led to its "revolutionary" present, revolutionary nationalism was a resolutely modern discourse that suggested a controlled and orderly future for a nation propelled forward by the always vaguely defined but vigorously defended principles of the Revolution.

Fox's victory in 2000 represented the culmination of a series of institutional, political, and economic reforms that occurred in fits and starts from the 1970s onward and came to form the basis of a new democratic nationalist mythology that traced its origins to government repression of student protestors in 1968. From the 1980s into the first two decades of the twenty-first century, popular pressure for democratization had, according to this new mythology, led to the dismantling of the corporatist hegemonic state party in favor of a pluralistic system in which multiple political parties competed for power. While I will discuss the impact of political and economic reform in the coming chapters, this is not chiefly an institutional history of the Mexican state, nor a history of economic ideas or demographic shifts. Instead, I examine Mexico's post–1968 history primarily through the lens of nationalism as one of the chief frameworks through which this history has been debated and understood at both an elite and popular level.

The choice of the Angel of Independence as the backdrop to Fox's victory celebrations was representative of how competing political actors strategically appropriated nationalist imagery to communicate their messages to a national audience as the PRI state disintegrated. Inaugurated by President Porfirio Díaz on September 16, 1910—the official centenary of the beginning of Mexico's independence insurgency— *el Ángel* commemorates the heroes of Mexico's struggle for independence (fig. I.1). Both the Angel and the Paseo de la Reforma served as sites for rituals designed to reinforce the state's legitimacy under the PRI, such as patriotic ceremonies and the annual Independence Day military parade. They also served as favored sites for spontaneous popular celebrations including soccer victories, as well as for protest marches that directly challenged the state's legitimacy. However, the relationship between a state and its memorials is not one-sided. Instead, monuments take on a life of their own once built and are subject to popular reinterpretation over time in ways that can challenge or resist the state's original intention.[4] This is also true of nationalist myths and symbols more generally.

The Fox campaign's intended message for Mexicans this time was one communicated throughout his campaign: that a Fox victory, like independence, signified a moment of rupture that would propel Mexico forward into a new and superior democratic stage of its history. Fox's government was not, however, able to simply will a democratic update to the national epic into existence, a desire reflected by Fox's 2005 proposal that the anniversary of his victory be commemorated annually as "Democracy Day." A turbulent twelve years of PAN rule ended with the PRI winning back the presidency in 2012 under Enrique Peña Nieto.

Figure I.1. Mexico City's Angel of Independence on the Paseo de la Reforma was a site for official and popular rituals of commemoration, celebration, and protest. Photo by author.

While Peña Nieto also situated his victory within a democratic narrative of Mexican history, this narrative did not celebrate July 2, 2000, as its main turning point. Instead, in his inaugural address President Peña Nieto cited the legacy of October 2, 1968, when a previous PRI administration had overseen the massacre of student protestors in Mexico City, as signifying a rupture that led to Mexico's democratic present.[5] During that year's presidential campaign, however, opposing candidate of the center-left Party of the Democratic Revolution (PRD), Andrés Manuel López Obrador, also used the mythology of 1968 to portray the potential return of the PRI to the presidency as an authoritarian regression.[6] The mythology of 1968 and Mexico's democratic transition thus exhibited a characteristic that had always been central to revolutionary nationalism: it provided a language of contestation as well as consent.

The term *mythology* is used throughout this book in reference to Mexican history and nationalism. However, this is not intended to imply falseness. Mythology is best described as a language used to make a complex world intelligible rather than one intended to deceive. As

French semiologist Roland Barthes argued, mythology functions as a system of communication that uses familiar images to communicate certain meanings.[7] Mythology therefore draws upon various sources of prior awareness to create what may be a simplified and idealized, but not inherently false, picture of the world.

In fashioning their revolutionary nationalist mythology, postrevolutionary nation- and state-builders drew upon local histories of rebellion, oppression, and productive relations with the state in a flexible and interactive fashion in villages and towns across Mexico. Once their meanings were broadly agreed upon, national heroes were evoked by elites and popular classes as mutually understood symbols through which they could communicate and negotiate over material issues such as access to land or labor conditions. This meant that, even if elite actors such as government officials promoted revolutionary nationalist discourse to legitimize their hold on power, it also became interwoven with popular cultures and legitimate popular demands, such that revolutionary nationalist myths and symbols could at times be used to resist the application of elite power or to contest state policy.

Statues of revolutionary heroes were therefore not toppled in the aftermath of the PRI's defeat in 2000. National holidays such as Revolution Day, mid-nineteenth-century liberal hero Benito Juárez's birthday, and Independence Day also remained part of Mexico's civic calendar. What mood did exist for iconoclasm directed at the heroes of revolutionary nationalism appeared mostly confined to intellectual circles, or groups that had maintained a counter-hegemonic conservative identity throughout the postrevolutionary period.

What had changed substantially by 2000 was the relationship between Mexico's hegemonic nationalism, the meaning of citizenship, and the institutions of the state. This process began prior to Fox's election, during the economic instability of the 1970s. In particular, following the 1982 Mexican debt crisis, successive Mexican governments embraced a neoliberal development model that unsettled the state's relationship with revolutionary nationalist mythology and associated collective citizenship rights. In response, independent social movements, opposition political parties, and armed insurgents in the case of the 1994 uprising of the Zapatista Army of National Liberation (EZLN) appropriated national myths and symbols such as the Mexican Revolution and its heroes, including Emiliano Zapata and Lázaro Cárdenas, to challenge the PRI's hold on power and, in many cases, its neoliberal reforms. Conservative opponents from the PAN, meanwhile, favored invoking revolutionary hero Francisco Madero and his struggle against the Porfirio Díaz regime to symbolize a nationalist democratic tradition that challenged PRI dominance of state institutions without necessarily contradicting neoliberal economic and social reforms enacted by post-1982 PRI administrations.

In this way, history and nationalist mythology have often been explicitly intertwined with debates over institutional and policy reform in Mexico. In the following chapters, we will see how the shared symbolic framework of revolutionary nationalism helped shape the boundaries within which different actors, ranging from state officials and private businesspeople to peasant groups, sexual minorities, and residents of poor urban neighborhoods, understood their interests and negotiated relations of power or access to resources from 1968 to the early years of the Peña Nieto administration. This includes the development in Mexico of a concept of democracy involving individualized notions of civil and political rights, a relatively novel concept following a postrevolutionary era when citizenship rights in Mexico were conceived of in collective terms.

Linking the Nation to the State

As the Paseo de la Reforma arrives at Mexico City's historic center, it comes to an intersection between the Avenida Juárez that leads into the historic center and another—the Avenida de la República—that heads westward and is dominated by the imposing Monument to the Revolution (fig. I.2). This monument is a solid stone structure built in an art deco style and topped with a bronze dome. Above its four columns are figures representing independence, the Reform laws, agrarian laws, and labor laws.[8] Dedicated in 1938, the Monument to the Revolution was built around the rusting framework of a legislative palace planned by the Díaz regime before it was overtaken and overthrown by the Mexican Revolution that began on November 20, 1910. When postrevolutionary state- and nation-builders commissioned a monument to commemorate the historical rupture in which they most directly located their own origins and legitimacy, they chose to sculpt into this monument representations of the past great ruptures of independence and the liberal Reform. The Monument to the Revolution thus provides a striking example of how the postrevolutionary state may have recast Díaz as a villain in Mexico's historical narrative but also built upon the

Figure I.2. Mexico City's Monument to the Revolution, seen from the junction of Avenida de la República and the Paseo de la Reforma. Photo by author.

framework laid down under his rule when constructing revolutionary nationalism.

The figures built into the structure of the Monument to the Revolution also provided a representation of the framework of class-based identities—specifically those of peasants and workers—that were central to revolutionary nationalism. These identities were associated with demands for collective citizenship rights symbolized in revolutionary nationalist discourse by great national heroes such as Zapata and Juárez and codified into the liberal and revolutionary constitutions. Revolutionary nationalism, in this way, provided a direct link between history, identity, citizenship, and the state, mediated through the great heroes of the past.

Revolutionary myths and symbols were therefore not simply bronze heroes Mexicans had been taught to admire. Instead, they symbolized the rights of groups and individuals that had been earned through historical struggles and that the state also symbolically (if often not practically) recognized. It was also through such heroes that Mexicans often debated the rights and obligations of both state and society implicit in the definition of Mexican citizenship as well as the extent to which this citizenship existed as a status versus a practice.[9] Institutionally, the corporatism of the postrevolutionary state was organized according to these identities.

The corporatism of the PRI state is defined here broadly in accordance with the definition of state corporatism developed by neo-corporatist theorists such as political scientist Philippe Schmitter. Under this system society is divided into a limited number of hierarchical and noncompetitive sectoral organizations. In return for a monopoly on representing a particular group, the state exercises certain controls, such as the selection of leaders or demands for political support. The state also plays the dominant role in coordinating these interests, with its role understood as ensuring economic and social order in the formulation of public policy.[10]

In postrevolutionary Mexico, not all sectors of society were equally integrated into the corporatist model. For example, representatives of big business were never granted an official sectoral organization despite requests. Other forms of interest representation and political rule also existed alongside and within corporatist mechanisms. Historian Jeffrey Rubin has, for example, highlighted the uneven presence of the state across Mexico's territory when suggesting the dominance by caciques, or political bosses, as more relevant than corporatism for understanding politics in many regions of Mexico under the PRI state.[11] However, corporatism was integral to the functioning of the postrevolutionary Mexican state. This importance was not solely or even principally due to the extent to which the corporate sectors practically integrated the masses into the state, but to the way in which a corporatist idiom of limited collective identities provided a cognitive framework of "legitimate" political interests and set boundaries within which negotiations between state and society over citizenship rights could take place.[12]

The close link between revolutionary nationalism and postrevolutionary state formation has meant that judgments about this state have tended to shape how historians have understood both revolutionary nationalism and the Mexican Revolution itself. Until the 1960s, the dominant view of historians about the Revolution was that it had been a genuinely popular uprising and, while its shortcomings were well noted, the postrevolutionary state was understood to represent a reformist and nationalist advance on the prerevolutionary Porfirian state.[13] During the 1960s and particularly following the 1968 Tlatelolco massacre, however, a growing number of historians came to see the postrevolutionary state as an authoritarian "philanthropic ogre" that used a combination of patronage and repression to underwrite its rule.[14] This encouraged a revisionist approach that challenged the Mexican Revolution's popular nature. Revisionist historians now emphasized what they broadly described as the PRI state's Machiavellian manipulation, exploitation, and repression of popular classes behind a false façade of revolutionary nationalist legitimacy.[15]

Despite such challenges to its legitimacy and a series of severe economic crises during the 1980s and 1990s, the PRI state and revolutionary nationalism showed a remarkable capacity for survival. Indeed, political historian Soledad Loaeza noted amid the post-1982 atmosphere of perpetual crisis that the relative stability of Mexico's political model despite public expressions of discontent was "the great enigma of Mexican political life."[16] While it had undeniably authoritarian features, the PRI's continued rule after 1968 seemed to rely most heavily on a significant and at times seemingly inexplicable degree of popular consent or at least resignation. The need to understand this enigma encouraged the development of a postrevisionist interpretation of Mexico's postrevolutionary history that provides the historical foundation for this examination of Mexican history after 1968.

For postrevisionist historians seeking to understand Mexico's general stability amid crisis without frequent or flagrant recourse to violent repression, the idea of consent and Antonio Gramsci's theory of hegemony was particularly suggestive. Hegemony is defined here in its broadest sense as a form of rule that includes the use of coercion, but which depends on the cultivation of consent through cultural means that permeate society and reinforce power structures.[17] Beginning in the late 1980s, historians of Mexico such as Alan Knight, Stephen Lewis, Catherine Nolan-Ferrel, and Mary Kay Vaughan applied the concept of hegemony to analyzing the foundations of the PRI state's rule. They found this rule to be based on a complex and multidirectional dynamic, involving a combination of popular revolt during the Mexican Revolution followed by subsequent processes of reform and negotiation as well as the selective deployment of coercive measures.[18]

Postrevisionist Mexican historians were further influenced by a growing body of literature aimed at understanding the symbolic aspects of state formation that became a topic of increasing interest for scholars during the 1980s.[19] Philip Corrigan and Derek Sayer's historical sociology of English state formation, *The Great Arch*, was a particularly influential work on this topic.[20] Corrigan and Sayer looked at how forms of social order were historically constructed and thus naturalized through what they defined as "a project of normalizing, rendering natural, taken for granted, in a word 'obvious,' what are in fact ontological and epistemological premises of a particular and historical form of social order."[21] This process of "moral regulation" was the social action (such as education, persuasion, and indoctrination) undertaken by state-building elites aimed at legitimizing the state form by naturalizing it through a process of cultural transformation. The resulting state form can also be understood as a symbolic accomplishment, with even apparently technical aspects of its functioning, such as banking systems or birth and death registries, having a cultural component.[22]

In Mexico, the moral ethos that naturalized the postrevolutionary state's routine functioning involved presenting the state as a representation in the present of the struggles and sacrifices of past generations of patriots, particularly those of the Independence, Reform, and Revolutionary struggles. One of the most novel aspects of postrevolutionary state formation compared to the prerevolutionary Porfirian state was the attention its architects paid to creating a nation-state in the sense of a cultural framework that would unite the entirety of the population to the institutions of the state, involving a mutual recognition of legitimacy between state and nonstate actors as well as at least the potential for a mutually beneficial negotiated relationship between the Mexican state and people.[23] The state promoted this cultural framework through an extensive calendar of patriotic civil celebrations, monuments, historical texts and research institutions, public instruction, the education system, and the use by government officials of a highly commodified political discourse of revolutionary myths and symbols. The cultivation of the myth of the Revolution and the public image of its main protagonists as national heroes was central to this framework, with the PRI state portrayed as the institutional manifestation of the will and interests of Mexico's "revolutionary majorities."[24]

Contrary to the neoliberal myth of the state as an oppressive leviathan, part of the reason the postrevolutionary state made such efforts to negotiate its reforms and win broad popular consent was its weakness. Knight, for example, disputes revisionist portrayals of the reformist Cardenista state of the 1930s as a steamroller that moved across Mexico enforcing its reforms, instead arguing that the postrevolutionary state resembled a jalopy more than it did a juggernaut.[25] The postrevolutionary state in fact demonstrated a weak real ability to implement its reform agenda when faced with strong and sustained resistance by local elites, meaning it often had to negotiate its expansion across the national territory. While such negotiations undoubtedly involved force and unequal power relations, they also included incentives such as legal, financial, and political support to local elites and organizations that allied with the PRI.[26]

Rubin's examination of the politics in the region around Juchitán, Oaxaca, during the 1970s and 1980s further highlighted the ongoing presence of regional counterweights to the national state's power under the PRI and the importance of multiple, everyday negotiations of power in cultural as well as political and economic spheres. According to Rubin, the PRI's hegemony was less absolute than revisionists had supposed and even electoral processes were an occasion for far livelier debates than a superficial glance at the traditional electoral hegemony of the PRI would indicate.[27] Thus, while the PRI's hegemony definitely existed, Rubin has argued that it was always full of holes, resembling swiss cheese.[28]

Understanding the postrevolutionary state as a jalopy with swiss cheese hegemony does not deny the use of authoritarian mechanisms to support the PRI state's rule. The ultimately successful revolutionary nationalist nation- and state-building project further involved distinct combinations of reform, repression, and negotiation in different parts of Mexico. However, the construction of revolutionary nationalism as a hegemonic nationalist framework can, in a general sense, be described as, in the words of Knight, a struggle in which "the common people of Mexico were both victims and participants."[29] It is this historical dynamic that led revolutionary nationalism to win undoubted popular legitimacy as a language of negotiation and helps to explain its survival beyond the political system with which it was originally associated.

Revolutionary nationalism set broad cognitive boundaries that contained what were considered legitimate courses of political action, both for elite and popular actors. These boundaries became central to how politics was conducted in Mexico during most of the twentieth century and encouraged significant continuities into the twenty-first. Even the PAN, with its ties to counter-hegemonic Catholic conservative nationalism, increasingly cultivated an association with revolutionary nationalist mythology as it sought to build popular support during the 1980s. During the first decade of the twenty-first century, PAN administrations also continued to face opponents brandishing nationalist symbols such as Lázaro Cárdenas to oppose plans for deepening free market reform. That such political battles continued to play out through the mainstream media, drawing public intellectuals and particularly historians into policy debates, demonstrates the need to understand the politics of history and nationalism in order to understand how politics functions more generally in Mexico.

In this book, I draw upon such insights gained from postrevisionist Mexican history and general theories of state formation to provide an interpretation of Mexican political history since 1968. This was not a period of dramatic revolution or state-building, but one in which the Mexican state sought to manage crisis and a political transition that increasingly became what geographer and social theorist David Harvey calls a process of neoliberal "creative destruction," through which the state organizes its retreat from rather than expansion into many areas of public life.[30] On the one hand, revolutionary nationalism played a role in helping to maintain social stability under the rule of the national state. On the other, the Mexican state had to deal with the symbolic boundaries of revolutionary nationalism as a framework that contained its scope for movement, thereby helping to shape how both neoliberal and democratizing political reform were implemented in Mexico.

Understanding the Mexican Nation

Facing away from the Avenida de la República on which the Monument to the Revolution stands, across the intersection with the Paseo de la Reforma, is the Avenida Juárez, which leads toward Mexico City's historic center. On the Avenida Juárez is located another of Mexico's most iconic patriotic monuments, the Juárez Hemiciclo (fig. I.3). Díaz dedicated this monument that pays tribute to Benito Juárez two days after the Angel of Independence. A struggle for power between liberals and conservatives had been a permanent feature of Mexican politics since independence in 1821 and, in 1872, governing liberals named the Paseo de la Reforma to commemorate the Reforma (Reform) period of civil war, foreign invasion, and liberal reforms out of which the liberals had recently emerged victorious. This ultimate liberal victory under the leadership of Juárez meant that it was to be liberal national heroes and narratives that shaped the hegemonic nationalism promoted by the Porfirian state and would later be built upon by postrevolutionary elites.

As Mexican electoral politics became increasingly plural during the 1980s and 1990s, Juárez remained perhaps the most divisive of revolutionary nationalism's heroes. This was due to Juárez's association with

Figure I.3. The Juárez Hemiciclo in Mexico City during a 2008 political rally led by Andrés Manuel López Obrador, then a member of the center-left PRD. Photo by author.

mid-nineteenth-century conflicts between liberals and conservatives, particularly the expansion of secular state institutions to the detriment of the Catholic Church's institutional power. By the 1990s all major Mexican political parties embraced a broadly liberal conception of politics that included support for the ideal of the secular state.[31] Juárez, in a broader sense, had also come to symbolize liberal state institutions and respect for the rule of law. When President Ernesto Zedillo appeared on televisions across Mexico on July 2000 to announce the effective end of PRI rule, he therefore chose to communicate the democratic convictions of the Mexican government and people while standing in front of a portrait of Benito Juárez in the presidential residence of Los Pinos.[32]

However, as the PAN began to win power, those within the party who identified with Catholic conservatism periodically caused controversy by casting doubt on Juárez's truly heroic status and patriotism, provoking strong criticism from the media and officials in the PRI and the relatively new center-left PRD. Juárez, the icon of Mexican liberalism and Mexico's most popularly acclaimed national hero, was thus still a figure of hostility for many who identified with a counterhegemonic conservative Catholic nationalism into the twenty-first century, even as many conservatives broadly agreed with the PRI's practical embrace of neoliberalism. On the other hand, the pro-neoliberal PRI administrations and largely antineoliberal PRD opposition united in their defense of Juárez. The division over the figure of Juárez in this way reveals the importance of identity in political conflict and decision-making in Mexico.

As historian Eric Van Young has argued, there is a danger of over-determinism in using materialist historical interpretation to explain the actions of groups or individuals. Van Young thus suggested that historians "launch our causal arrows" in the other direction to begin with questions such as collective mental representation, religious world view, constituent elements of group identity, and political culture, and to work from there to understand forms of collective political action.[33] By taking revolutionary nationalism as the lens through which to view post-1968 Mexican history, I explore how established notions of identity and meaning helped to shape the way in which Mexico experienced and adapted to the neoliberal age as well as the associated "third wave" of democratization in Latin America and Eastern Europe during the 1980s and 1990s.[34]

Reifying culture can also lead to a form of cultural overdeterminism that presupposes a fixed cultural reality impervious to influence from conjunctural forces, persuasion, or, indeed, material pressures. As I am focusing on the way in which nationalism articulates cultural identity to citizenship, I examine changing institutional and economic power structures alongside nationalist discourse in a way that allows for a coaction between material structures and meaning systems.[35] In this respect, I understand culture and cultural practice as a medium that pervades social orders—including economic and political practice—rather than as a reified force or discrete and exotic lumps that can be separated out and decoded from other forms of social relations.[36] Such a position helps to make sense of the heated debates about figures such as Juárez during the 1990s and 2000s that seem to have no direct material implications for their protagonists.

The success of nationalism as a hegemonic framework that established the popular plausibility of Mexico as a nation is borne out by the fact that no major actors sought to secede from or challenge the idea of Mexico as a nation-state during the period of this study. As happened with the expanding literature on state formation, during the 1990s scholars of Latin American history began to consider theories of nationalism developed in relation to non–Latin American case studies to understand how this form of social organization came to have meaning in the region. Among the prominent theorists of nationalism, Benedict Anderson and Eric Hobsbawm most noticeably influenced the ensuing debates over the role of the nation in Latin American culture and politics.

Hobsbawm's work placed a modernist emphasis on the construction of nationalism as interrelated with elite-directed projects of industrialization and capitalist development. In his most influential work on the topic, Hobsbawm focused on the development of "invented traditions," or rituals that, through repetition and reference to the past, were used by elites to naturalize what were deemed appropriate values for a nation's citizens.[37] In a region where the state is understood to have preceded and then created the nation, this constructionist theory has obvious appeal.

In this book, I take annual commemoration ceremonies such as the highly ritualized Independence Day celebrations as a major focus of examination. The invented traditions of Mexican nationalism center around an extensive calendar of patriotic festivals that, from the president emerging on the balcony of the National Palace to issue the *grito* (cry) on Independence Day to the annual sporting parade on Revolution Day, proved remarkably resilient. What particularly characterized these dates under the pre-2000 PRI administrations was the explicit nature of appeals to historical continuity to legitimize the sectoral and hierarchical organization of the postrevolutionary state and its political program.[38] Such appeals to history became increasingly explicit during times of crisis when the need to maintain group cohesion across a diverse territory became particularly acute, as "if the conflicts [or problems] of the present seemed intractable, the past offered a screen on which desires for unity and continuity . . . could be projected."[39] The heroes and events of the past thus provided the form for what is in reality a mythologizing of current power relations rather than of history, resulting in the paradoxical attempt to depoliticize a political party through a revolutionary "end of history," of which the PRI state was the natural outcome.[40]

The dynamic of negotiation that underpinned revolutionary nationalism's popular legitimacy, however, suggests that Hobsbawm's ideas are only partially relevant to Mexico. Particularly following the 1982 debt crisis, a new generation of state elites adapted the language of their commemorative speeches and historians offered reinterpretations of the national history as existing social arrangements were weakened by neo-liberal reform and demographic change. Nevertheless, these established nationalist myths and symbols appeared to be something of a straight-jacket from which even the post-2000 PAN administrations were unable to completely break free. The difficulty of reinventing established traditions highlights the way in which state-promoted nationalism gained legitimacy through dialogue and negotiation, meaning that it went through a process of popular appropriation on its route to popular acceptance. For this reason, nationalist mythology could be projected back at elites from below to challenge or renegotiate the state's legitimacy.

Anderson's *Imagined Communities* outlined a more nuanced theory of nationalism. His ideas are useful for this study, as they have been for the study of Latin American nationalism more generally, due to the way he acknowledges the nation as a hegemonic sociological construct. While strongly connected to the forces of modernity and capitalism, Anderson views nationalism as functioning through an ongoing process better described as collective imagining than elite manipulation.[41] Whereas nineteenth-century French intellectual Ernst Renan's famous treatise on the nation described it as a form of "daily plebiscite," Anderson argued that nationalism functioned in a more innate, subconscious fashion than a plebiscite would suggest.[42] A nation's existence still, however, depends on the extent of its ongoing plausibility for its members.

Anderson also moved away from the preoccupation with the falseness or genuineness of the nation often present in earlier debates over nationalism.[43] As historian Mauricio Tenorio Trillo put it, "debating the falseness or authenticity of nations resembles discussing what God really looks like. In our post-Nietzschean era God has died and we understand this, but we know that nevertheless he/she somehow exists and is part of our understanding of the world."[44] In a similar sense, whether a Mexican state preceded a Mexican nation does not diminish the importance of nationalism to how Mexicans understand their own place in the world.

Claudio Lomnitz's influential critique of *Imagined Communities* has further expanded understandings of Mexican nationalism.[45] Lomnitz found Anderson's description of the nation as a community always imagined to be horizontal and fraternal in nature to be highly problematic. Instead, he drew attention to a characteristic feature of Spanish American nationalism: the interrelation between bonds of fraternity and dependence, and weak citizens and strong citizens.[46] Similarly, collectivist institutions such as indigenous communities, haciendas, and guilds have been important in how the Mexican nation has traditionally been imagined as a series of interrelated institutions and collectivities. In Lomnitz's view, the precise nature of bonds of fraternity and citizenship are important to the study of nationalism because "it is in the articulation between citizenship and nationality that various nationalisms derive their power."[47] The focus of this book is the dynamics of this link between citizenship —understood as legitimate rights and responsibilities—and revolutionary nationalist cultural identity and the insights this dynamic provides to the study of post-1968 Mexican politics and history.

Existing studies of revolutionary nationalism, most notably those of Ilene O'Malley and Thomas Benjamin, have primarily focused on how it developed and was used in an instrumentalist sense to reinforce the power of the postrevolutionary Mexican state.[48] Looking more closely at popular uses of revolutionary nationalism, a 2008 book by Samuel Brunk compellingly examines the *Posthumous Career of Emiliano Zapata*.[49] Anthropologist Lynn Stephen has further explored the relationship between nationalism and political action through reference to Zapata in rural Oaxaca and Chiapas during the 1990s based on a historical examination of how state educational and agrarian institutions socialized peasants into the nation during the 1930s and 1940s.[50] However, Brunk and Stephen focused on a specific hero that represented one, albeit important, aspect of revolutionary nationalism's role in left wing and particularly peasant politics.

Indeed, the evocative case studies of Zapata and the 1994 "neo-Zapatista" EZLN uprising have dominated the work of scholars who have examined the politics of Mexican nationalism since the 1980s.[51] Illustrative of the gap between what may be of most interest to foreign scholars and that which is most relevant to Mexicans themselves is the scholarly neglect of Benito Juárez as a Mexican national hero. An April 2011 poll found Juárez to be by a wide margin the national hero with whom Mexicans most identified.[52] The previous month, Google also announced that Juárez had consistently been the most searched for Mexican national hero since tracking began in 2004, except when during the September and November 2010 bicentenary of independence and centenary of the Revolution he was briefly overtaken by search requests for independence hero Miguel Hidalgo and the revolutionary Zapata.[53] Despite this, since Charles Week's 1987 work *The Juárez*

Myth in Mexico, no major study has been published exploring the significance of Juárez as Mexican nationalist mythology.[54] Similarly, it was not EZLN figurehead Subcomandante Marcos who defeated the PRI in 2000. Instead, Vicente Fox, a conservative, Catholic businessman from the PAN became the face of Mexico's democratic transition. Yet there has been no detailed study so far of the relationship between conservative nationalism and revolutionary nationalism in the context of the PRI state's decline.

In the following chapters, I therefore extend the discussions of the relationship between nationalism, politics, and culture in Mexico beyond the more obviously evocative examples of revolutionary heroes and left-wing politics to include perspectives usually excluded. In particular, I examine how conservative identities, Catholicism, and private enterprise played a crucial role in shaping Mexico's political transition. Leaving such perspectives out would, I argue, simply reinforce the relatively restricted framework of acceptable collective identities promoted by the postrevolutionary state and ignore the ways in which forces such as religion or transnational discourses of democracy played a role in the continuous construction of a hegemonic Mexican nationalism during the period under study. In terms of transnational discourses of democracy, I also consider the emergence of new categories of legitimate political identities with attendant citizenship rights based on gender or cultural and sexual diversity. This topic, however, deserves far more detailed analysis than I have been able to include here.

Organization of This Book

When writing about nationalism and how it interacts with political, social, and economic changes, I faced a situation similar to that of Tenorio Trillo when writing his engaging history of Porfirian nationalist representations at world's fairs: a need for "constant interaction between a general, provocative, abstract, and speculative realm and a concrete, empirical, and temporally and spatially confined domain." I am indebted to his example in providing a conceptual model for writing a history that allows the reader to "shift from account to account, detecting concepts, characters, or arguments that gradually become familiar."[55] Some subjective selection is necessary to deal with a topic as vast as Mexican politics and nationalism, so I have chosen to concentrate on the political use of certain national heroes such as Juárez, Cárdenas, and Zapata as well as national holidays such as Independence Day and Revolution Day that will become familiar to readers as they weave through the text. These heroes and dates have been chosen on the basis of their prominence, permanence, or divisiveness in the context of Mexico's post-1968 history and the ways in which they can shed light on the major political and social developments of the period.

Each chapter begins with what I call a "snapshot," which is a narrative account of a given conjuncture that I judged particularly evocative and representative of one or more of the themes discussed within the chapter. By immersing the reader in a narrative account of a particular conjuncture before undertaking a more thematic analysis of the period, I hope to provide both greater context for the analysis as well as a richer feel for the mood(s) of the period being discussed. The chapters themselves are not strictly divided into presidential terms (called *sexenios* in Mexico) so much as contexts in which different aspects of how nationalism was woven into Mexican politics came most clearly into view. In a general sense, however, the need to give a coherent and comprehensible picture of the themes and events has led me to structure my analysis of post-1968 history in a way that moves forward through time in a roughly linear sense.

I begin this study with a snapshot examining the mythologizing of the state repression of the student movement of 1968 as the starting point for a new, arguably hegemonic, though heavily contested, narrative of Mexican history that arose during the final two decades of the twentieth century. The chapter then explores how the concept of a Mexican national identity came to have popular meaning from independence until the 1960s. Through this analysis, revolutionary nationalism is revealed as a discourse with deep historical roots that combines questions of culture and identity with material concerns as a framework of negotiation between elite and popular as well as local and national actors.

The second snapshot describes the last triumphant gasp of revolutionary nationalism: the nationalization of the Mexican banking system by President José López Portillo in September 1982. Chapter 2 then focuses on how the state used revolutionary nationalist discourse to legitimize its power in the aftermath of the 1982 debt crisis. I provide context for Mexico's neoliberal transition by examining the changes in domestic elite networks and international ideological currents that assisted the shift toward a neoliberal development model in Mexico beginning in the 1970s. The focus then shifts to historical commemoration ceremonies to explain how the state sought to legitimize the PRI's continued hold on power amid economic crisis, neoliberal reform, and austerity measures.

Snapshot 3 describes the heated 1986 campaign for the governorship of the northern state of Chihuahua between the PAN and PRI. Within the chapter, I describe the rise of an increasingly assertive conservative opposition during the 1980s that had as its most visible face the PAN, but also involved significant participation by ecclesiastical authorities and private enterprise. I then discuss the relative weakness of the Mexican left and the contrasting rise of civil society movements as an alternative mechanism of negotiating power and access to resources in Mexico through reference to identity and citizenship rights. Finally, I detail the split in the PRI and 1988 presidential campaign to show how a movement seeking a return to revolutionary nationalist values led by Cuauhtémoc Cárdenas became the biggest electoral threat to the PRI by 1988.

The fourth snapshot shows how the protest movement sparked by allegations of electoral fraud against Cárdenas in 1988 spilled over into that year's Independence Day ceremonies. In chapter 4, I examine the connection between the institutional framework of the state and nationalism by exploring the most novel attempt at adapting revolutionary nationalism to neoliberalism: the social liberalism of the Carlos Salinas presidency (1988–1994). While social liberalism initially appeared remarkably successful, the limits of this administration's ability to reshape popular understandings of Mexican nationalism is also revealed through an examination of the controversy caused by government attempts to change school history textbooks.

Snapshot 5 details the explosion of the neo-Zapatista EZLN insurgency in Chiapas on the day the crowning achievement of Salinas's modernizing reforms—the North American Free Trade Agreement (NAFTA)—was due to come into effect. Chapter 5 then looks at the connection between class and racial identities to the notion of collective rights within revolutionary nationalism and how this shaped popular responses to neoliberal reform, particularly in the context of the EZLN uprising. This includes examining how the racial ideas established in revolutionary nationalism were mixed with new, transnational discourses of freedom, democracy, and multiculturalism by peasant and indigenous groups to contest access to rights such as political autonomy and resources such as land.

The final chapter brings together the issues of nationalism, political pluralism, and neoliberal reform to understand the nature of Mexico's political transition in 2000 and the return of the PRI to the presidency in 2012. Snapshot 6 explores the problematic celebration of the bicentenary of Mexican Independence and the centenary of the Revolution under President Felipe Calderón (2006–2010). The chapter then shows how nationalist symbols were woven into the political battles of the Ernesto Zedillo administration (1994–2000) as opposition parties began to win greater spaces of power. The contested nature of Mexico's democratic transition and the post-2000 presence of revolutionary nationalism is then explored in the context of disputes over electoral results, the persistence of corruption and impunity in state institutions, weak economic growth, mass violence unleashed by the Calderón administration's war with drug cartels, and the PRI's return the presidency in 2012.

The national and international press widely reported the defeat of the PRI's candidate in the 2000 elections as the confirmation of Mexico's transition to democracy and, as one Mexican newspaper headlined its front page, a "good-bye to the PRI."[56] With the PRI no longer in Los Pinos, the "Revolución hecha gobierno" (Revolution made government) formula that tied national identity to the institutions of the state through revolutionary nationalism also appeared to have died a final death. Peruvian novelist Mario Vargas Llosa described this transition the day following Fox's victory as being one from a "perfect dictatorship" to a "difficult democracy."[57] What exactly this democracy would be beyond difficult was, however, unclear. The post-election front cover of weekly newsmagazine *Proceso* reflected this uncertainty, showing an image of the coffin decorated in the colors and logo of the PRI held aloft by Fox supporters at the Angel of Independence with the headline, "And now what?"[58]

Amid the triumphalism and uncertainty that greeted the PRI's defeat in 2000, the Revolution, Zapata, and Juárez remained ever present in the Mexican popular imagination and political discourse. The PRI itself survived defeat in 2000, and won back the presidency after only two terms in opposition. The nation also remained central to how people in Mexico and beyond understood the world in an early twenty-first-century era of free-trade agreements and cultural globalization. When historians, politicians, activists, and ordinary people tried to explain, understand, and challenge the various crises and transformations that accompanied the collapse of the old certainties of the PRI system, they indeed often turned precisely to the nation and its history for guidance. In the chapters that follow, we will look at these continuities that belied talk of a great rupture in 2000. We will also see how different actors called upon the great heroes and myths of the national history and attempted to promote new ones in the struggle to construct a post-PRI state Mexico as a way of understanding history as not just a process of institutional, economic, or demographic shifts but also a process of continual conflict and negotiation in the construction of collective meanings.

Dos de octubre no se olvida

During the 1980s and 1990s, the massacre of student protesters on October 2, 1968, by state security forces in Mexico City became a standard reference point for writers, historians, politicians, activists, and others from across the political spectrum as a symbol of the authoritarianism of the PRI state. While there is much room to debate its practical impact or popular resonance at the time, there is little doubt about the symbolic importance of the massacre that took place in the Plaza de las Tres Culturas in the Mexico City neighborhood of Tlatelolco for understanding twentieth-century Mexican history. More than any other single event, Tlatelolco came to symbolize a historical rupture that set Mexico on the path to democracy by shattering the benevolent façade of the PRI state.

The Tlatelolco massacre's symbolic power was strengthened by its proximity to the October 1968 Mexico City Olympiad. Hoping to use the Olympic Games as a showcase for Mexico's rise to the status of a stable and modern nation under the PRI's rule, the Mexico City Olympic Organizing Committee chose peace and friendship as the central themes of the games. The aesthetic sensibility of the Olympic iconography was suitably modern and progressive, most strikingly displayed in the games' logos of "Mexico '68" composed of concentric circles to provide the sensation of motion typical of the contemporary op art style (fig. 1.1).[1] The contrast between modern graphic design, streets lined with banners featuring silhouettes of a white dove—the other main symbol of the games—and the decidedly unmodern and nonpeaceful state violence toward student protesters on the streets of Mexico City was thus powerfully stark.

The escalation of the 1968 student protests themselves can be traced most directly to the violent intervention of riot police in a July 1968 conflict at the National Polytechnic Institute (IPN) in Mexico City. This

Figure 1.1. A model demonstrates the outfits designed for tour guides at Mexico City's 1968 Olympic Games featuring the op art logo through which organizers hoped to project a modern image of Mexico to the world. Courtesy Bettman/ Corbis.

set in motion a chain of events in which conflicts between university students and the government escalated during the following months into mass protests that met with a violent response from state security forces.[2] As the Olympic Games approached, the Mexican government grew increasingly nervous at the prospect of world attention being focused not on an orderly and modern capital city, but on running street battles between the government and students. Ominously, President Gustavo Díaz Ordaz (1964–1970) warned on September 1 during his annual presidential address to the nation—called the *informe*—that "we have no wish to see ourselves in a position that will mean taking measures that we do not want to take, but that we will take if necessary; whatever it is our duty to do we will do, whatever lengths we are obliged to go to, we will."[3]

On the night of October 2, ten days before the opening ceremony of the Olympic Games, the government acted on that threat. A crowd of roughly ten thousand students gathered during the late afternoon in the Plaza de las Tres Culturas to listen to political speeches and protest continuing government repression. The crowd challenged the PRI's plan to use the Olympic Games as a showcase of Mexico's modernity, with one of the recurrent chants of the 1968 student movement being "we don't want the Olympics, we want revolution!"[4] As the meeting came to an end, white-gloved security officers and tanks began to appear at the plaza's exits while soldiers watched over the scene from their positions on surrounding buildings. At roughly 6:10 p.m., shots began to ring out across the plaza.[5]

The Díaz Ordaz government claimed, and the news on private television monopoly XEW dutifully reported, that students fired at government troops first. Eyewitnesses, however, told of a helicopter flying low over the crowd and dropping two flares—one red and one green—before soldiers stationed on surrounding buildings began to fire on the crowd below.[6] As gunfire rained down, the crowd broke apart and tried to flee. However, a never-confirmed total generally considered to number over one hundred people were killed.[7] When the shooting stopped, members of the "Olympic Battalion" paramilitary group created by the government to provide security for the Olympic Games moved in. They swept through surrounding homes and buildings, rounding up protesters, whom they beat and arrested.[8]

While the Tlatelolco massacre was by no means the first example of violent repression by the PRI state, Tlatelolco was unique in that repression was directed at a movement largely made up of the urban middle class rather than peasants or workers.[9] Furthermore, the violence occurred in the heart of the national capital, in view of the national and international media. The tension this caused between educated middle classes—particularly urban intellectuals—and the postrevolutionary state was decisive in the subsequent mythologizing of 1968 as a turning point in contemporary Mexican history.[10]

In the decade following the massacre, the arts and sections of the press provided spaces for these critical voices to take aim at the PRI state. While television and newspaper reports on the evening of October 2 and in the following days minimized the number of deaths and generally blamed students for the violence, student and other left-wing political organizations supported by sympathetic cultural figures protested and kept memories of the massacre alive. Journalist and novelist Elena Poniatowska's collection of testimonies regarding the student movement and massacre, *La noche de Tlatelolco* (The Night of Tlatelolco, 1971), became one of the most read accounts of the student protest and continued to be reprinted into the twenty-first century.[11] Octavio Paz, another icon of twentieth-century Mexican literature, resigned as Mexico's ambassador to India in protest of the massacre and became a vocal supporter of the liberal democratic cause in Mexico.[12]

During the 1970s, annual commemorations of the Tlatelolco massacre took place, organized by students and teachers from Mexico's major universities. The principal demands of the marchers were freedom for political prisoners, an end to government repression, and that the massacre not be forgotten. The last demand led to the phrase most associated with this movement: "2 de octubre no se olvida."[13] During this decade, Tlatelolco commemorations remained small-scale. As the PRI attempted to distance itself from the public display of state violence at Tlatelolco, it largely ignored the marches. The Mexican state did, however, continue to wage a "dirty war" through the 1970s against the extra-parliamentary left, some of whose members had joined guerrilla movements in the aftermath of the massacre.[14]

Following electoral reforms in 1977, the PRI successfully channeled much of this left-wing opposition back into the institutions of the state by legalizing parties such as the Mexican Communist Party (PCM) and opening greater spaces for opposition parties within institutions such as the legislature. Among new parties of the left, both the Mexican Workers' Party (PMT) and Revolutionary Workers' Party (PRT) located their origins in the 1968 student movement.[15] Following this political opening, the commemoration of Tlatelolco became increasingly ritualized. Opposition parties and other left-wing social organizations that experienced greater state toleration became increasingly central actors in 1968 commemorations, using the marches to denounce government repression of left-wing activists as well as appealing for electoral support.

By the early 1980s Tlatelolco commemorations generally involved a march from the Plaza de las Tres Culturas to the Zócalo, where antigovernment speakers would address the crowds in the shadow of the National Palace. Marches also took place in major cities outside the capital, particularly those with large university student populations, such as Puebla.[16] However, the ritual of commemorating 1968 reinforced the rising symbolic importance of Mexico City and the city more generally to notions of national identity following Mexico's rapid urbanization during the postrevolutionary period.[17]

Independent worker and peasant movements united their contemporary economic and social demands with the demands of the 1968 movement in slogans, banners, and speeches. For example, in 1984 protesters called for a just salary and an end to rising prices alongside the traditional calls to free political prisoners and end government repression.[18] The first public appearance of a unified gay and lesbian movement in Mexico occurred at the commemoration of the tenth anniversary of the Tlatelolco massacre in 1978, with marchers connecting calls for an end to political repression associated with the date to their own calls for an end to police harassment and persecution of gay and lesbian Mexicans.[19] Another leading twentieth-century intellectual of the Mexican left, writer and journalist Carlos Monsiváis, described October 2, 1978, as holding its own symbolic importance for Mexican sexual minorities as "the date of an opening of urban tolerance, restricted as possible, but irreversible."[20]

During the 1980s, national newspapers gave significant coverage to the marches and more directly acknowledged the events of October 2 as a massacre than during the 1970s.[21] Such coverage was important in shaping and diffusing a standard interpretation of the significance of the date throughout Mexico as a rupture in Mexican history that set Mexico on the path toward democracy. For example, an editorial in left-leaning newspaper *Unomásuno* argued on the fifteenth anniversary of the massacre that following Tlatelolco, Mexico was no longer the same.[22] A 1984 headline in the generally progovernment newspaper *Excélsior*, meanwhile, proclaimed that "the popular movement of 1968 awoke the civic consciousness of Mexico."[23]

An extensive number of books and articles by historians, political scientists and ex-leaders of the movement examining the events of 1968 also began to emerge during the 1980s. By the massacre's twentieth anniversary books dealing with 1968 had indeed come to form something of a subgenre of Mexican writing that crossed the borders of history, memoir, politics, and literature.[24] Mexican filmmakers also began to deal with the events of 1968 and their aftermath, most notably in *Rojo amanecer* (1988) and *El Bulto* (1992), the latter of which dealt with the 1971 assassination of student activists during the Luis Echeverría administration (1970–1976) by state agents in the Jueves de Corpus violence. While both movies faced some government censorship, they eventually found cinematic release.[25]

The anniversary of the Tlatelolco massacre also became a date for debate and reflection in the increasingly plural Mexican congress. On October 2, 1984, left-wing Unified Socialist Party of Mexico (PSUM) federal deputy and political philosopher and historian Arnaldo Córdova cited the student movement of 1968 as a watershed in Mexican politics that led the PRI to open some democratic spaces to ensure its own survival.[26] Conservative political groups also embraced the anniversary of Tlatelolco as a date for renewing calls for democratic reform. PAN deputy Alberto Ling Altamirano used his intervention in the congress on October 2, 1984, to call on Mexicans to fight in order to make sure that the Tlatelolco massacre was not repeated.[27] Another important political actor in Mexico, the clergy, by this time used the association between 1968 and a fight for democracy to make public pronouncements on October 2 calling for greater state tolerance of political action by ecclesiastical authorities.[28]

For the new technocratic PRI leadership of the 1980s, the mythology of Tlatelolco also served some legitimizing purpose for reducing the state's role in the economy. Members of the PRI began to refer to the Tlatelolco massacre on its anniversary as a turning point that had led to democratic reforms that were part of their current political agenda.[29] In 1986 the PRI even chose the date of October 2 to announce a new wave of reforms aimed at giving greater representation to smaller parties in the legislature.[30] The mythology of Tlatelolco in this way provided a new generation of PRI leaders a language for expressing measured self-criticism to differentiate the current administration from the excesses of past PRI administrations and legitimize contemporary reform measures. The example of the massacre was also cited by those arguing for the need to channel political debate into state institutions rather than the "violence" of independent protest movements.[31]

By the early 1990s the mythologizing of 1968 was linked above all with calls for democracy. At least superficially, by this time a discourse of democracy bridged ideological divides between mainstream political parties competing for power in Mexico. While pro–free market conservative groups embraced this democratic discourse as early as the mid-1970s, the formation of a new center-left Party of the Democratic Revolution (PRD) in 1989 marked a later and more or less definitive turning point for parties of the left away from a language of socialism and revolution toward a focus on achieving democracy. During the 1990s, commemorations of 1968 thus often included calls to continue a "fight for democracy" attributed to the 1968 student movement from all major political parties.[32]

As the discourse of democracy became increasingly hegemonic in Mexico, the commemoration of 1968 become increasingly public and mainstream. On the massacre's twenty-fifth anniversary in 1993, the Carlos Salinas administration (1988–1994) permitted the construction of a monument to the students of 1968 in the Plaza de las Tres Culturas (fig. 1.2). Government officials did not, however, attend its unveiling.

Figure 1.2. Members of dissident teacher union National Coordinator for Educational Workers (CNTE) commemorate the fallen of October 2, 1968, at the monument to the victims of the Tlatelolco Massacre during a 2013 protest march. Courtesy Eneas De Troya.

Enthusiasm for commemorating Tlatelolco reached its peak around the massacre's thirtieth anniversary in 1998. This was also a time of heightened democratic exuberance, as one year earlier the PRI had for the first time lost control of the Mexico City government and its majority in the Federal Chamber of Deputies. The upcoming 2000 presidential elections also appeared to hold the potential for a definitive "transition to democracy" with the end of PRI rule. In 1998 Mexico City bookstores thus reported that the multitude of new and republished texts dealing with the events of 1968 were among the year's best sellers.[33] Photos were also released showing then-president Ernesto Zedillo (1994–2000) being accosted by state security forces during 1968, reinforcing the president's claims of a democratic and antiauthoritarian vocation.[34]

One of the most high-profile examinations of the events of 1968 during 1998 was a documentary broadcast on the highest rating channel of the Televisa television consortium. The documentary was produced by historian Enrique Krauze, a leading figure in public debates over the need to reinterpret Mexican history in the service of democratization. While this program was part of a longer series called *México Siglo XX* (Twentieth-Century Mexico), Krauze explained the choice of

"Díaz Ordaz and 1968" for the first episode as intended to prove his seriousness in producing a show that was "designed from the beginning to push democratic change of television and from television."[35] Demonstrating an interpretation of 1968 in tune with antistatist neoliberal discourses of freedom, Krauze described the cause of the violence as "the clash between a libertarian youth and an authoritarian president."[36]

Televisa had, in fact, historically served as one of the key institutions that supported hegemonic PRI rule, having evolved from the XEW network that broadcast censored news of the massacre in 1968. The previous year, Emilio Azcárraga Milmo, Televisa's president since 1972 and son of the company's founder, had died, signaling an apparent end of an era. However, his son, Emilio Azcárraga Jean, succeeded him as company president. Moreover, while Televisa no longer enjoyed a monopoly over commercial television in Mexico, the state had only licensed one competitor, TV Azteca.[37] Mexican commercial television had thus made a relatively small jump from monopoly to duopoly and Televisa had been passed down from father to son.

A continued concentration of media ownership in Mexico and the close relationship between the major television consortiums and the state hinted at the limits of electoral reform in pluralizing Mexican politics. Krauze, an enthusiastic public advocate for democracy and at the time a member of the board of Televisa, however, offered as proof of the new Televisa president's democratic sincerity that it had been Azcárraga Jean himself who had suggested that *México Siglo XX* should begin with an examination of 1968.[38] This proved a popular decision, as the episode was remarkably successful when broadcast on April 26, 1998, and achieved ratings comparable to those of a soccer game.[39]

That a television documentary about government repression of student protesters in 1968 was broadcast on Mexico's most powerful television network and was a ratings success thirty years after the fact is a testament to Tlatelolco's symbolic elevation as a central turning point in Mexico's twentieth-century history by 1998. Despite being largely a symbol of the left during the 1970s, Tlatelolco by the 1980s was also mythology of the right. Those on the right projected the aim of achieving of democracy in the face of an authoritarian state onto the student movement of 1968 whose democratic demands, they argued, could only be fulfilled through the dismantling of the PRI state. However, Tlatelolco simultaneously served as a mythology of the left, deployed by those such as the PRD, who supported political opening but opposed the neoliberal retreat of the state from interventionist economic and social policies.

The development of Tlatelolco as a revisionist national myth demonstrates both the importance and complexity of myth to how the nation, the state, and the connections between them are imagined in contemporary Mexico. More than for its direct practical repercussions, the importance of October 2, 1968, in Mexican history lies in its elevation as a new point of rupture in a nationalist historical narrative built around such ruptures traditionally portrayed as periodically correcting the nation's march toward progress and modernity. The myth of the Revolution that dominated pre-1968 Mexican political discourse had symbolized both a rupture and kind of "end of history" that resulted in the postrevolutionary state. Understanding the importance of the Tlatelolco massacre to Mexican history therefore involves appreciating how Mexicans came to understand this importance. Similarly, understanding the importance of the historical nationalist myths and symbols amongst which the events of October 2, 1968, came to sit necessarily involves understanding how and why they came to be remembered, understood, and renegotiated.

CHAPTER ONE

Imagining and Inventing Mexico

M any of the myths and symbols that gave revolutionary nationalism its power as a way to imagine Mexico as a nation with a
shared past, present, and future had their roots in Mexico's prerevolutionary history. The evolution of these myths and symbols and how
they gained legitimacy reveals much about the evolution of the overarching political and cultural systems that have historically structured
Mexico as a nation. This chapter focuses on how the revolutionary
nationalist framework promoted by the PRI state gained its symbolic
legitimacy by first looking at how Mexico as a country that emerged
from colonial rule geographically, linguistically, and ethnically divided
came to resemble the modern ideal of a nation-state. Such an historical
background demystifies terms such as *nation* and *nationalism* that, like
democracy, are often used even in scholarly work in an offhand fashion
as established facts with little indication of how (or if) they came to
have any popular meaning.

In this chapter, I introduce many of the historical myths and symbols
that recur in subsequent chapters and explain how they became part of
a hegemonic symbolic framework for imagining Mexico as a nation
through interactions between cultural, political, and material forces.
This dynamic helps explain why nationalist myths and symbols continued to feature so prominently in Mexican political debates as economic
crisis and the transnational currents of neoliberal ideology undermined
old certainties from the late 1960s onward. It also provides clues as to
why no iconoclastic popular rejection of the heroes and myths with
which the PRI was most closely associated accompanied the party's electoral defeat in 2000.

¡Vivan los héroes que nos dieron patria!

According to the narrative of Mexican history promoted by the postrevolutionary state, Mexico's march forward as an independent nation
began with the "Grito de Dolores" of "father of the *patria*" and Catholic priest Miguel Hidalgo in the town of Dolores, Guanajuato, on September 16, 1810. On this date, Hidalgo rang the bells of the parish
church to assemble the town's residents and call on them to join his
uprising with a rousing indictment of the Spanish colonial government.
The call of this independence movement—collectively known as the
Insurgentes (Insurgents)—did inspire significant popular mobilization,
with thousands of largely rural followers such as peasants, hacienda
peons, artisans, and miners participating in the spectacular and bloody
military battles of the ensuing war.[1] Many of the symbols employed—
though not invented—by the Insurgentes, such as the image of an eagle
on a nopal cactus attacking a snake, also became fundamental symbols
of Mexican national identity.[2] However, the process through which this
narrative was structured and these symbols came to have popular
meaning was prolonged and tightly interwoven with the outcomes of
later political battles during the nineteenth century.

While the Insurgente struggle and leaders are today privileged in the
official narrative of Mexican independence, the Trigarante (Three
Guarantees) army led by former royalist general Agustín de Iturbide
played the dominant role in the final stage of the conflict that achieved
Mexico's formal independence in 1821.[3] Formed as a coalition dominated by ex-royalist troops and elites, Iturbide led those who wished to
retain as much as possible of the colonial political and social order once
the decline of Spanish viceregal authority appeared irreversible. These
conservative forces allied with the battle-weary Insurgentes with the
shared goal of making a final, ultimately successful military push
against colonial authorities.[4] Iturbide then rode into Mexico City on
September 27 to declare Mexico an independent nation and the following July was crowned Constitutional Emperor of Mexico.[5]

Mexico had, however, emerged from colonialism poorly integrated
in an economic, political, cultural, and geographical sense and the
majority of the population had a weak sense of national affinity.[6] An
ongoing essentially inter-elite conflict between two broad groups that
came to be known as liberals and conservatives, supporting different
conceptions of the political and cultural organization of the nation,
ensured that the Mexican state remained weak and unable to serve as a

unifying force for much of the first half-century of Mexico's post-independence life.[7] The prevailing conservative ideal for Mexico's political model involved a centralized state unified behind the domestic and international legitimacy of a (preferably European) monarch.[8] The liberals, meanwhile, sought to emulate the republican federalist model of the United States, reduce the size of state bureaucracy, attack corporate privileges, enshrine freedom of the press and religion, guarantee the rule of law, and expand education.[9]

Divisions between liberals and conservatives extended to disagreement over which national heroes should be venerated and the most appropriate date for celebrating Mexico's independence. Liberals traced their lineage to and thus venerated the exploits of the Insurgente heroes and celebrated the anniversary of the grito of Hidalgo as Mexico's Independence Day. While displaying little affinity for the contemporary indigenous population, liberals also promoted a narrative of independence that portrayed Spanish colonialism as a period of brutal, repressive, and backward rule while using the glories of the indigenous (Aztec) civilization to symbolize native American genius. In this narrative, the Insurgente struggle was linked to Aztec resistance against Spanish rule, most notably symbolized by the heroic resistance shown by the last Aztec ruler, Cuauhtémoc.[10] Conservatives, meanwhile, privileged Mexico's Catholic and Hispanic heritage in their interpretation of the national history and proposed the entry of Iturbide into Mexico City as the date of Mexican independence.[11]

Reforming and Restoring the Republic

The general failure of liberals and conservatives to settle on a definition of political sovereignty left successive governments largely impotent in the face of frequent uprisings and subversive plots that arose in local contexts with national implications. Furthermore, a poorly integrated national economy and the state's ruinous finances made Mexico's long-term economic survival precarious.[12] Mexico's disastrous defeat in the Mexican-American War (1846–1848), in which the country lost roughly half of its territory to the United States, marked a significant turning point in this context that further sharpened debates between liberals and conservatives as Mexico's survival as an independent country seemed increasingly doubtful.

At heart, both conservative and liberal groups aimed to build a viable state that could unify Mexico's territory in a political and economic sense and so achieve the stability, prosperity, and international esteem necessary to avoid the nation's disintegration and subjugation to foreign rule. Both groups also inextricably connected the fate of the nation as a cultural community to that of the state to the extent that they often described armed rebellions following the Mexican-American war as threats to Mexican nationality.[13] However, disagreements over which models of political organization and national identity would best resolve Mexico's political and cultural disunity remained deeply entrenched.

Civil war thus broke out between liberals and conservatives in the post–Mexican-American War decade. The increasingly centralist and dictatorial nature of the final Antonio López de Santa Ana (1853–1855) government sparked a liberal response in the Revolution of Ayutla (1854), following which Mexico again lurched into a period of mass violence known as the War of Reform (1857–1861).[14] United behind the banner of the Constitution of 1857, liberals led by Benito Juárez ultimately emerged victorious and began to implement a new code of citizenship through a series of laws dubbed the Reform Laws.[15]

The Reform Laws broadly sought to increase the modernizing state's exclusive administration of a range of functions by usurping those of existing institutions.[16] The most powerful competing institutions were the military and, particularly, the church, which both had their legal privileges revoked by the liberal government. Despite forming the basis for an enduring Catholic conservative hostility to the myths and symbols of the Reform period and the figure of Benito Juárez in particular, nineteenth-century liberal anticlericalism in this sense implied a secularization of the state and an expansion of its authority over national life rather than an outright repudiation of Catholicism.[17]

In a general sense, the aim of the liberal government was to bind Mexicans together in a single framework of citizenship rights under a federalist state. Indigenous communal property and distinct corporate privileges that had existed since colonial times were thus a target for liberal reformists. The prevailing liberal attitude to the indigenous population was that it existed outside of the civilized nation, but could be redeemed and thus permitted to "progress" with the nation through modernizing instruction that would permit participation in the marketplace and exercise of liberal citizenship rights.[18] Liberal officials used methods such as surveying and mapping coupled with onerous taxation of communal lands in an attempt to force indigenous communities to disband and privatize established systems of communal land holdings in a project as much aimed at social engineering as economic development or state-building.[19]

Connecting the *Patria Chica* to the *Patria Grande*

Initial liberal victory in the Reform War did not in itself resolve Mexico's political fragmentation and instability. Conservative groups continued to resist the application of the new laws and, in the aftermath of their defeat in the Reform War, looked abroad for support. The conservatives found a willing collaborator in French Emperor Napoleon III, who used the pretext of a moratorium announced by President Juárez in 1861 on debt repayments to France, Great Britain, and Spain to launch a successful invasion of Mexico and appoint Austrian Archduke Ferdinand Maximilian of Hapsburg as Mexico's second emperor. This period is described by historians as the French Intervention or Second Mexican Empire (1864–1867). Liberals formed a government in exile led by Juárez and continued to implement the Reform Laws and Constitution of 1857 where it held power while militarily resisting Maximilian's rule.

The Mexican state from independence to the Reform War generally had an at most fragmentary presence through much of Mexico. Mexican society's fragmentation along political, geographic, and cultural lines had also been one of the most significant barriers to the establishment of a hegemonic political or cultural project across Mexico's vast territory since independence. State modernization projects and elite debates about liberal and conservative ideology therefore likely had limited impact on the majority of Mexico's largely rural population. Instead, the primary loci of symbolic and affective as well as material and economic relations remained the *patria chica* (small homeland) of the village or region.[20]

In order to win popular support and mobilize communities during the conflicts of the 1850s and 1860s, liberal and conservative leaders negotiated with community leaders over specific local demands. For example, liberal leaders made promises of land redistribution, access to resources, or the right of communities to elect their own leaders to win local support for their cause. On the conservative side, the link between ideology and identity ran primarily through Catholicism, such that parish priests who were trusted local authorities often emerged as antiliberal political leaders.[21] New political and social institutions were also established during the fighting, such as liberal national guard units that helped mediate between communities and the national leadership.[22]

Through direct experiences of negotiating support particularly for the victorious liberal cause during the Reform and Intervention periods, the inhabitants of many of Mexico's multiple patrias chicas began to form cognitive connections between their interests and identities and those of an overarching (liberal) *patria grande*. The civil wars of the mid-nineteenth century are thus most relevant to the long-term development of Mexican nationalism for the way in which mass violence and popular mobilization opened channels used with particular success by liberal leaders to establish a workable framework of negotiation between national and local political actors.

The French Intervention ended in 1867 with the defeat and execution of Maximilian and Juárez resuming the presidency. During this period, known as the Restoration of the Republic (1867–1876), villages in a collective sense invoked their support of the liberal cause, Juárez, and the Constitution of 1857 to regional and national political leaders when demanding the recognition of citizenship rights they had earned through this support. As they related to the lived experiences of much of Mexico's rural population, these struggles represented an opportunity to negotiate the terms of accepting the legitimacy of external political authorities inhabiting a weak state and still heavily dependent on popular support for their survival.[23]

A dynamic of conflict and negotiation with both national and local dimensions in this way helped build a cognitive framework connecting subnational categories of identity (such as family, community, and ethnicity) to a larger nation and made connections between local and national interests popularly plausible. Political infrastructure formed during the struggle also helped connect local political interests to the national state, albeit often tenuously. Furthermore, different villages and regions were now able to relate to one another through reference to histories of patriotic loyalty based upon their affiliation and participation during past national struggles.[24] This was an unstable and uneven process, but one that for the first time provided mechanisms for negotiation between national and local interests in many parts of Mexico.[25]

Once the fighting had ended and the state-building elite's priority changed from popular mobilization to imposing order, negotiation between communities and the state often ended in half- or unfulfilled promises and was increasingly replaced by coercion. Indeed, liberalism became notably less popular and the liberal government increasingly centralist after 1867. This in turn provoked several uprisings against the liberal state by communities that had previously mobilized in defense of liberalism.[26] However, in a general sense, popular mobilization during the Reform and French Intervention wars established a pattern of negotiation between local and national actors through community and regional political leaders that laid the foundations for a more durable national state than had the more ephemeral coalitions of the independence struggle.

The wars of the mid-nineteenth century also brought about a relatively durable resolution of the conflict between liberals and conservatives in favor of the liberal cause. Liberalism and specifically *Juarismo* emerged from the Reform and Restoration period with their symbolic legitimacy as a patriotic discourse greatly enhanced.[27] Conversely, the conservative cause was left demoralized and largely discredited following the failure of the French Intervention. In one of many disappointments with the Second Mexican Empire for conservatives, Emperor Maximilian confirmed the anniversary of Hidalgo's grito rather than Iturbide's entry into Mexico City as Mexico's unique official date to commemorate independence.[28] For the remainder of the nineteenth century, when major political conflicts with national implications occurred, they were largely between competing forces that broadly identified with the liberal cause, while conservative nationalism remained a counter-hegemonic force and Iturbide a counter-hegemonic national hero eclipsed by Hidalgo (fig. 1.3).

The Porfiriato: Peace, Progress, and the Cult of Benito Juárez

Benito Juárez's death in office in July 1872 ushered in a new period of instability between rival liberal leaders. Sebastián Lerdo de Tejada initially succeeded Juárez before being overthrown by Porfirio Díaz, who assumed the presidency in 1876 following the Rebellion of Tuxtepec. Díaz was a military hero who led the cavalry at one of the great liberal victories against the French Intervention at the Battle of Puebla on May 5, 1862. He had, however, subsequently launched an unsuccessful rebellion against Juárez's government when his political ambitions were thwarted. With Díaz's ascension to the presidency, a new stage in Mexico's history known as the Porfiriato began, which extended until the outbreak of the Mexican Revolution in 1910.

Under Díaz's rule Mexico experienced a prolonged period of relative

Figure 1.3. Fragment of Juan O'Gorman, *Altarpiece of Independence* (1961).
This mural painted for Mexico's National History Museum at Chapultepec
Castle shows a twentieth-century revolutionary nationalist reading of Mexico's
independence struggle that builds on the nineteenth-century liberal interpretation. Miguel Hidalgo (center) is depicted leading a popular movement that
crossed barriers of class, race, and ethnicity against Mexico's colonial Spanish
rulers. Photo by author.

political stability and economic growth. Porfirian elites built on frameworks of political negotiation between the center and regions established during the Reform and French Intervention wars to promote the
modernization of the Mexican economy and society according to the
dictates of particularly European discourses of liberal modernity.
Complementing efforts to expand state and economic infrastructure,
the Porfirian government dedicated unprecedented effort to cultivating
a unifying framework of nationalism. Again, European intellectual
treatises on nationalism such as that of philosopher Ernst Renan, which
treated nationalism as a necessary condition of modernity, strongly
influenced Porfirian state-builders in this regard.[29]

One element of this strategy was state-sponsored written historical
works that promoted an integrative and evolutionary narrative of
national history.[30] Dubbed the "liberal synthesis," this narrative

maintained the link between the struggle of the Aztecs and Insurgentes against Spanish colonialism present in earlier liberal histories, but extended its reach to include the patriotic struggles of the liberal Reform and Restoration period.[31] This narrative embraced the idea of great ruptures, described as "revolutions," as a positive force that propelled the nation forward. Historical texts, patriotic commemorations, and monuments thus promoted the idea of revolutions—specifically the independence struggle of 1810 and the Reform Wars—as turning points that structured the nation's onward march through history by periodically correcting its course.[32]

Historical texts could have a limited effect in shaping popular attitudes in a country where the majority of the population was still illiterate. The state thus relied on other means to communicate its nationalist vision. Throughout the Porfiriato, the heroes of the Reform period and events such as the Battle of Puebla were promoted across the national territory in paintings, statues, and monuments, with particular emphasis on local heroes who had participated in great national events.[33] The cult of national heroes served a didactic purpose as heroes were imbued with appropriate patriotic values that were highlighted during popular celebrations of their exploits. Heroes also became a channel for reconciliation as political rivalries in life dissolved into unified expressions of respect and reverence by erstwhile political rivals.[34]

The central hero of the Porfirian myth of national unity was liberal president Benito Juárez. Despite the fact Díaz had broken his alliance with Juárez and indeed attempted to overthrow him in the rebellion of the Plan de Noria in 1871, the Porfirian regime dedicated significant effort to promoting Juárez as a national hero. Juárez's death in office meant that controversies surrounding his rule were quickly laid to rest and he became a shared reference point that liberal groups began to deploy selectively when justifying opposing stances on contentious topics such as reelection and anticlericalism.[35] In death, Juárez became a symbol that enjoyed broad legitimacy and had the potential to symbolize that which united over that which divided liberals (fig. 1.4).

While political divisions in life or the truly heroic status of newly deceased and canonized liberals were at times openly questioned in the press, historic rivalries with Juárez were off limits due to the centrality of Juárez to the Porfirian the myth of national unity.[36] This mythology presented Juárez as the leader of the Reform struggle who propelled the nation forward from independence through the achievement of liberty. Díaz, meanwhile, was presented as the heir to Juárez who added to the

Figure 1.4. Antonio González Orozco, *Juárez, Symbol of the Republic Against the French Intervention* (1972). This mural painted for Mexico's National History Museum depicts Benito Juárez (center) symbolically leading liberal soldiers facing foreign invaders as a defender and symbol of Mexico's sovereignty. Photo by author.

nation's progress through the achievement of peace.[37] In Porfirian nationalist mythology, then, the Juárez period was an era of transition while the Porfiriato represented one of resolution in which the peace necessary for progress and the fulfillment of Juárez's ideals had been achieved.

One of the principal occasions for reaffirming a connection between Juárez and Díaz was historical commemoration ceremonies. The first of these to occur on a large scale was on the fifteenth anniversary of Juárez's death, when artillery charges rang over the national capital every quarter hour throughout the day, parades rolled through the streets, and public speeches were delivered lauding Juárez's contributions to the nation. Newspaper editorials reinforced the modernizing and patriotic message of the official commemoration, stressing the importance of remembering the work of Juárez as a guide and an inspiration for the Mexican people and government to remain on the correct path of progress.[38] The expansion of communication and transportation infrastructure, such as the railway and telegraph, assisted the mass diffusion and standardization of such nationalist commemorations.[39] Centrally appointed local political leaders further ensured that civic celebrations were observed appropriately outside of state capitals.[40]

During the Porfiriato, the date of the Independence Day grito ceremony was moved forward to the night of September 15 to coincide with Díaz's birthday and the form of the ceremony maintained by the post-revolutionary state was established. In 1896 state officials transferred the bell purportedly rung by Hidalgo from the church in Dolores, Guanajuato, to Mexico City's National Palace. Henceforth, Mexican presidents would emerge on the balcony of the National Palace at 11:00 p.m. on September 15 to proclaim a series of "vivas" to Mexican independence and national heroes, culminating with the repetition of "¡Viva México!" to which the crowds below would shout "¡Viva!" The president would then ring the bell that symbolized Mexico's birth as a nation.[41] As historian Robert Duncan noted, the Independence Day ceremony developed during the Porfiriato and continued thereafter hierarchically fused the nation, the state, and its leader together in a patriarchal fashion.[42]

The centenary of Hidalgo's grito somewhat paradoxically represented both the apotheosis of a triumphant Porfirian nationalism and the last gasp of a state about to be demolished during a prolonged period of armed uprising. To celebrate the centennial of independence, a flurry of monuments and public works were inaugurated amid parades and festivals promoting the Porfirian ideals of peace and progress, reaching a crescendo in September 1910, the month of the centennial. Foreign dignitaries gathered to pay tribute to Mexico's modernity and, in symbolic recognition of Mexico being judged sufficiently stable and modern to earn its sovereignty, Spain returned to the Mexican government the personal belongs of Insurgente hero José María Morelos, and France the keys to Mexico City somewhat implausibly claimed to have been stolen by French invaders in 1862.[43] Two months later, however, Mexico would be in the early stages of what came to be known as the Mexican Revolution.

From Peace and Progress to Revolution

The Porfirian state in its early years had attracted significant popular support, particularly from those who felt the promised citizenship rights of the Reform and Restoration periods had not been fulfilled under previous administrations. However, popular discontent with the state grew from the 1890s onward. Generational change was one reason for the breakdown of the state's popular legitimacy. At the local level, a new generation of leaders prone to a heavy-handed and corrupt form of rule replaced veteran political operators, alienating local communities.[44] At the national level, a new generation of elites guided by a positivist form of liberalism, dubbed *cientíﬁcos* (scientists), also became dominant among the *camarillas* (factions) within the Porﬁrian government. Porﬁrian cientíﬁcos sought to implement European theories of a scientific and objective management of state and society in Mexico by strengthening centralized and hierarchical power structures with little appreciation for past political arrangements built on cooperation and consensus at the local level.[45] Progress became almost exclusively defined in an economic determinist sense for the cientíﬁcos, who aimed to set in motion a virtuous circle of peace, order, and progress that would eventually turn Mexico into a "modern" country.[46]

As railways and communications improved their reach into rural Mexico, commercial expansion and industrialization further changed local dynamics by reorganizing land and labor patterns. This sharpened conflicts over land, labor, and natural resources between villages and between communities and outside commercial interests. The state also accelerated efforts to redistribute collective peasant landholdings, which had previously been resisted with some success by peasants.[47] Rather than laissez-faire, Porﬁrian elites influenced by European ideas about racial hierarchies were interventionist in their prescriptions for economic progress, which included transforming popular cultural values. This meant that, in the words of historian Richard Weiner, "not market forces but rather education, immigration, and coercion were deemed necessary to transform the 'lazy' natives into capitalist workers."[48]

A drift toward authoritarian centralist government accompanied such interventionism and provided another major cause for the outbreak of revolution. As historian Laurens Ballard Perry argued, the great challenge for nineteenth-century Mexican liberals in power had been "the subordination of regionalism to nationalism without destroying federalism with centralism."[49] Particularly from 1890 onward, frameworks of negotiation forged during the Reform and Restoration period, as incomplete and contested as they were, broke down. The increasingly centralist state relied ever more heavily, to paraphrase the Porﬁrian administrative slogan of "pan o palo," on the threat of the stick over the promise of bread.[50]

As accounts of enthusiastic popular participation in Porfirian patriotic celebrations and the survival of many of its central myths and symbols demonstrate, Porfirian nationalism did enjoy significant popular legitimacy.[51] Indeed, distinctive features of Porfirian Mexican nationalism, including a cult of heroes, a long calendar of civic celebrations, and the construction of monuments that transformed public spaces into accessible lessons in national history and values, survived the Revolution. As historian Mauricio Tenorio Trillo notes, these were all aspects of a Porfirian strategy to project ideal views of the nation as a framework within which social, political, cultural, and economic realities could be discussed.[52] It is likely that, as at no time before, Mexicans during the Porfiriato moved from being conscious of having a nationality to having some national consciousness defined in terms of shared values and culture. This, however, proved a double-edged sword for the Porfirian state.

The Díaz regime promoted a history of popular mobilization to represent the ideal of individual sacrifice on behalf of the greater good of the nation's interests. However, popular nationalist discourse during this period displayed a particular characteristic of Mexican nationalism noted by Claudio Lomnitz: it has historically been popularly invoked most frequently to call upon the state to respect or fulfill the rights of individuals or communities.[53] Across Mexico, years of commemorating the historical sacrifices of living and dead veterans on dates such as Independence Day and the Cinco de Mayo anniversary of the Battle of Puebla reinforced a notion of citizenship rights earned through popular sacrifice on behalf of the nation.[54]

As veterans of these wars began to die and direct memories began to fade, historical symbols and commemorations of patriotic nationalism became more important to communities. A self-representation as heir to these veterans legitimized the community's claim to citizenship rights earned by their forebears and nationalist symbols such as Juárez and the Reform were evoked to legitimize opposition to a state that did not effectively guarantee these rights. Historical commemorations could in this way be transformed from an occasion for reaffirming common bonds between state and society to occasions for highlighting the breaking of these bonds.[55]

The use of a nationalist discourse of citizenship rights extended beyond those who had directly participated in the Intervention and Reform wars, demonstrating the extent to which it had spread as a form of national consciousness. For example, historian Friedrich Katz noted that villagers in remote Namiquipa, Chihuahua, argued for their right to land on the basis of their past patriotic service. However, these villagers argued that their patriotic service involved "preserving civilization against the barbarians" in historic clashes with Apache Indians rather than support for Liberals or Insurgentes.[56] The residents of Namiquipa would thus justify their subsequent support for revolutionary Francisco "Pancho" Villa's uprising against the Díaz government on the basis that the regime had disrespected the rights and honor they had earned through such service to the nation.[57]

The Mexican Revolution

As did the Reform and Independence wars, the uprising that began with Francisco Madero's call in the Plan de San Luis Potosí for a revolution on November 20, 1910, to overthrow the Díaz regime served as a catalyst for multiple grievances that were often intensely local or regional. Madero himself did not come from a popular background, but a wealthy business family from the northern state of Coahuila. The Maderos were, in fact, reasonably representative of increasingly frustrated sections of Mexico's middle class and businesspeople, who felt excluded from the closed Porfirian political system and in competition with the foreign investors the Porfirian state sought to attract.[58] Madero's call for revolution thus offered little in the way of social reform, but rather a return to the principles of the Constitution of 1857 through a democratic opening of the political system that in itself would bring about a renewal of social and political life.

Conceived largely as an urban rebellion by Madero and his immediate group of supporters, the Díaz regime was in reality defeated in rural Mexico. Military leaders recruited to the Maderista cause, such as Villa and Pascual Orozco in the state of Chihuahua, quickly achieved significant success against the federal army.[59] A series of relatively small movements across Mexico loosely united by their support for the Plan de San Luis Potosí continued to gather momentum and by early 1911 the Porfirian state was on the brink of collapse. The uprising that coalesced around the Maderista cause thus corresponded to the nineteenth-century model of rebellion in Mexico in that it provided a window of national upheaval within which many local struggles organized to overthrow an unpopular regime. A tired and defeated Díaz soon capitulated, beginning negotiations with Madero and resigning the presidency almost exactly five months after the Mexican Revolution began on May 21, 1911.

While urban and labor revolts were not central to the Revolution, anarchist currents associated with important intellectual and political leader Ricardo Flores Magón's movement influenced the development of a wave of labor strikes beginning in 1906.[60] Far more central to the revolutionary upheaval were the often intertwined themes of political autonomy and land that had been a trigger for uprisings throughout the nineteenth century.[61] In particular, the expansion of the hacienda system, which in many areas employed coercive labor practices such as debt peonage and operated in collusion with state authorities, was a central cause of rural rebellion. The most significant of these rebellions was that of Emiliano Zapata and his followers in the state of Morelos, located to the southwest of Mexico City.[62]

Once in power, Madero proved less of a reformer than those who rebelled demanding land and labor reforms had hoped. The Madero government prioritized restoring peace and order often to the detriment of political reform, reinstating many Porfirian political leaders and institutions. Nowhere was Madero's misunderstanding of the social motivations of popular uprising more evident than in his dealings with those who had risen up behind Zapata. Madero refused to accede to demands for land redistribution, instead calling on the Zapatistas to disarm and trust in the legal system that had previously overseen the distribution of their communal lands to haciendas.[63]

Hostilities thus soon resumed between Zapatista rebels and the Madero-led national government. On November 8, 1911, the Zapatistas issued the Plan de Ayala that savaged Madero as a tyrant unfit to carry out the principles of the Revolution of November 20, 1910. The Zapatistas called on the people of Mexico to rise up against Madero, claimed Madero's Plan de San Luis Potosí on behalf of the oppressed people of Mexico and outlined a plan for a comprehensive redistribution of land and natural resources to towns and citizens through special land redistribution tribunals. The Plan de Ayala further invoked the redistribution of ecclesiastical properties under the Reform laws to connect Zapatista plans for land redistribution to the established national symbol of "the immortal Juárez."[64]

Sailing off to exile in France, Díaz is popularly remembered as having remarked, "Madero has unleashed a tiger, now let's see if he can control it."[65] A failure to address or perhaps general incomprehension of the social and political motivations that led so many to rise up in support of his movement in 1910 ultimately doomed the Madero government.[66] Madero and his vice president José María Pino Suárez were assassinated in a coup led by leaders of the old regime, who installed Porfirian General Victoriano Huerta as the new president on February 19, 1913.

Despite its relative lack of success, the brief Maderista presidency had a lasting political impact in its successful promotion of a notion of the Revolution as an autonomous, positive, and national force. The Zapatistas' Plan de Ayala, for example, spoke of the Revolution as a force that transcended the actions of the Madero government to the point of appropriating Madero's Plan de San Luis Potosí to legitimize their anti-Maderista rebellion. The Zapatistas also linked Juárez to the reified Revolution, with a link between the Revolution, Reform, and Independence struggles emphasizing the patriotic association between revolutionaries fighting against unpatriotic "conservatives and despots," who were those who opposed national and popular interests and sought to hold back the march of history.[67] The brutal martyrdom of Madero, subsequently dubbed "the Apostle of Democracy" in patriotic discourse, meanwhile, meant that his stature grew as a symbol for rallying popular support and unifying revolutionary groups in their opposition to the Huerta government.[68]

The period following the Huerta coup was the bloodiest phase of the revolutionary struggle and during this phase what remained of the Porfirian state was destroyed. In the north, Maderista governor of Coahuila and landowner Venustiano Carranza and the military command of Álvaro Obregón formed a coalition called the Constitucionalistas. The Constitutionalistas fought in alliance with Villa's Division of the North. In the south, the Zapatistas brought the Revolution to Mexico City's doorstep from their base in Morelos.

Despite the later mythologizing of the Revolution as a single movement, it was in reality divided into different groups with often-conflicting agendas. The Constitucionalistas under Carranza, who hailed from the states of Sonora and Coahuila, was a movement in which hacendados and middle class professionals led the opposition to Huerta. The Zapatistas, by contrast, were mostly peasants from free villages resisting encroachment on their land by the expansion of the hacienda system. The Villistas, meanwhile, represented the most diverse group, including members from all social classes but excluding hacendados.[69]

Reflecting the divisions between revolutionary groups, when the Huerta government fell in July 1914, a new period of revolution within a revolution began that lasted until about July 1915. During this period,

Figure 1.5. Francisco Villa and Emiliano Zapata in Mexico City's National Palace in December 1914, after forming an alliance at the Convention of Aguascalientes to take power. Courtesy Archivo Casasola/Fototeca Nacional de México.

competing revolutionary factions fought amongst themselves for power. Villa's tenuous alliance with Carranza under the Constitucionalista banner soon collapsed. When revolutionary leaders met at the Convention of Aguascalientes in October 1914 to determine the post-revolutionary political order, Villistas and Zapatistas formed an alliance. The Constitucionalistas withdrew from the conference in response and the Villista and Zapatista forces marched on Mexico City, with pro-Villista Governor of San Luis Potosí General Eulalio Gutiérrez assuming the presidency (fig. 1.5).

Establishing their capital in Veracruz, the Constitucionalistas began to fight and negotiate their way back into power. Carranza moved to undercut peasant support of both Villa and Zapata by issuing the Law of January 6, 1915, calling for a radical redistribution of land and wealth framed as a fulfillment of the Reform Laws. Obregón, mean-while, allied with the anarcho-syndicalist Casa del Obrero Mundial (House of the World Worker), who formed red battalions to fight along-side the Constitucionalistas, laying the foundations for a lasting rela-tionship with the urban labor movement.[70] This strategy proved successful, with the Constitucionalistas soon taking control of Mexico City following a series of military victories that left the Villistas and Zapatistas weak and isolated.[71] A particularly important symbolic moment in the early formation of a new revolutionary state was then overseen by the Carranza administration (1917–1920) with the drafting of the Constitution of 1917 that codified a new, revolutionary contract of citizenship between state and society.

A period of yet more fratricidal violence between the leading figures of what the state would later promote as a "revolutionary family" followed the Constitucionalista victory. In 1919, with Carranza as president, the government was involved in a successful plot to assassinate Zapata in Chinameca, Morelos. The following year, Obregón overthrew Carranza, who was assassinated as he fled to Veracruz. In 1923, with Obregón as president, Villa was gunned down in his home state of Chihuahua with the likely consent of the state.[72] One of the remarkable aspects of the revolutionary nationalist narrative of history is therefore that all of these leaders came to be remembered as national heroes who fought for largely the same cause and laid the foundations for a state that claimed legitimacy as heir to all of these often-violently conflicting movements.

Building a Revolutionary State

The decade of revolutionary upheaval largely demolished the Porfirian state, and during the early postrevolutionary decades, the Mexican state was rebuilt in three overlapping phases that aimed to avoid the turmoil of the early independence period, the technocratic authoritarianism of the late Porfiriato, and the timid liberalism of the Madero government. The first of these phases occurred from roughly 1920 to 1929, when the victorious elite attempted a moralist cultural transformation of the nation under the presidencies of Constitucionalista General Álvaro Obregón (1920–1924) and Plutarco Elías Calles (1924–1928). During an interim known as the Maximato, Calles dominated attempts at the greater institutionalization of power. In the next phase, under President Lázaro Cárdenas (1934–1940), the state paid greatest attention to cultivating a popular support base that would form the lasting political, social, and institutional foundations of the postrevolutionary state.

While there were significant ruptures between the Porfirian and postrevolutionary state, the political and cultural reforms of the postrevolutionary decades aimed at a similar goal of laying the foundations for development by eliminating precapitalist obstacles to modernization.[73] With the outbreak of the Revolution evidencing the limited ability of an enlightened modernizing state to impose its dictates, the postrevolutionary state-building project was based on the notion of winning popular legitimacy and consent as the principle (though not the only) basis for the exercise of state power.[74] How this process unfolded broadly accorded to the theory of moral regulation developed by Philip Corrigan and Derek Sayer, through which forms of social order are historically constructed and rendered natural through a process of cultural transformation.[75]

Particularly in regions with well-established local elite networks and a tradition of autonomy from the national government, the relatively weak postrevolutionary state depended from its earliest phase upon successfully negotiating its reforms through local political authorities to implement its modernization project. Negotiating recognition of the central government was often a delicate process and state cultural and political projects did not find success in a dramatic, sweeping fashion, nor were they entirely imposed on a hapless populace.[76] Rather, as historian Mary Kay Vaughan observed, particularly during the 1920s and 1930s, "contesting and reshaping central state directives became part of the reconstruction of power, knowledge, and everyday life."[77]

While post-1890 Porfirian developmental liberalism generally unfolded in a top-down fashion and was heavily oriented toward foreign investment and immigration, the postrevolutionary state paid significant attention to tying development projects to national self-sufficiency, and national projects to local needs. For example, following the creation of the National Roads Commission in 1925, the government encouraged communities to form committees to directly participate in the construction of roads. This encouraged not just local participation in national development projects, but also discussions about the economic, cultural, or social benefits that could come with links to surrounding communities, commercial centers, religious shrines, or educational institutions. The government would also build the road network using national revenue sources and with preference for utilizing and improving the design expertise and labor of Mexicans.[78]

Studies in the states of Morelos, Mexico State, Puebla, and Michoacán further show that infrastructure such as roads led to individuals becoming increasingly exposed to market forces and institutions of state and federal governments. This in turn weakened the power of existing local political and economic leaders and institutions, including the hacienda.[79] State infrastructure projects in this way supported the overarching aim of establishing the popular idea of the national state as a guiding force in local economic and social development and an important, potentially beneficial, and naturalized presence in the daily lives of millions of Mexicans.

A need for dialogue and negotiation also shaped the political model of the postrevolutionary state. Obregón's assassination at the hands of a Catholic fanatic in 1928 as he prepared to resume the presidency gave particular urgency to the governing elite's efforts to politically unify Mexico and lower the intensity of its conflict with militant Catholicism.[80] The model developed by the outgoing administration of Plutarco Elías Calles (1924–1928) involved a national revolutionary party that would provide political stability by uniting different revolutionary factions within the state. The foundations of what became the PRI were thus laid under Calles, with the National Revolutionary Party (PNR) founded on March 4, 1929.

Under this new political model the executive played the dominant role of conciliation between social groups and classes. Power was centralized in the figure of the president, while judicial and legislative branches as well as state and municipal governments were assigned a subordinate role. By 1933 the postrevolutionary electoral model had also taken its general shape. Among its principle features were presidential terms of six years (sexenios) and the constitutional impossibility of reelection for the offices of the federal and state executives.

President Lázaro Cárdenas (1934–1940) further reformed the postrevolutionary state to broaden its popular base by promoting mass incorporation into the party according to a collectivist corporatist model. The four institutional pillars on which the party—renamed the Party of the Mexican Revolution (PRM) in 1938—rested were the labor unions, peasants, the popular sector, and the military. The corporatist system formed a structure that was pyramidal and patriarchal in nature, with power flowing from the sectoral organizations through the party to the powerful executive at its peak.[81]

While regular elections were held and registration granted to some opposition parties, the postrevolutionary political system was hegemonic in that it attempted to provide institutional channels for social inconformity while the revolutionary party retained firm control of the state. Cárdenas strengthened the power of the Executive, introducing such trademarks of the Mexican *presidencialismo* as the *destape* (unveiling), which was the process by which the president chose his successor before publicly retiring from national political life. After Mexico's long history of *caudillismo*—personalistic rule by charismatic strongmen—and the instability surrounding the transfer of power that resulted from this form of rule, the Cárdenas reforms brought a greater institutionalization to the transfer of power and paved the way for the transition to civilian control of the presidency in 1946. In this sense, the Cárdenas reforms signified a transition in Mexico's model of political rule from caudillismo to presidencialismo.[82]

During the Cárdenas period, a massive land redistribution program also occurred that reinforced the privileged role in national economic and social life as well as the symbolic importance in revolutionary nationalism of a collective village landholding system called the ejido. Through agrarian bureaucrats and rural teachers, the state encouraged the adoption of a peasant identity and the formation of peasant organizations in rural Mexico as part of its effort to attack established local power structures. Symbolically, this legitimized the peasant within the nation as a subject with associated citizenship rights earned through the struggle of past heroes, most notably Emiliano Zapata. In a practical sense, Cardenista agrarianism assisted the formation of alliances between groups within communities seeking land redistribution and the national state against despised local authorities, with land redistribution often going hand in hand with a redistribution of power at the expense of traditional politico-religious authorities.[83] In a broader sense, as historian Jocelyn Olcott has argued, Cárdenas's emphasis on "mobilization and collective organizing over individualism and competition" constituted a defining Cardenista contribution to the character of legitimate revolutionary identities and their associated citizenship rights as collectivist and class based.[84]

The economic model established during the 1930s aimed to stimulate national economic development through various mechanisms of state intervention and protectionism. The National Polytechnic Institute (IPN) in Mexico City—a central battleground between students and state security forces in 1968—was formed in 1937 by the Cárdenas administration to train a new generation of Mexican scientists, technicians, and engineers who would drive the country's development. The creation of the IPN further connected revolutionary values to this project, being formed in part to counterbalance the National Autonomous University (UNAM), then a center of conservative politics.[85]

The nationalization by Cárdenas of Mexico's oil resources on March

Figure 1.6. Sectoral organizations gather in the Mexico City Zócalo on the first anniversary of the Lázaro Cárdenas administration's expropriation of Mexico's oil resources. A banner on the cathedral includes an image of Hidalgo and draws a connection between the *grito* of Independence in 1810 and the oil expropriation of 1938. Courtesy Archivo Casasola/Fototeca Nacional de México.

18, 1938, particularly came to symbolize Cardenista economic nationalism, with the date accordingly added to Mexico's extended postrevolutionary calendar of annual patriotic commemorations (fig. 1.6). Further symbolizing Mexico's control over its own development, gas stations owned by state oil company Petroleos Mexicanos (Pemex), painted in the colors of the national flag, soon dotted the new highways built by the National Roads Commission.[86] The construction of exclusively state-owned gas stations decorated in the national colors along state-built highways thus transformed the landscape in a way that reinforced the state's central role in promoting national development and protecting Mexico's economic sovereignty.

Following the Cárdenas presidency, the Mexican state also showed greater openness to the private sector and an increasingly procapitalist economic orientation. Virtually from the moment Cárdenas chose him as his successor, President Manuel Ávila Camacho (1940–1946) moved to establish a close and cooperative relationship with business interests that had been hostile to the Cárdenas administration.[87] From the 1940s to the 1960s, compulsory business associations such as the Confederation of Industrial Chambers (CONCAMIN) and the National Chamber of the Manufacturing Industry (CANACINTRA) were formed through government legislation as a way of incorporating private enterprise into the political system.[88] However, the PRI rebuffed repeated petitions from leaders of business organizations for the creation of an official PRI-affiliated corporatist business sector due to the party's self-presentation as representing popular rather than elite interests. A relatively harmonious relationship between the PRI state and private business interests nevertheless lasted into the 1970s, with big business accepting a reduced role in politics and symbolically reinforcing the centrality of the state to Mexico's national development in exchange for a guarantee of profits and a respect for property rights.

Democracy, Elections, and the Opposition under the PRI State

A fundamental shift between the postrevolutionary political model and that of the Porfiriato was the embrace of collectivist institutions that added a political idiom of nationalist inclusion to the prevailing ideal of the enlightened and progressive state.[89] The revolutionary party was organized in a multi-class fashion as an institutional framework designed to avoid political and social fragmentation, and class, rather than competing categories of identity such as race or gender, structured postrevolutionary political discourse regarding citizenship rights. Under Ávila Camacho greater efforts were made to diminish factionalism and increase discipline within the hegemonic revolutionary party, with the independence of affiliated sectors increasingly subordinated to the state in a hierarchical fashion. The power of the left in worker and peasant organizations was also diminished in favor of more conservative urban professionals in the popular sector.[90] To promote a public image of a united revolutionary governing party, the state further set as the permanent parameter for political conflict a division between the revolutionary majority incorporated into the institutions of the party and counterrevolutionary minorities whose presence was tolerated within the system.[91] Within this framework, the state party, renamed the Institutional Revolutionary Party (PRI) in 1946, was conceived of not as one of many parties operating in a competitive electoral system, but as the institutional manifestation of the revolutionary majority and, by association, the nation.

Calles specifically invited opposing groups to organize and

participate in the battle of ideas by integrating into the institutionalized political system while the preliminary institutional bases of the PRI system were being laid.[92] The Mexican state took a relatively benign stance toward conservative opponents and supported the survival of allied satellite parties nominally of the left as a necessary component of a binary revolutionary/reactionary form of multiparty democracy. Opposition parties were not only symbolically but also institutionally subordinated to the PRI state, upon which they relied for party registration and recognition of voting totals. The state would then focus its harshest attacks on opposition figures that had emerged from within the revolutionary elite or the left who most significantly challenged the state's privileged claim to revolutionary legitimacy.[93]

Until the 1980s, elections in postrevolutionary Mexico are best understood as a civic ritual aimed at the periodic renewal of the PRI state's legitimacy and organized around one of this system's most successful features: the regular and orderly transfer of power between presidents and their supporters within the system. In a functional sense, it was the hegemonic state party, corporatist organizations, and central state bureaucracy that incorporated the masses into the formal political system and determined public policy. During election campaigns, party officials and leaders of sectoral organizations arranged lavish displays of electoral propaganda and mobilized members to attend rallies in towns and cities across Mexico. On election day, people were again mobilized to go to the ballot box more to confirm their allegiance to the revolutionary cause than to choose between competing political projects.

The presence of opposition parties was actively encouraged within this political model, not just as a relief valve for political tensions, but also to strengthen the legitimizing power of the electoral ritual for the PRI. Party president and veteran PRI ideologue Jesús Reyes Héroles accordingly explained the logic of state support for a viable opposition presence in 1972: "we do not want to fight against the wind, against the air: that which resists supports."[94] On a symbolic level, the Revolution needed to triumph once more over its opponents in the reaction for the electoral ritual to fulfill its legitimizing role, while low public participation—encouraged by the lack of a viable opposition—also threatened to undermine the appearance of popular support for the system. This helps to explain not only the massive amounts of money spent by the PRI on campaign propaganda, but also why the most significant pluralizing reforms of Mexico's political system under the PRI occurred when the opposition appeared at its weakest.

Entwining Revolution, Nation, and State

For postrevolutionary state-builders, revolutionary nationalism assisted the process of establishing interconnections with nonstate actors and institutions by providing a symbolic framework that subjectified citizens as, for example, peasants or workers whose rights were legitimated through a language of revolutionary myths and symbols. This was structurally supported by class-based corporatist sectoral organizations and central state bureaucracy that communicated and reinforced this subjectification of identity and rights through direct contact with communities. Postrevolutionary state- and nation-building in this sense operated in accordance with Philip Gorski's description of "organizational entwining," in which states seek to establish *connections with* beyond simple *authority over* civil society.[95]

The temporal congruence between state development and the transformation of popular nationalism following the Revolution greatly enhanced the state's ability to successfully instill revolutionary nationalism into everyday frames of reference. Mexican postrevolutionary elites faced relatively little established institutional resistance outside of the church due to the destruction of the Porfirian state during the Revolution. State cultural machinery was thus built more than reformed by the teachers, corporatist sectoral organizers, and state officials who fanned out across the country during the 1920s and 1930s. These officials acted as the main communicators of the new revolutionary nationalist mythology who directly connected its myths and symbols to established nationalist mythology and the postrevolutionary state's modernizing policies in a practical sense.[96]

Founded in 1921, the Secretary of Public Education (SEP) was one of the most influential actors in the process of intertwining the myths and symbols of revolutionary nationalism with the institutions of the postrevolutionary state. As the SEP absorbed existing rural schools into a national system and built new schools, the public education system reinforced subjectivities of peasants, workers, and oppressed classes, presenting them as the protagonists of Mexican history. The values of national citizenship were thus redefined from the liberal individualism of the Porfiriato to one of collective national solidarities.[97] The Programa de Libros de Texto Gratuitos (Free Textbook Program) that began during the presidency of Adolfo López Mateos (1958–1964), meanwhile, reaffirmed the socializing role of the education system by providing free and compulsory textbooks for all Mexican school children aimed at molding appropriate values and understandings of the national history.[98]

Historian Catherine Nolan-Ferrell has shown how this socialization into the revolutionary nation occurred in her case study of rural Soconusco, Chiapas. State education officials first promoted a revolutionary template of national identity through textbooks and public classes for Soconusco's residents. State agrarian officials then reinforced revolutionary nationalism by effectively restricting the benefits of reforms—particularly land redistribution—to those peasants who self-identified as supporters of the Mexican Revolution. An invocation by peasant communities of revolutionary language in turn compelled politicians to address peasant concerns in order to maintain popular legitimacy for themselves and for the postrevolutionary political system as a whole.[99] This established a framework of communication between communities and the state in which, for example, a community from the state of Veracruz would request resources for a new road from President Cárdenas through phrases such as "Easy communication is one of the benefits of the Revolution."[100]

The way in which central state policies were implemented and the Revolution taught was further filtered through local histories, popular culture, and political power structures.[101] Particularly from the 1930s onward, representatives of the Mexican state made many concessions to local sensibilities in the application of national cultural policies and reform projects more generally, forging new identities and links between state and society through negotiation. For their part, communities selectively appropriated, discarded, or emphasized portions of the state's cultural project according to their own subjectivities and needs, weaving local culture, memories, and power relations into understandings of the revolutionary nation and state.[102] Thus, while the postrevolutionary state increasingly structured the acceptable remembering of the past as its infrastructural power grew, individuals and communities conditioned their ongoing acceptance of external state authorities in distinct ways across Mexico in a fashion that belied state-centered notions of political power.[103]

In regard to Mexico's ethnic and cultural identity, the state promoted a notion of *mestizaje* (racial and cultural mixing) associated with the idea of what intellectual and collaborator with the Obregón administration José Vasconcelos described as "the cosmic race."[104] For Mexico's indigenous population, mestizaje implied acculturation more than mixing. Under the guidance of intellectuals such as Manuel Gamio postrevolutionary politicians and intellectuals understood anthropology as a science that could promote cross-cultural comprehension between European and indigenous forms of thinking and bridge remaining divisions between Mexico's indigenous and Spanish pasts to create a mestizo national culture.[105] Documenting and preserving select elements of indigenous culture considered particularly worthy, postrevolutionary anthropologists helped provide revolutionary nationalism with an *indigenista* (pro-Indian) aesthetic sensibility, as expressed in the works of postrevolutionary muralists such as Diego Rivera or the incorporation of indigenista elements into the midcentury Mexican modern architecture of public buildings such as the National Museum of Anthropology (1964) and the UNAM buildings of the 1950s.[106] At the same time, state anthropologists aimed to educate out "premodern" elements of indigenous culture.[107]

The National Indigenous Institute (INI), created in 1948, became the main vehicle for direct engagement between the state and the indigenous population under the idea that it would exercise temporary tutelage over indigenous communities until they assimilated the national culture and were thus placed on the path to progress through the disappearance of traditional indigenous authorities in favor of participation in municipal politics and corporatist institutions.[108] Other institutions reinforced this process of integration into the state and the adoption of a mestizo, revolutionary identity. For example, agrarian officials largely ignored land claims made on the basis of ancestral or indigenous identity, with communities instead encouraged to adopt a class-based peasant identity and register with corporatist peasant federations.[109]

In terms of the historical narrative that accompanied this state- and nation-building project, revolutionary nationalism built upon the liberal nationalism of the Porfiriato but recast the Porfirian state as a deviation from the ideals of Juárez. Within this narrative, the Revolution represented a new great rupture that had corrected the nation's course by adding social justice concerns to the freedom and modernity of the Insurgente and Reform struggles. Revolution Day on the November 20 anniversary of Madero's uprising was further added to Mexico's patriotic calendar as a national holiday in 1920, joining annual commemorations of the Independence and the Reform movements.

Within the dominant postrevolutionary historical narrative, the Revolution represented more an end of history than one more historical rupture for Mexico. Mexico's new state elite directly connected their legitimacy with being heirs to the popular struggle of the Revolution and its main heroes, with the Obregón government promoting the notion of a "revolutionary family" to symbolize the new political class's unity and ongoing connection to the revolutionary struggle. The tombs of Madero and his vice president, Pino Suárez, quickly became sites of official state commemorations on the anniversary of their assassination. Obregón used such occasions to justify his overthrow of Carranza as a return to the Maderista path and a restoration of the Revolution's aims after the Carrancista deviation.[110] A rehabilitation of Zapata's image by the state also occurred after Carranza's overthrow, with both Obregón and Calles using commemorations of Zapata's assassination in Morelos to connect their agrarian reform agenda to the principles of Zapata. In this way, postrevolutionary elites selectively cultivated the images of and popular meanings connected to different heroes. Within revolutionary nationalism, Zapata would henceforth symbolize the popular agrarianism of the Revolution taken up by the postrevolutionary state.[111]

In a final official reconciliation between the Revolution's main leaders, Carranza and Villa joined the pantheon of revolutionary heroes following the formation of the state revolutionary party in 1929. Carranza came to symbolize the revolutionary citizenship contract of the Constitution of 1917, while Villa maintained a less clear relationship to the state but enjoyed a thriving career in comic books, novels, and movies.[112] As had been the case under the Porfirian state, official commemorations of the heroes of rival factions were used to heal old wounds and promote unity between revolutionary factions.[113]

With direct connections between state officials and the armed struggle of the Revolution beginning to weaken, Calles oversaw a further reworking of nationalist discourse from a focus on political legitimacy flowing from personal membership in the revolutionary family to emphasize a conception of the state as "la Revolución hecha gobierno" (the Revolution made government). This concept implied a reified, living Revolution that existed above the actions of individuals and had as its institutional manifestation the state revolutionary party.[114] The Revolution was now not just an armed struggle, but a modernizing force that encompassed all of the initiatives undertaken by the postrevolutionary state.[115] Cárdenas as state-builder became the last major hero of revolutionary nationalism, symbolizing the fulfillment by the postrevolutionary state of the promises of popular justice and economic sovereignty through his administration's massive redistribution of land to peasant communities and nationalization of Mexico's oil reserves.

The state further paid significant attention to promoting methods of mass communication such as newspaper, radio, cinema, and television to diffuse a shared national culture and identity. A state radio station was created in 1924 to be run by the SEP, which broadcast cultural and educational programming, and in 1936, the government introduced a law requiring that all commercial stations broadcast 25 percent "typical" (mestizo and Indian) Mexican music. Both public and commercial stations also broadcast other mandated programming such as presidential speeches, with commercial stations required by law to broadcast some state programming.[116]

The formal and informal government oversight of radio broadcasting set the pattern for the relationship between the mass media and the state for most of the twentieth century. While historical commemorations may still have been repeated in small towns across Mexico, the state could now also rely on television newscasts and national newspapers to relay the same images and key quotes from these ceremonies to a national audience of people who might never attend one personally. Commercial operators such as Emilio Azcárraga Vidaurreta— who began operating radio stations and founded the forerunner to Mexico's powerful Televisa television consortium—learned to promote the preferred cultural and political values of the government in order to retain the favorable disposition of the state toward their business operations.[117]

The post–World War II economic growth of the "Mexican Miracle" lasting into the 1960s and the explosion of mass media assisted a process of massification and commodification of culture. Mexican cinema—heavily supported by state funds and also subject to censorship—experienced a boom from the 1930s until the early 1950s. Mexican films such as *Río escondido* (1948) reinforced the revolutionary nationalist framework through their frequent use of the trope of the good representatives of the modern and enlightened central state battling the bad figures of backward and irrational local power holders in rural settings. As Mexico became increasingly urbanized after 1940, film plotlines and heroes also increasingly migrated to the city. However, the same dynamic of the honest and enlightened state official versus retrograde elements in society or the system remained.[118]

Compromise was central to this cultural dynamic and the sharper edges of the 1920s and 1930s projects of cultural reform were quickly softened. For example, while formal anticlericalism remained a part of patriotic political discourse President Manuel Ávila Camacho (1940–1946) proclaimed himself "a believer," patriotic films such as *¡Mexicanos* *al grito de guerra!* (1943) mixed liberal Juarista and Catholic symbolism under the state's approving gaze, and frequent references were made to the Catholicism of PRI presidential candidate Miguel de la Madrid's wife during the 1982 campaign.[119] Without ignoring the existence of blunt mechanisms of coercion and domination, it was this ability to adapt and compromise that most significantly underwrote the PRI's prolonged period of rule.

While the distribution of wealth grew increasingly unequal, the state increasingly repressive, cities more crowded, and agriculture stagnant, the period from 1940 until the political shock of 1968 and economic shocks of the 1970s also saw a period of sustained economic growth, renewed national confidence, and blossoming cultural production. This period thus took on the aura of a golden age in which a mass, popular culture of movie stars, telenovelas, well-remembered songs, and tourist sites mixed with historical patriotic myths and symbols to create a broadly understood ideal of *lo mexicano*, or that which was distinctly Mexican. Within this general panorama of postrevolutionary Mexico's cultural florescence, Mexico's distinct political model was presented alongside mariachis, modern beach resorts such as Acapulco, and movie stars like Cantinflas as integral to Mexico's distinctive national identity.

Revolution and Revision

From the 1950s onward and particularly following 1968, revolutionary nationalism became a target for cynicism. This was influenced by the generational trends that had contributed to the 1968 student movement itself, including the emergence of an increasingly prosperous, urban, and cosmopolitan middle class that began to look upon Villa, Zapata, and Juárez as little more than distant, "bronze" heroes cynically dusted off at regular intervals to legitimize an equally fossilized and authoritarian state.[120] The creation of revolutionary nationalism as a durable and dominant public framework for imagining a whole range of social relations in Mexico is, however, best understood as a process of negotiation shaped by the interaction between elites and popular actors. Since independence, state-building elites struggled to reconcile divisions of race, class, culture, and identity to promote the idea of a single nation with shared interests that corresponded to Mexico's political boundaries. Following the Revolution, the reworking of social, economic, and political relationships included promoting new myths and symbols to inspire national integration while building on prior nationalist frameworks that also involved negotiation between state-directed cultural initiatives and popular values and memories.

Revolutionary nationalism's enduring legitimacy lay principally in the way in which its myths and symbols served both to strengthen a sense of national identity and order under the state from above and also an instrumental political tool that could be invoked from below to demand fulfillment of collective citizenship rights. For many Mexicans, memories of the sacrifices of popular heroes or land granted by Cárdenas and his successors legitimized their citizenship rights and place within the national community. The postrevolutionary political and economic model, furthermore, proved relatively successful at mediating between popular opinion and elite design, minimizing the reliance on open coercion and maximizing the appearance of consent.

With their deep roots in popular historical experiences, it is perhaps not surprising that revolutionary nationalist myths and symbols survived moments of crisis and experiences of the betrayal of the citizenship rights these myths traditionally symbolized. Rather than dying away, figures such as Lázaro Cárdenas, Francisco Madero, Emiliano Zapata, and Agustín de Iturbide continued to surface in Mexico's post-1968 political battles. Accordingly, when the postrevolutionary political and economic model was plunged into profound crises following the 1982 debt crisis, PRI government officials used the very same symbols to justify government austerity measures and neoliberal reform. However, independent peasant and workers' organizations also brandished these same revolutionary nationalist symbols to contest what they saw as a betrayal of their citizenship rights.

JoLoPo and the Bank Nationalization

Marking the beginning of an era characterized by a sense of permanent crisis and intense public debate over the meaning of the nation's history, the final months of President José López Portillo's administration represented the last gasp of a triumphant revolutionary nationalism. On September 1, 1982, President López Portillo addressed the Mexican Congress and the nation for his sixth and final informe before handing over power to his successor, Miguel de la Madrid. The annual presidential informe under the PRI generally involved a statistics-laden recounting of the government's successes to date, an outline of its current agenda, and reaffirmation of the current administration's status as heir and continuation of Mexico's revolutionary tradition. Largely a summary of and response to the 1982 debt crisis from the state's perspective, López Portillo's final informe did not foreshadow the significant shift in Mexico's economic development model that would occur under his successors during the 1980s and 1990s. Instead, this speech throws into sharp relief the fraught relationship between the revolutionary nationalist discourse that traditionally legitimated the PRI's rule and the free market neoliberal reforms that followed.

Taking office in 1976 during an economic crisis involving currency devaluations, rising inflation, enormous government deficits and an increasingly hostile and politically organized private sector, López Portillo initially appeared to have dramatically turned Mexico's economy around.[1] A sudden return to economic boom times during the López Portillo administration was mostly due to the discovery of vast new oil reserves along Mexico's gulf coast in 1974, just as oil prices began to rise precipitously following the formation of OPEC and instability in the Middle East. As oil prices soared, US banks also found themselves awash in the "petrodollars" of oil-rich Middle Eastern states and sought to turn a profit on these reserves by offering generous loans at favorable rates to countries such as Mexico.[2] Mexico's changing economic outlook in turn earned López Portillo the praise of international financial publications such as *The Economist* and *Fortune*, which lauded his pragmatism and competence.[3] The López Portillo administration also expanded efforts begun during the previous administration of Luis Echeverría (1970–1976) to shore up faltering public confidence in the PRI system through the introduction of ambitious new schemes to address Mexico's endemic problems of poverty and under-development.[4]

The government initially had to accept some austerity measures negotiated with the International Monetary Fund (IMF) in 1976 during the dying days of the Echeverría presidency. However, by 1977 the situation had changed, such that López Portillo now had the resources at his disposal to pursue policies designed to rapidly accelerate Mexico's economic growth and announce to the nation that it was now Mexico's auspicious responsibility "to administer abundance!"[5] The government accordingly discarded plans to control debt and rein in government spending, instead taking full advantage of the favorable circumstances to increase public spending on infrastructure and social programs, vastly expanding the role of the government in the economy.[6] This rapid growth in public spending far outpaced extra income from oil exports, leading the Mexican government to borrow ever-higher amounts from international financial institutions.

The illusion of endless prosperity was short-lived, and by June 1981 it was becoming clear that a confluence of factors was bringing about a worst-case scenario for Mexico. Following the 1974 discoveries, Mexico had the world's fourth-largest oil reserves and oil exports became increasingly important to the economy, accounting for 61 percent of the value of its exports in 1981, up from 27 percent in 1977.[7] However, a glut of Middle-Eastern oil following the reentry of Iran and Iraq into international oil markets, coupled with an increasing global emphasis on energy saving in industrial development, saw oil prices in steady decline by mid-1981.[8] This coincided with falling international prices for Mexico's other major exports such as silver, coffee, and lead.[9]

At the same time, interest rates began to climb dramatically in central economies, most significantly in Mexico's main creditor, the United States, where the Federal Reserve under Paul Volker kept rates at record highs between 1979 and 1981, reaching a peak of 16 percent in 1980. Mexico, whose foreign debt had quadrupled between 1976 and 1982 to $80 billion—the equivalent to 50.7 percent of GDP—was thus caught by the increasing emphasis in macroeconomic policy in creditor countries such as the United States toward containing inflation. High interest rates also made the United States attractive for Mexican investors, who increasingly moved their money out of Mexico.[10] Inflation further became a significant problem in Mexico during the second half of the López Portillo presidency, rising from 17.8 percent in 1978 to 98.8 percent in 1982.[11] This left the administration scrambling to announce a series of drastic measures to control inflation and tackle the country's balance of payments crisis as it entered its final year.[12]

The election year of 1982 began in horrific fashion as López Portillo prepared to hand over the presidency to his anointed successor. López Portillo was keenly aware of the potential political implications of the economic crisis for himself and the postrevolutionary political system. After the February peso devaluation, the president told representatives of private business lobby groups, "I know that a president who devalues [the peso] devalues himself; I know that a president who makes decisions in times like the present loses credibility for many sections of society and, of course, loses the faith of many others."[13] A symptom of the growing crisis of public confidence, López Portillo's final informe was preceded by weeks of rumors and calls for a return to economic nationalism amid concern over the growing interference in Mexican economic policy by international interests, chiefly the IMF.[14] The president himself gave little clue as to what he would announce in the days prior to the address. He did, however, affirm that in the three months ahead he would act "always thinking that the Mexican Revolution is alive and it deserves that we give it its proper historical presence because it is the doorway to our future."[15]

During his informe, López Portillo justified his government's efforts to accelerate economic growth through debt, arguing that it was necessary to take advantage of the favorable circumstances as "in Mexico opportunity and time have a different dimension than in rich countries. . . . The international current against the weak is too strong for swimming slowly."[16] Thus, he argued, "I made the decision to launch the country forward to save it from the trap that a hostile world, set up by powerful countries for their own benefit, permanently has readied for underdeveloped countries."[17] The president proudly explained that Mexico had rejected what he argued would have been the easy route by submitting to international pressures to dismantle trade barriers, enter the General Agreement on Trades and Tariffs (GATT), and reduce social spending.[18]

According to López Portillo, Mexico's current problems could be blamed on a "financial plague" that, "as in medieval times, brings country after country to its knees. It is transmitted by rats and its result is unemployment and misery, industrial collapse, and speculative profiteering. The cure of the healers is to deprive the patient of food, to force him to rest."[19] The president also took aim at internal enemies of Mexico's economic stability who speculated against and destabilized the peso, invested in property and businesses in the United States, and converted their earnings in pesos to savings in bank accounts denominated in US dollars.

López Portillo then outlined a strategy for his final three months in office designed to cement his place in history. Invoking the last Aztec emperor, the Mexican Revolution, the 1917 constitution, and the 1938 oil nationalization decreed by President Lázaro Cárdenas, the president employed the familiar rhetorical device of identifying the state and the nation as one to justify state control of the economy as a "Mexicanized economy."[20] López Portillo stressed the central role played by speculative financial institutions in the present crisis and the continued threat they posed to Mexico's economic health. López Portillo's solution was to issue two presidential decrees that would signal a dramatic return to economic nationalism: one putting in place government-controlled currency exchange rates and, most significantly, another nationalizing Mexico's banking system.

The speech was comparatively brief and abstract in its references to the Revolution. However, it signified a strong reassertion of revolutionary time that was immediately greeted with both shocked disbelief from business groups and the conservative PAN and a sudden outbreak of nationalist fervor from the media, intellectuals, and the left, who presented the move as a reassertion of national (popular) sovereignty. The 1982 economic crisis's culmination in the bank nationalization in this way encouraged in Mexico what Claudio Lomnitz describes as a period of historical excess often characteristic of the process of mourning and recovery that follow national trauma. As Lomnitz notes, the most noticeable characteristic of this historical obsession is a messianic historical sensibility that frames the present in terms of a leap to and from a moment of past possibility.[21] Just as historical consciousness is a hallmark of modernity, an excess of or obsession with history is in this way a hallmark of failed modernities. Mexico in 1982 experienced such a failure as another illusion of progress and prosperity collapsed into economic failure and dependency.

The leap between past and present possibility is evident in the press coverage during the days following the nationalization. One newspaper headlined its report the following day "The Beginning of Another Historical Battle" and argued for national unity behind the government in explicitly historical terms, stating, "When Juárez resolved that foreign debt could not be paid and faced the risk of invasion, he had the Mexicans behind him, even the majority of those who had been until shortly beforehand his adversaries. And the national memory is still fresh of the scenes of broad, exciting popular support for the oil expropriation decreed by Cárdenas."[22] This same schematic connecting Juárez to the present government via Cárdenas was employed by a commentator in a series of articles in another newspaper entitled, "1859–1938–1982: Decisive Years."[23] Heberto Castillo, veteran leftist activist in opposition to the PRI and a founder of the Mexican Worker's Party (PMT), joined other commentators in *Proceso* magazine in describing the bank nationalization as "the most transcendental action taken by the Mexican government since that March 18, 1938."[24] The left more generally rallied to the call of unity, with the most significant independent party of the left, the Unified Socialist Party of Mexico (PSUM), a party formed in part from the old Mexican Communist Party, calling for "solidarity of the left with the nationalized bank" and warning people to "beware of the reaction of the oligarchy."[25]

The response from public intellectuals employed similar themes. Historian and novelist Héctor Aguilar Camín noted that "the expropriation of the banks has impressed upon many people the sense of being in the presence of the greatest national event of the past forty years and nevertheless not knowing how to live it." He believed it was "an authentic return to history."[26] A historian generally much more sympathetic to neoliberal ideology, Enrique Krauze, was careful to outline his doubts about the correctness of the nationalization or comparisons to Cárdenas. He argued, however, that the present crisis was a moment during which Mexicans should look to their national history as "the source of our wisdom."[27]

Two days after the informe, the government held a rally in Mexico City's central square, the Zócalo, with a reported half million people gathering in support of the nationalization (fig. 2.1).[28] A separate rally of supportive independent organizations of the left followed several hours afterward. The official gathering closely followed the historical script of the 1938 oil expropriation when enthusiastic crowds gathered in the Zócalo to support Cárdenas. Members of PRI-affiliated peasant,

Figure 2.1. In scenes reminiscent of public displays of support for President Lázaro Cárdenas's nationalization of Mexico's oil reserves in 1938, crowds gathered in the Mexico City Zócalo to express support for López Portillo's bank nationalization on September 3, 1982. Courtesy Sergio Dorantes/Corbis.

worker, and popular sectors gathered in 1982 as they had in 1938 to hear their leaders deliver rousing speeches denouncing "reactionaries'" opposition to the measure and drawing comparisons between current events and those of 1938. The president himself spoke last from the balcony of the National Palace, declaring that "on this side are the majority who demand justice, who demand the values of our nationality; on the other, those who wish to leave with their beloved treasure."[29] As would be customary during Mexico's annual Independence Day ceremony, the president followed his address by waving the national flag to the crowds assembled below.[30]

Evoking the most emblematic historical assertion of Mexico's economic sovereignty and the country's annual celebration of its independence, the López Portillo administration staged a symbolically charged event designed to reaffirm the state's revolutionary nationalist identity.

As noted in the press, the images of 1938 were well established in the popular memory as a moment when Mexico asserted its national sovereignty in the face of intense international pressure, and comparisons between López Portillo and Cárdenas were "the order of the day."[31]

Calling upon the nation to unite behind it, as it had in past moments of crisis united behind Cárdenas and Juárez, the López Portillo administration aimed to allay fears it was beholden to the interests of international capital through a leap back to revolutionary historical time. The national villain in 1982 was sometimes referred to by a new name, *sacadólares*, people who bet against the Mexican economy by transferring their wealth abroad. But it was essentially the same forces of imperialism, reaction, and oligarchic conservatism that Mexican heroes from Cuauhtémoc to Hidalgo and Juárez to Cárdenas had battled since the birth of the Mexican nation. López Portillo reiterated the triumphant reassertion of the nation's control over its destiny when reopening the nationalized banks with a ceremony in which he raised the Mexican flag in the central Banamex branch in Mexico City. National flags were also prominently hung in all of the reopened and newly nationalized banks.[32] As López Portillo had pronounced in his final informe, the loud and clear message was that "we have broken the taboos. The Revolution is liberated from fears and accelerates its march."[33]

CHAPTER TWO

Making the Revolution Realistic

Despite the initial flourish of nationalist enthusiasm with which the bank nationalization was greeted, a range of domestic and international factors had converged to make the likelihood of a sustained swing back toward economic nationalism unlikely. Convinced of the scientific correctness of their prescriptions for modernizing the country's economy and society, a new technocratic leadership assumed power in December 1982 under President Miguel de la Madrid. This leadership was far more favorably predisposed than the López Portillo administration to reaching agreements with international financial institutions to renegotiate Mexico's foreign debt and open up its economy to foreign investment and competition.[1]

Revolutionary nationalist mythology emphasized the idea of a paternalistic, state-directed economy and society deriving from the Revolution as a third and final stage of the Mexican national epic crystallized into "the Revolution made government." Austerity measures and neoliberal reforms, however, undermined old linkages between the nation and the state, increasing tensions between organized labor and peasant groups and the presidency. These measures also failed to reignite economic growth and contributed to rising poverty and the increasing polarization of income distribution. This chapter examines how the state attempted to maintain national unity and social stability under the hegemonic PRI state in this context during the de la Madrid administration (1982–1988). I will particularly focus on the use of historical commemorations to reinforce symbolic ties between the nation and the PRI state as it retreated from direct economic intervention.

While appeals to revolutionary nationalism help to explain how the state was able to maintain a surprising degree of social and political stability during this period, revolutionary nationalism also provided a broadly understood language that was used to rally opposition to neoliberal reform and demand the fulfillment of citizenship rights. The dynamics of an established nationalist ideology at odds with neoliberal conceptions of the relationship between state, market, and individual, but upon which the state depended for its legitimacy, is therefore an important element of Mexico's neoliberal moment following the 1982 debt crisis. To understand this dynamic, I will first explain why the incoming de la Madrid administration was predisposed to embracing an economic ideology that seemed destined to undermine the symbolic and the institutional structures that had historically underwritten PRI rule.

Explaining Mexico's Neoliberal Shift

Different perspectives exist on why such a significant, almost simultaneous, shift in social and economic policy toward neoliberalism occurred in Mexico and other lower-income countries during the 1970s and 1980s. A dominant analytical framework employed by critics of neoliberalism has been influenced by Marxist thought. This is unsurprising given that weakening the power of organized labor is a central goal of neoliberal economic policy and a spectacular rise in already pronounced income inequality was a defining social characteristic of Mexico and other lower-income countries in the neoliberal era. In a broad sense, such critiques understand neoliberalism as a project aimed at the restoration of the power of the owners of capital through the centralization of upper-class control over the means through which wealth is accumulated and the privileging of the protection of capital over other economic and social policy aims.[2]

Structuralist and dependency theories of economics, which had dominated economic thinking in Latin America from at least the 1950s, have also often been employed in a complementary fashion to the Marxist critique by those analyzing Latin America's neoliberal shift. A popular critical perspective in this vein sees the factors leading up to the implementation of neoliberalism in "periphery" countries like Mexico as reflecting an international economy built according to unequal and exploitative relations between central and peripheral economies. Economic and political actors in "center" countries, according to this interpretation, cultivated and used instruments such as international financial institutions and transnational corporations alongside relaxed barriers to the movement of capital to entrench and exploit bonds of economic dependency that entangled countries such as Mexico. The greater their integration into global capitalism, the more vulnerable peripheral economies were to changes within central economies and governments could therefore be coerced into implementing neoliberal policies by threats to withdraw capital, particularly during times of crisis.[3] Successive generations of Mexican leaders had been taught such approaches to economic theory through public schools and universities.[4] It is therefore not surprising that López Portillo chose to use this analytical framework to explain why the Mexican economy had faltered during the final years of his presidency and to justify greater rather than less state direction of the economy.

These analytical approaches are useful for understanding the rise of neoliberalism in Mexico. Even allowing for a reckless approach to spending as well as flagrant corruption within the López Portillo administration, Mexico ultimately found itself at the mercy of forces beyond its control as proponents of neoliberalism gained control of US and global financial institutions, using them to force economic "adjustment" by raising interest rates to historic highs. Relatively open financial markets simultaneously permitted investors to precipitously withdraw billions of dollars from the national economy. Future credit was then conditioned on the application of neoliberal reform in negotiations which often brutally assigned the blame for debt crises on those who had taken advantage instead of those who had provided massive amounts of credit.[5] It is also worth noting that it is precisely this moment of third-world debt crisis that is most typical of the Mexican shift to neoliberalism among other developing countries that also underwent neoliberal transitions, such as Brazil, Bolivia, and Venezuela. As Fourcade-Gourinchas and Babb have noted, this debt crisis was itself "part of the larger historical process of financial globalization, which has changed the structure of constraints and opportunities within which governments must operate."[6]

It is important, however, to avoid a mechanistic determinism in the adoption of dependency and class-based analyses when explaining the Mexican state's ideological shift toward neoliberalism.[7] Some analysts have cited the rising importance of debt to Mexican governments during the 1970s as the chief explanation for the shifting patterns of elite recruitment at the highest levels of the state to the benefit of officials with particular economic education credentials who were to usher in Mexico's neoliberal era.[8] The particular preference for officials with at least graduate-level qualifications from US universities, where neoliberal theory was in vogue, has also been attributed, at least in part, to the lack of graduate-level economics courses in Mexico until the 1970s and the dominance of Marxist analysis in the economics faculty of the UNAM.[9] However, during the ten or fifteen years prior to the 1982 debt crisis, domestic political pressures also led to a reconfiguration of Mexico's political elite within the PRI. In particular, the need to distance the state from the images of the violent repression of the student movement of 1968 played a vital role in this reconfiguration.

The process of internal realignment began with President Luis Echeverría, who had served as interior minister in the Gustavo Díaz Ordaz administration (1964–1970) and was directly implicated in the Tlatelolco massacre of 1968. Following a particularly extensive election campaign based around the idea of ushering in a new era for Mexico, Echeverría conducted a thorough purge of Díaz Ordaz loyalists at the highest levels of the bureaucracy.[10] Bypassing traditional recruitment criteria privileging grassroots political and internal party experience, Echeverría sought to consolidate personal loyalty to himself by promoting a young and relatively politically inexperienced group of bureaucrats with fewer ties within the party. The incoming administration thus represented a lower than average level of continuity from the previous administration and, significantly, this reorganization of the state included a thorough change of personnel in the treasury, something that was uncommon in the changeover between administrations and that effectively sidelined many traditional economists.[11]

Echeverría also oversaw a strengthening of the power of the presidency relative to other wings of the bureaucracy, particularly in its control over economic policy. A process of relative marginalization of the treasury's influence culminated shortly after López Portillo took office with the formation of the Ministry of Programming and Budget (SPP), which was granted broad powers over the allocation of government funds.[12] This weakened the power over economic policy relative to the presidency of traditional state economists and existing internal power networks.

The objective of both Echeverría and López Portillo was likely far from instituting a neoliberal revolution in Mexico. They had, however, strengthened the ability of the presidency to dictate economic policy while facilitating the meteoric rise of a new generation of PRI technocrats who formed their own networks of political alliances with others from a similar intellectual background. The selection by López Portillo of Miguel de la Madrid—whom he had appointed as head of the SPP in 1979—to succeed him as president meant that the final piece of the puzzle fell into place for the rise of the technocrats to the top of the political system. Following de la Madrid's rapid rise from head of the SPP to the presidency, the ministry became the incubator for a new generation of PRI technocratic leadership that guided Mexican economic and development policy for close to twenty years, with all three of Mexico's presidents from 1982 to 2000 having previously served as head of the SPP.

Shared educational characteristics among a new generation of technocrats within the bureaucratic elite was also notable. These characteristics included graduate degrees in economics and a rising preference for private Mexican universities over the UNAM in Mexico City, which had traditionally served as the most important university in the recruitment of political elites. Internationally, the United States was by a wide margin the preferred destination for Mexican elites seeking graduate-level degrees.[13]

The privileging of a specific type of knowledge and educational title at the highest levels of bureaucracy accords with sociologist Pierre Bourdieu's characterization of the neoliberal state as having as its basis the rise of a new state nobility that bases its claim to rearrange society on its superior knowledge and economists' approach. The increasing importance of "expert knowledge" in neoliberal economic thought to this state further encouraged an increasing marginalization of PRI traditionalists at the highest levels of the state.[14] Such an environment appears to have been cultivated by early international proponents of neoliberalism who specifically identified the development of scientific neoliberal knowledge through think tanks and educational institutions as a core strategy in countering what they considered a socialist monopoly of the disseminators of knowledge such as universities, institutions, journals, and the media.[15]

Thus, despite the adverse institutional setting for neoliberalism of a pyramidal corporatist system dependent on internal negotiations of power and government patronage, Mexico found itself by December 1982 with a governing elite that, whatever the external pressures, had shared educational and socializing experiences that for the most part convinced them of the need to implement a neoliberal economic reform agenda. This group was also convinced of its superior claim to govern based on its specialist economic knowledge. Indicating this confidence in their abilities, the new PRI leadership even attracted attacks for a lack of consultation and technocratic arrogance from representatives of the private sector.[16] On a popular and symbolic level, however, the legitimacy of the government and the connection between the nation and the state still ran through revolutionary nationalism, which had traditionally been identified with statist and nationalist economic policies.

While the moment of crisis in itself might have stirred up an increased historical obsession with the revolutionary nationalist narrative, López Portillo encouraged this process by programmatically and rhetorically tying his response to a reassertion of strong economic nationalism. Despite this, popular expectations of a dramatic return to an assertive economic nationalism failed to survive far beyond the newly national-ized banks. Negotiations with the IMF continued and further austerity measures such as cuts to social spending were adopted during the final months of the López Portillo administration. By December enthusiastic supporters of the bank nationalization, such as historian Aguilar Camín, were describing those final months as a "no-man's land" during which the government appeared paralyzed, unwilling to proceed further down the road of economic nationalism but also unwilling to sign a new agreement with the IMF.[17]

For his part, incoming president de la Madrid had specifically iden-tified during his campaign a break with populism as an aim of his gov-ernment. In the context of Latin American neoliberal discourse, this suggested lifting the design of public policy above popular political pressures by limiting expectations that the state could effectively address these pressures.[18] This would allow the state to operate, in the words of de la Madrid, "with realism in the analysis and design of practicable policies . . . with imagination but [avoiding] fantasies."[19] Unlike nineteenth-century liberals who attacked the centralism and paternal-ism of monarchical rule, twentieth-century neoliberals globally aimed to dismantle states pressured by social demands they were held to be ill suited to solving.[20]

Whereas debates had raged within López Portillo's economic cabinet between structuralists and monetarists over an active role for the state in stimulating economic growth and consumption versus a preference for monetary controls in response to the crisis, the de la Madrid admin-istration clearly favored the latter approach. In its initial response, the Immediate Program for Economic Reorganization, the government identified inflation as the most important threat facing Mexico and con-tinued to stress controlling inflation, frugality, and integration into the global economy over stimulating domestic demand in its economic strategy.[21]

By the end of his first month in office, de la Madrid had replaced Bank of Mexico general director Carlos Tello, an economist inspired by structuralist and dependency theories, with Miguel Mancera Aguayo, a former economics student and lecturer at private Mexico City university the Autonomous Technical Institute of Mexico (ITAM) with an MA in economics from Yale.[22] De la Madrid also began to reverse the bank nationalization by issuing 34 percent of the stock of the nationalized banks to the public.[23] Throughout its term, the de la Madrid administration further reduced public expenditures excluding debt service by 62.9 percent and closed or privatized 750 of the 1,155 publically owned companies that existed in 1982.[24] At the same time, the administration continued and in some respects strengthened the centralization of decision and policy making in the executive branch of government.

With the economic crisis deepening and the new administration convinced of the need to radically reform Mexico's economic model in a way that would weaken the state's traditional methods of distributing government patronage, the PRI faced an uncertain panorama for political stability. Internally, representatives of PRI-affiliated workers' groups in the Congress were opposing and voting against reform proposals that they felt would be prejudicial to their members while others were exiting the chamber to avoid voting for measures they did not support.[25] Outside of the PRI, the government faced popular discontent and an increasingly organized and vocal opposition from the conservative PAN and private business groups. In response, state officials attempted to adapt revolutionary nationalism to their new project for modernizing the Mexican state and society.

Unity, History, and Reconciling Continuity with Crisis

The continuing crisis complicated a teleology of the nation, or simply the Revolution, marching ever forward toward progress and modernity, as was traditional in revolutionary nationalist discourse. This crisis, moreover, was widely blamed on the incompetence and corruption of the López Portillo administration, if not the culmination of successive incompetent PRI governments and the exhaustion of the PRI system generally. As the de la Madrid administration continued, revelations of the extreme corruption of top officials in the López Portillo administration reinforced the impression of a corrupt and rotten system. This sensation was compounded by the strident antistatist discourse of an emboldened PAN and private business lobby groups that increasingly coincided on the key concept of the state as the source of society's problems and a threat to personal freedom and economic development.

The irony inherent in the political conflicts between conservative opponents and the PRI was that the government was attempting to implement an economic reform project largely identical to that proposed by these opponents, leading to a situation described by historian Lorenzo Meyer as "an opposition between two groups of politicians, of individuals, but not of fundamental programs or projects."[26] Even so, maintaining unity behind the PRI system was a central preoccupation of the state during the first years of the de la Madrid presidency because, as Roderic Ai Camp notes, the belief in economic liberalism that the technocrats brought with them from foreign and domestic private university economics departments did not, at least initially, extend to a belief in the need for substantial political liberalization.[27] This was an important aspect of neoliberal reform in Mexico as the Mexican government still sought to play an active role in directing economic development, even if the strategies followed free market and monetarist principles. Indeed, the implementation of neoliberal reform required the maintenance of a relatively strong state in the face of popular resistance.

The model for the new PRI state under de la Madrid reduced the state's direct participation in the economy through privatizations and austerity measures, but retained a powerful role for the state in actively orienting even private capital toward broad strategic economic development goals by, for example, exerting pressure on private producers and retailers to restrain prices. While the government had limited success in gaining the cooperation of these producers and retailers, it had greater success pressuring business leaders to fall in line with its strategies for controlling inflation and liberalizing trade, often using threats such as audits or loss of government contracts. In the latter years of the presidency, it also used its corporatist mechanisms to establish pacts with the labor movement to suppress demand for wage increases.[28] This marriage of neoliberalism and a relatively strong state required a delicate renegotiation if not dismantling of the corporatist and government patronage mechanisms that integrated broad sections of society into the state during the postrevolutionary period while maintaining the centrality of the Revolution to the way in which the nation-state relationship was imagined.

References to corporatist methods of group integration into the state through the PRI did still feature in government speeches aimed at demonstrating the truly representative nature of the PRI system versus the alternatives. The speech offered during the official ceremony for Independence Day at Mexico City's Angel of Independence monument in 1983 by Interior Minister Manuel Bartlett provides a particularly neat summary of this construction. The PRI regime was, according to Bartlett, analogous to the "national society" as "the workers' movement, the peasants, [and] the popular classes all have in our regime an instrument for the promotion of their interests, they are the base, the allies, the destiny of the Revolutionary State."[29] This statement also highlighted the genuine lack of national or cross-class reach of other political parties such as the PSUM on the left and PAN on the right. The PRI was indeed the only truly national political party in Mexico during the 1980s. Thus, as the principal speaker at the 1984 Revolution Day celebrations argued, the Revolution continued to be a truly national idiom for politics and society in Mexico as it included "different classes; women, men, and young people of the north, south, central, east, and west of the country, contributing to give a national character to the collective project of Mexicans."[30]

From the earliest moments of the de la Madrid presidency, the historical emphasis in official rhetoric changed from the triumphal tones of comparisons between the 1938 oil expropriation and the 1982 bank nationalization to more subdued reassurances of the ability of the state with the nation united behind it to overcome the present crisis. Thus, during the Juárez commemorations at San Pablo Guelatao, Oaxaca, in March 1983, Secretary of Foreign Affairs Bernardo Sepúlveda Amor was careful to stress that the current crisis was less severe than that faced and overcome by Juárez.[31] In May, at the annual Carranza commemoration in Tlaxcalantongo, Puebla, where Carranza was assassinated in 1920, the drafting of the 1917 constitution amid crisis served as an example of Mexico knowing how to overcome its most difficult moments, while the chief speaker at the Cárdenas commemoration in Mexico City argued that, as in 1938, Mexicans needed to strengthen their unity in order to overcome the economic crisis.[32] This established one of the main ways in which the government sought to maintain the symbolic ties between the state and the nation during an administration characterized by almost perpetual crisis: by stressing links between the present and past moments of difficulty and the example of the heroes of the past whose project had culminated in the postrevolutionary state to overcome these crises.

In the historicizing of present difficulties, there was an implicit fusion of the state with Mexican national identity. By extension, during the 1980s government representatives portrayed attacks against the government as by extension attacks on "Mexicanness," as the PRI system was an "organic" expression of "the national political being."[33] If the historic lineage of the present administration could be traced back to historic national triumphs and heroes, then that of its opponents could also be connected to those who had worked to undermine such victories and heroes. When some attempted to dispute the official version of Mexican history, government representatives further decried this as a profane assault on Mexican national identity.[34]

Counterrevolutionaries and Anti-Mexicans

Counterrevolutionaries and reactionaries served as a common foil against whose machinations postrevolutionary governments would warn since the very conception of the Revolution as such following the Maderista victory in 1911.[35] Postrevolutionary state-builders presented a Revolution/reaction fracture as a majority/minority split, fusing a reified notion of the Mexican Revolution with national history, symbols, values, and traditions to claim moral authority for their actions as the authentic representative as the popular traditions and identity of the majority of Mexicans. That the almost always unspecified figure of the reactionary continued to feature in revolutionary nationalist discourse in the 1980s is a testament to the successful commodification of a discourse which provided a genealogy not only for the state, but for those with competing claims to power.

During commemorations of Juárez's birth on March 21 during the 1980s, government speakers thus compared their opponents to nineteenth-century conservatives who collaborated with the French invasion and occupation of Mexico and who continued to "diligently eat away at the columns of the Republic."[36] They were those who "aspire toward regaining old privileges."[37] More direct aim was sometimes taken at specific groups, such as organized business lobby groups, that were politically active and vocal in their criticisms of the PRI state during this period. As one speaker noted, "since the triumph of the [liberal] Republic, the nation overcame the spurious tradition of the so-called assemblies 'of notables.' The national will is opposed to the pretensions of business leadership and rejects all authoritarian conceptions based upon the supposed sovereignty of notable individu-als."[38] In conclusion, however, it could always be said, as stated during the 1984 Revolution Day commemoration speech, that counterrevolu-tionaries had failed in the past and those who tried to defeat the Revolution would fail in the future.[39]

As Mexico's economic and political stability worsened during the de la Madrid presidency, this line of attack became more specific and aggressive. One speaker likened current detractors of the government to the historical enemies of Mexico's national heroes being commemorated as "the landholders, the conservatives, the liars, the unrealistic dream-ers of foreign paradises, the deserters, the supporters of foreign inter-ests; in sum, the anti-Mexicans."[40] In another speech in the lead-up to the 1986 state elections in Zacatecas, the national president of the PRI argued that it was "the usual adversaries" working against the Mexican Revolution and the social rights of the people, however, as Juárez had sentenced, "the triumph of the reaction is morally impossible."[41]

The defeat or even criticism of the PRI state and its policies was thus the defeat, criticism, or abandonment of the Revolution itself as, accord-ing to a 1985 Revolution Day speech, "the Revolution cannot be reduced to its original violence nor to the whole of the new institutions: within it has to be included the social project, the realization of which is the object of the entire effort which was undertaken. Only the consumma-tion of this project or its abandoning, will lead to the end of the Revolution."[42] Furthermore, the speaker argued, "this is the Revolution, this is our country. In our calculations, in our actions, we do not bet on its ruin, we bet on its victory because we are going to triumph."[43] Such a conception implied a state that transcended the current political moment and instead inhabited the same realm of the reified Revolution/ nation marching ever forward toward progress, with those who bet against the success of the PRI state thus betting against Mexico. In the same way as Francis Fukuyama would later proclaim the teleology of a neoliberal "end of history" that could only be derailed by a regressive last man, the Mexican state continued to promote the idea of a revolu-tionary end of history that could only be derailed by the figure of the last man as the reactionary who wished to frustrate history's grand designs.[44]

Another common charge against opponents was that they were act-ing on behalf of foreign interests, particularly those of the United States. If all nationalisms define themselves at least partly in relation to com-peting nationalisms, then the perennial other for Mexico has been its powerful northern neighbor. American imperialism had left deep scars on the national psyche following the Mexican-American War (1846–1848) and US interventions during the Revolution, particularly the invasion and occupation of Veracruz in 1914.

During the roughly concurrent de la Madrid and Ronald Reagan administrations, allusions to US intervention in Mexican affairs increased as relations between the two countries deteriorated notably from 1984 onward. The deterioration was chiefly due to Mexican opposition to US military intervention in Central America, the torture and murder in Mexico of US Drug Enforcement Agency agent Enrique Camarena, and the resurgence of economic crisis in 1985, aggravating US concerns over possible instability on its southern border and the increasing flow of immigrants.[45] The Reagan government applied increasing pressure on the de la Madrid administration over these issues from 1985 onward, including the threat to cease buying fifty thousand barrels a day of Mexican oil for "security reasons."[46] Comments by the US ambassador to Mexico, John Gavin, further increased tensions as he criticized Mexican officials for a "lack of vigor" in the war against drugs and called Mexico a "safe haven" for Soviet spies.[47]

In the lead-up to the hotly contested 1986 gubernatorial elections in the state of Chihuahua, US Republican senator Jesse Helms organized a series of hearings on Mexico in the Senate Foreign Relations Committee during which Reagan administration officials lined up to criticize Mexico for electoral fraud, corruption, and the drug trade. One official linked the family of the president to drug trafficking and accused the governor of Sonora of growing marijuana and opium poppies. Helms himself claimed that the 1982 presidential elections had been fraudulent and called for the Mexican president to step down (fig. 2.2).[48]

These hearings sparked outrage in Mexico and, once again, the PRI and the independent left found themselves on the same side as both participated in a Great Popular March in Defense of National Sovereignty from the Monument to the Revolution to the Mexico City Zócalo on the anniversary of Cárdenas's birth. Tens of thousands of people gathered to hear speakers such as actress Ofelia Medina—a veteran supporter of left-wing causes—denounce those who in the Reagan era "want to modify the constitutional juridical regime that we Mexicans have given ourselves; they want to push the country into crisis . . . looking to impose a system of parties without options for real transformation, desiring a mono-political economic regime that offers a paradise for foreign investment and speculation."[49]

Figure 2.2. A circa 1986 political sign in Mexico City inverts statements in the US Senate Foreign Relations Committee linking Mexican government politicians to the drug trade. Instead, US senator and critic of the Mexican government Jesse Helms is described as the *capo* (drug lord) of the United States trying to impose a narco PAN government on Mexico. The sign further calls for the end of Mexico's debt repayments and continental unity against drug trafficking. Courtesy Sergio Dorantes/Corbis.

As was implicit in the comments by Medina, the deteriorating relationship between the two countries included increased US interest in Mexico's domestic politics. Mexico's political system was generally denounced as fraudulent and undemocratic from north of the border. Elections, particularly in northern states such as Chihuahua, Coahuila, and Nuevo León, where the PAN was most electorally strong, were followed to an unprecedented extent by the US media during the mid-1980s, with coverage generally critical of the PRI and sympathetic to the PAN.[50] The PAN maintained that it was perfectly reasonable for US politicians and the media to opine about Mexico as this was how open democratic societies operate.[51] However, the support shown in the US media for the PAN's cause and the attendance of a PAN delegation to the Republican National Convention in 1985 left the party vulnerable to nationalist attacks over its closeness to an interventionist US government.[52]

This was a favorable context for government seeking to strengthen its symbolic ties to the nation, in this case as a bulwark against US imperialism, while implementing significant reforms amid economic crisis. Defense against foreign interference had been a feature of state discourse prior to this escalation in tensions. Such references became more urgent in tone, however, at occasions such as the May 1986 Carranza commemoration, in which the principal speaker took aim at US interference, arguing: "Today as in the past, there are fading foreign politicians, looked upon poorly by their compatriots as intolerant and reactionary, who in collusion with venal and disreputable journalists try to tarnish the image of our country and its institutions with false and misleading information. They will never succeed! The irreproachable national and international conduct of Mexico and its President Miguel de la Madrid are the most rotund and objective retort to these mercenary attacks."[53]

Historical commemorations thus began to take on a particularly aggressive tone in their denunciations of unpatriotic opposition. The principal speaker at the 1986 Juárez commemoration denounced "internal and external enemies," noting that "in every part of the world opposition parties try to capitalize on errors and weaknesses of the current government. What is not acceptable is that they look for echo chambers outside national borders and even less so that they ally themselves with interest groups who are attempting to weaken the country."[54] During the Independence Day celebrations of the same year, Mexico's Attorney General Sergio García Ramírez warned against the loss of Mexican identity and independence before taking aim at the "hall of shame" that looked for support outside of Mexico and were offended by the Constitution of 1917, Juárez, and the Revolution.[55]

The attorney general's comments would be easily understood as referring to many of the PAN's policies, including proposals to change the constitution to permit a greater role for the Catholic Church in education and politics—with Juárez being the historical figure most associated with attacking church privileges—and proposals to abolish the collective land ownership ejido system for rural communities, with the institution of the ejido also enshrined in the constitution and strongly associated with the revolutionary struggle. To underscore his argument, García concluded by summing up the revolutionary nationalist synthesis: "Mexico has an experience of combat, distinguished by social liberalism, constitutionalism and, more recently, revolutionary nationalism and all of them, seen from the point of view of the patria, are nationalism. . . . They are revolution marching forward."[56]

Crafting a Realistic Revolution as the Crisis Deepens

At the same time Mexico's relationship with the United States began to deteriorate, the country plunged into economic crisis after a brief upturn during 1984. The aggressive stance taken by US politicians toward Mexico likely served more than anything to strengthen the de la Madrid government domestically during a new period of economic crisis by providing it with an external aggressor against which it could assert its nationalist credentials. As will be seen in the next chapter, the state had also come under significant domestic criticism, particularly for its response to the September 1985 Mexico City earthquake, which exposed profound government corruption and inefficiency. Even prior to the earthquake, however, Mexico had begun to slip into crisis.

Once again, both internal and external events precipitated this crisis. A relative relaxation of government austerity programs in the lead-up to the 1985 midterm elections contributed to a sharp rise in inflation, while Saudi Arabia's decision to flood oil markets led to an even more drastic drop in oil prices than that which had triggered the economic crisis of 1981–1982.[57] The drop in oil prices more than wiped out any savings made by Mexico on servicing its debt due to lower interest rates in the United States, leaving Mexico to renegotiate its debt once again as it found itself unable to make payments of around $700 million per month in debt servicing.[58]

By now Mexico's debt obligations had become the greatest impediment to economic recovery as severe cuts to government spending were not enough to cover even interest payments and creditors continued pressing for deeper cuts while refusing to negotiate lower interest rates. Again, speculation grew during 1985 about the possibility of a dramatic nationalist gesture such as a unilateral debt moratorium. Instead, weak compromise agreements were reached with international financial institutions and private banks, which somewhat relaxed demands for the government to deepen austerity programs. These agreements did, however, commit the Mexican government to move further toward market liberalization—including through reductions in government subsidies, lowering restrictions on foreign investment, and more privatizations of state-owned enterprises—in return for new loans.[59] While this gave the government some breathing space, the new loans increased its overall debt burden by tens of billions of dollars.

Despite the lack of flexibility shown by its creditors, the Mexican government does not appear to have seriously considered a radical change from the economic strategy employed following the 1982 debt crisis. It was for the most part a model debtor, and trade liberalization continued to the point that in 1986 the de la Madrid administration overturned López Portillo's earlier rejections on economic nationalist grounds to joining the General Agreement on Trades and Tariffs (GATT). While much of the political discourse used by supporters of neoliberalism elsewhere centered on ideas of individual freedom, such a discourse was problematic for a government attempting to maintain the integrity of a highly centralized hegemonic political system. This was particularly true when its chief political opponents employed precisely this language to attack the PRI state for the limitations placed on political plurality and as the origin of Mexico's current economic problems. US verbal aggression had bought the government some space, but it faced an increasingly problematic future in terms of maintaining social stability amid deteriorating economic conditions and sharp cuts in social spending without any visible reward in the short or medium term for these austerity measures.

In attempting to integrate its development strategy into the established symbolism of revolutionary nationalism, the government thus employed a different element of neoliberal political discourse that was applicable to its circumstances: the idea of neoliberalism as an objective science of economics such that "there is no alternative." This idea would likely have held innate appeal to the government's technocratic leadership on a personal level, as it underscored their privileged relationship to power owing to their possession of this knowledge. It is also likely the key to why the PRI technocrats were willing to acquiesce to the demands of international capital, as, beyond any conscious defense of class interest, the economic orthodoxy being applied was also the methodological lens through which they saw and analyzed the crisis.[60] Such a discourse in itself held little symbolic power and would not have necessarily been accepted outside the relatively small elite schooled in neoliberal economics. However, officials from the de la Madrid administration linked the concept to revolutionary nationalism in an attempt to portray its reform project as essentially nationalist.

The discourse of the inevitability of neoliberal reform appeared from the very first year of the de la Madrid presidency. During Independence Day commemorations, the Interior Minister began to adjectivize the economic reform as "revolutionary" when arguing that "the austerity policy which has been implemented is an indisputable expression of revolutionary realism, of responsibility and courage, of a sense of history."[61] This revolutionary realism involved, according to the speaker at the 1986 Cárdenas commemoration, "finding the equilibrium between a utopian nationalism, disconnected from the cold international economic reality, and an excessive pragmatism that forgets our most valuable political principals."[62]

In a discursive strategy that perhaps best established the argument for the continued relevance of the PRI state in an era of economic austerity measures that undermined its traditional rhetorical commitments to social justice, director of the SPP Carlos Salinas de Gortari asserted during the 1983 Revolution Day commemorations that "there is no real alternative to Revolutionary austerity."[63] Within his speech, Salinas differentiated between what he called "reactionary austerity" and the revolutionary variety, arguing that revolutionary austerity seeks the reordering of the economy, creates the conditions for Mexico to overcome the structural difficulties and deficiencies, and prepares the country for the future. On the other hand, reactionary or regressive austerity "is the option of economic reform without social aims; it is the pillaging of the majorities and the renouncing of national sovereignty; it is the re-establishing of a liberalism without restriction; the law of profit as the motor of social life."[64] In other words, even if "there is no alternative," things might still be worse without the postrevolutionary state to at least moderate some of the more pernicious social effects of austerity and economic reform.

As to whether this austerity could really be considered revolutionary, the PRI argued that it in fact reflected a core strength of the Revolution as the guiding force in Mexico's continued development: its ability to adapt and evolve according to changing circumstances. According to this view, as articulated at a 1985 Carranza commemoration, change is necessary and "it has to be admitted that the Revolution is alive because it has known how to recognize and correct with careful restraint its deviations; because it has been able to renew itself."[65] After all, "revolutions, social movements, are just that: movements. Revolutionary motionlessness does not exist, because motionlessness is the tomb of revolutions."[66]

A notion of the PRI state as an organic political expression of the nation's history that protected the nation from the constant threat that reactionaries and external enemies posed to the social conquests of the Revolution was well established before the 1982 debt crisis. The major innovation in revolutionary nationalist discourse during the de la

Madrid administration was the idea of revolutionary realism, which justified harsh government austerity programs in place of economic nationalist solutions. Using a variation of global neoliberal discourse that spoke of an economic science that provided the only viable option for economic development, the state situated economic reform involving a significant reduction in the government's commitment to ameliorating social and economic inequality as the latest stage of the revolutionary nation's unstoppable march toward modernity.

In this way, the continuity of the state helped justify what could have been an otherwise unpalatable economic reform agenda as the state's heritage in the Revolution fused it with the extension of revolutionary land and labor rights as well as the economic growth of earlier decades. By extension, those opposing this government could be fused with those who had fought against the popular struggles and gains of Mexico's past. The PRI state's historical roots in this way helped it survive the immediate effects of its reforms through the historicizing of political power as a reified expression of the nation that transcended present contingencies. The intent was that, even if its ends are not immediately apparent, many Mexicans might continue to give the government the benefit of the doubt.

The Limits of Nationalist Legitimization of State Power

The PRI state was not entirely convincing in its efforts to legitimize its reform agenda using nationalist discourse in the face of a precipitous decline in living standards for the majority of Mexicans. While the mythology of the Revolution had promoted a patriarchal relationship between the state and the nation that the PRI wished to retain, the events and heroes being commemorated continued to hold symbolic power in part because they could be rooted in the intended audience's prior awareness of these heroes and their histories, whether they were Cárdenas's economic nationalism or Emiliano Zapata's fight for land and liberty alongside the peasants of Morelos. They were also tied symbolically to political structures and reforms now being reversed.

The example of Zapata is particularly instructive of how revolutionary nationalist mythology could be turned into a symbolic weapon against the PRI state. In the immediate aftermath of the 1982 debt crisis, protest movements adopting the figure of Zapata (fig. 2.3) provided the most visible antecedent for the later strategic use of revolutionary

Figure 2.3. Statue of
Emiliano Zapata in
Cuautla, Morelos, where
his remains are
entombed and official
government commemo-
rations are held on the
anniversary of his death.
Photo by author.

nationalism to challenge the state's legitimacy. The use of Zapata as a weapon against the state was most clearly in evidence during the de la Madrid period on the annual commemorations of Zapata's assassination.

The failure of successive Mexican governments to improve the living standards of peasants had long been cited both by PRI officials and critics of the system as one of the postrevolutionary state's biggest failures. If past administrations represented unfulfilled promises, then the de la Madrid administration did not seem to be offering even promises. At the 1983 Zapata commemoration in Cuautla, Morelos, the subsecretary of agrarian reform proclaimed that there was simply no more land left to redistribute, despite the demands of peasants and that "today the revolutionary thing to do is not redistributing land but increasing agricultural production to decrease the deficit in foodstuffs and improve the situation of the peasant."[67]

Such rhetoric was contrasted in press coverage, such as that of the newspaper *Unomásuno* that accompanied its coverage of the official ceremonies with images of old veterans of Zapata's Army of the South in humble clothing and often staring straight ahead in an accusatory manner. Alongside the official comments were also printed the counter-claims of peasant groups that there were still large extensions of land in private hands that the government was obliged to redistribute under Article 27 of the constitution. Through such coverage, the commemo-ration of Zapata's death served to reveal the failures of the post-revolutionary regimes to match a revolutionary agrarian rhetoric with real improvement in the conditions of peasants. Reporting of the Zapata commemoration more than any other thus tended to focus on the gap between an official revolutionary nationalist rhetoric and the reality of how the system functioned.

As land redistribution slowed and the de la Madrid administration dismantled protectionist measures such as price controls and trade bar-riers, the Zapata commemorations increasingly became an occasion for protest against government agrarian policy. In 1984 two large groups of peasant and political organizations converged on Mexico City to form a protest camp in the Zócalo in front of the National Palace and stage protest marches from the Escuela Normal and Monument to the Revolution to the Zócalo.[68] Similar protests also took place in cities such as San Luis Potosí and Tuxtla Gutiérrez, Chiapas.[69] Peasant orga-nizations used the occasion to denounce what they referred to as an agrarian counterreform, which allowed the persistence of large concen-trations of land in few hands and pushed peasants into low-paid jobs with poor conditions.[70]

With the protest marches in Mexico City continuing to grow in size, the government began to pay more attention to official Zapata com-memorations. During the midterm election year of 1985, high profile defections and public expressions of discontent from the PRI-affiliated National Peasant Confederation (CNC) over the underrepresentation of peasant leaders in the PRI's candidate lists preceded the Zapata com-memoration.[71] At the official commemoration in Cuautla only months before the elections, the subsecretary of agricultural reform criticized "those who take advantage of this moment of economic hardship, of the confusion to which the crisis gives rise, to provoke and preach what they consider politically opportunistic: agitation, showy and disruptive pro-tests."[72] Meanwhile, in Mexico City an estimated thirty thousand peo-ple, many of whom had traveled from other states, participated in protest marches that progressed from the edges of the city to key venues such as the US embassy and the buildings of the secretariat of agrarian reform before ending with a rally in the Zócalo.[73] Asked directly about the protests following the ceremony in Cuautla, Secretary of Agricultural Reform Luis Martínez Villicaña cast doubt on the motives behind the marches, remarking, "I am convinced that this is not a march of authentic peasants: this has a high political content judging by its timing."[74] Zapata's son Mateo, now speaking as secretary of mixed agriculture in the state of Morelos, also pronounced himself against such independent peasant organizations as it was "easier to obtain solutions from government, the solution is within the government."[75]

The government did not have much effect in dissuading the protesters, however, and began to increase the scale of official commemorations of Zapata's assassination as a counteroffensive measure. In 1987 a parallel Zapata commemoration ceremony to the one in Cuautla was held in Mexico City where protestors had begun to dominate commemorations of the date. The official commemoration was held at the offices of the CNC and attended by President de la Madrid. This commemoration involved three separate ceremonies, including one outside the building attended by an estimated twenty-five thousand peasants and another attended by state governors, senators, and federal deputies inside the building. The president took advantage of the occasion to submit 115 presidential resolutions of land disputes and witness the signing of agreements between the CNC and various government institutions, including peasant housing projects, rural infrastructure, and scholarships for peasant children. To further emphasize the message of this display, the secretary of agrarian reform asked all peasant leaders during his speech to join the government's efforts because "only through the path of respect toward [state] institutions can authentic agrarian justice be achieved."[76]

Despite the government's increased attention to Zapata commemorations, protest marches around this date continued to grow. On the same day government officials commemorated Zapata at CNC headquarters in Mexico City and in Cuautla, protest marches were held in states such as Jalisco, Guerrero, Michoacán, and Chiapas.[77] Three separate protest marches were also held in Mexico City, where about two dozen representatives of independent peasant groups completed a hunger strike next to the Mexico City cathedral in protest of the government's lack of attention to peasant demands. While the government had moved the focus of their commemorations to Mexico City, the protestors retained control of the symbolically important public spaces of the Monument to the Revolution and the Zócalo, chanting slogans such as, "If Zapata were alive, he would be with us."[78]

These dueling Zapata commemorations revealed a key weakness in the use of historical nationalist discourse for perpetuating the legitimacy of a state regardless of significant swings in policy. A myth or hero such as Zapata continually needs to be rooted in some kind of history because, if he is read as an empty symbol or alibi for the PRI, for example, then his use is discredited in the eyes of the intended audience by the obviousness of its motivation. What is essential for symbolic language to work is for it to appear that the symbol, in this case Zapata, naturally conjured up the concept, the PRI. In other words, it was necessary for the audience to hold an understanding that the PRI resulted from the Revolution and Zapata *was* an important part of that Revolution. Once this is understood, the use of Zapata by the PRI appears perfectly natural.

The Zapata myth, propagated throughout Mexico as part of the nationalist project of the postrevolutionary regime, also showed the multidirectional and dynamic nature of how mythology functions. As Zapata *did* lead indigenous and mestizo peasants in defense of their rights to land and social and economic justice, his connection to present day peasant groups independent from the PRI was also a natural one. It was necessary for the PRI to keep this aspect of the Zapata myth alive so that it could promote the image of a benevolent patriarchal state taking care of the needs of peasants, who should view their material interests as best met through state institutions rather than through other forms of independent action. However, this meant that, as historian Samuel Brunk has argued, "even as Zapata helped people imagine a national community, in Mexico's various corners ritual observances of his death gradually created the conditions wherein communities of protest could form around him and use him to challenge the state's legitimacy."[79]

This opened up a problem for the PRI as neoliberal reforms undermined the structural mechanisms that reinforced the symbolic linkages between the nation and the state. Revolutionary nationalism potentially provided raw material for the creation of new, broadly recognizable symbolic languages of protest which could be used to oppose the hegemonic PRI state and its modernization project. Such contestations of the true meaning of the official national culture promoted by the state raise the broader question of how beliefs and practices are implanted and legitimated in a society, "whether by imposition from above (hegemony) or by some more open-ended, chaotic process of contestation and negotiation in which groups of social actors may each have a fairly open-eyed vision of what they want their culture (or their segment of it) to be like."[80] The contestation of the date of the Zapata commemoration on a national scale during a period of crisis and reform suggests that this contestation and negotiation formed an important and ongoing element of the legitimization of the hegemonic PRI state. In this way, the symbolic language of revolutionary nationalism was not simply a tool of manipulation as, to be successful, its audience had to be complicit in the construction of its meaning by accepting its underpinning assumptions. When groups or individuals withdrew this complicity, nationalist discourse could well be redefined by groups seeking to undermine the state's attempts to promote order and unity.

An Excessively Historical Crisis

In addition to aggressive anti-Mexican posturing by some US politicians and the lack of an obviously viable alternative national modernization project, the continued power of revolutionary nationalism as a framework for imagining the Mexican nation likely played an important role in maintaining a surprisingly high level of political stability during the de la Madrid administration. If confidence in the PRI was waning, it did not necessarily follow that the Revolution's symbolic power declined along with it. If anything, reflections on national history and identity became increasingly central to national political debate during this time of crisis and the Revolution was by now an unavoidable component of such reflections. While there was increasing recognition and commentary about the way in which the Revolution had been relegated to mere rhetoric by the PRI, it does not follow that the general concept of the Revolution had ceased to have its own power grounded in a collective sense of national identity or in local identities and histories.

The continuing symbolic power of the Revolution did not, however, necessarily ensure the PRI's privileged hold on power. Increasing discussion of the failures or deviations from the Revolution showed the risk to the PRI system of opponents who could contest not just the party's control of the state but also its privileged relationship to the Revolution. As the Zapata counter-commemorations show, an anti-PRI revolutionary nationalist discourse became increasingly prominent following the debt crisis of 1982. Thus, while the PRI was initially remarkably successful in preserving social stability in spite of an almost perpetual sense of crisis, during the de la Madrid presidency the links between the nation and the state became increasingly frayed. These weakening links occurred in the realm of direct, material assistance to Mexican citizens and found clear expression in the symbolic realm of history and nationalism. The widening gap between the actions of the PRI state and the discourse that traditionally legitimized its rule also provided an opening for opposition parties who during the 1980s harnessed both revolutionary nationalism and transnational discourses of freedom and democracy associated with neoliberalism to contest the PRI's continued hold on power.

¡Ya es tiempo!: Chihuahua, 1986

As it approached the July 1986 elections for governor, state legislature, and municipal governments, the northern border state of Chihuahua was the focus of intense national and international attention as a central battleground for democracy in Mexico. Under the PRI system gubernatorial elections had the predictability of presidential elections as state governorships helped tie the national territory together politically through the hegemonic state party. In Chihuahua, home of Pancho Villa and a key battleground of the Mexican Revolution, the mechanisms, social pacts, and rituals of the PRI system had historically functioned relatively effectively.[1] However, Chihuahua emerged in the 1980s as a state where the PRI system's survival faced one of its greatest tests. Following local elections in 1983, the PAN opposition held municipal governments encompassing more than half of the state's population, including the two largest and most symbolically important cities: state capital Chihuahua and border city Ciudad Juárez.[2] Thus, with the electoral fortunes of the PAN on the rise and a PRI that looked to be in potentially terminal decline across northern Mexico, the 1986 Chihuahua elections appeared as a key test of the limits of revolutionary nationalist appeals to legitimacy for the PRI.

Chihuahua was also representative of regional cultural and economic differences that were increasingly manifested in local political conflicts and through anti-center/anti-PRI sentiment. By the mid-1980s Chihuahua was experiencing a boom in maquiladoras, which were mostly foreign-owned assembly plants concentrated near the border in cities like Ciudad Juárez, where imported goods would be assembled and then exported as finished products. The maquiladora economy defied the national downturn to experience rising growth following the 1982 debt crisis, with the peso devaluation and domestic crisis improving the competitiveness of maquiladoras as a source of cheap labor for transnational companies.[3] Chihuahua's greater integration with the US economy, however, also meant that the price of basic goods sourced from the United States, as well as the interest payments on the dollar-denominated loans of northern businesspeople, rose following the crisis. This, along with the higher cost of public services relative to central Mexico, fed anti–Mexico City resentment.[4]

Strong social links with the United States were also an important factor in Chihuahua's distinct political culture. These links included the education of many middle- and upper-class students in US schools and universities that culturally reinforced a conception of democratic politics distinct from the Mexican model and weakened the normative power of the Mexican public education system.[5] Taken together, this context of growing social, cultural, and economic separation from the center of state power in Mexico City and the onset of a severe national economic crisis saw Chihuahua reemerge during the 1980s as a state where local grievances took on national implications.

The PAN's candidate for the governorship in 1986 was Francisco Barrio Terrazas, a descendent of the Terrazas-Creel family that during the Porfiriato rose to dominate the economic and political life of Chihuahua. Indeed, this dominance of the local economy and politics was a central motivation for many small ranchers and businessmen to rebel during the Revolution. Villista forces also specifically targeted the Terrazas-Creel family for expropriation of lands and businesses.[6] Following the Revolution, the local Porfirian elite—including the Terrazas-Creel family—soon regained prominence in the regional economy; however, the family did not regain their political dominance of the state.[7] Barrio Terrazas's progression from private enterprise to politics was thus representative of a longer historical convergence between pre- and postrevolutionary economic and political elites in Chihuahua. The candidate was further emblematic of a new group of *neopanista* leaders, having entered the PAN in 1983 from the business world to immediately compete for a high profile and strategically important elected position as mayor of Ciudad Juárez.

The PRI chose as their gubernatorial candidate Fernando Baeza Meléndez, a Jesuit-educated professional with a background in his youth of Christian democratic activism. In this way, he resembled more a traditional PAN than PRI politician. Indeed, the PRI's candidate to succeed Barrio Terrazas as Ciudad Juárez's mayor, high-profile industrialist Jaime Bermúdez Cuarón, argued that the PRI and PAN were essentially pursuing the same objectives; however, "what is different is the path: we are realists and they are idealists."[8] The selection of Bermúdez Cuarón was part of a broader PRI strategy to win the support of private enterprise, which had increasingly supported the PAN in recent elections.[9] This candidate was furthermore a member of one of the most powerful families to emerge in Chihuahua following the Revolution, with patriarch Antonio J. Bermúdez using his wealth to build political connections that led to his appointment as director general of Pemex by President Miguel Alemán in 1947.[10] In this sense, the Bermúdez Cuarón candidature was representative of the traditionally cozy relationship that belied a revolutionary nationalist discourse distancing the PRI from business elites.

While not a central point of contention during the elections, revolutionary nationalist claims to legitimacy did feature in the PRI's campaign. For example, the campaign director used the standard revolution/ reaction dichotomy to argue that the PRI was "the heir of the Independence campaign, of the men of the Reform, and of the hopes and aspirations of the people of Mexico expressed in the Revolution. The PAN is heir to everything opposed to all this; they are incorrect Mexicans."[11] The leader of PRI-affiliated Revolutionary Confederation of Workers and Peasants (CROC) further appealed to the historical legacy of the PRI state's achievements to win support, denouncing the fact that "a great number of Chihuahuenses are against the PRI and the system. How do they dare react with ingratitude against the system that gave them everything: ISSTE, IMSS,[12] almost free higher education, freedom to say what they want?"[13]

The swearing in of the PRI's local candidates was, however, noted in the press for striking steel workers shouting for a solution to their demands. Members of affiliated sectoral organizations who were bussed to the state capital for the event also emptied out of the venue once they had registered their attendance and claimed their free lunch.[14] A breakdown of the traditional corporatist mechanisms of negotiation between state and society thus bubbled to the surface in Chihuahua during the usual rituals of the electoral process designed as displays of party unity.[15]

Against an exhausted PRI system, the PAN offered change to Chihuahua. This change was defined as democracy and freedom versus the entrenched fraud, corruption, and authoritarianism of the PRI. Democracy was, by the mid-1980s, established as a central discourse for the legitimization of political power crossing ideological lines, linked strongly by the PAN to the concept of freedom. The act of voting for the PAN was portrayed in the party's campaign material as in and of itself a brief experience of freedom from the repressiveness of the PRI, with one pamphlet produced by the PAN telling voters that "on July 6, you have ten seconds of freedom to vote according to your convictions."[16] The fight for a new era of freedom and democracy was linked to another core theme of the PAN campaign: the opportunity for the people of Chihuahua to vote against "the system," which was centered in Mexico City, undemocratic, long insensitive to local problems, and had caused the current economic crisis. Barrio Terrazas's campaign summed up this call for change with the slogan, "¡Ya es tiempo!" (It's time!).[17]

As political sociologist Alberto Aziz Nassif noted, there was little debate during the campaign about the policy platforms of the PAN and PRI candidates, which, while containing important structural differences in the realm of governance, coincided on the fundamentals of the state's development model. Instead, debate focused on the electoral process itself.[18] This was representative of a broader discursive strategy adopted by the PAN across Mexico to legitimize its claim to power on the basis of liberal democratic criteria. Change was a central discursive theme, as democracy necessarily required alternation in power, and such an alternation required the PRI to lose elections for them to be considered democratic. Reinforcing the centrality of democracy and electoral pluralism in the Chihuahua campaign was the further formation by a broad coalition of non-PRI opposition groups ranging from conservative Catholic to independent worker and peasant organizations into the Democratic Electoral Movement (MDE).[19]

Two months before the elections, the PAN began a campaign of civil disobedience directed at reversing December 1985 state electoral reforms that increased the discretional power of PRI-affiliated electoral officials and weakened the opposition's ability to monitor the election process. Proposed actions included writing on banknotes, "In Chihuahua we demand that the vote be respected"; placing stickers on car license plates with the slogan, "I am a civil disobedient"; and instructing supporters not to pay water or electricity bills.[20] The intensity of the denunciations of fraud increased as the election approached, with actions including a hunger strike led by PAN mayor of the state capital Luis H. Álvarez, and the occupation of the offices of the National Registry of Electors in protest of apparent PRI manipulation of the electoral system.[21]

After decades of subtle politicking over a limited range of issues, the Catholic clergy emerged during the early 1980s as an increasingly vocal political actor. Political scientist Roderic Ai Camp has cited the 1986

Chihuahua elections as the tipping point for the church's full adoption of an activist political posture.[22] In Chihuahua, the clergy released guides for Catholic voters, *Vote with Responsibility* in 1983 and *Christian Coherence in Politics* in 1986. The shift in tone from the first document, which dealt with more general questions regarding Christian morality and politics, to the second, which focused on electoral fraud as "the greatest corruption" affecting Mexico, mirrored a similar evolution in PAN opposition discourse in the 1980s.[23] Before the election, the archbishop of Chihuahua, Adalberto Almeida y Merino, proclaimed that the church was "with the people against electoral fraud" and supported the civil disobedience campaign, arguing, "they can legalize but not moralize fraud. An immoral law is not binding."[24]

Baeza, meanwhile, minimized or omitted the PRI logo from his campaign material and adopted the slogans, "Baeza is ours" and "Baeza is different."[25] The PRI candidate also argued for a federalism in which Chihuahua "lives its own individuality . . . strongly joined to a national project. Without the centralism that depletes our resources."[26] Furthermore, the PRI sidestepped direct conflict with the church in Chihuahua. Baeza in fact frequently professed his own religious beliefs and adopted a tone of offence toward attacks on his campaign that used religious motifs, including at one rally offering up a prayer for these detractors: "forgive them, Lord, for they know not what they do."[27]

International press paid attention. Seven weeks before the elections, US television network PBS broadcast a documentary called *Standoff in Mexico*. This documentary detailed electoral processes in northern states, presenting the PRI system as corrupt and violent while featuring PAN candidates and then-Ciudad Juárez mayor Francisco Barrio Terrazas as fighting for democracy. The producer and director of the show told Sonora newspaper *El Norte* the documentary showed that "undeniably, the PAN is gaining ground in states like Sonora, Chihuahua, and Nuevo León. The PRI must open the doors to democracy. If electoral frauds continue, then violence could erupt."[28] Again, although attacking this press coverage as the result of an antinationalist alliance between the PAN and US interests, the PRI attempted to emulate its strategy by contracting a US public relations firm to provide favorable biographical information about its candidate to the media north of the border.[29]

On election day July 6, 1986, reports surfaced of "urnas embarazadas" (pregnant ballot boxes), boxes already full of completed ballots when polling stations opened.[30] Over the following days, opposition groups complained about the expulsion of their election observers, irregular locations and opening hours of polling stations, and violent reactions by security forces when local communities protested such irregularities.[31] At 7:00 p.m. on election night, national PRI delegate Manuel Gurría Ordoñez announced the PRI's victory after just 28 of 1789 ballot box totals had been registered. However, PRI candidate Baeza cautioned at another press conference that night that candidates would have to wait for further vote counting before proclaiming victory.[32]

Two days later, President Miguel de la Madrid downplayed the importance of the electoral process during an unofficial confirmation of a PRI victory in Chihuahua. He described the victory as a sign that "we Mexicans have reaffirmed our confidence in the ideology and the doctrine of the Mexican Revolution, and we demonstrate this as much through electoral processes as in the daily realizing of the duties that correspond to each and every one of us."[33] When official results were released on Sunday, July 13, they showed Baeza winning the governorship with 401,905 votes against 231,063 for Barrio Terrazas. The PRI also won back all municipal governments previously held by the PAN, including Ciudad Juárez.[34]

The PAN called for the elections to be annulled and antifraud protests began two days following the elections. Chihuahua's archbishop again added his voice to the protests, arguing that a candidate who professes to be a Christian could not accept a governorship won through fraud. On Wednesday, July 9, the Democratic Electoral Movement's first march took place in the capital from the city's Plaza de Armas to the Francisco Villa monument with an estimated attendance of eight thousand people.[35] On Thursday, the Christian Family Movement civil organization arranged a mass in the Chihuahua cathedral to pray for those still on a hunger strike. Following the mass, Barrio Terrazas held a protest meeting attended by an estimated crowd of up to thirty thousand people. In his speech, the ex-candidate warned that the president and central authorities were going to have to face the consequences of trying to mess with Chihuahua.[36]

Whereas private enterprise had constituted the main independent support for the PAN in other states, in Chihuahua the Catholic Church filled this role while private enterprise seemed more reluctant to join the PAN's protests. Chihuahua's bishops released a joint statement the day after the elections, declaring them fraudulent and supporting civil disobedience as a response. A week following the elections, bishops declared that masses would be suspended the next Sunday to protest the electoral fraud. In a homily read in all of Chihuahua's Catholic churches announcing the suspension, the bishops proclaimed, "Last Sunday, July 6, someone fell into the hands of some robbers; someone suffered all manner of abuse, mistreatment, derision; someone was assaulted in the most delicate aspect of their dignity, someone was threatened, lied to, had their human rights disrespected. That someone is the people of Chihuahua."[37] Answering accusations that the church was supporting the PAN, on August 7 Archbishop Almeida and the bishops of Ciudad Juárez and Tarahumara released a joint statement entitled "A Moral Judgment" that argued "the dissatisfaction that reigns among a large majority of the people of Chihuahua has gone beyond the limits of a confrontation between political parties and is now located in the realm of human rights and moral principles affecting all of us."[38]

The sixty-seven-year-old PAN mayor of the state capital remained on a hunger strike for forty-one days into early August, stating that he was willing to die but still "stubbornly clinging to the idea of living as a free man."[39] The decision to abandon the strike at the urging of supporters and following the final declaration of election results on August 11 represented a turning point in post-election Chihuahua. There was a gradual move back toward governability as protest actions decreased in scale and increasingly moved into the institutional realm as formal complaints to electoral authorities.[40] With the formal swearing in of Baeza as governor on October 3 in a ceremony attended by de la Madrid and surrounded by tight security, the Chihuahua electoral process effectively came to an end. Both Baeza and Barrio Terrazas in their respective speeches in different venues on inauguration night called for reconciliation amongst Chihuahuenses, though in Barrio Terrazas's case this was to be directed toward a longer-term struggle for democracy.[41]

The 1986 Chihuahua elections were notable for the way in which the contest for political legitimacy between the PRI and PAN moved away from a discourse of historical myths and symbols to one of democracy and freedom. President de la Madrid did adopt the standard revolutionary nationalist legitimizing discourse that minimized the importance of the electoral process relative to the ideals of the Revolution. However, the PRI ultimately found that the effectiveness of these traditional appeals was limited by the ongoing economic crisis and an inability or unwillingness of the state to satisfy the demands of labor, peasant, and student groups. By selecting as its gubernatorial candidate a businessperson who offered up prayers for his opponents during campaign rallies, the PRI further revealed the increasing programmatic convergence between it and the PAN, which was masked by the rising intensity of electoral competition between the two parties.

With the support of the Catholic Church and the US media, the PAN argued that legitimate power sprang only from clean elections, which represented the fundamental human right of freedom. The party thus elevated the electoral process to the realm of human rights and morality and placed it at the center of political debate. Despite not winning power, the PAN in this way won an important symbolic victory in Chihuahua by turning the elections into a referendum on democracy that the PRI could not win without democracy losing. This meant that the PRI subjectively lost the elections before the voting had even begun.[42]

Open political activism by the Catholic Church was another important element in the 1986 Chihuahua elections. With few exceptions, the church emerged as supportive of the PAN and discourses of freedom and democracy during political battles in subsequent decades. However, the definition of democracy and freedom wielded by the PAN and the church was limited, focusing mostly on the civic right to vote rather than the social and economic rights of revolutionary nationalist discourse or the diversity promoted by activists challenging traditional social values related to gender and sexuality. It also relied on the negative counterpoint of crisis, which give an abstract promise of change undoubted appeal. This strategy met with significant success in attracting support, particularly in northern states such as Chihuahua. However, its limitations as an alternative framework to revolutionary nationalism for imagining the relationship between the nation and the state would become spectacularly apparent by the end of the de la Madrid administration.

CHAPTER THREE

Opposing the PRI

Freedom, Democracy, and Revolution

Change, democracy, and a vindication of the original aims of the Revolution were central themes of opposition political discourse during the de la Madrid administration as the electoral process became more competitive and opposition parties began to play a greater role in national politics. These domestic developments were strongly influenced by an international discourse of democracy that placed particular emphasis on notions of individual freedom and electoral pluralism in defining a political system as democratic, which, in turn, signified its legitimacy. Such a conception challenged the self-definition as democratic of a political system built around a hegemonic state party, collectivist corporatist institutions, and a binary notion of a ruling revolutionary majority and tolerated reactionary minority.

This chapter examines how opposition political parties, peasant, urban popular, and workers' movements wielded the discourse of democracy against the PRI state and how this strategy related to questions of identity. Widespread popular discontent with the PRI during the prolonged economic crises of the 1980s and 1990s increased the appeal of calls for change in Mexico. However, the success of the postrevolutionary state-building and cultural projects meant that by this time all actors were to some extent bound by the broad cultural parameters of the Revolution that helped to legitimize the exercise of state power, shape social relations, and define legitimate identities connected to specific citizenship rights. Discourses of change and democracy were therefore often interwoven with the symbolic language of revolutionary nationalism by opposition movements, who increasingly legitimized their claims for power or resources as a fulfillment of the principles of the Revolution betrayed by the PRI in power.

Democratizing the Political Platypus

The PRI state was a political model that defied easy categorization based on a simple dichotomy between democracy and authoritarianism. Democracy was part of the postrevolutionary state's discourse from its earliest stages. However, the democratic ideal of the PRI system was essentially a majoritarian model in which the state represented and executed the will of a national majority while respecting—within certain limits—the rights of minority groups. Though the PRI model involved hegemonic rule by one party, it also actively encouraged the survival of certain opposition parties and their participation in regular elections. Under the PRI there was also relative freedom of speech and political association; however, the state had at its disposal coercive mechanisms that could be activated when it judged certain forms of opposition overly threatening or disruptive to its hegemonic rule. Economist and historian Jesús Silva-Herzog Márquez for this reason evoked the Australian mammal that confounded scientists upon its discovery due to its apparent mix of bird, mammal, and reptile features to describe the PRI state as a "political platypus."[1]

As detailed in the previous chapter, a confluence of domestic and international forces created the environment in which Mexico's development model was increasingly shaped by neoliberal ideology after 1982. These forces also set in motion a process whereby the significance of voting increasingly shifted from a form of plebiscite reaffirming support for the revolutionary state into an act of protest or a sometimes highly charged contest between groups for state power.[2] Domestic political developments also encouraged this process.

After the failure of the PAN to put forward a presidential candidate in 1976 left José López Portillo running officially unopposed, in 1977 the PRI introduced sweeping electoral reforms to improve the democratic legitimacy of the political system. These reforms took a carrot and stick approach to incorporating opposition groups into the formal political system by encouraging electoral participation and effectively punishing electoral abstention.[3] The immediate impact of the reforms was to open up electoral politics to a more ideologically diverse range of actors and increase electoral participation. De la Madrid was thus elected president in 1982 after facing opponents from both the left and right and able to claim upon taking office that he had won "the elections with the highest turnout in our history."[4]

Coming to power amid severe economic crisis, de la Madrid

promised to lead Mexico forward with a project that included administrative decentralization, democratic reform, and a "moral renovation" of national life aimed at attacking corruption. When the administration issued the National Development Plan outlining its policy agenda, it listed preserving and strengthening Mexico's democratic institutions as its first priority, while overcoming the economic crisis was listed second.[5] As the new administration sought to respond to the crisis through less rather than more direct state intervention aimed at ameliorating material hardship, democratic and administrative reform were in this way held up as an alternative source of legitimacy for the state.

De la Madrid communicated his commitment to institutional reform and the rule of law by professing a particularly close personal affinity for Insurgente hero José María Morelos, who helped draft Mexico's first constitution. This was not unusual for Mexican presidents, who often adopted a totemic hero as early as the presidential campaign to establish their personal patriotic values and leadership style. For example, Luis Echeverría publically identified with the nationalist and reformist mythology of Lázaro Cárdenas, while José López Portillo professed a more extravagant affinity for the Aztec deity Quetzalcóatl, after whom he named his presidential aircraft.[6] From the beginning of his electoral campaign, de la Madrid claimed to be guided by the moral rectitude of Morelos, even naming Mexico's first communications satellites, launched in 1985, Morelos I and II in honor of his totemic hero.

De la Madrid's political reform agenda, however, represented a significant shift from the aims and ideas according to which the postrevolutionary state had been designed. Postrevolutionary state-builders had aimed to avoid the regional, political, and social fragmentation that had previously characterized Mexico's republican history. Now, the president cited the encouragement of political pluralism and a geographical decentralization of power as key goals.[7] In his first informe, de la Madrid thus argued that "if the transformation planned by the Revolution implied [a process of] concentrating forces, the complexity of the social fabric and the necessity of a more even territorial development today demand that they be dispersed."[8]

Encouraged by global discourses of democracy and the PRI's selective opening of critical spaces within the formal political system and press, an assertive opposition presence grew in strength during the 1980s. This opposition challenged the PRI's hegemonic hold on power on the basis of the democratic ideal of pluralism. While the presence of the independent left within the formal political system was the most novel change to electoral politics following the 1977 reforms, the established conservative opposition of the PAN initially proved most successful at adapting its political strategy to this new era. In alliance with other actors, such as private enterprise and the Catholic Church, the PAN used discourses of freedom and democracy to reinvigorate its historical competition for power with the PRI state.

The Catholic Church and Private Enterprise: Making Freedom a National Value

The PAN's success during the 1980s was not entirely tied to the rise of neoliberal ideology or alliances with other powerful actors. A long-term demographic shift toward a growing urban middle class had provided the party with a potentially important constituency that was not directly integrated to the state's representative mechanisms and hard-hit by the economic crisis.[9] Urban popular movements that organized independently and pressured the state for access to services and resources in northern urban areas, such as the border cities of Tijuana and Ciudad Juárez, also at times formed strong links with the PAN.[10] Furthermore, the PAN appealed to deep cultural and regional identities that persisted beneath the surface of hegemonic frameworks of liberal or revolutionary nationalist identity. In particular, in regions such as the state of Jalisco and the Bajío regions of Guanajuato, Michoacán, and Querétaro, the reemergence of a historical conservative Catholic identity marginalized or discouraged under the PRI state played a central role in reenergizing political opposition to the PRI, often to the benefit of the PAN.[11]

Catholicism remained in 1980s Mexico one of the most significant sources of cultural power, or power based around cultural resources such as symbolism, ideology, moral authority, and cultural meanings. Despite the anticlerical aspects of the postrevolutionary state's legal and discursive framework, the Catholic Church also remained a powerful institution that competed with the state over control of the minds and souls of Mexicans. As well as its privileged symbolic relationship to Catholicism, the church as an institution retained ties to a significant proportion of Mexico's citizens through a network of mostly parish-level organizations.[12] Prior to the 1980s, however, ecclesiastical authorities largely abstained from high-profile public interventions in electoral politics.

During the 1980s, discourses of freedom and democracy associated with neoliberal ideology opened up symbolic spaces within which the church could legitimize attacks on the Mexican state without necessarily attacking revolutionary nationalism. The appeal to the church of discourses connecting individual freedom to a reduction of state intervention citizens' lives also had solid historical foundations. Mexico's Catholic hierarchy had traditionally exhibited a marked lack of sympathy if not outright hostility toward Vatican II and its social doctrines, including those that inspired liberation theology.[13] The Church instead adopted a deeply conservative theological orientation that considered social justice issues in a way that, according to sociologist Joseph Palacios, "largely emphasizes the educational and spiritual formation of social actors, promotes a system based on charity, and does not allow strategies to address the structural issues of social justice."[14] Pope John Paul II's conception of the church as providing an antiauthoritarian defense of society against the state and particularly communism reinforced an affinity between neoliberalism and Catholicism.[15] In this context, the church often willingly used its symbolic capital to lend the electoral process generally and the PAN specifically a sense of moral righteousness.

Another group that played a central role in the advance of conservative opposition to the PRI after 1982 was Mexican private business interests. Private business associations had been a feature of Mexico's political landscape since the 1920s and their formation was indeed encouraged by the PRI as a mechanism for dialogue between the state and private enterprise. Privileged access to government officials and inclusion in public committees was then granted for members of associations such as Mexican Employers' Association (Coparmex), formed in 1929, and the Council of Mexican Businessmen (CMHN), formed in 1962.[16] While lacking the official incorporation into the political system of corporatist sectoral organizations, these associations allowed for an orderly process of organization and homogenization of powerful interests outside of the PRI state into groups that could be formally and informally engaged in negotiation and policy-making processes.

Symbolically, revolutionary nationalism and the disrepute it cast upon right-wing politics as the preserve of reactionaries and counterrevolutionaries had helped to contain opposition activities by big business. For example, Mexican National Confederation of Industrial Chambers president Jorge Sánchez Mejorado famously signaled in 1975 the identification of big business with the revolutionary majorities when stating that, whatever class they may technically belong to, "Mexican businessmen are of the left."[17] By the time he made this comment, however, the institutional and discursive links between private enterprise and the state were beginning to loosen.

In Latin America, the United States, Europe, and elsewhere, private enterprise was by the mid-1970s formally organizing to lobby for policy change and to diffuse free market ideology as governments experimented with statist solutions to the apparent collapse of Keynesian economic orthodoxy.[18] These groups used a discourse of individual freedom and democracy associated with free market economics to counter established justifications for state intervention in the economy on the basis of collective social rights, such as those embedded in revolutionary nationalism.[19] This signified a strategic shift from the emphasis on scientific correctness of neoliberal policies used in the authoritarian contexts of 1970s Chile and Argentina toward promoting neoliberal reform as an antidote against authoritarianism and tyranny wielded by the state.[20] In Mexico, the move toward this political strategy was most clearly signaled by the formation of the Business Coordinating Council (CCE) in May 1975. Formed primarily as an initiative of the Council of Mexican Businessmen in response to the Luis Echeverría administration's statist economic policies, the CCE listed among its aims the promotion and defense of ideological principles that supported fundamental liberties against "arguments in favor of establishing a totalitarian dictatorship in our country."[21]

The response to the 1982 bank nationalization from private enterprise demonstrated both the increasing political organization of the private sector and its antistatist political discourse. Coparmex organized a series of meetings around the country titled "México en la Libertad" (Mexico in Freedom) to coordinate private enterprise's strategy to influence public opinion against the nationalization as a lurch toward authoritarianism.[22] Business associations launched a broader campaign titled "Movimiento de Libertad y Solidaridad" (Movement of Freedom and Solidarity), which exhorted Mexicans to "fight for your freedom" in pamphlets that contained such ominous warnings as "yesterday it was the telephones, electricity, water . . . today it is the banks, tomorrow it will be the newspapers, the radio, food; later it will be your house, and then . . ."[23] In full-page newspaper announcements, the CCE argued that the encroachment of the state into the private sector signified "inefficiency, bureaucratization, corruption, and a totalitarian threat" pointing Mexico toward socialism.[24]

The defense of freedom was further framed as a nationalist cause by business organizations. While supporters portrayed the bank national-ization as Mexico taking back control of its economic destiny from disloyal and antinationalist financial interests, the president of the National Confederation of Chambers of Commerce (Concanaco), Emilio Goicoechea, retorted that "we are nationalist and patriotic Mexicans. We were born and we generate wealth and employment here . . . and here we will fight to preserve human liberty, not for us but for all Mexicans, freedom in the economic and political spheres, [and] free-dom of expression and beliefs that together make up freedom in capital letters."[25] The CCE's brash president Manuel Clouthier—who emerged as a particularly forceful advocate for big business in the wake of the nationalization—similarly defended the private owners of the banks by arguing that the banks already were nationalized and that the move instead signified their *estatización* ("statization").[26] Business activists in this way redefined national values to move away from revolutionary nationalist ideas of collective social rights guaranteed by the state to the right of all Mexicans as individuals to a personal freedom threatened by the interventionist state.[27]

Despite this increasingly critical antistatist language and occasional vindications of conservative counter-hegemonic heroes including Agustín de Iturbide in publications such as *Negocios y Bancos* (Business and Banks), private enterprise did not definitively split from traditional working arrangements with the PRI state during the de la Madrid administration. Beyond the most ideologically driven actors, business interests continued to negotiate with and even financially support the PRI.[28] What is most significant about the changing participation of Mexican business people during the 1980s is therefore the philosophical cohesiveness of a business discourse that entailed a significant reformu-lation of nationalism and citizenship rights from the collectivist values of revolutionary nationalism toward the focus on individual freedoms of neoliberal political discourse.[29]

After 1982, private business interests further began to see the useful-ness of the PAN as a potential representative of its interests, or at least as a method through which they could place pressure on the PRI through selective public and/or financial support in sensitive contests. Historically, private business associations also had close ties to conser-vative Catholicism. This continued to be in evidence through the pre-sentation of conservative Catholic views alongside the new neoliberal political discourse in forums such as the tri-annual Atalaya (Watchtower) conferences organized by the CCE and the magazine *Negocios y*

Bancos.[30] The rising political assertiveness of private enterprise and the Catholic Church harnessing transnational discourses of democracy thus provided strong sources of support for the PAN during the 1980s. As elections had traditionally implied an impossible competition with the Mexican state rather than with another political party, the PAN tended to focus its political work on advocating its values, particularly at a local level.[31] For the first time in its history, the party now began to seriously compete for power beyond the level of municipal government.

Neopanismo

As private enterprise organized politically and refined its discursive strategies during the 1970s, the PAN was also going through an internal process of ideological redefinition. Two main internal currents emerged, defined by political scientist Francisco Reveles Vázquez as pragmatic and dogmatic based on, respectively, an embrace of liberal pragmatism inclined toward electoral participation and one based on a moral critique of the state based on Catholic social philosophy.[32] Meanwhile, the 1977 electoral reforms made the PAN's survival largely dependent on rebuilding its electoral viability in competition with a broader field of newly legalized opposition parties. This strengthened the position of the pragmatic current and in 1978, an important group of the Catholic dogmatic current left the party. This marked a turning point in the PAN's history from being a rigidly organized party of cadres guided by strict ideological principles into one that increasingly sought mass popular appeal through the electoral process in the mold of a US-style catchall party.[33]

In 1982 the PAN adopted an almost identical stance to business groups in opposition to the bank nationalization. Party leaders characterized the bankers as a sacrificial lamb for the government's failings and the move as one that "draws us closer to dictatorship and further away from democracy."[34] Such appeals for freedom and democracy more generally characterized the political discourse of the PAN during the 1980s associated with a new pragmatic and less dogmatic style of PAN politics that became known as *neopanismo*. As an electoral strategy, neopanismo also meant an aggressive style of campaigning designed to apply maximum pressure on the government to open up spaces of power to the party, including civil disobedience actions and the courting of international (mainly US) support.[35]

Figure 3.1. Archetypal Panista Bárbaro del Norte and former business leader
Manuel Clouthier campaigns in the 1984 Coahuila gubernatorial elections under
a banner promising change. Courtesy Greg Smith/Corbis.

The most emblematic representatives of neopanismo were prominent
business figures who joined the party during the 1980s and were often
given preference over veteran party members in the selection of candidates for high-profile election contests (fig. 3.1). This group was also
sometimes called the Bárbaros del Norte (Northern Barbarians), reflecting a sense of resentment at the takeover of the party by individuals not
educated in traditional *panista* ideology and who embraced a rougher
style of politics in the "wilder" northern states. The name also reflected
the simple fact that much of this business support was centered in northern states where the PAN most benefited from inter-elite conflicts as
well as anti-Mexico City sentiment.[36]

As electoral democracy implied alternation in power between parties, the PAN used the electoral process to highlight the undemocratic
nature of the PRI's perpetuation in power while establishing a democratic identity for itself as representing this alternation.[37] Denunciations
of an electoral fraud already in progress became the most common
theme of PAN election campaigns during the 1980s and marches,
encampments, building occupations, and caravans in defense of democracy along with a language of struggle characterized its political style.[38]

The PAN also selectively invoked the historical myths and symbols of revolutionary nationalism. Adopting a rhetorical defense of the institutions of the state and the Constitution of 1917 against the abuses of the PRI, the PAN challenged the PRI's centrality to Mexico's political model and sought to portray its struggle as antisystem rather than antinationalist. The party also positioned itself within the revolutionary nationalist tradition that formed the symbolic boundaries of Mexico's hegemonic political model not as a representative of the reaction but as a defender of the original, democratic aims of the Revolution.

The most prominent revolutionary reference point for neopanistas in this respect was Francisco Madero and his banner of "effective suffrage, no reelection." In 1982 the PAN chose as its presidential candidate Pablo Emilio Madero, a party veteran and nephew of Francisco Madero. Pablo Madero argued on the campaign trail that the PRI system was the result of the principles of the Revolution winning on the battlefield but losing in peacetime. Rather than signaling a defeat of the Mexican Revolution as a political and social project, Pablo Madero thus characterized a victory of the PAN over the PRI as a fulfillment of the goals of the Revolution, defined as a fight for democracy against dictatorship.[39]

Pablo Madero was subsequently sworn in as PAN party president in February 1984. At his swearing-in, the party's National Council declared that it remained in favor of electoral participation partly on the basis that effective suffrage was "the cleanest and original purpose of the Mexican Revolution of 1910."[40] As party president, Madero continued to make reference to his revolutionary heritage, arguing, "If my uncle Francisco Madero were alive he would surely be a member of the PAN, because we fight for the same objectives as he did."[41] In the context of a disputed 1985 electoral contest in the state of Nuevo León, the defeated PAN candidate and fellow party members further forced their way into the Monterrey Revolution Day parade and identified their cause as being "like that of Francisco I. Madero, because after seventy-five years the demand for clean elections has not been fulfilled."[42] In their embrace of Madero, the PAN implicitly and explicitly connected the PRI government to the Porfirio Díaz dictatorship. The 1984 party platform indeed stated that, despite the "phraseology" of the de la Madrid administration, "the states of the federation are as free and sovereign as they were during the Porfiriato."[43]

Identification with the pure origins rather than the corrupted outcome of the Revolution represented a public acknowledgement of the broad legitimacy of revolutionary nationalism as a cultural and political framework relative to counter-hegemonic conservative frameworks. As they won power in northern Mexican towns that had been central to the revolutionary struggle, local PAN governments at times raised money to erect monuments to local heroes who played an important role in creating Mexico's postrevolutionary political model, such as Álvaro Obregón and Plutarco Elías Calles. In campaign speeches, PAN candidates would further now declare that "we are fighting today for that which the heroes of the Revolution fought."[44] While the PRI grappled with reworking revolutionary nationalism for a realistic but still revolutionary neoliberal era, the PAN sought to capitalize on economic crisis, growing anti-PRI sentiment, and international neoliberal political discourse to legitimize its claim to power on the basis of democratic pluralism as a key revolutionary value.

Despite the combative tone of electoral processes during the 1980s, the PRI and PAN were in fact growing increasingly similar in both their embrace of revolutionary nationalist mythology and their policy prescriptions. This led Octavio Paz to conclude that "the growth of the PAN does not express so much an ideological tendency as the discontent of many citizens."[45] The success of the PAN's appeals for popular support rested to a significant extent on the deliberate vagueness of a language of freedom and democracy that at times adopted a revolutionary nationalist form, allowing for diverse interpretations of the change on offer. The newly legalized parties of the left, meanwhile, struggled to articulate a clear alternative to the PRI, and this lack of a strong alternative opposition in electoral politics further helped direct popular discontent toward the PAN.

The Mexican Left: Democracy, Nationalism, and the State

After decades of illegality, repression, and extra-parliamentary activism, the Mexican left entered the 1980s far more ideologically and organizationally divided than did the right. After 1968, the left had fragmented into groups that participated in clandestine guerrilla movements, formed political parties generally banned from electoral participation, or concentrated on political organizing within worker, peasant, and urban popular movements.[46] In general, however, these groups had struggled to build deep roots outside of universities, teachers' unions, and relatively small sections of the worker and peasant movement.[47] At the time of the 1982 debt crisis, the Mexican left remained deeply divided over the usefulness of electoral participation and had a far less clear view than did the right on the appropriate role of the state. This ambiguity meant left-wing groups were poorly placed to take advantage of electoral reform and the crisis of the PRI system to build support.

An ambiguous relationship between the Mexican left and the post-revolutionary state had deep roots that stretched back at least to the state's most radical phase under President Lázaro Cárdenas.[48] As historian Barry Carr has argued, such ambiguity led to a situation in which "the productivist and statist strains within the culture of Mexican socialism weakened the left's critical stand and enhanced the 'revolutionary' state's capacity to assume the role of sole legitimate interpreter of what was 'national' and 'popular.'"[49] There was also a significant tradition within the Mexican left of identification with revolutionary nationalism.[50]

The Mexican Workers' Party (PMT) and its leader Heberto Castillo were particularly important in seeking to develop a "pragmatic socialism" with mass appeal that included adopting national heroes of Independence, the Reform, and the Revolution as the PMT's banner from its foundation in 1974 onward.[51] The Mexican state in turn often appropriated the language and symbolism of the left. This meant that the Mexican left often found itself supporting the PRI state's expansion as a nationalization of society and resources and battled the Mexican right—including the PAN—using the same antireactionary and anti-oligarchy language as the PRI.

The most successful party of the left formed in the wake of the 1977 electoral reforms was the Mexican Unified Socialist Party (PSUM). This party was formed in 1981 through a merger of the Mexican Communist Party (PCM), which achieved legal registration in 1978, and other left-wing groups.[52] The party would routinely attack the PRI government; however, it supported the interventionist state in a general sense as a positive force.[53] Consistent with this position, independent left parties, including the PSUM, allied with the PRI during the final months of López Portillo's presidency to support the bank nationalization and rigid exchange controls against the "oligarchy" represented by the PAN, clergy, and business groups.[54] In the final months of 1982, when conservative opposition was particularly intense, the independent left further voted to recognize de la Madrid's electoral victory and in favor of PRI antidefamation legislation, both of which the PAN opposed on democratic and free-speech grounds.[55]

During this pivotal period, the left thus struggled to articulate a coherent anti-PRI, prostatist position and had relatively weak connections to civil society upon which to draw. It was therefore far less able than the PAN to harness popular anger as the government swung from the dramatic gesture of economic nationalism in the bank nationalization to neoliberal reform and austerity measures under de la Madrid. Intellectuals who adopted an antistatist liberal posture, such as Octavio Paz and Enrique Krauze organized around the literary and political journal *Vuelta*, also tended to adopt a sympathetic view of the PAN's electoral struggles while characterizing the Mexican left as intrinsically antidemocratic.[56]

Continuing internal disagreement within the Mexican left over the definition of key concepts including democracy and references to Soviet communism further divided and blunted the effectiveness of the left's electoral participation in the immediate aftermath of the 1982 debt crisis.[57] Cooperation between the PSUM and the PMT, for example, was hampered by disagreement over the use of the symbols of international socialism such as the hammer and sickle. These parties ended their formal alliance in the lead-up to the 1985 legislative elections, during which the PMT adopted the nationalist slogan, "We want to continue being Mexicans."[58] This helps to explain the relatively slow electoral growth of the left relative to the PAN, which was quicker to embrace electoral pragmatism, construct broader social alliances, and deal relatively efficiently with the internal divisions electoral pragmatism caused.[59]

New Social Movements, Civil Society, and Superbarrio

Another force that helped shape Mexican politics during the 1980s were new social movements that formed beginning in the late 1970s.[60] These were movements that organized independently in response to the failure of the state to meet popular needs. In urban contexts, groups organized around demands such as affordable housing or the provision of basic services as rural-urban migration swelled the ranks of the urban poor. In the countryside, independent peasant groups organized around demands including land or support for agriculture. While these movements responded to historically new situations, in their political strategies and negotiated acceptance of external authorities, they also reflected an historical feature of the hegemonic rule of the postrevolutionary political system that was the constant presence of various sites of resistance and contestation, which were often deeply rooted in local cultural and material contexts.

The tactics of these social movements generally involved popular mobilization for actions ranging from protest marches to occupying or obstructing public buildings in order to pressure state institutions often by raising public awareness of their demands and embarrassing public officials into addressing them.[61] The movements also drew on the mythology of the Revolution. For example, the Land and Liberty Popular Front formed in Monterrey, Nuevo León, in 1976 and the Plan de Ayala National Confederation formed in Milpa Alta near Mexico City in 1979 explicitly drew on the mythology of Zapata to, in the latter case, symbolize peasant demands and, in the former, communicate the needs of recent urban migrants who "invaded" vacant land, built their own neighborhoods, and sought formalization of land titles and provision of basic services.[62]

More so than factories or mines, these movements were based in contexts such as popular neighborhoods and fields and suggested a new conception of political organizing focused on the "politics of consumption" rather than the traditional focus on the workplace and the "politics of production."[63] This characteristic also resulted in these movements becoming mechanisms for increased political participation by Mexican women in politics.[64] As traditional gender roles placed women as most responsible for caring for the family and managing the household, women often most immediately and acutely suffered the impact of problems such as the rising price of household goods or lack of services including water, public transport, medical clinics, and electricity. Women were therefore also often the first to react and mobilize to seek attention to their demands.[65]

Since the Cardenista state-building years, women had made significant political gains in Mexico. However, Mexican women's political activism often tended to draw on traditional self-sacrificing and maternal notions of Mexican womanhood and eschewed challenges to the gendered nature of power in favor of agitating for citizenship rights on the basis of a productive, class-based, and patriotic commitment to the Revolution.[66] During the 1980s, initiatives such as the Women's Regional Council, formed by the National Council of the Urban Popular Movement in 1982, now incorporated challenges to traditional gendered social and political roles to address problems such as domestic and sexual violence and issues related to health and nutrition that particularly affected women. One impact of the breakdown of limited class-based notions of rights and identities of Mexico's postrevolutionary political and nationalist framework during this period, then, was the opening for increasingly diverse forms of political action demanding citizenship rights denied on the basis of identities such as gender, sexuality, or ethnicity.[67]

The new social movements were, initially at least, largely independent not just from the PRI but from the party political system more generally. Left-wing parties attempted to ally with these movements as the decade wore on and in northern cities such as Ciudad Juárez urban movements did develop links to the PAN.[68] However, as these movements based their popular legitimacy on their ability to negotiate with state authorities on behalf of those whom they represented, alliances with opposition parties were likely advantageous only in an ephemeral sense to place greater pressure on PRI officials.[69] Instead, new social movements strategically benefited from an increasingly competitive electoral system and tensions between different political currents within the PRI to gain leverage over state officials.[70]

The Mexico City earthquake of September 19, 1985, which killed more than ten thousand people and left hundreds of thousands injured and homeless, led to further popular mobilizing and organization outside of the state. The earthquake also had a profound symbolic impact on the state-society relationship. As the 1968 Tlatelolco massacre came to symbolize an ogre hiding behind revolutionary philanthropy, the government's response to the Mexico City earthquake exposed an inefficient and corrupt state hiding behind a facade of strength.

Poorly constructed public buildings collapsed during the earthquake, killing thousands of people and serving as a testament to the practices of corruption that saw funds siphoned off from public projects into state officials' personal bank accounts. In the hours and days following the earthquake, the government appeared paralyzed in the face of mass destruction and the president appeared aloof amid the suffering of Mexico City's residents. The declining symbolic power of the figure of the Mexican president in particular was manifested in open displays of contempt during public appearances following the earthquake, for example at the opening ceremony of the 1986 Mexico City soccer World Cup, when the mere mention of the president's name by speakers and the president's entire opening speech were drowned out by the crowd's boos and jeers.[71]

Following the earthquake, citizens were left to independently organize and begin rescue operations and then pressure the state to provide housing and services. Women again emerged in key leadership roles within organizations created in response to the earthquake, such as the Coordinating Committee of Earthquake Victims (CUD) and the September 19th Garment Workers' Union.[72] This political activism again displayed a more nuanced understanding of how power functioned to include gender, with the CUD in one slogan demanding "Democracy in the city and in the home."[73]

The spontaneous popular organizing in response to the earthquake also reinforced the importance of a notion of civil society to Mexican political discourse during the 1980s. This concept was popularized by writers such as left-wing intellectual Carlos Monsiváis, who chronicled the tales of the spontaneous organization by Mexico City residents following the 1985 earthquake.[74] Civil society came to represent in political discourse a social sphere separate from and in competition with the state for power, with Monsiváis describing the spontaneous organization following the earthquake as a popular "taking of power" from the state.[75]

Monsiváis in a broader sense identified a new nationalism that reflected the growing economic precariousness and urbanization of Mexico's population by the 1980s. This nationalism, according to Monsiváis, still built upon the shared referents communicated by the state through institutions such as the education system. It had, however, become fragmented and depoliticized, rejecting unifying panoramas and centering instead on a renewed faith in localism, but a localism that meant not the rural *pueblito* but the urban suburb, barrio, or gang.[76]

The hero to emerge out of the intersection of a new urban nationalism and social movements was Superbarrio (super neighborhood). Portrayed as a *lucha libre* wrestler in red and yellow tights and mask, Superbarrio first appeared at rallies organized by the Asamblea de Barrios (Assembly of Neighborhoods) movement created to support those demanding services and housing following the earthquake (fig. 3.2). This movement evolved over time into one that more generally challenged economic policies that left Mexico City's low-income residents in a precarious position.[77]

Superbarrio was cast as a defender of the poor residents of Mexico City against those such as the landlords and politicians who had the apparatus of the state and legal system to defend them. His name was designed to juxtapose the powerful and the popular with "super" implying the hero's strength equal to that of the ruling elite who lived in impunity while "barrio" referred to the residents of popular

Figure 3.2. Superbarrio Gómez. Courtesy Sergio Dorantes/Sygma/Corbis.

neighborhoods whom he represented. Superbarrio was then given the surname Gómez on the basis that such a common surname would reiterate the collective, popular identity behind the mask.[78] Rather than relying on the traditional language of the left to articulate opposition to neoliberal free market reform and austerity measures, Superbarrio used wrestling metaphors. Conjuring up the referee, who in lucha libre favors the villains against the virtuous wrestlers, Superbarrio argued that "in the barrio the government wants to be the referee and it supports the landlords and lends them riot police to assist in the eviction of families."[79]

Taking his persona from a decidedly popular form of culture, Superbarrio was an important symbolic weapon of the Assembly in framing a dynamic whereby the people had to fight in order to obtain basic rights from a state that protected only the interests of the powerful. The effectiveness of such symbolism was such that Superbarrio traveled to California in 1989 to highlight the condition of Mexicans who had been "practically driven into economic exile" in the United States, where they lacked basic labor rights and were fearful of persecution by US immigration authorities. This visit provoked significant press coverage, Superbarrio's own temporary detention by US immigration authorities, and a minor diplomatic conflict between the Mexican and Los

Angeles city governments after city council members awarded a commendation to Superbarrio.[80] Most significantly, however, Superbarrio's activism and reception north of the border demonstrated the increasingly transnational scope of Mexican experiences of economic and social marginalization during 1980s. This experience extended beyond Mexico's national borders to encompass poor residents of Mexico City and Los Angeles barrios alike.[81]

When introduced into contexts of formal negotiation or confrontation with state authorities and politicians, the mere presence of Superbarrio in red and yellow tights and mask further served to ridicule political formalities. As the 1988 presidential elections approached, in November 1987 the Assembly held a mock ceremony announcing Superbarrio's candidature for the presidency at Mexico City's Juárez Hemiciclo. Parodying the PRI's rituals for handing over power to a new president, the three sectors of the Assembly gathered at the ceremony to pledge support for their candidate as would the PRI state's corporatist sectors at the destape of the PRI's presidential candidate every six years.[82]

In the months following the earthquake, the de la Madrid administration made extra funding available for housing for the urban poor; however, it did not create mechanisms for distributing this funding. This role was instead adopted by urban social movements such as the CUD and the National Coordinating Committee of the Urban Popular Movement. These movements were thus strengthened and developed their own system of horizontal and sectoral alliances in the barrios of Mexico City.[83] Rather than political parties, the new social movements of the urban barrios and impoverished countryside most effectively channeled popular discontent against the negative effects of state economic policy into action and opened spaces of participation outside of the state. At the same time, divisions within the PRI between those who supported the neoliberal direction of the de la Madrid administration and those who argued in favor of the social justice ideals of the Mexican Revolution were becoming increasingly evident.

The Democratic Current and the Rupture of the Revolutionary Family

The dominance of the PRI by a new generation of neoliberal technocrats was by 1986 causing serious concern for members of the party associated with traditionalist revolutionary nationalist perspectives. Porfirio Muñoz Ledo, a former party president and Mexican ambassador to the

United Nations, and Cuauhtémoc Cárdenas, outgoing governor of Michoacán and son of ex-president Lázaro Cárdenas, became the public faces of an internal group that attempted to unite PRI members critical of the neoliberal development model. The group called itself the Democratic Current and planned to frustrate the usual practice of the president nominating his own successor by applying democratic discourse to internal party politics in order to challenge the dominance of the party by proponents of neoliberalism.[84]

The Democratic Current essentially endorsed the traditional postrevolutionary conception of representative democracy that saw party mechanisms as providing spaces for negotiation between different interest groups, arguing that its proposal was to strengthen rather than weaken the PRI. One of the most immediate impacts of the Democratic Current's emergence was a demystification of the internal unwritten rules of the PRI state, particularly the ritual of selecting the party's presidential candidate. Traditionally, unofficial pre-candidates would conduct mostly internal politicking for the presidential nomination. The nomination was then ultimately left to the discretion of the president and revealed to the public in a ritual called the destape, or unveiling. This led to the president being given the nickname "the great elector," as it was he who ultimately chose the next president.[85] However, Democratic Current leaders proposed the nomination of Cuauhtémoc Cárdenas as PRI presidential candidate in 1988, choosing Cárdenas to represent those within the PRI who opposed the policies of the party's new technocratic leadership due to the broad legitimacy he enjoyed amongst party members as political heir apparent to one of revolutionary nationalism's greatest heroes.[86]

PRI leadership initially vacillated between criticism and cautious tolerance of the Current while refusing to accept its proposals for new internal mechanisms for electing party candidates.[87] Instead, PRI leadership modified the traditional process of selecting the party's candidate by announcing an official list of the six front-running candidates on August 13, 1987. However, the president was still to ultimately choose the PRI's 1988 presidential candidate by advising the party's National Political Coordinating Commission of his preference. Moreover, this official list did not include Cárdenas.[88]

While the Democratic Current continued its campaign from within the PRI, it now began to outline the possibility of acting outside the party. On September 17, sympathizers began a One Hundred Hour March for Democracy from the Mexico City Lázaro Cárdenas monument to the Zócalo where the protestors camped before, on September 21, marching to a rally at the Monument to the Revolution.[89] Through such actions, the Democratic Current became arguably the first national political movement opposed to neoliberalism to effectively utilize the discourse of democracy to attack not so much the PRI state, but the party's technocratic leadership and its neoliberal development model. It did this by appealing to the established mythology of revolutionary nationalism and most directly to the figure of Lázaro Cárdenas.

On Saturday, October 3, President de la Madrid informed PRI leadership of his choice of successor, which was publically announced the following morning in front of a crowd of around twenty-five thousand party members in the Benito Juárez plaza at the PRI's Mexico City headquarters.[90] The president had chosen Carlos Salinas de Gortari and the PRI and its sectoral organizations showed the usual discipline in publically pledging their support for the party's candidate. The Democratic Current was now left with few options but to either fall into line with party procedures or leave the PRI. Many supporters of the Current did remain within the PRI; however, its leadership, including Cárdenas and Muñoz Ledo, immediately began to organize an external candidature.

The Democratic Current accepted the approach of the Authentic Party of the Mexican Revolution (PARM) for an electoral alliance that was soon joined by the Popular Socialist Party (PPS) and the Party of the Cardenista Front of National Reconstruction (PFCRN). All of these were satellite parties of the PRI who had previously taken on its candidates as their own, providing yet another blow to the legitimacy of the new technocratic leadership of the PRI. Members of the Democratic Current indeed described themselves as "the legitimate part of the PRI and . . . still *priístas*" who were mobilizing to support Cuauhtémoc Cárdenas.[91] After a series of small parties who had not yet achieved registration added their support to the Cárdenas candidacy, the electoral alliance adopted the name National Democratic Front (FDN) in December 1987. So began the presidential campaign of the son of one of revolutionary nationalism's great heroes in opposition to the candidate nominated by the party that had spent decades promoting this hero's mythology.

The 1988 Presidential Elections: *Se Cayó el Sistema*

The PRI headed into the election year of 1988 facing not just an ascendant and aggressive conservative opposition, but also the most significant internal rupture in its history. This rupture initially seemed to strengthen the electoral potential of the PAN, which elected Manuel Clouthier as its presidential candidate in November 1987. With a background as a prominent agribusiness leader from the northern state of Sinaloa, ex-president of both Coparmex and CCE as well as a prominent member of the conservative Christian Family Movement in his home state, Clouthier was the very embodiment of 1980s neopanismo. He had only joined the PAN in 1984, but two years later ran as the party's gubernatorial candidate for his home state and had a reputation for a frank, informal, and at times aggressive style, often campaigning under his nickname Maquío.[92]

As the 1988 electoral year began, press attention focused mainly on the contest between the PRI and PAN candidates. If Clouthier was emblematic of a neopanista *Bárbaro del norte*, then Salinas was the archetypal representative of another 1980s Mexican political stereotype: the *delamadridista* technocrat. As rumors swirled of Salinas's substitution due to his uninspiring campaign style, the PRI scrambled to recast the candidate as a popular and dynamic leader.[93] Voters were invited to submit their thoughts on Mexico's problems to Salinas, who would then respond directly to selected correspondence through the media in an initiative called "Let Mexico Speak."[94] Salinas, however, also continued with de la Madrid's more general thesis of realistic revolution to legitimize continuing neoliberal reform.

Clouthier adopted the central campaign theme of the PAN's electoral strategy during the 1980s in his campaign slogan "Join the Change." The candidate focused his campaign rhetoric on democracy, including through verbal attacks and protest marches against media outlets to highlight the unequal access granted to non-PRI candidates and thus the undemocratic nature of the contest. Most notably, Clouthier targeted the Televisa broadcasting monopoly, whose owner Emilio Azcarraga declared his loyalty to the PRI in early 1988.[95] Clouthier instructed his followers, "Don't watch Televisa because it never tells the truth."[96]

The Clouthier campaign also made significant appeals to nationalist sentiment. While campaigning in Morelia in January 1988, Clouthier laid a floral wreath at the house of Insurgente hero José María Morelos and told the directors of local popular movements that they could be the Villas and Zapatas of this age by supporting change.[97] Francisco Madero emerged again during this campaign to link the PAN with a nationalist tradition of confronting undemocratic authority. During a Clouthier rally in Mérida, Yucatán, the local PAN leader promoted a narrative linking the PAN's struggle against the PRI to Madero and specifically Yucatán's Maderista governor José María Pino Suárez (1910–1911). In his own speech, Clouthier expanded this narrative to include recent electoral protests in northern Mexico and the 1968 Mexico City student movement.[98] More directly conjuring up images of Madero's fight against the Porfirian state, Clouthier issued a Manifesto of San Luis Potosí at a February campaign rally in that city, calling for a new social pact based on smaller government and democracy.[99] Later at a campaign rally in Puebla, Clouthier read from Madero's 1910 Plan of San Luis Potosí as if it were his own campaign speech and, upon revealing its provenance, commented to the crowd that it "seems as though it refers to the present, doesn't it?"[100]

One historical figure that caused clear problems for the Clouthier campaign, however, was Benito Juárez. Following a campaign event at the Autonomous Benito Juárez University in Oaxaca when the PAN candidate failed to pay homage to Juárez, Clouthier's press secretary explained the lack of homage to reporters by venturing that "in my very personal opinion, I believe it is because [Juárez] has been the greatest historical traitor."[101] Such a response conjured up traditional historical narratives of conservative hostility toward the liberal Reform and the Revolution, and commentary about the candidate's attitude toward Juárez continued to shadow Clouthier through the campaign. Clouthier was thus forced to declare as the election approached, "I don't have anything against Juárez. I have paid and will continue to pay homage to him, but we should leave the past where it belongs. I am more interested in the present and the future."[102]

The annual commemorations of Juárez's birth occurred during the campaign while Salinas, Clouthier, and Cárdenas were all in the state of Chihuahua. This provided a contrast not just between their respective relationship to the figure of Juárez, but also of their more general strategic use of the symbols of revolutionary nationalism to communicate and legitimize their political projects. Cárdenas linked the struggles of Juárez and the Reform to a contemporary need to regain national autonomy by first regaining economic autonomy. Salinas in Ciudad Juárez, meanwhile, used the occasion to outline a vision of Mexico's relationship with the United States involving cooperation for economic development and uncompromising defense of national interests, including the human rights of migrants.[103] Also in Ciudad Juárez, Clouthier laid a wreath and led an honor guard at a Juárez monument; however, he neglected to mention Juárez by name in his speech and instead specified that "we are here to pay homage to the idea or the ideal of the Republic."[104] Clouthier's main campaign event of the day, in fact, involved mocking Salinas's campaign slogan by addressing a crowd at an international bridge and leading followers in shouting "let Mexico speak . . . Heeeelp!" toward El Paso, Texas.[105]

By late February Clouthier began to release a single white dove at the end of speeches and compared his presidential campaign to the popular liberation movements led by Gandhi, Martin Luther King, and against apartheid in South Africa.[106] Clouthier also criticized the state's use of an historical legitimizing discourse during the campaign, arguing at one rally that "this confusion between government and party, between president and cacique, and the association of history and patriotic symbols is a fascism that has grown in our land."[107] The grandiosity and aggressiveness of this language and of Clouthier's style more generally emphasized the drawbacks of a neopanista political strategy that was effective at galvanizing supporters and attracting press coverage but also polarized and alienated many from the PAN's cause.

In an apparent misreading of the popular mood, Clouthier caused particular controversy when he identified the Philippines as "the path to follow" at a political meeting in Puebla.[108] The example of the Philippines to some extent seemed fitting. The overthrow of the Ferdinand Marcos dictatorship by the Philippine People's Power Revolution in 1986 arose out of a series of circumstances that combined economic crisis brought about by foreign debt pressures, involvement by international financial institutions such as the IMF, and a broad popular alliance that began with a military coup but grew to include politicians, middle-class intellectuals, the Catholic Church, defectors from the regime, and business elites. Moreover, the uprising was framed internationally as a struggle for freedom and democracy against authoritarianism and tyranny that included the introduction of neoliberal economic reforms following Marcos's overthrow.[109] Opponents of Clouthier, however, alleged that references to the Philippines were proof that the PAN represented a conservative fanaticism that sought to destabilize Mexico in the service of foreign ideology.[110] In response, Clouthier attempted to soften his call by suggesting followers instead *Chihuahuizar* (Chihuahuanize) the entire country with civil disobedience actions.[111]

By February it was in fact the Cárdenas campaign's call for a return to the postrevolutionary state's founding principles along with a repudiation of neoliberal reform that was gaining momentum. As the son of a revolutionary nationalist hero, it was relatively unproblematic for

Cuauhtémoc Cárdenas to draw upon revolutionary nationalism in his campaign against the current PRI leadership. Although Cuauhtémoc Cárdenas rejected criticisms that he was capitalizing on the Cárdenas surname by arguing it was the only one he had, the figure of Lázaro Cárdenas was a constant presence in the FDN campaign.[112] One campaign poster directly evoked the idea of Lázaro Cárdenas's return in the figure of his son, featuring a profile image of Cuauhtémoc Cárdenas with the distinctive silhouette of his father cast behind him like a shadow.[113] The popular appeal of such references to Cardenismo became particularly evident as the campaign progressed into a region with a close historical association with the land redistribution program of Lázaro Cárdenas: the Laguna region of Coahuila.

Salinas had faced his most hostile reception of the campaign in this region as his appearances and speeches were greeted with jeers, shouts of support for Cuauhtémoc Cárdenas and, according to press reports, objects thrown at the PRI candidate.[114] The press was taken by surprise by the contrasting images of large, enthusiastic crowds of tens of thousands that received Cárdenas across Coahuila in the days following Salinas's appearances. They printed accounts of emotional scenes as the candidate was greeted with comments such as "this hand received land from your father" and "this hand shook the hand of the general [Lázaro Cárdenas] when he came with you in 1956."[115] Local monuments and murals dedicated to Lázaro Cárdenas had been cleaned for the visit and crowds pressed close to be able to see and touch the son of the ex-president. In his speeches, Cuauhtémoc Cárdenas evoked a return to the values of Cardenismo and the Mexican Revolution as a framework of productive negotiation and mutual respect, stating "it was here that the Revolution tried to deepen agrarian reform, making the land productive in the hands of the peasants. Here the peasants responded to the government, a revolutionary government . . . we know full well what side the peasants of the Laguna are on. They have always been with the Mexican Revolution."[116]

Similar accounts of local memories of Lázaro Cárdenas emerged throughout the rest of the campaign, including when Cárdenas toured small Mixtec towns in the mountains of Oaxaca where Lázaro Cárdenas spent much of the last decade of his life.[117] In the town of Juxtlahuaca, Cuauhtémoc Cárdenas was shown a bed, chair, and two tables that had been in his father's residence and were now displayed in a kiosk in the town square. This display was accompanied by quotes and photos of Lázaro Cárdenas, including one that showed Cuauhtémoc Cárdenas standing at the foot of his father's coffin.[118] In another town, a local resident remembered, "I saw the general himself pushing the vehicles that break down in the Mixteca region. He was the greatest authority in the country and here he was with us! We thought that things would continue like this, but afterwards no one again took it upon himself to offer solutions."[119] These positive personal recollections of Lázaro Cárdenas were thus spontaneously evoked by the campaign of his son in many parts of Mexico, and one Mixteca local expressed their effect when informing Cuauhtémoc Cárdenas, "We believe we can trust the general's whelp."[120]

In the midst of economic crisis and neoliberal adjustment, the return of "the general" in the form of his son to advocate a return to the path of revolutionary nationalism significantly resonated with the experiences and memories of many people, particularly in rural Mexico. Unlike PRI candidates who generally adopted a totemic national hero, as Monsiváis noted, the deeply rooted memory and mythology of his father meant that Cuauhtémoc Cárdenas was one of the few figures in Mexican political life that did not require translation.[121] Along with the 1982 bank nationalization, the 1988 election campaign was in this way one of the events during which the excess of history that characterized Mexico's post-1982 sense of permanent crisis became most evident. Indeed, in both cases the moment of past possibility most frequently evoked in the face of crisis was the Lázaro Cárdenas presidency and an ideology of Cardenismo that centered on an assertive economic nationalism and social justice guided by an interventionist state.[122]

Following the campaign, historian Adolfo Gilly edited a collection of letters sent to Cuauhtémoc Cárdenas during 1988 that revealed the importance of Cardenista mythology in inspiring people to support his candidacy.[123] Most letters came from rural areas and demonstrated a sense that the Revolution had been betrayed by the PRI and that Cuauhtémoc Cárdenas represented the possibility to resume the Revolution's true path in favor of the majority of (poor) Mexicans. The letters also revealed how Cardenista mythology within the broader framework of revolutionary nationalism had been worked into local histories in a strikingly similar fashion in different parts of Mexico.

Many of the letters recounted a vision of Mexico's postrevolutionary history that cited the Cárdenas presidency as a golden age followed by a long period of betrayal that led to current hardships. A cognitive separation between the PRI and the Revolution thus seemed to already exist in the minds of many Mexicans, with the 1988 Cárdenas campaign acting as a catalyst for the public expression of this separation. Anthropologist JoAnn Martin found a similar dynamic at work in the community of Tepoztlán, Morelos, where residents identified Mexico's postrevolutionary agrarian reform laws as just, but those administering it in the present dishonest and their legal documents illegitimate. In 1988 Tepoztlán community members voted five to one in favor of Cárdenas.[124] The disconnect between the nation, the Revolution, and particularly the most recent PRI governments was so deep that many of the letters referred to those in government as "foreigners" or "Spaniards" while using phrases such as "Mexican Indian" or "of Revolutionary blood" when describing Cuauhtémoc Cárdenas.[125]

The PRI's concern over the potential power of the symbol of Lázaro Cárdenas became obvious through two main responses. On one hand, the government attempted to outline the differences between its "legitimate" use of history to inspire Mexico's modernizing march forward and its "opportunistic" use by the FDN. Salinas argued that "those of us [in the PRI] who invoke Lázaro Cárdenas . . . don't look for votes by exploiting the nostalgias of times already gone. . . . If we invoke history it is . . . to give us inspiration and confidence that, despite the difficult problems we are living, generations that came before us also faced difficult challenges and they knew how to take Mexico forward."[126] For his part, de la Madrid attempted to reformulate the revolutionary/reactionary dichotomy to one between a "modern and up-to-date conception of the Mexican Revolution" versus a "profoundly reactionary" neopopulism that "tried to find solutions in 1980 . . . [believing] the more bureaucrats that we have and the more money we lose on inefficient supposed social programs, the more revolutionary we will be."[127]

Corporatist peasant sector leaders were the most vocal in their denunciations of Cuauhtémoc Cárdenas's use of his father as a source of legitimacy as it was the connection between the PRI and peasant sectors communicated through Zapata and Cárdenas that was most threatened by the *neocardenista* opposition. At the annual commemoration of Zapata's death in April, the CNC national leader accordingly railed against "factions poorly protected by the surname of an illustrious revolutionary that is patrimony of the peasants and people of Mexico . . . and that they now want to sell to us when it is ours."[128] In response, Cuauhtémoc Cárdenas on the same date attacked the legitimacy of PRI-affiliated peasant organizations and called for the creation of a new peasant organization based on the principles of Article 27 of the constitution, closely associated with both Zapata and the land redistribution program of his father.[129]

The commemoration of the fiftieth anniversary of the 1938 oil expropriation during the 1988 campaign, however, revealed the difficulty now faced by the PRI in claiming legitimacy through the symbol of Lázaro Cárdenas. Newspaper *La Jornada* noted the ambiguity of a banner displayed at the anniversary ceremony made by local Pemex union leaders rumored to be hostile to Salinas's candidacy, which stated, "1938 Cárdenas gave birth to us. 1988 Cárdenas continues to guide us in the defense of Pemex."[130] The FDN, meanwhile, used the occasion to stage its own rally in Mexico City attended by an estimated seventy thousand to one hundred thousand people that demonstrated the greater ease with which it could connect its campaign to traditional revolutionary nationalist mythology than could a neoliberal, proglobalization, and privatization candidate.[131] Demonstrating the support the Cárdenas campaign received from urban social movements as well as rural peasants, Superbarrio spectacularly arrived at the rally preceded by a group of marching tambourine players dressed in his colors of red and yellow and leading a group of ten thousand Mexico City residents into the Zócalo.[132]

Despite the official ceremonies, a series of television advertisements commemorating the anniversary of Mexico's oil expropriation that referenced Lázaro Cárdenas were taken off air and a campaign began to emerge in the media that sought to minimize if not tarnish the heroic status of Lázaro Cárdenas. On March 23, the Televisa program *24 Horas* broadcast an interview with two people who claimed to be previously unrecognized children of Lázaro Cárdenas born to separate mothers. Both openly criticized their alleged half brother Cuauhtémoc Cárdenas for misusing their father's name and praised the PRI system.[133] In July, following the elections, all references to the Cárdenas presidency were edited from a rebroadcasting of epic historical soap opera *Senda de Gloria* on the Televisa network.[134] Clouthier, discounting an electoral alliance with the FDN, also attempted to muddy the image of Lázaro Cárdenas by accusing the ex-president of electoral fraud in 1940 against opposition candidate Juan Andrew Almazán.[135]

As the campaign entered its final months, the focus of attention increasingly became the contest between Cuauhtémoc Cárdenas and Carlos Salinas. Cárdenas continued to tour the country before ever-greater displays of popular support, with particularly large crowds greeting him in the state of Michoacán and at the UNAM in Mexico City, traditional bastions of Cardenismo and the left respectively.[136] From the left, Cárdenas's main competition was Heberto Castillo as candidate of the new Mexican Socialist Party (PMS).[137] As polls emerged showing Cárdenas clearly ahead of Clouthier and gaining on Salinas as voters' preferred presidential candidate, Castillo renounced his candidature so that his party could join the FDN coalition behind Cárdenas.[138] In announcing his support, Castillo stated that "the spirit of Lázaro Cárdenas is running through the Republic, and it runs in his son Cuauhtémoc."[139] This provided the left with its first broad, viable electoral coalition unquestionably grounded in Mexican historical myths and traditions after a long tradition of sectarianism, leaving only the Trotskyite Revolutionary Workers, Party's (PRT) candidate Rosario Ibarra de Piedra outside.

To draw his campaign to a close, Cárdenas opted for a rally in the Mexico City Zócalo followed by further mass rallies in the Laguna region and Michoacán (fig. 3.3). All were attended by tens of thousands of supporters, whom Cárdenas called upon to reconstruct the nation based on the example of Lázaro Cárdenas and other heroes from independence, the liberal Reform, and the Revolution.[140] Cárdenas stated, "Our proposal has been very clear: we fight to regain the abandoned and denied path of the Mexican Revolution, whose principles and objectives, we argue, maintain their relevance."[141] The central argument of Salinas's final campaign speech also drew upon revolutionary nationalism, but as a call to unite behind the state's modernization project, declaring "as during Independence, the Reform, as in the Revolution, today arises from the struggle of our people the need to modernize ourselves to build a Mexico more just, stronger, and more sovereign."[142] Clouthier, meanwhile, used his closing campaign speech to draw comparisons between the authoritarian options of the PRI's "more of the same" and FDN's "nostalgic confusion" and "*neopriísmo*" with "the democratic option" of the PAN.[143]

Election day, July 6, 1988, came to have long repercussions for Mexico's political system due to the spectacular manner in which the postrevolutionary state failed one of the greatest tests of its democratic legitimacy. As initial results were released showing significant opposition victories, chaotic scenes unfolded as the new computerized system for tabulating votes was abruptly shut off. Opposition representatives marched to the room where the Federal Electoral Commission was meeting to complain and were greeted with an announcement that has been attributed to different people with different phrasing but that became synonymous with the events of 1988 as "se cayó el sistema" (the system crashed).[144]

As the computer system failed to come back online, opposition

Figure 3.3. "Cárdenas with the ideals of Zapata." A sign at a Mexico City electoral rally held by a Cuauhtémoc Cárdenas supporter from Axochiapan in Emiliano Zapata's home state of Morelos. Courtesy Sergio Dorantes/Corbis.

complaints grew. Candidates Cárdenas, Clouthier, and Ibarra de Piedra united to personally present a declaration denouncing electoral fraud and calling for the restoration of legality in the electoral process to interior minister Manuel Bartlett before addressing the press and supporters outside the Interior Ministry offices.[145] Despite the lack of official results, shortly after 1:35 a.m. the PRI's national president declared the clear victory of Carlos Salinas de Gortari. This inflamed accusations of fraud and over the next few days, opposition groups began to organize protest actions and release their own results.[146]

Even the official results, when finally released, implied significant erosion in support for the PRI system and its incoming president. Salinas officially won 50.31 percent of the vote—by far the lowest of any candidate in the PRI's history—to Cárdenas's 31.11 and Clouthier's 17 percent. The official figures thus implied a significant change in Mexico's political landscape since de la Madrid won the presidency with over 70 percent of votes in 1982 and the conservative PAN had been the most significant opposition party with almost 16 percent of votes.[147] It was now a revolutionary nationalist opposition that most significantly challenged not just the PRI's hold on power, but its symbolic relationship to the Revolution. Cárdenas was officially recognized to have won the largest share of votes in four states and Mexico City, including clear majorities in Michoacán (63.8 percent), Zapata's home state of Morelos (57.7 percent)—both with large rural peasant populations—and the predominantly urban Mexico State (51.6 percent).[148] As for his own vote, Cárdenas told reporters after emerging from the polling station that he had voted for Superbarrio.[149]

Neocardenismo, Neopanismo, and Neoliberalism

The unexpected success of Cárdenas and the FDN in 1988 drew upon something deeper than mere dissatisfaction with the PRI and challenged revisionist views of the postrevolutionary state and its associated revolutionary nationalist discourse as operating in a largely top-down fashion. Memories of Lázaro Cárdenas and Cardenismo that emerged during the campaign revealed processes through which connections had been established between state and society in both an instrumental and symbolic sense. Letters to Cuauhtémoc Cárdenas from across Mexico contained frequent references to the promises of Cardenismo betrayed through the PRI's failure to fulfill the legitimate citizenship rights symbolized within revolutionary nationalism by Lázaro Cárdenas.[150] Cuauhtémoc Cárdenas in this way emerged as a leader who physically embodied one of the key symbols legitimizing the rights of millions of Mexicans, and represented the possibility of regaining citizenship rights unfulfilled if not threatened by the current government.

The popular swing away from the PRI to the FDN in 1988 further represented a rupture between popular understandings of revolutionary nationalism and the actions of the PRI in government. However, it also reinforced revolutionary nationalism's role in defining broad cognitive boundaries that contained political action in Mexico. Neocardenismo's success further challenged the popular appeal of definitions of democracy based on individualist liberal principles and essentially nonideological multiparty electoral competition. The relative weakness of Clouthier and the PAN in 1988 hinted at an ultimately shallow and limited appeal for the neopanista anti-PRI message of "change" as well as the limited support for a wholesale overthrow of Mexico's postrevolutionary political system.

In the aftermath of the 1988 elections, the incoming Salinas administration faced a difficult task in establishing its legitimacy. In an international environment in which clean, pluralistic elections were increasingly important for the legitimacy of political systems, the continued ability of the corporatist infrastructure to guarantee PRI electoral victories had proven doubtful. As it was still convinced of the correctness of neoliberal formulas for reorganizing Mexico's economy and society, the Salinas administration also needed to define a political project that could mitigate the gap between the revolutionary nationalism that symbolically legitimized the PRI state and the administration's neoliberal policy agenda. The weakness of the often-haphazard nature of the de la Madrid administration's attempts to ameliorate tensions between revolutionary nationalism, neoliberal austerity measures, and international discourses of democracy had been revealed in the 1988 elections. The Salinas administration thus undertook a sustained project to reconfigure relations between the nation and state in an institutional and symbolic sense. This project drew upon both revolutionary nationalist and populist political traditions and was the most extensive project for reworking state-society relations since that of President Lázaro Cárdenas.

Independence Day, 1988

At 11:00 p.m. on September 15, 1988, Miguel de la Madrid was due to step out onto the balcony of the National Palace in Mexico City for the sixth and final time as president to preside over the official grito ceremony to commemorate Mexico's independence. As the high point of Mexico's annual calendar of nationalist commemorations, during the grito the president emerged high above the cheering crowds in the Zócalo to reenact Miguel Hidalgo's 1810 call for an uprising against Spanish colonial authorities. Mexican writer and PRI senator Andrés Henestrosa described this ceremony as one in which "the President of the Republic is Hidalgo, revived, the bell that chimes is that of Dolores, the people who chant the grito are the same [people] who followed the insurgent banners."[1] Once the formal ceremony concluded, however, the crowd below took control of the occasion in often eclectic, chaotic, and irreverent popular patriotic celebrations.[2] Like many aspects of Mexican nationalism, the grito combined formal ritual with popular expressions in a way that blurred the line between elite invention and popular culture. Alongside extensive reporting of official ceremonies, every year national newspapers also printed a balance sheet of this unplanned chaos in Mexico City in terms of the crimes committed and deaths recorded during the evening.[3]

The limits of the PRI's traditional rituals for legitimizing state power were evident in the aftermath of the 1988 elections. For the hegemonic state party, presidential elections historically served to symbolically legitimize the transfer of power every six years from the outgoing president to his successor. The federal elections of 1988 had the opposite effect, as ideologically opposed political groups united against the PRI to contest the victory of its candidate. The PRI's corporatist sectors also proved incapable of mobilizing a sufficient number of citizens to achieve a clear electoral victory and the outgoing de la Madrid administration was discredited by the implication it had intervened to alter the election results. Compounding this crisis of legitimacy was the fact that Salinas's most significant opposition had arisen from within the PRI itself in the form of the National Democratic Front (FDN) organized behind the candidature of Cuauhtémoc Cárdenas.

Ten days following the chaotic election night of July 6, supporters of Cuauhtémoc Cárdenas gathered at Mexico City's Monument to the Revolution and then marched to the Zócalo to hear the ex-candidate address hundreds of thousands of assembled supporters. At the rally, Cárdenas told supporters that the ratification of the official voting totals would constitute "a coup d'état to impose a usurping government that would lack legitimacy, weak in the face of international pressure and [pressure from] diverse and contradictory internal interests."[4] Once Cárdenas's speech finished, the crowd sang the Mexican national anthem and dispersed through the streets of Mexico City's Historic Centre in what newsmagazine *Proceso* described as a festive spirit. Two *judas* were burnt, one with the face of Carlos Salinas and the other in the form of a cardboard rat with the logo of the PRI around its neck.[5] In reference to Salinas, choruses of "Let's get rid of the baldy with the big ears" were sung through the streets until the crowd reached the Juárez Hemiciclo. Once at the Hemiciclo, the gathering was described as almost breaking out into a popular celebration.[6]

Cárdenas next began a national tour in the states of Morelos and Guerrero with meetings in public plazas, some attended by tens of thousands of supporters. This mobilization of supporters aimed to keep pressure on the government to recognize the votes received by the FDN, culminating in a day of national mobilization on August 15, when the electoral college in the legislature would meet to begin the process of ratifying the election results.[7] On August 4, ex-candidates of the PAN and PRT, Manuel Clouthier and Rosario Ibarra de Piedra respectively, joined with Cárdenas in releasing a statement titled "Declaration for Democracy" calling for the annulment of the elections if irregularities were not corrected and asking that authorities elected through fraudulent elections not be recognized.[8] PRI officials, meanwhile, responded to the protests with increasingly threatening language, describing the opposition movement as engaging in "verbal terrorism" and behavior that was undemocratic, disrespectful of the law, and, most ominously, a threat to social order that could lead to violence.[9]

On August 15, the congressional electoral college began a disorderly process of ratifying the electoral results for the legislature while the

FDN and PMS set up a protest camp outside the congress to demand that their victories be recognized. The ratification was due to be completed within four days. However, the process stretched on for two weeks in chaotic sessions characterized by mutual recriminations for undemocratic behavior between PRI representatives and an opposition block of FDN and PAN representatives.[10] Meanwhile, PRI supporters took part in marches in Mexico City on August 24 in support of Salinas's victory, which was formalized with the final ratification of the election results on August 29. The unprecedentedly pluralist LIV Legislature that resulted from these elections was then formally inaugurated on August 31, just one day before Miguel de la Madrid was due to present his final informe to the Chamber of Deputies.[11] In response to the tense political climate, the PRI announced that president-elect Salinas would break with tradition and not attend the final informe of his predecessor.

In Mexican politics, the sixth informe traditionally serves as the final opportunity for a Mexican president to provide a justification for and shape future interpretations of the actions taken during their presidency. José López Portillo's final informe in 1982 involved a particularly dramatic effort to shore up his legitimacy with a bank nationalization decree initially greeted by mass public displays of support. In contrast, the content of de la Madrid's final address to the nation six years later was largely overshadowed by the spectacle of opposition members of congress shouting recriminations at the outgoing president.

De la Madrid described the recent elections as "the beginning of a new and improved stage in our political development" and argued that "our political adversaries and academics working from cubicles or watching from cafés should make no mistake: the recent elections gave us fewer votes, but the Mexican Revolution remained in power."[12] However, opposition legislators yelled rebuttals to de la Madrid's statements. When the president spoke of the recently concluded electoral process, opposition legislators responded by chanting "total repudiation of the electoral fraud!" and when he mentioned the reduction of the public sector, FDN legislators shouted "the Revolution has been betrayed!"[13] Finally, FDN senator Porfirio Muñoz Ledo led an opposition walkout that provoked angry shouts of "traitor" from former colleagues in the PRI.[14] Such rowdiness during a presidential informe was unprecedented.

The day before President de la Madrid's final grito, Cuauhtémoc Cárdenas held another rally in the Zócalo attended by hundreds of thousands of supporters calling on Carlos Salinas to renounce the presidency. Cárdenas located in the FDN movement "the great ideals of the Mexican Revolution [that] run through the entire history of the nation" and presented the movement as an opportunity to "recuperate the historic ideals of the Revolution, the full rule of the Constitution, and the legitimacy of our government and our elected representatives."[15] Alluding to the restoration of liberal rule under Juárez following the French Intervention in 1867, Cárdenas concluded by calling on his followers to "let us restore the Republic by founding its new institutions in a political culture of freedom, reason, and tolerance."[16]

The PAN had enthusiastically joined post-electoral protesting of electoral fraud; however, it did so only in a general sense and refused to specify which candidate's victory had been prevented by this fraud. During the post-election turmoil, an estimated fifteen thousand people gathered at the Angel of Independence on Independence Day 1988 for a grito organized by the PAN that the party described as an event "that signifies the authentic freedom of Mexico" and that focused on repudiating electoral fraud.[17] Manuel Clouthier gave this rival grito, which began with a phrase attributed to Hidalgo during the original "Grito de Dolores" in 1810 but had been omitted from official ceremonies: "Death to bad government!"[18] Yet another element in this grito taken from the original but absent from the official ceremony was Clouthier's cry of "Viva the Virgin of Guadalupe!," which was by the 1980s a customary panista addition to the traditional secular *vivas*.[19] Another symbol of conservative nationalism that had been marginalized from official nationalist discourse for well over a century was also present: one supporter in the crowd held aloft between the panista banners and Mexican flags a placard that read, "Viva Agustín de Iturbide, consummator of Independence. Union, religion, independence."[20]

Miguel de la Madrid, meanwhile, appeared before the crowds in the Mexico City Zócalo to lead the official Independence Day celebrations one day after Cárdenas had in the same square declared the PRI system in terminal crisis and claimed the principles of revolutionary nationalism for his own movement. Like many other nationalist rituals designed to legitimize the state, the grito also provided a space within which inconformity with the state could be expressed. Due to the tense situation, soldiers and police officers were stationed around the Zócalo and plain-clothed security forces deployed throughout the crowd. Nevertheless, hundreds of Cárdenas supporters concentrated below the balcony of the National Palace. When de la Madrid emerged to give the traditional grito, to "the heroes that gave us patria," these supporters greeted the president with cries from below of "fraud!," "Cárdenas!," and "Viva Cárdenas, death to the PRI!"[21] The president, however, observed the usual formalities of the ceremony undeterred and remained on the balcony of the National Palace after the grito for roughly fifteen minutes for the singing of the national anthem and until the fireworks display concluded.

Following the fireworks, the president retired from the balcony and tensions between opposition supporters and security forces in the Zócalo began to escalate. The military police formed a line in front of the National Palace and attempted to push back Cárdenas supporters shouting antigovernment messages and waving the banners of opposition organizations. Amid this struggle, a reporter from the newspaper *Excélsior* was dragged along the ground by officers and hit in the stomach with their firearms, while a press photographer had his camera forcibly taken away despite loud protests from Mexican and foreign reporters covering the event.[22]

As the conflict intensified, scuffles broke out between security forces in uniform or civilian clothing and shouting protesters. Some of these protestors were pulled bloodied and handcuffed from the crowd by security officers and rushed to waiting police vehicles.[23] One case detailed in the press the following day involved Red Cross ambulance officers successfully pleading with security forces to release a bloodied protester to them for medical treatment rather than taking him away.[24] However, the official account of the evening, as described in a statement issued by the police, was that a small group of less than one hundred, possibly under the influence of drugs or alcohol, were trying to enter the National Palace before being stopped, without arrests or further incident.[25]

The next day, the Independence Day holiday, Secretary of Agrarian Reform Rafael Rodríguez Barrera gave the official Independence Day address. As the government representative, Rodríguez Barrera used his speech in 1988 to reiterate that "the Mexican political system is and will be inalterable" while affirming the incoming government's dedication to push forward with an agenda of change and greater closeness between the government and the people.[26] The traditional Independence Day military parade marched down the Paseo de la Reforma following the speech, with a group of PAN members who remained camped at the Angel of Independence shouting at each group, "Total repudiation of the electoral fraud," and, in reference to the relative hirsuteness of the

PAN and clean-shaven and balding PRI representatives in the 1988 presidential elections, "Yes to beards, no to baldies."[27]

Such a spectacle amid the annual highlight of Mexico's patriotic calendar suggested the limits of the PRI's traditional rituals for legitimizing state power. In 1988 the electoral process proved counterproductive for legitimizing the renewal of the state through the transfer of power between administrations. An annual tradition of obedient legislators attentively listening to and applauding the president's informe, simultaneously broadcast across the nation's television screens, was also marred by noisy recriminations and accusations from a reinvigorated opposition within the political system. Finally, the ritual of the grito in which the president took on the paternal act of leading the nation in the annual celebration of its independence was the scene of popular protest and clashes between protestors and state security forces.

The emergence of a new opposition movement that combined discourses of democracy and freedom with appeals to the established myths and symbols of revolutionary nationalism contributed greatly to this crisis of legitimacy. In particular, the Cárdenas opposition appealed to Mexicans by vindicating the established symbolic framework of revolutionary nationalist citizenship rights. Such rights may have only been imperfectly fulfilled by the PRI state in the past, but under de la Madrid, the Mexican state appeared to retreat from accepting even the principle that the state should guarantee such rights. This left the incoming Salinas administration facing the challenge of restoring the legitimacy of the PRI state and reconciling their neoliberal reform project with the established framework of revolutionary nationalism.

CHAPTER FOUR

Carlos Salinas and Mexico's New Era of Solidarity and *Concertación*

The PRI system demonstrated a remarkable capacity for renewal following the turbulent 1988 electoral process and, contrary to initial indications, strengthened its hold on power in many respects during the Carlos Salinas administration. As the postrevolutionary state promoted a symbolic language tied to social and political rights, so too did the Salinas administration promote a new language characterized by terms such as solidarity, social liberalism, and *concertación* (consensus). While embracing a liberal language of democracy, pluralism, and individual rights, the Salinas administration also strengthened the relative power of the presidency in a political style that came to be described by political scientists as "neoliberal populism."

More than any other Mexican administration of the post-1982 neoliberal era, the Salinas administration also paid attention—initially with significant success—to reworking both the symbolic and institutional relationship between state and society under a neoliberal populist style of leadership. Dramatic economic reform along free market neoliberal lines continued and in fact became bolder under Salinas. Initiatives such as the North American Free Trade Agreement (NAFTA), which came into effect in January 1994, and the abandonment of previously untouchable elements of revolutionary nationalism's economic program, such as the end of land redistribution, went beyond anything attempted during the de la Madrid administration and challenged core principles of revolutionary nationalism. The Salinas administration, however, complemented such reforms with new social spending initiatives and made a concerted effort to craft a new nationalist discourse drawing on revolutionary nationalism to explain this changing relationship between state and society. This project was reinforced by a relatively supportive international environment for the reforms and discourse of the administration and a mix of repression and negotiation with domestic opposition political parties. The Salinas administration also, however, provides a case study of the limits of the Mexican state's power to reshape popular understandings of nationalism, most spectacularly displayed in 1992, when the administration attempted to alter Mexico's compulsory school history textbooks.

Salinas and Neoliberal Populism

As Mexico's shift toward neoliberalism took place in an international context of a third-world debt crisis involving austerity measures and free market reform, the style of rule embraced by Salinas that came to be known as neoliberal populism was not a uniquely Mexican phenomenon. This style of rule emerged during the 1990s as a broader Latin American response to transnational currents of neoliberalism and found its most developed expressions in the administrations of Salinas in Mexico (1988–1994), Carlos Menem in Argentina (1989–1999), and Alberto Fujimori in Peru (1990–2000). The rise of neoliberal populism in this way underlines the need to understand the actions of Mexican policy makers as responding to transnational as well as domestic forces that encouraged certain responses that were echoed by other national governments.

Populism has traditionally been a vaguely defined term, with scholarly approaches most broadly divided into those that treat it as primarily an economic phenomenon, or at least one with a significant identifiable economic component, and those who treat it as a political phenomenon based on a particular style of rule.[1] The economic perspective on populism, which dominated analysis prior to the 1990s, saw Latin American populism as a twentieth-century phenomenon associated with the industrializing drive of the region's elites tied to mechanisms of government intervention in the economy, including import substitution industrialization, price controls, and income redistribution. Such mechanisms ostensibly aimed at boosting internal markets were also, it was argued, used to target benefits at key sectors of society, which would then function as the populist leader's core support base. This dynamic generally implied a reciprocal relationship ranging from less formal expectations of voting and mass mobilization by those who benefited from the leader's largesse to outright clientelism. The classic Mexican populist according to this definition was Lázaro Cárdenas.[2]

The neoliberal view of populism was generally highly critical of its effects on economic development, with the corollary that a positive effect of neoliberal free market reform in Latin America would be the eventual eradication of this destructive phenomenon blamed for the region's twentieth-century cycles of boom and bust.[3] This argument held that national economies opened up to transnational capital flows and the laws of the free market would encourage responsible economic policy in the global competition to attract investment and reduce a government's ability to pursue irresponsible economic policy for short-term political gain.[4] Critics of populism in Mexico particularly pointed to the development policies of Echeverría and López Portillo, which they argued obeyed a political rather than economic logic and eventually led to the 1982 debt crisis.[5] This neoliberal teleology thus promised Latin America not only prosperity through capitalist modernity but also freedom from the whims of populist leaders through political modernity.

In the earlier phases of neoliberal reform throughout Latin America, populism was thus generally a label attached by commentators from various fields to political movements of the left that opposed neoliberalism.[6] The Cárdenas campaign in 1988 and that of Luiz Inácio Lula da Silva in the 1989 Brazilian elections were thus dismissed as populist and anachronistic, while their victorious pro-neoliberal opponents such as Salinas and Fernando Collor de Mello in Brazil legitimized their economic reform agenda based on a need to resist populist temptations and pursue responsible reforms.[7] However, when a style of political leadership that certainly *looked* like classic Latin American populism did begin to flourish once again in Latin America during the 1990s, it was in fact led by the region's most successful neoliberal reformers, including Salinas (fig. 4.1).

Around the same time that neoliberal populism emerged, so too did new approaches in the scholarly literature that unlinked populism from a particular historical and socioeconomic context or specific economic policy prescriptions.[8] This interpretation instead emphasized political style, with populism being most clearly characterized by the establishment of a personalized and direct bond between a leader and their followers, whose mobilization functions as the key legitimizing tool for this leadership.[9] Proponents of this viewpoint argued that populist leaders generally pursue a reformist rather than revolutionary agenda, bypassing established institutional structures such as political parties in favor of a more direct form of communication with "the people," generally a heterogeneous mass concentrated in lower socioeconomic sectors of society. New networks are thus built around the leadership and,

Figure 4.1. President Carlos Salinas greets local residents on a working tour in
Tetla, Tlaxcala. Salinas cultivated the image as a popular leader in a style
emblematic of neoliberal populist government. Courtesy Keith Dannemiller/
Corbis.

though such networks can eventually undergo a process of institutionalization, they tend toward a low degree of it.[10] A populist leader still has
to offer *something* to followers beyond simple charisma. However, what
this implies in terms of economic or social policy is a matter open to
empirical investigation in individual cases rather than implying
direct associations between the populist style and specific economic
policies.[11]

One of the innovative arguments made by scholars who analyzed the
rise of neoliberal populism in Latin America during the 1990s was that,
rather than being irreconcilable, neoliberalism and populism in fact
shared certain inherent qualities. The remarkable rebound of the Salinas
presidency's popularity following the 1988 elections is in part explained
by the administration's identification of such affinities. As Weyland
argues, both neoliberalism and populism share an antiorganizational
bent: the former in its desire to protect the equilibrium of the market
from interference by special interest and rent-seeking groups and the
latter in cultivating popular legitimacy by identifying with a heterodox
mass of the people against selfish political factions and elites. Populist

and neoliberal approaches to concepts of freedom and democracy, at least on a rhetorical level, thus share common ground in validating unstructured or minimally structured forms of political and economic activity as preferable to the intervention of organized interest groups or bureaucratic red tape, which distort outcomes for selfish gain.[12]

To break down entrenched organized interests, both neoliberals and populists rely on a strong state. This factor also helps explain neoliberalism's initial expressions in Latin America within the context of Chile and Argentina following the military coups of 1973 and 1976, respectively, where authoritarian rule was justified precisely on the basis of being necessary to guard against organized socialist influences threatening social and economic equilibrium and development.[13] By the 1980s the developed discursive association between neoliberalism and ideas of freedom and democracy made alliances between neoliberal economic experts and genuinely popular political leaders a far more justifiable form of coalition to alliances with military dictatorships. This was particularly so in the context of the end of the Cold War, when the justification of communist subversion disappeared virtually overnight.[14] Neopopulist regimes such as that of Salinas thus operated in a relatively welcoming international environment. The weakening of traditional representative mechanisms for subaltern sectors of society by economic crisis and neoliberal adjustment also created suitable conditions in which a populist leader with unmediated access to the masses could thrive.[15]

The technocratic true believers of the Salinas administration were always unlikely to consider returning to nationalist political and economic solutions as a viable option. Furthermore, the 1988 elections had exposed the limitations of the PRI's established corporatist infrastructure for guaranteeing election victories and retaining power. The growth of popular movements among the urban poor outside of the PRI-affiliated sectoral organizations, meanwhile, represented a potential risk to the incoming administration's stability if Cárdenas and the PAN maintained and/or built upon the significant support they received from these movements in the 1980s.[16] An alternative formula for linking the state to the nation was therefore needed, and Salinas found it in a populist framework that sidelined existing corporatist entities in favor of a direct relationship between a dynamic, reformist, and socially committed president and the masses tired of declining living standards, crisis, and uncertainty.

Solidarity: A New Relationship between State and Society

Salinas took office in December 1988 promising to modernize Mexico. The president defined this modernization as the central project of his presidency during his inaugural speech to the congress, directly referencing the theme of modernizing everything from Mexico's health system to its armed forces no fewer than twenty-five times. Mexico's national history was to be, according to the president, "a motivator and a stimulant" for this modernization.[17] The new president thus cast himself as a reformist nationalist and set out to transform the meaning of Mexico's historical traditions as an integral element of building support for his sweeping reform program.[18]

The first major action designed to reinforce the Salinas administration's modernizing zeal involved a symbolically powerful attack on the entrenched and often informal power structures of the corporatist sectors with the arrest on January 10, 1989, of Pemex workers' union boss Joaquín Hernández Galicia. Popularly known as La Quina and based in Ciudad Madero, Tamaulipas, where the Petroleum Workers of the Mexican Republic Union (STPRM) headquarters were located, Hernández Galicia was emblematic of the corruption and impunity embedded within the PRI system that de la Madrid's moral renovation project was supposed to target.[19] Using revenues from the publically owned Pemex to build a business empire and powerbase amongst workers, La Quina had been accused in the press of assassinating rivals and importing arms shipments for his own personal security since the late 1970s, but authorities neglected to investigate such charges.[20]

Little more than a month after Salinas became president, a combined federal police and army force stormed Hernández Galicia's home to be greeted, according to the official accounts, by a hail of bullets from the union leader's bodyguards, leaving one detective dead. Hernández Galicia was charged with murder and illegal possession of firearms, with police claiming to have found a cache including two hundred Uzi submachine guns and thirty thousand rounds of ammunition in his home.[21] In 1992 the once untouchable union leader and PRI corporatist ally was then sentenced to thirty-five years in prison for homicide and illegal arms possession.

Despite a two-day oil workers' strike in protest, the arrest was broadly greeted as a positive move by the new government against impunity and corruption, helping to shore up the image of a powerful, legitimate, and effective president after months of uncertainty following the contested electoral result. Prominent intellectuals such as Octavio Paz and Enrique Krauze signed a public letter to this effect, arguing that the arrest showed Mexico "would advance, no doubt, on the road to democracy."[22] However, the de la Madrid administration had claimed a similarly high-profile scalp for moral renovation soon after taking office when Mexico City police chief under López Portillo, Arturo Durazo Moreno, was arrested for massive corruption while other powerful officials suspected of corruption were left untouched. It therefore remained to be seen if such arrests were more than simply a newer form of political ritual accompanying the transition between presidential administrations.

President Salinas from his inaugural address also promoted the concept of a new relationship between state and society based on a principle of *concertación social* (social consensus) that in practice meant a direct dialogue and partnership between the executive and different interest groups. The administration justified this streamlining of communication in the language of neoliberalism by arguing for the need to strip away a paternalistic and inefficient bureaucracy in order to empower the people in a relationship of co-responsibility with the state. In practice, this strategy reinforced the centralization of state power in the presidency that began under Echeverría.

Salinas also drew upon revolutionary nationalism to support this formulation, arguing that it had been the original aim of the Revolution to create not only a strong state to defend national sovereignty and popular social rights, but also an emancipated population in place of one suffocated by bureaucracy and state tutelage. A leaner, less bureaucratic state would therefore be more able to fulfill the goals of the Revolution while adapting Mexico to global change in a way that protected its national sovereignty.[23] The signature social policy of the administration was the National Program of Social Solidarity (Pronasol), incorporated into a new Secretary of Social Development (Sedesol) in 1992, which provided the institutional framework that underpinned this discourse.[24]

The aims of Pronasol formally outlined on December 6, 1988, were to raise living standards, specifically those of peasants, indigenous people, and the urban poor. This would be achieved through a strategy of equilibrated regional development and by creating the conditions for the improvement of living conditions while strengthening the participation of civil society organizations and local authorities in development initiatives.[25] The Salinas administration in a broader sense promoted

Pronasol as implying "a new relationship between society and government," and it did indeed differ from the traditional pyramidal form of state-society relations that had underpinned the postrevolutionary political system.

Whereas the postrevolutionary state had traditionally depended on a hierarchy of local PRI and PRI-affiliated union officials through whom patronage would trickle down in return for local support, the Salinas administration constructed a parallel bureaucracy of local Pronasol (later Sedesol) officials intended to manage resources independently from the local party organization and promote the program to local communities (fig. 4.2). Communities would make proposals for Pronasol projects through a local Solidarity committee, either to the local Solidarity official or the town government. Requests would then be analyzed by Solidarity officials for technical revisions before final approval of funding would be granted either directly to community organizations or public institutions where appropriate. In order for state governments to receive Solidarity funds, governors were further required each year to sign a social development agreement directly with Salinas, which included a Solidarity clause according to which state and municipal government officials would hold regular meetings with Pronasol/Sedesol officials for the evaluation of Pronasol projects.[26] This was designed to give state and local officials less discretion over the targeting of social spending and less personal patronage to distribute.

In the targeting of resources, critics pointed to an apparently political logic that belied talk of modernizing and democratizing reform. Many described Pronasol as the latest in a long line of PRI social development projects based on patronage and clientelism, albeit now expanded to include urban and indigenous groups beyond the poor rural communities primarily targeted by the Echeverría and López Portillo administrations' Pider and Coplamar antipoverty programs.[27] While considerable, the financial resources committed to the program—said to derive from the privatization of state-owned businesses and savings from increased government efficiency—were still less than pre-1982 social spending. Rather than its real ability to ameliorate the hardships suffered due to budget austerity, the success of Pronasol instead derived from the targeting of the program to important social and political actors to mitigate their opposition to the Salinas administration and its usefulness as a communications strategy.[28]

Pronasol resources were most visibly distributed to groups that formed the basis for civil society movements during the late 1970s

Figure 4.2. Photo from a Pronasol pamphlet showing the solidarity literature distributed through local Sedesol offices across Mexico. Large amounts of printed material were distributed through the Sedesol bureaucracy explaining the government's new reforms and commitment to social justice.

through the 1980s and were outside the traditional corporatist mechanisms for negotiation between state and society. These social sectors had provided a significant source of support for opposition parties such as the PAN in northern cities and the center-left Party of the Democratic Revolution (PRD) that evolved from the FDN in 1989 around Mexico City.[29] Pronasol, which the administration stated aimed to empower grassroots organizing, effectively split popular movements between those who refused to deal with Salinas and those who would. As well as raising the costs for groups that allied with opposition parties, the Salinas administration sought to limit the number of grassroots organizations by strategically allying with the stronger ones while continuing to marginalize weaker organizations.[30]

Those organizations that did cooperate with the administration argued that Pronasol represented a concession from the state that recognized the growing importance of popular movements independent from the PRI's corporatist framework. Movements such as the COCEI in Juchitán, Oaxaca, that had come into conflict with the previous administration further argued that their political actions should respond to the immediate needs of their supporters and that the organization had always strengthened itself by taking advantage of concessions offered by the state.[31]

The ability to secure funding on behalf of those they represented did strengthen those organizations that chose to participate in Pronasol relative to those that did not. For example, political scientist Paul Haber compared the Popular Defense Committee (CDP) in Durango, which participated in Pronasol, and the Assembly of Neighborhoods (ABP) in Mexico City, which did not. Whereas the CDP experienced significant growth under Salinas, the ABP remained loyal to the PRD and saw membership decline as it faced greater obstacles in securing resources.[32] This further underscored the conditionality of access to public resources on maintaining good relations with the presidency through concertación social. Pronasol in this way had significant success in disarticulating the national multiclass front that organized behind the Cárdenas campaign in 1988 by encouraging popular mobilization around local issues such as funding for housing, education, or infrastructure rather than national issues such as critiques of the state's macroeconomic policy.

Despite the goal of Pronasol being to address poverty, spending was targeted most at urban areas where less than 30 percent of extremely poor households were located, but where the PRI's share of voting totals had most significantly declined and Cárdenas had found his greatest support in 1988.[33] The issue of housing for the urban poor had been central to the rise of urban popular movements during the 1980s and Pronasol spending was used to strengthen those movements that developed a good relationship with the Salinas administration.[34] The Valle de Chalco settlement on the outskirts of Mexico City received particularly personal attention from Salinas, who visited the neighborhood in January 1990 to switch on the electricity supply provided under the program in a public ceremony. The president also spent the night in a local home, something he was to repeat on two further occasions as he returned to launch other Pronasol projects. Salinas further invited Pope John Paul II to say mass in Chalco during his 1990 tour of Mexico and the area, which had been emblematic of rising poverty following the 1982 crisis, was now touted to both domestic and international audiences as a showcase for the government's commitment to fighting poverty.[35]

The Chalco development and events such as the visit of Pope John Paul II are particularly emblematic of how Pronasol could symbolically communicate the president's modernizing attack on poverty even to those who did not directly benefit from social spending. Another part of this communications strategy was the annual National Solidarity Week instituted by the government in September 1990. During this week, the president would promote the achievements of the program by touring Solidarity projects and communal working days programmed for the week. Following the first Solidarity Week, the president proudly announced that more than fifty thousand activities had taken place involving the participation of ten million Mexicans.[36] To underscore the importance of the notion of solidarity to its modernization project, the Salinas administration launched two satellites into orbit named Solidarity I and II as part of its modernization of telecommunications.[37]

Following the 1988 debacle, the PRI's electoral fortunes rebounded spectacularly in areas such as Chalco and Ixtapalapa in Mexico City, which received particular attention under Pronasol. In a more general sense, midterm electoral results in 1991 showed a shift back toward the PRI majority government/conservative PAN opposition dichotomy following the 1988 Cárdenas upset.[38] This was an arrangement supported under the concertación social formula for direct negotiation of the recognition of PAN electoral victories but continued hostility toward the PRD.

The concertación formula was also applied to relations between the presidency and corporatist bodies to privilege direct negotiation over party mechanisms, most significantly in relation to workers' groups. Good relations with the presidency became more important for unions during this period and traditionally powerful labor organizations, particularly the Confederation of Mexican Workers (CTM) and its secretary general since 1941, Fidel Velázquez, saw themselves increasingly marginalized within the party structure and in presidential decision-making. At the same time, others more amenable to direct negotiation, such as the Mexican Telephone Workers' Union (STRM), received direct presidential support.[39] The risk of intransigence for union leaders was in this sense the same as it was for leaders of independent social organizations: marginalization and ineffectiveness.[40]

The elimination of corporatist sectoral quotas for internal governing bodies of the PRI, such as the National Executive Committee and the National Political Committee, in favor of open internal elections, further reduced the influence of the sectors within the party, and even more so relative to the executive.[41] However, corporatism was not completely dismantled during this phase of neoliberal reform and indeed its mechanisms were often used to ensure sufficient social stability for reforms. The Salinas administration's overall approach to unions and the corporatist sectors was in fact largely strategic and aimed to weaken the power of individual sectoral leaders or unions relative to the presidency rather than eliminating either the sectors or the corporatist system of state-sector relations outright.[42]

The high-profile arrest of Hernández Galicia, for example, took place against a backdrop of the STPRM oil workers' union being particularly hostile to neoliberal reform. La Quina was also personally a vocal critic of the PRI's recent neoliberal turn and had been accused of supporting the Cuauhtémoc Cárdenas campaign in 1988.[43] The arrest is therefore more accurately understood as a strike against destabilizing elements within the PRI system and as a public relations strategy than evidence of a wider drive toward democratizing reform.[44] Moreover, the Salinas administration installed a more compliant official in Sebastian Guzmán Cabrera as leader of the STPRM whose election was marked by the same practices of intimidation and vote rigging that occurred under La Quina, but who subsequently consented to the Salinas administration's plans to restructure Pemex that included the firing of more than thirty thousand oil workers in 1991.[45]

From Revolutionary Nationalism to Social Liberalism

As well as reworking the institutional relationship between the state and society, the Salinas administration placed significant importance on creating a new cultural project to accompany neoliberal reform under the name of social liberalism. Emerging after Pronasol and the associated emphasis on solidarity was already established in Salinista discourse, the administration expended considerable effort developing a new nationalist framework of social liberalism. This discourse drew upon nineteenth-century liberal traditions to juxtapose Salinista social liberalism with neoliberalism as a distinctly Mexican response to global instability and currents of change. Social liberalism wove established historical myths and symbols into the Salinas administration's reform agenda to communicate the message that the state's modernization project constituted a nationalist and popular response to an uncertain post–Cold War international panorama and was, as Salinas explained in his first informe, "the best defense of [Mexico's] sovereignty."[46] Rather than a radical new reform agenda, then, the president argued that he was implementing a "social liberalism [that] is within the very edification of our nation, because it is what has constructed our national conscience."[47]

The Salinas reforms included a broader reorganizing of Mexican cultural institutions, most significantly the founding of the National Council for Culture and the Arts (Conaculta) within the first week of the Salinas term. Conaculta's first president, Rafael Tovar y de Teresa, explained the council's mission as being tightly bound to the broader modernization project of the administration. According to Tovar y de Teresa, Conaculta aimed to promote national culture as "a point of reference, unique and unsubstitutable" during an era in which traditional collective identities were weakened by transnational forces such as liberalized global trade.[48] The creation of Conaculta, moreover, provided an organization through which the government could coordinate cultural policy with civil society actors, most notably providing a channel for dialogue with influential Mexican intellectuals.[49]

During the first years of the Salinas presidency, the PRI also launched the magazine *Examen* and think tank Cambio XXI as forums for debating and publishing material outlining the intellectual foundations of the Salinas reforms.[50] The social liberalism interpretation of history promoted in such forums hinged on the idea that the defining event of Mexico's republican history had been the victory of the nineteenth-century Liberal Reform movement. Mexican liberals were credited with introducing reforms that overcame post-independence chaos and division to create a nation of individuals living under the rule of law in a secular, sovereign state.

The social liberalist reading of Mexico's liberal tradition identified the need for state intervention to ensure equality and social justice as a central concern of Mexican liberals. Nineteenth-century debates about social justice were then portrayed as having been interrupted by the coming to power of Porfirio Díaz. It was the Revolution and, most significantly, the Constitution of 1917 that finally attempted harmonizing individual guarantees under the rule of law with social and political rights, in this way signifying Mexico's movement from a nation of individuals to one of citizens. While the Independence and Revolutionary struggles were both included in this schematic, their significance was defined respectively in terms of their initial outline and then later fulfillment of core ideals championed by Reform-era liberals.[51] Social liberalism was in this way presented as the rediscovery of an authentically Mexican political tradition that had been championed by some of its greatest heroes and that bridged the gap between individualist neoliberal reform and the traditional collectivist values of revolutionary nationalism.

As Alan Knight identified, an obvious appeal of returning to the liberal reform movement for historical legitimacy with only halfhearted reference to the Revolution was that it offered a means to downplay the government's revolutionary heritage without falling into the trap of neo-Porfirismo.[52] This was especially useful as comparisons between government technocrats and the positivist científicos of the Díaz regime were commonly hurled at the Salinas and de la Madrid administrations.[53]

Salinas further sought to co-opt some aspects of the nationalist leftist critiques of neoliberalism associated with neo-Cardenismo. Rejecting characterizations of its reforms as guided by doctrinaire positivism, supporters of the Salinista reform project enunciated their own rejection of what they described as a laissez-faire neoliberal false dichotomy between an economically and a socially responsible state.[54] The president instead argued in favor of a model in which the invisible hand of the market was accompanied by a *mano solidaria* (hand of solidarity) that included an active role for the state in protecting national sovereignty, encouraging community and individual initiative, and ensuring the fulfillment of citizenship rights for marginalized and vulnerable groups.[55] As a cultural project, proponents of social liberalism argued for a modern nationalism that conserved historic values without remaining tied to obsolete public policies.[56] This clear distinction was repeatedly made in social liberal discourse between a *social* liberalism oriented toward achieving social justice and an insensitive, homogenous globalizing *neo*liberalism.

This dichotomy between a neoliberalism and state social programs was not as clear as Salinas sought to portray. The question of how to balance social citizenship rights with neoliberal free market reform was, in fact, a central topic of concern for neoliberal reformers globally. In relatively wealthy economies such as the United Kingdom, the response often took the form of involving private enterprise, or at least a private enterprise mentality, in welfare programs alongside initiatives of co-responsibility between state and welfare recipients such as welfare-to-work programs.[57] By the late 1980s social justice initiatives such as Pronasol that centered on the idea of self-help projects were also increasingly seen by proponents of neoliberal reform in developing economies as a necessary element of economic reform for preserving political stability and encouraging a less dependent, more entrepreneurial attitude among subaltern groups.[58]

For a Mexican audience, the president and his supporters set up a phantom battle with neoliberal ideology in which they cast themselves as championing a practical, moderate, and realistic program that neither fell into the trap of neo-Porfirismo nor an outdated, nostalgic path to failure endorsed by neo-Cardenistas. For an international audience, Pronasol and Salinas's populist political style gave the president a pragmatic, modern, and reformist image within the neoliberal mainstream. Further strengthening the international rehabilitation of the Mexican government's image following the turbulence of the 1980s was the Salinas administration's most ambitious reform agenda: the negotiation of a free-trade agreement with its powerful northern neighbor.

From South to North: Reframing the Relationship between Mexico and the United States

The negotiation of the North American Free Trade Agreement (NAFTA), announced by Salinas and US President George H. W. Bush in June 1990, and growing to include Canada the following year, represented to its supporters not just a way of locking free market reform into the Mexican economy, but a symbolic entry into the first world of the north and exit from the third world of the south.[59] This had been the dream of Mexican elites since the nineteenth century. A free-trade agreement with the United States, however, also represented another minefield for a president seeking to refashion nationalist discourse for the neoliberal era.

Successive PRI administrations up to that of de la Madrid had publically emphasized Mexico's cultural and political affinities with Latin America and asserted an independent attitude toward the United States, regardless of the realities of often very close cooperation between the two governments.[60] Indeed, Mexican nationalism had been significantly shaped by a juxtaposition with the United States as its primary external other.[61] In Mexico's nationalist mythology, the great martyrs were the Niños Héroes, young cadets who had given their lives rather than surrender to US invaders during the Mexican-American war of 1846–1848. The military academy at which they were martyred later became the

Figure 4.3. The Monument to the Niños Héroes in Mexico City. In the background is Chapultepec Castle, formerly the military academy where the Niños Héroes were said to have fought to the death before the last surviving soldier wrapped himself in the national flag and plunged to his death rather than surrender to US invaders during the Mexican-American War (1846–1848). Photo by author.

Castillo de Chapultepec that looms over the monument-lined central stretch of the Paseo de la Reforma in Mexico City and the Monument to the Niños Héroes at its base is another of the capital's most iconic monuments (fig. 4.3). The PRI had also historically played upon such images of the United States as threatening and interventionist to promote unity behind the national state.

Mexican-US integration had in fact already begun to increase markedly both economically and in terms of immigration in the decade prior to NAFTA coming into effect. Political scientist Stephen Morris identified the three major responses to this integration as being one that saw it as a threat to national identity and political sovereignty, another that saw integration as positive and enriching for both the United States and Mexico, and, finally, one that fell between the two categories by recognizing some impact on culture and sovereignty but saw it as relatively contained and nonthreatening.[62] Analysis of polling by political scientists Charles Davis and Horace Bartilow further found that positive and negative attitudes toward the United States more generally strongly correlated to whether Mexicans supported or opposed NAFTA prior to its implementation.[63]

As in other areas of reform, the Salinas administration showed sensitivity to such sentiments and adopted the in-between position described by Morris. Opinion polls taken in 1992 suggested that popular sentiment was in sync with this strategy, with most respondents believing that, while NAFTA would have some impact in diluting national culture and traditions, it would be minimal.[64] Government officials from the president down assured Mexicans that they would defend Mexico's culture and sovereignty through the negotiations and that this push into modernity would be *Mexican* and guided by the lessons of Mexico's history.[65]

The administration further argued that it was acting to protect Mexico's sovereignty through a realistic response to both the immediate context of post–Cold War global instability and the unchanging reality of Mexico's geographical location next to the world's only remaining military superpower. In this context, Salinas argued that neither "protectionist barriers nor . . . aggressive rhetoric defend us."[66] Instead, Mexico had to remain internally united while embracing, always in reference to its distinctive nationality, global currents of change as "today, this threat is to remain outside, at the margin of new integrative world processes, [and] from the great currents of trade and resources."[67]

To help address concerns of economic sovereignty, the Salinas administration established as one of its key negotiating points the protection of Pemex as a state-owned oil monopoly and used its success on this point to reaffirm that the government would not allow Mexico's sovereignty to be compromised by the agreement.[68] This was thus another "reform of the Revolution" in which Juárez was evoked to symbolize the administration's continued concern for sovereignty and Zapata to symbolize its concern for social justice in public statements.[69] Through all of this, the administration emphasized that NAFTA would benefit Mexicans and relied on favorable coverage in the media, particularly television, to promote this message.[70]

Opposition to NAFTA came from a variety of groups of the left, from independent peasant organizations to dissident teachers' unions.[71] The PRD argued that NAFTA signified an agreement built on the exploitation of Mexico's cheap labor and natural resources, keeping it in a position of dependence and worsening the conditions of Mexican workers.[72] Launching his second bid for the presidency on November 20, 1993, Cuauhtémoc Cárdenas described the negotiation of the agreement as "one of the most serious and humiliating episodes for our country" and called for a referendum.[73] This was consistent with the PRD's generally suspicious attitude toward US political and economic interests as taking advantage of Mexico's relative weakness to ally with the PRI and local capitalists to form deals to the detriment of most Mexicans.[74] Others, such as political theorist, ex-communist, and then-PRD member Jorge Castañeda, argued against the idea that such an agreement was inevitable and suggested that Mexico was compromising its own interests for a mirage of modernity.[75] While broadly supportive, even the PAN expressed concerns over the loss of *mexicanidad* (Mexicanness) through greater integration with the United States.[76]

Such criticisms were not a reflexive anti-Americanism so much as based on concerns about protecting national culture, sovereignty, and citizenship rights against a much more powerful country. While Cárdenas and the PRD might have seen the United States as a potential threat, they did not reject the idea of a trade agreement with Mexico's northern neighbor completely. Instead, they argued that the deal being negotiated by the PRI was a bad one for most Mexicans. A significant reason for this reticence to engage in open anti-Americanism was the growing symbolic and political recognition within Mexico of the large Mexican migrant population living in the United States as Mexicans who both retained Mexican citizenship rights and were worthy of admiration for making sacrifices to financially support their families and communities at home. Cárdenas and the PRD thus now campaigned both on Mexican and US territory for votes and, though the issue had been publically discussed since the Echeverría administration, it was PRD legislators who in 1994 formally introduced an initiative into the federal Chamber of Deputies to give voting rights to Mexicans living outside the national borders.[77]

While Mexican emigration to the United States had a long history, Mexico became increasingly dependent on the income sent home by migrants as their numbers greatly increased from the mid-1970s onward. A series of changes to US immigration legislation as well as the restructuring of both economies and Mexico's post-1982 economic crisis during this time had led to a qualitative change in Mexican immigration from short-term and formal toward more permanent yet increasingly informal settlement in the United States.[78] The resulting cross-border economic, social, and political bonds increasingly defied a grounding of the Mexican nation within the territorial borders of the Mexican state. Anthropologists and demographers, for example, noted the increasingly important role during the 1980s and 1990s of migrants living in the United States in the financial, political, and cultural affairs of particularly rural towns in Mexico. Mexican attitudes to the United States and NAFTA, meanwhile, also became closely linked to perceptions of how Mexicans living in the United States were treated.[79]

Political actors responded to this situation by broadening both the symbolic and legal framework of the Mexican nation and citizenship. By the end of the de la Madrid administration prominent representatives of the Mexican government routinely led Independence Day grito ceremonies in cities around the United States with large Mexican immigrant communities. Indeed, Salinas had led the grito in Los Angeles as the secretary of planning and budget in 1983.[80] The Mexican government had also begun to expand constitutional guarantees to Mexicans living informally in the United States, which by 1998 included amending the constitution to allow dual citizenship for Mexicans living outside the national borders.[81] As evidenced by Salinas's comments, however, the government approached integration with the outside world and particularly the United States with a somewhat ambivalent message of inevitability.

Some commentators, however, viewed increased integration with the United States in an almost unqualified positive light. Historian Héctor Aguilar Camín, for example, described revolutionary nationalism as being significantly driven by an anti-gringo impulse that ignored the positive impacts of US ideas and culture on Mexico stretching back to nineteenth-century liberalism and independence. He further sentenced that Mexico would benefit greatly from becoming more like the United States in areas such as health, education, living standards, and democratic institutions. Aguilar Camín thus called on Mexicans to embrace greater integration with the United States by throwing off notions of an inert, fixed identity and instead embrace a progressive, forward-looking perspective.[82]

This call was made not just in the context of NAFTA, but within a broader debate on the national history that was taking place during the Salinas period and in which Aguilar Camín was a central actor. These discussions revealed a deepening divide among Mexican intellectuals over established revolutionary nationalist framework of national identity and whether it represented principles to which the nation should return or which were holding it back. In 1992 this divide provoked a significant public controversy centering on government plans to modify school history textbooks.

The Demythification of Mexican History
and the History Textbook Controversy

As part of its effort to restore legitimacy to the presidency, the Salinas administration actively courted cultural elites to support its modernization project, in part by using state patronage through Conaculta. The Salinas reforms in the cultural sphere encouraged a reinterpretation of Mexico's history, particularly the significance of the Revolution, that extended beyond government-promoted social liberalism. The tone of much of the era's historical analysis is encapsulated in the contention in Aguilar Camín and Lorenzo Meyer's 1989 book *A la sombra de la Revolución Mexicana* (In the Shadow of the Mexican Revolution) that Mexico was entering into "a new historical age bidding farewell to the most cherished traditions and intolerable vices of the historic tradition that we know as the Mexican Revolution."[83]

One of the more general themes of historical debate that emerged at this time centered on the issue of the "myths" or "lies" of Mexican history and the need to produce a new, objective history for the nation to reflect its modernization. The monthly journals *Nexos* and *Vuelta* were important participants in this debate. *Nexos*, for example, ran a series of interviews with prominent historians titled "Mexico through Its Myths" from October 1993 to January 1994 that focused on identifying and debunking the myths of the national history.[84]

The most significant attempt to reinterpret the national history for the neoliberal era was the Salinas administration's commissioning of a new series of free history textbooks for schoolchildren in 1992 for the first time since the Echeverría administration. During the presidency of Adolfo López Mateos (1958–1964), the Mexican state began the Programa de Libros de Texto Gratuitos (Free Textbook Program) that became an important part of the ongoing hegemonic cultural project of the postrevolutionary state.[85] The hegemonic rather than totalitarian nature of the PRI's cultural project was displayed in debates that greeted each new round of texts during the 1960s and 1970s during which nonrevolutionary identities emerged to contest the state's perspective. Specifically, the persistence of Catholicism and conservative identities were represented by groups including the PAN and ecclesiastical authorities who were traditionally the most vocal critics of the free text-books and the manner in which they presented sensitive issues such as history and sexual education.[86] The texts in this way had traditionally formed a key battleground of domination in postrevolutionary Mexico, with the very fact that the government selected texts from which all Mexican schoolchildren were supposed to learn arousing complaints of indoctrination.[87]

When Salinas and Secretary of Education Ernesto Zedillo launched the National Agreement for the Modernization of Basic Education in May 1992, the production of new history textbooks was given particu-lar priority and new texts titled *Mi libro de historia de México* (My Book of Mexico's History) for fourth, fifth, and sixth grades of primary school were rushed into production to be ready for the 1992–1993 school year beginning in August.[88] Although the history texts were tra-ditionally produced by the secretariat of public education itself, Salinas and Zedillo selected high-profile historians Enrique Florescano and Aguilar Camín, both associated with *Nexos*, to oversee the editing of the new texts and a private publisher, Ultra, to print them.[89] Both the president and education minister—at the time regarded as a leading potential candidate for the PRI's 1994 presidential nomination—took a strong personal interest in the texts, which extended to selecting the authors and cover images, and approving the final texts.[90]

Not long after Salinas and Zedillo launched the history texts and copies began to circulate, public criticism exploded. While some out-right exclusions of events or heroes caused controversy, Mexico's defined narrative of history along with its key heroes and events remained largely in place. The main source of debate over the new texts therefore centered on the presentation of these events and heroes in a manner that altered their significance. Specifically, the flashpoints for conflict were the discussion of events in which the ideological reorientation of the Mexican state toward neoliberal globalization could be most clearly read. These included the presentation of US military interventions in Mexico, the relationship between social injustice and a development model privileging foreign and private investment under Porfirio Díaz, and an obscuring of the causes championed by revolutionary leaders, particularly the agrarian cause of Emiliano Zapata. It was also argued by opponents that the history texts engaged in direct propaganda in favor of the current administration in their discussion of the 1988 elec-tions, the initial years of the Salinas government, and the educational reforms that led to the production of the texts themselves.[91]

A column by Miguel Ángel Granados Chapa in newspaper *La Jornada* on August 20, 1992, set the tone for much of the criticism that followed when he described the motivation for the texts as being "in order to avoid being accused of running counter to Mexican history, the government resolved to alter it through a vast operation of ideological revision."[92] Joining in this criticism were many of those historians not among the group who had formed a close relationship with the Salinas administration. A former National History Prize winner and author of influential works on the Mexican Revolution and Cuba, Paco Ignacio Taibó II, was particularly prominent among these critics. Taibó participated in a series of public debates on the texts during which he argued that the texts "defend the darkest figures from the nation's past" and constituted a "pro-American view of history on the eve of the [North American] Free Trade Agreement."[93] Adding to these critiques, agrarian historians Margarita Carbó, Esperanza Fujigaki, and Iván Gomezcésar Hernández argued from their perspective that the texts presented a vision of Mexico as a cosmopolitan country in which the indigenous and peasant populations were "excrement and backwards."[94]

Within Mexico's intellectual establishment, the selection of Florescano and Aguilar Camín to oversee the production of the texts provided another motive for criticism, even from those otherwise largely sympathetic to the content and tone of the texts. These criticisms centered on the perception of government patronage being showered upon the *Nexos* group, particularly from intellectuals associated with the rival monthly publication *Vuelta*. Both the *Nexos* and *Vuelta* groups operated largely as private producers of culture, with Aguilar Camín and the *Nexos* group owning television station Channel 22 and publishing house Cal y Arena. The *Vuelta* group, of which Octavio Paz and Enrique Krauze were the most prominent members, were associated with the Clio publishing house, which produced historical soap operas as part of a close working relationship between Krauze and television consortium Televisa. This conflict can therefore be understood as at least in part resulting from the increasing privatization of cultural production after 1982, which created a new class of public intellectuals as commercial producers of knowledge and culture vying for government and corporate support.[95]

Accusations of government favoritism for the *Nexos* group were also made by critics including Granados Chapa, who portrayed the *Nexos* historians as "authorized voices" for the state.[96] *Vuelta*'s Krauze, meanwhile, attacked both those who criticized the new interpretation of history in the texts as appearing "more like defenders of the sacred official history and the ideologies that died in 1989 than of the truth," while criticizing the books as poorly written and training his guns firmly on the decision to use historians associated with *Nexos*. Both Krauze and Paz portrayed the *Nexos* group as attempting to seize control of the national culture by allying themselves with the government.[97] Aguilar Camín responded that such critics were engaging in a bitter cultural guerrilla war based on envies and rivalries generated by the *Nexos* group's recent successes.[98]

Within the political system, the PRD was one of most prominent and earliest critics of the texts. For example, PRD federal deputy René Bejarano ironically observed of the texts that "it turns out that Texas was not captured nor sold, but sought its 'separation.'"[99] Bejarano further criticized the treatment of revolutionary heroes Villa and Zapata and the omissions of any reference to the constitutional article mandating that education offered by the state must be free at all levels, Madero's slogan of "effective suffrage, no reelection," the Zapatistas' Plan de Ayala, and Zapatista-influenced agrarian laws.

The PRD also took exception to how its own place in history was represented. Failure to note the disputed election in 1988 that led to the PRD's formation was highlighted in party members' arguments, as were references in the texts to the PRD as a continuation of the disbanded Mexican Communist Party.[100] Stepping into the role of patriotic defenders of national history, the PRD and sympathetic historians began a series of public classes for teachers to "correct" the new texts. These classes began on September 7, 1992, with a class given by Taibó in the Plaza Santo Domingo in Mexico City, directly across from the offices of the secretary of public education.[101]

Arousing some of the most heated debate was the omission that seemed most obviously aimed at changing the presentation of historical US-Mexico relations: that of the Niños Héroes. Critics argued that the young martyrs had been removed from the national epic as they now sat uncomfortably with the political and ideological aims of the Salinas administration as it pursued greater economic integration with the United States. While the PRI responded that the Niños Héroes were in fact mentioned in the book for fourth grade students, this response did not satisfy critics such as Taibó, who placed a sign in the front window of his home reading, "Who killed the Niños Héroes? The new Books of Mexico's History."[102]

The Niños Héroes were used by critics as perhaps the most

emblematic and traitorous example of the administration's attempts to alter the national history to fit its neoliberal ideological agenda. PRD senator Raymundo Cárdenas, for example, argued that "evident in the texts is the ideological-political intention which seeks to refashion Mexicans within [the context of] a new relationship with the United States [by] falsifying historical events."[103] An ex-PRD senator further claimed that a US embassy official had revealed to her at an embassy dinner that Washington had pressured the Mexican government to change school history textbooks as they considered them unfriendly to the United States.[104] Such allegations added to the debate the suggestion that a subservient Mexican state had changed school texts due to pressure from Mexico's powerful northern neighbor.

How the dictatorship of Porfirio Díaz was presented also attracted strong criticisms of ideological revisionism. This attack revived the comparisons between the neoliberal technocrats of the de la Madrid and Salinas administrations and positivist científicos of the Porfirian era that Salinas had attempted to avoid through social liberalism. It also followed wider debates within political and intellectual circles about the recent rehabilitation of the public image of the Porfiriato, with Krauze's 1987 biography *Porfirio Díaz: Místico de la Autoridad* (Porfirio Díaz: The Mystique of Authority), one of the highest profile and earliest examples of this revisionist view of Díaz.[105]

The main emphasis in discussion of the Porfiriato in the 1960s and 1970s texts had been on the injustice and inequality produced by a development model that, while resulting in significant material and cultural advancements, privileged the needs of a wealthy few—most notably foreign investors—to the detriment of the majority. In the 1992 texts, the foreign investment and economic development of the Porfiriato are positively portrayed while class conflict is given little coverage.[106] PRD federal deputy Bejarano used the controversy over the new texts' more sympathetic portrayal of the Porfiriato to ironically suggest that, according to the Salinas administration's new school history texts, Porfirio Díaz "only needed Pronasol in order to be perfect."[107]

Another front in the fight against the new texts came from within the corporatist structure involving the New Unionism Democratic Movement and National Coordinator of Educational Workers (CNTE), both dissident factions of the SNTE teacher's union that had recently emerged from strikes during the Salinas administration's first year.[108] These unions organized public forums criticizing and calling upon teachers to reject the new texts. The arguments used were largely the same as those deployed by the PRD and critical historians of the left, with New Unionism, for example, calling the new texts dogmatic, criticizing the presentation of the 1988 elections, and again highlighting that Porfirio Díaz had "by neoliberal decree ceased to be a dictator."[109]

In the first weeks of the textbook controversy, the SNTE and its powerful secretary Elba Esther Gordillo, a Salinas ally appointed following the 1989 teacher strikes, made only guarded remarks that avoided directly criticizing the new texts.[110] However, it appears that the effectiveness of the political use of the issue by dissident factions and the potential for instability within the union led Gordillo to adopt a critical stance toward the texts. By the end of August Gordillo announced a meeting of SNTE leaders to examine the new texts after which the union would announce its official position.[111] After Gordillo ventured further criticisms of the texts following these meetings, the government began to back away from the content of the books and the secretariat of public education (SEP) joined with the SNTE to form commissions for revising the texts.[112]

Members of the PRI itself were notably weak in their defense of the new texts. The response from PRI legislators to withering attacks from the PRD and other parties of the left during debates in the legislature ranged from awkwardly reading prepared statements from the SEP to simply remaining silent.[113] By late September 1992 the party's official publication *La República* was calling for the modification of the texts as "the alterations and historical omissions [in the new texts] break with Mexico's nationalism and cultural identity."[114] While party discipline prevented public criticism, the growing controversy threatened to reopen the wounds that had led to the formation of the FDN in 1987 as many in the PRI seemed uncomfortable with the tone of the new texts and the neoliberal orientation of the PRI leadership they suggested. The silence of PRI legislators during congressional debates was accordingly read in the media as an expression of sympathy for the PRD's arguments.[115] Furthermore, the Mexican armed forces complained about the presentation of its role in the 1968 Tlatelolco massacre.[116]

The resistance shown by public school teachers to the new texts revealed a deeper difficulty that the Salinas administration faced in turning a neoliberal reformist economic and political project into a hegemonic nationalist cultural project. As sociologist Mattias vom Hau notes, the infrastructural power of a state is vital in its project of legitimizing its authority through nationalism, as this power determines to a great extent the state's ability to intervene in the socialization of its citizens. However, an already infrastructurally powerful state can also limit a reformist nationalist project by harboring pockets of resistance.[117]

Postrevolutionary state-builders during the 1920s and 1930s had reconstructed state infrastructure destroyed during the Revolution, at the same time attempting to instill a hegemonic revolutionary nationalist identity, including through the expansion of the education system. In contrast, the Salinas administration was attempting to transform national identity through school history textbooks within the context of a comparatively infrastructurally powerful state. This project therefore faced a different challenge of significant and organized pockets of resistance within the state's cultural machinery that had broader implications for its economic and political reforms.

The most vocal defenders of the content of the new texts were those who had presented the strongest opposition to the 1960s and 1970s editions: the Catholic Church, PAN, and business groups.[118] The response from the church and conservative Catholic educational interest groups emphasized most of all that the new texts presented "the true history" of Mexico and promoted unity.[119] The Mexican Episcopal Conference (CEM) called them "an initial movement toward a reconciliation with our history" while criticizing as reproachable and immoral "the attitude of those who are trying to take advantage of this polemic to confuse public opinion."[120] Furthermore, the head of the Catholic National Parents' Union (UNPF), an organization that had led opposition to the previous two rounds of texts, in 1992 called on teachers to defy a boycott of the new texts called by dissident teachers' unions.[121]

More so than the PRI, the PAN mounted a strong defense of the texts. Senator Diego Fernández de Cevallos argued the PRD opposed the texts because they "are no longer adapted to [a] black and white view, socialist education is no longer imposed, no longer is the love of a certain type of person or conduct promoted, no longer is a certain political bias imprinting upon the youth an absolutely Manichean vision [of history]."[122] The national secretary of the PAN, Carlos Castillo Peraza, similarly voiced the party's support for the new texts as a move away from PRI state efforts "to coercively unify the popular memory" and toward "the democratic ideas the PAN has supported."[123] Private business lobby group Coparmex also adopted the stance that the texts represented "an advance."[124] The debates surrounding the 1992 history texts thus provided a particularly visible image of the realignment of interest groups within the nation as expressed in the cultural project of the state. Uncomfortably for the Salinas administration, the relative alignment of interests for and against the texts seemed to reinforce the idea of a revolutionary/reactionary dichotomy promoted for decades in PRI discourse. However, this time the Salinas administration was on the same side as the reaction.

The government appeared not to anticipate that the new texts would generate such controversy and proved remarkably sensitive to accusations of hostility to the established myths and symbols of national history. Initially, Zedillo and other officials at the SEP simply dismissed charges of ideological revisionism and argued that revised texts were needed to meet standards of modern scholarship. However, as the controversy continued to grow during August and September, the government became increasingly nervous and Zedillo began to qualify his support for their content.[125]

Salinas himself remained largely absent from the debate surrounding the new texts. However, he seemed particularly sensitive to the accusation that the government was attempting to erase the patriotic sacrifice of the Niños Héroes from the national memory while negotiating a free-trade deal with the United States. To this end, Salinas took care during interviews following the September 1992 Mexico City commemorative ceremony of the Niños Héroes to underline that the government was "always predisposed toward . . . honoring the memory of the Niños Héroes of Chapultepec" as a "fundamental part" of the national history.[126] At the 1992 Independence Day celebrations, the president also added a viva to the Niños Héroes for only the second time in a presidential grito ceremony, and this was included in the grito ceremony for the rest of Salinas's presidency.[127] As the government's official orator at the 1992 Independence Day celebrations, Zedillo also made specific reference in his speech both to the Niños Héroes and Zapata, whose roles in Mexican history were claimed to have been minimized in the new texts. In the crowd, however, there appeared placards featuring slogans supporting the Niños Héroes and demanding that the memory of national history be defended.[128]

By early September Zedillo agreed that, although the current texts would remain in circulation during the 1992–1993 school year, they were "clearly of a transitory nature" and would be reviewed by an expert panel before the next school year, for which new history textbooks would be produced.[129] Toward the end of the month, Zedillo announced that a new workbook would be available by December for teachers, featuring a list of corrections based on consultations with the

SNTE and other sources.[130] By January 1993 the texts were abandoned altogether, with Zedillo canceling plans for their revision and announcing a juried competition for historians to write a new series of texts for the 1993–1994 school year.[131] Showing greater caution than it had in 1992, the administration eventually discarded the winning entries of the 1993 competition and commissioned a new series of texts that proved more ideologically acceptable to critics of the 1992 versions.[132] A wounded Aguilar Camín was left to defend the texts he helped oversee by leveling accusations of base politicking at the "retro left" in the PRD, corporatist resistance to change from the SNTE, and professional jealousy from historians and journalists.[133]

The Limits of Solidarity

In the attention it paid to a cultural project of social liberalism and neoliberal populist framework of Pronasol, the Salinas administration demonstrated an understanding of the ongoing need to negotiate its hegemonic rule in both a symbolic and material sense. The Salinista reform project involved a delicate balancing of dramatic economic and social reforms with new neoliberal populist mechanisms for communicating with civil society and distributing state patronage. The Salinas administration further dedicated significant effort to renegotiating its historical and nationalist legitimacy by reworking the revolutionary nationalist framework into social liberalism. This new framework retained but shifted the emphasis between the established myths and symbols of Mexican nationalism in a far more sophisticated manner than had the realistic revolution discourse of the de la Madrid administration. The rebounding of the PRI's fortunes in elections and opinion polls following the debacle of the 1988 elections suggests that the Salinas administration had some initial success in its efforts to combine policy reform and promote a new symbolic framework connecting state and society for the neoliberal era.

In its efforts to adapt school history textbooks to its modernization project, however, the administration ultimately judged that it had pushed too far. The school history textbook controversy demonstrated the potential of the established revolutionary nationalist discourse to limit as well as legitimize state power in Mexico. Heroes such as Zapata or the Niños Héroes were elements of a rich language of myths through which opposition groups could communicate messages that transcended the immediate issue of the content of the texts, including the impact of neoliberal economic reform on the rural economy or the impact that NAFTA would have on Mexico's economic and cultural independence. Groups such as peasants, workers, the armed forces, and even PRI officials were also able to read their own marginalization within the new political and economic order into the falling fortunes of the heroes and events through which their rights and status had historically been legitimized. Conversely, groups such as the Catholic Church and private business interests could see their relative status rising and thus in 1992 switched from a traditionally critical to supportive stance regarding the state's presentation of the nation's history. That this controversy took place amid the general success of social liberalism exhibits both the flexibility of revolutionary nationalism as a symbolic framework of negotiation and the way in which it symbolically contained political action within certain boundaries.

On January 1, 1994, NAFTA was due to come into effect and in July of that year presidential elections would be held to choose Salinas's successor. Whereas de la Madrid entered his final year as president with Mexico still submerged in the crisis that began in 1982, Salinas looked to be entering his final year having presided over not just a renewal of the PRI but of the Mexican political and economic system's legitimacy more generally. However, once again the PRI state was to face a severe crisis of legitimacy as it approached the transfer of power between presidents. Revolutionary nationalism and particularly the figure of Emiliano Zapata were also again at the center of a challenge to the PRI system and neoliberalism. However, unlike in 1988, this challenge arose not from within the PRI, but far away from the national capital, in the mountains of the Mexican southeast.

¡Ya basta!

On New Year's Day 1994, the crowning achievement of the Salinas administration's modernization project—the North American Free Trade Agreement (NAFTA) between Mexico, the United States, and Canada—was due to come into effect after almost four years of negotiation. Having successfully reached a deal for a broad-ranging new trade agreement with two advanced economies, Mexico had placed itself at the vanguard of neoliberal economic globalization. Through the apparent success of social liberalism and its centerpiece social program, Pronasol, the Salinas administration also appeared to have provided a model for neoliberalizing developing economies that avoided the political and social instability provoked by earlier waves of harsh structural adjustment programs. There was thus a generally triumphant mood within the administration as it entered its final year promoting the idea that Mexico was not only emerging from the prolonged post-1982 crisis but had ended up on the cusp of once and for all leaving behind the third world of the south for the first world of the north.[1] As a further sign of its ascendency in the global economic order, during the first half of 1994 Mexico was to be officially admitted to the club of developed economies, the Organization of Economic Cooperation and Development (OECD).

Rather than waking up on January 1, 1994, to find themselves part of a great leap forward into prosperous modernity, Mexicans instead awoke to reports of a dramatic return to the country's revolutionary past. A guerrilla army had appeared during the early hours of the morning in the southeastern state of Chiapas to declare war on the Mexican Army and the government led by Carlos Salinas. The rebels had met little resistance, quickly seizing control of seven towns, including the state's historical capital, San Cristóbal de las Casas.

A spokesperson for the rebels emerged at 6:00 a.m. in a ski mask on the balcony of the Palacio Municipal of San Cristóbal de las Casas to announce to Mexico and the world who this group was and why it had risen up in rebellion. Introducing himself as Subcomandante Marcos, the spokesperson read a statement that outlined a historical narrative identifying the movement as the product of five hundred years of struggle: "First against slavery, then during the War of Independence against Spain led by the Insurgentes, then to avoid being absorbed by North American imperialism, then to promulgate our constitution and expel the French empire from our soil, and later the dictatorship of Porfirio Díaz denied us the just application of the Reform laws and the people rebelled and leaders like Villa and Zapata emerged, poor men just like us."[2] Faced with a lack of housing, land, work, health care, food, education, and the democratic right to elect their leaders, Marcos continued, the poor people of Chiapas were today saying, "¡Ya basta!" (Enough is enough!).[3]

Calling itself the Zapatista Army of National Liberation (EZLN), the movement's declaration employed the myths and symbols of state-sponsored Mexican nationalism to legitimize war against the Mexican state. "We are the inheritors of the true builders of our nation," Marcos declared, while the PRI state was a seventy-year-old dictatorship led by conservative traitors who resembled the reaction of PRI discourse. According to the new Zapatistas, the PRI government led by Salinas was heir to those "that opposed Hidalgo and Morelos, the same ones that betrayed [Insurgente] Vicente Guerrero . . . that sold half our country to the foreign invader . . . that imported a European prince to rule our country . . . that formed the 'scientific' Porfirista dictatorship . . . that opposed the Petroleum Expropriation . . . that massacred the railroad workers in 1958 and the students in 1968, the same ones that today take everything from us, absolutely everything."[4]

This "First Declaration from the Lacandón Jungle" was read aloud in several Maya and Zoque languages by Zapatista leaders in towns seized by the rebels across Chiapas. Through this declaration, the Zapatistas also sought legitimacy in the Mexican Constitution of 1917. The declaration specifically cited Article 39, which stated that national sovereignty resides in the people, who had an inalienable right to alter or modify their form of government. Invoking the Geneva Accords and identifying itself as a formal army, the EZLN also appealed to international organizations, including the International Red Cross, to watch over and regulate its formally declared war against the Mexican Army and aimed at capturing the national capital. The EZLN assured

Mexicans that "the beloved tri-colored [Mexican] flag [is] highly respected by our fighters" alongside the movement's own symbols, and invited all sympathetic Mexicans to join its struggle.[5]

Following its spectacular appearance, the EZLN was quickly beaten back into the mountains and jungles of Chiapas by the Mexican Army. The rebels began their retreat on January 2, attacking the nearby military base of Rancho Grande as they abandoned San Cristóbal while thousands of federal troops moved in to the state. Chiapas became increasingly militarized and reports by the press and nongovernmental organizations (NGOs) soon emerged of the military conducting indiscriminate air attacks against mountain towns, summarily executing captured rebels, and firing at press and aid vehicles.[6] The town of Ocosingo was the site of the most intense fighting, with thousands of troops surrounding the town and finally taking full control on January 4.[7]

During the days immediately following the uprising, uncertainty over the identity of the rebels and nature of the rebellion in Chiapas contributed to a cautious rejection of the EZLN in many of the comments in the press and from within the formal political system. Campaigning ahead of the July presidential elections, PRI, PAN, and PRD candidates and spokespeople recognized Chiapas's chronic poverty and underdevelopment, but defended institutional politics over violence. The National Executive Committee of the PAN blamed the local (PRI) politicians for failing to provide adequate channels for political expression and, in an attitude that characterized much of the early response that denied the agency of the indigenous population, for the ignorance in which local authorities had left them, which made them "easy prey for manipulation by false redeemers."[8]

With the notable exception of the bishop of the diocese of San Cristóbal de las Casas Samuel Ruiz, local ecclesiastical authorities took a similar stance to the PAN, criticizing EZLN leadership for exploiting the ignorance and poverty of an indigenous population they portrayed as puppets in the war. The prelate of state capital Tuxtla Gutiérrez argued that the rebellion's leaders had taken advantage of a "situation of poverty [for] sowing amongst the indigenous people feelings of hate, anger, vengeance, ideologizing them," while the bishop of Tapachula said in a statement that "we lament that they [EZLN leaders] are stirring up the indigenous people and leading them into a massacre."[9] In the PRD, the uprising sparked more sympathetic internal debates over how much support the party should give to the Zapatista cause and over the right to rebellion, with PRD president Porfirio Muñoz Ledo at the party's second National Council in January stating, "We recognize our-selves in them."[10]

While many intellectuals on the left joined this debate with a tone sympathetic to the Zapatista movement, those associated with the *Nexos* and *Vuelta* groups strongly rejected the movement's aims and tactics as an assault on the modernization of Mexico. Writing in *Nexos*, Héctor Aguilar Camín provided perhaps the most robust defense of the success of the Salinas modernization project against the EZLN move-ment and its supporters.[11] As Aguilar Camín saw it, the Zapatistas were ideologically "an extravagant mix of fossil formulas of the left . . . with echoes of liberation theology, a plebeian and schoolbook vision of the national history, and a democratic demand that repeats the Cardenista discourse from 1988."[12] According to Aguilar Camín, the EZLN's sup-porters were largely an anachronistic left for whom "the successes of the Salinas government seem excessive."[13]

Writing in *Vuelta*, Octavio Paz fiercely attacked intellectuals who expressed sympathy for the EZLN, whom he accused of learning noth-ing from the collapse of communist totalitarianism. Enrique Krauze also advanced a similar notion to the PAN and conservative ecclesiasti-cal authorities that there existed a division within the EZLN between indigenous people from below manipulated by university graduate com-manders from above. Krauze further situated the EZLN within a single antidemocratic tradition that included a violent millenarian Christian uprising in Chiapas in 1712, Central American guerrillas of the 1980s, and the Peruvian Shining Path insurgency of 1980s and 1990s.[14]

In the midst of the conflict, President Salinas gave the traditional presidential New Year's address on January 6 not from the usual loca-tion of the presidential residence of Los Pinos but from the National Palace in the center of Mexico City. Surrounded by the symbols of state power, Salinas sat in the presidential chair with the national coat of arms visible behind him and declared the rebellion an affront and embarrassment to Mexico that did not constitute an indigenous uprising but the action of a violent armed group. In reference to the ripping away of the veil of first-world modernity, the president described the move-ment as seeking "to tarnish the name of Mexico that has taken so much work and effort to build."[15] Rather than, as they claimed, a movement of national liberation, the president described the uprising as "an action against the national interest. This armed group is against Mexico."[16]

National and international solidarity movements became the most important source of support for the Zapatistas from the beginning of the conflict. The EZLN's communications strategy involved circumventing mainstream media by releasing information to civilian supporters who helped distribute them, including uploading them to the Internet and distributing them among NGOs in Mexico and abroad.[17] The electronic distribution of information about the EZLN's struggle led to marches during January 1994 in cities such as Ottawa, Madrid, and Washington, DC, demanding an end to the Mexican army's campaign in Chiapas.[18] As reports of abuses committed by the federal army reached a global audience, members of the US congress began to pressure the Mexican government to respect human rights through congressional hearings, public statements, delegations to Chiapas, and official letters directed to President Salinas.[19] All of these tied the viability of NAFTA to Mexico's respect for human rights and attention to the issues of inequality and a lack of democracy raised by the uprising.

The Mexican government thus found itself immediately on the defensive despite early military victories against the EZLN. President Salinas had attempted to cultivate a modern, progressive image not just for Mexico but for himself. When the Zapatistas placed the issue of human rights—central to contemporary discourses of liberal modernity—at the heart of their struggle, they aimed at a sensitive area for the legitimacy of the government and Salinas himself. Indeed, the administration had created a National Human Rights Commission the previous year as part of its project for modernizing the Mexican state.

Allegations of torture, disappearances, and mass graves in Chiapas recalled the worst human-rights abuses of Latin America's violent twentieth-century history. The highlighting of the social and political conditions in Chiapas also revealed the persistence of historical problems of economic inequality, injustice, and corruption that meant social citizenship rights were denied to millions of Mexicans.[20] For a Mexican audience, the Zapatistas criticized Pronasol—a program designed to enhance Salinas's social justice credentials—as not simply inadequate but "a cruel joke that brings tears of blood to the eyes of those who, under these suns and rains, are barely able to survive."[21] In its strategy, the EZLN therefore turned not just the myths and symbols of the Mexican Revolution against the state, but also discourses of democracy and human rights embedded in Latin America's third wave of democratization against the associated neoliberal development model.

Facing an obvious disparity in strength with the federal army and popular rejection of armed conflict, the EZLN's strategy developed over the following months to one that emphasized cultural over armed struggle, using what they termed "the weapon of the word." This strategy followed the Gramscian notion of a war of position in which civil society alliances and the use of language are critical resources in a revolution involving struggle for the cultural transformation necessary to bring about social transformation. The EZLN's public statements to this end employed a discourse described by Marcos as one that "connects with a tradition of struggle, with a cultural tradition, and produces this language that succeeds in penetrating strata of society through symbols."[22]

The EZLN embraced a radical politics that discarded the traditional language and symbolism of socialist revolution in favor of "a Marxism-Leninism more practical than theoretical" based on an analysis of the Mexican state, society, and national history.[23] Instead of the slogans of international revolution, the EZLN took as its battle cry a phrase of Insurgente leader Vicente Guerrero from Mexico's war of independence: Live for the patria, die for freedom.[24] Instead of state intervention to ameliorate social hardship, the EZLN further emphasized the right to self-determination.

The romantic image of Subcomandante Marcos as a ski-mask–clad, pipe-smoking rebel typing his correspondence on a laptop in the mountains of Chiapas further caught the imagination of the world beyond Chiapas and indeed Mexico. So too did the style of the movement's writings, which moved from dryly ironic indictments of government hypocrisy to whimsical tales of Marcos conversing with a beetle named Durito on his marches through the jungle.[25] The EZLN maintained communication with the outside world through media interviews, press conferences, and a steady stream of declarations, communiqués, and letters generally signed either by Subcomandante Marcos or "from the mountains of the Mexican southeast." As explained by Marcos, the language used was deliberately evocative and nonideological to direct the EZLN's appeals to the heart and lower theory to the level of the human being.[26]

Finding his legitimacy attacked on multiple fronts, President Salinas tried to diffuse the conflict politically while maintaining a steady military pressure on the EZLN. The president's language softened from the aggressive tone of his initial declarations, and during January a series of concessions were made to the Zapatistas in order to reach an agreement for peace talks. On January 10, Salinas dismissed the hard-line interior minister and ex-governor of Chiapas Patricio González Garrido and replaced him with Jorge Carpizo, the person Salinas had previously named the first head of Mexico's National Human Rights Commission. The serving governor of Chiapas was also soon replaced and high-profile former regent of Mexico City and then-secretary of foreign affairs Manuel Camacho was named commissioner for peace and reconciliation. Two days later, as tens of thousands of people gathered in Mexico City to march for peace in Chiapas, the president preemptively declared a unilateral ceasefire and on January 16 announced an offer of amnesty to the Zapatista rebels in a televised address.[27]

The EZLN responded to this offer of amnesty with a stinging rebuke that asked, "Why do we have to be pardoned? What are we going to be pardoned for? For not dying of hunger? For not being silent in our misery? For not humbly accepting our historic role of being the despised and outcast?"[28] Moreover, Salinas had announced his offer of amnesty in front of a portrait of Venustiano Carranza, presumably seeking to draw upon Carranza's symbolic association with the Constitution of 1917 and thus the rule of law. Marcos instead responded by drawing attention to another element of Carranza's biography: his role in the assassination of Emiliano Zapata in 1919.[29] However, after having expected to receive either support or rejection by Mexican society and instead being faced with a sympathetic public that was nonetheless in favor of ending the armed conflict, the EZLN adapted its strategy to increasingly emphasize dialogue.[30]

After negotiations that included a prisoner swap between the EZLN and Chiapas state authorities, it was agreed that peace talks would begin on February 21 and be moderated by progressive San Cristóbal de las Casas bishop Samuel Ruíz in the city's cathedral. By now the indigenous identity of the majority of the EZLN's members and the rights of Mexico's indigenous population to political and cultural independence within the Mexican nation were increasingly prominent in the movement's discourse. Acculturation into a homogenous mestizo culture had been encouraged under revolutionary nationalism as the pathway to full membership in the nation for Mexico's indigenous population. The EZLN threw this dynamic into reverse by using mestizo nationalist symbolism to legitimize the right to cultural, economic, and social autonomy for Mexico's indigenous populations. Demonstrating a multifaceted notion of identity, at the peace conference one EZLN representative identified himself according to name, ethnicity, region, and country as "David, Tzotzil, one hundred percent Chiapaneco, one hundred percent Mexican."[31] Further connecting the recognition of indigenous and local identities and concerns to the

Figure 5.1. Mexican Government negotiator Manuel Camacho Solís holds a corner of the Mexican flag with Subcomandante Marcos during peace negotiations in San Cristóbal de las Casas, Chiapas. Courtesy Gerardo Magallon/AFP.

Figure 5.2. Superbarrio, seen here with Subcomandante Marcos, was one of more than six thousand who journeyed to Aguascalientes II in the Lacandón jungle for the EZLN's National Democratic Convention in August 1994. Courtesy Gerardo Magallon/AFP.

strength of the nation, during negotiations Zapatista representatives unfurled a Mexican flag, which obliged Camacho as the government negotiator to either join them by holding up one corner of the flag or let it fall. Camacho, of course, joined with the rebels to hold a corner of the flag (fig. 5.1).[32]

The EZLN took advantage of the presence of the media and independent observers during the peace talks to communicate the movement's message to a global audience. Zapatista leaders conducted interviews with the national and international press and contacts were built with many of the NGOs and civil society organizations observing the negotiations. The peace talks thus became an important event in the political metamorphosis of the EZLN from an armed insurgency to a transnational civil society movement.[33] When negotiations concluded on March 2, the Zapatista delegates returned to their communities for consultations about whether the EZLN should accept the proposed peace treaty. Civil society and media organizations followed closely behind and were soon spreading images and stories of Zapatista communities deep in the Lacandón jungle far beyond Chiapas and indeed Mexico.[34]

In August 1994 more than six thousand people followed the call of the EZLN into the Lacandón jungle to attend a "National Democratic Convention" held by the EZLN. The convention was held in a venue cleared out of the jungle and baptized "Aguascalientes II" in honor of the location of the 1914 conference where Villista and Zapatista forces formed an alliance (fig. 5.2).[35] Addressing the crowd, Marcos explained the purpose of the convention: "to debate and to agree on the organization of a civil, peaceful, and popular national struggle for democracy, freedom, and justice." Marcos then adopted perhaps the most transcendent symbol of the Mexican nation, telling the assembled crowd, "The General Command of the Revolutionary Indigenous Clandestine Committee of the EZLN now gives you the national flag in order to remind you of what it means: Country, history, and nation. And we commit ourselves to that which it ought to mean: democracy, freedom, justice."[36]

CHAPTER FIVE

Land, Liberty, and the Mestizo Nation

At the time of the EZLN uprising, peasants continued to hold an important symbolic position within revolutionary nationalism, despite their practical economic and social marginalization that stretched back before the 1982 debt crisis, because they represented the popular origins of the Mexican Revolution. As the disintegration of the PRI state and nationalist economic model accelerated after 1982, peasant groups in turn invoked revolutionary nationalism in their struggles with the state to legitimize citizenship rights associated with the Revolution. These rights included political autonomy and access to resources, particularly land. Furthermore, the postrevolutionary state's policy of *indigenismo* had sought to acculturate the indigenous populations into a mainstream mestizo national culture.[1] However, indigenous organizations from the 1970s onward increasingly legitimized a range of material and cultural demands precisely on the basis of distinct indigenous ethnoracial identities that had been selectively appropriated and woven into a mestizo Mexican identity. To support this cause, indigenous activists during the 1980s and 1990s also harnessed transnational discourses of multiculturalism, democracy, and human rights.

In this chapter, I discuss how peasant and indigenous populations responded to changes in Mexico's development model to renegotiate their position within the nation both in terms of economic rights and cultural identity. Revolutionary nationalism connected economic, political, and cultural practices to the state through the concept of citizenship, but also drew symbolic boundaries of inclusion or exclusion that traditionally left indigenous groups on the margins of, if not excluded from, the mestizo nation. I therefore explore how the language of nationalist mythology functioned as one of the central discursive frameworks through which both conflicts and negotiations between marginalized actors and the Salinas administration reformists took place. The varied experiences of state-society relations within Chiapas itself also highlights the contrasting dynamics of state-society relations in different parts of the Mexican countryside, showing the long-term effects of the uneven nature of postrevolutionary state formation and its swiss cheese hegemony.[2] Finally, I examine how the neo-Zapatista revolution of 1994 drew on all of these dynamics, combining revolutionary nationalism with contemporary transnational discourses of liberal democracy to attack both the PRI state and an association between neoliberal economic policies and ideas of democracy, freedom, and human rights.

Land and Freedom from Bureaucracy:
Salinas, Zapata, and Agrarian Reform

Although conditions for peasants and the percentage of Mexicans living in rural areas steadily declined from the 1940s onward, the peasant army led by Emiliano Zapata remained one of revolutionary nationalism's most powerful and enduring mythologies. So too did the ejido, a communally held and inalienable form of land ownership that was an important social, political, and economic institution in postrevolutionary Mexico. The ejido was also a key site of confrontation and negotiation over access to resources between local and nonlocal groups, including the national state and private economic interests.[3] By 1990 ejidos accounted for over half of Mexico's arable land and benefited more than 3.1 million *ejidatarios* and their dependents.[4] Moreover, ejidatarios had a privileged status in communities due to the practical ability that participation in peasant sectoral organizations and credit programs gave them to form political connections as well as the symbolic link between the ejido and the Revolution.[5]

By the time Luis Echeverría assumed the presidency in 1970 frustration with the slow progress of land redistribution and the declining efficacy of the corporatist National Peasant Confederation (CNC) as a representative of peasant interests was manifested in protest actions such as the occupation of government agrarian offices and land invasions. Furthermore, peasants began to organize local and regional fronts in defense of their interests. The response of the López Portillo administration to the worsening crisis of Mexican agriculture was to shift the focus of state agrarian policy from land redistribution to improving the productivity of Mexican agriculture with the aim of regaining national self-sufficiency in basic foodstuffs such as corn, sorghum, and beans.[6] López Portillo employed a nationalist discourse to tie food security to national sovereignty and the social rights of popular classes to guaranteeing that their basic nutritional requirements were met.[7] After 1980, the administration's agrarian policy's emphasis increasingly shifted toward encouraging private investment in agriculture through measures such as the partial legalization of the commercial rental of ejido land and a broader move toward ending land redistribution and repressing peasant protests.[8]

The de la Madrid administration further withdrew state support from the agricultural sector and dismantled protectionist measures following the 1982 debt crisis. In a highly symbolic move, the government altered the constitution to recognize agricultural private property alongside the ejido long enshrined in Article 27, in itself a powerful revolutionary nationalist symbol.[9] Privatizing and austerity measures were then deepened by the Economic Solidarity Pact (1987) and continued into the Salinas administration in the form of the Reform of the Countryside initiative. By the end of 1993 the financing and marketing of rural production had been substantially reorganized to favor private rather than public organizations, with profitability and efficiency the main criteria when allocating credit. The dismantling of trade restrictions in accordance with GATT and NAFTA provisions further privileged a globalized logic of competitive advantage over food security. Small-scale farmers now found themselves increasingly without access to government credit and unable to compete with cheaper foreign imports.[10] Mexico's agricultural sector thus experienced growth below even the generally flat level of national economic growth during the 1980s and 1990s.[11]

Independent peasant organizations responded during the 1970s and 1980s by forming national movements to demand government attention to petitions for land redistribution and support for peasant agriculture.[12] These organizations demanded more state support and protested against neoliberal reform behind the unifying banner of the hero who most directly symbolized peasants' rights under revolutionary nationalism: Emiliano Zapata. In response, the Salinas administration made a concerted effort to reclaim Zapata for the PRI state and Salinas adopted Zapata as his totemic national hero. President Salinas had a son named Emiliano, called his presidential aircraft the *Emiliano Zapata*, and during his administration gave strong personal attention to ceremonies commemorating Zapata's assassination. Salinas was in fact personally present in Morelos for every annual Zapata commemoration of his presidency except when out of the country in 1991 and 1993. President de la Madrid, in contrast, only attended the final two Zapata commemorations of his presidency and only those held in Mexico City.

The reclaiming of Zapata from independent peasant organizations by the Salinas administration was particularly important in the context of the administration's symbolically charged agrarian reform initiative. In November 1991 the president sent a bill to Congress that would alter Article 27 of the Mexican constitution so as to end the state's responsibility to redistribute land to rural communities for ejido farming plots. This reform also proposed to allow existing ejidos to be divided among community members into private parcels and then rented or sold to domestic or foreign investors.[13]

Objections were immediately raised by independent peasant organizations and the PRD (among others) who argued that these reforms effectively legalized the use of various mechanisms such as credit default to force peasants into relinquishing land rights. Abolishing the ejido's inalienable status would therefore eventually reverse the gains of the Revolution, resulting in a reconcentration of land either in the hands of private interests or community elites, recalling the expanding hacienda system of the Porfiriato. Concerns were also voiced that unresolved land petitions would now simply be rejected, affecting thousands of peasants whose position would suddenly become even more precarious.[14] Furthermore, the goal of "food sovereignty" (self-sufficiency) remained part of Mexican nationalist discourse linked to economic nationalism and from this perspective the liberalizing of Mexican agriculture appeared to condemn the nation to dependency.[15]

On the other hand, supporters of the reform maintained that the inalienable ejido was a barrier to agricultural efficiency and progress due to its relatively small size. Supporters further argued that collective ownership and government oversight restricted peasant freedom to put their land and labor to its most efficient use. The reform of the ejido was thus designed to unleash market forces and bring about the development of agriculture according to the logic of competitive advantage and a niche marketing trade strategy, leading to a more efficient distribution of land and labor in Mexico. Finally, supporters argued, the new law placed limits on the size of private agricultural landholdings and required agreement of two-thirds of ejido assembly members for land to be sold as a way of guarding against involuntary privatizations and the reconcentration of land.[16]

These reforms generated such fierce debate in large part because the ejido was one of the key institutions that legitimized collective citizen-ship rights for a major sector of the population. Within the symbolic framework of revolutionary nationalism, Zapata fought and died for the land rights right of peasants. Article 27 of the Constitution of 1917, meanwhile, symbolized the state's acceptance of this right, which was then put into practice beginning with the massive land redistribution of President Cárdenas. A symbolic link was in this way traced through Zapata and Cárdenas from the local peasant community to the state through Article 27 of the constitution and the institution of the ejido. Sociologist Luin Goldring's description of the main building of an ejido in Zamora, Michoacán, showed how this was physically manifested in that community, with "the interior assembly hall . . . dominated by a huge mural of Emiliano Zapata and *campesinos* [peasants] struggling for, receiving, and working land . . . [while] a statue of General Lázaro Cárdenas graced the courtyard."[17] Within this mythology, "ejido" was virtually synonymous with "peasant" in discussion of agrarian issues in Mexico.[18]

The administration argued that its reform to Article 27 did not rep-resent the retreat of the state as a defender of peasants' rights, but rather the state's renewed commitment to the rights of peasants as individuals. Instead of collective citizenship rights, the government proposed an individualist conception of citizenship guaranteed by a theoretically universal right to private property and individual freedom. The original bill presented to congress also directly referenced Zapata, the Zapatistas' 1911 Plan de Ayala, and postrevolutionary land redistribution as "a motive for national pride."[19] However, due to demographic, social, and economic changes in the intervening years, the document stated, "to pretend that in the current circumstances the nationalist path should stay the same as yesterday, that of land redistribution, puts at risk the very same objectives pursued by the agrarian reform and the Mexican Revolution."[20]

Seeking to demonstrate his commitment to the rural economy, President Salinas followed the reform proposal's release with a ten-point plan to reactivate the countryside that he announced standing in front of a portrait of Emiliano Zapata in the presidential residence of Los Pinos. In his speech, Salinas argued that "the only reactionary option is to propose that nothing changes in the countryside, that everything is untouchable. Myths today bring poverty to the rural sphere. . . . I invite everyone to join the proposal of justice and liberty as they have [joined] past great agrarian visions of Mexico."[21] Continuing in this spirit, the secretary of agrarian reform praised the president for retaking the agrarian reform banner of Lázaro Cárdenas in that hero's home state of Michoacán while pointing out that "Cárdenas himself said that land redistribution should be accelerated so it could end."[22]

Liberty and Justice: Building New Links between the State and Rural Society

As the Mexican state had under Cárdenas used the agrarian bureaucracy to build links with peasants, the Salinas administration established new institutions to execute its agrarian reforms. These institutions were designed not just to communicate the specifics of the policy changes but to link these reforms to nationalist values and a new form of citizenship for peasants. As part of the overall framework of Pronasol, the Program of Direct Support for the Countryside (Procampo) was established to provide some subsidies for rural agriculture in accordance with Pronasol's orientation toward self-help initiatives. More directly related to the reform of Article 27 was the creation of the Program for the Certification of Ejidal Land Rights and the Titling of Urban House Lots (Procede) that was mostly implemented through the new Agrarian Attorney General's Office created in 1992. The administration appointed well-known anthropologist Arturo Warman as head of the Agrarian Attorney General's Office and in the office's magazine *Espacio*, he communicated the state's message that this new institution would empower peasants by freeing them from the corruption and inefficiency that had previously characterized their dealings with state agrarian institutions. The Agrarian Attorney General's Office's aim was in this way explained as being to "play a key role in creating a new agrarian culture that rejects paternalism and puts peasants in charge of their own lives."[23]

By March 1993 the Agrarian Attorney General's Office had grown to employ 3,161 people in a hierarchical structure of officials that stretched from a local coordinator working in regional offices to auxiliary *becarios campesinos* (peasant bursaries), who undertook local research, mapping, organizing, and training work with ejidatarios. The aim of the Procede officials was in this way to measure and map existing ejido borders and their internal plots, following which ejidatarios could decide whether to change to a private ownership regime.[24] This army of state employees spread across the Mexican countryside to assist local communities to implement the reforms and, in the process, officials of the Agrarian Attorney General's Office became the chief communicators of the Procede program and reform of Article 27.

Government publications distributed by these agencies also reshaped the "Land and Liberty" message of Zapata, which had previously been used to encourage peasants to collectively organize to petition the government for land. The new slogan of agrarian reform was "Liberty and Justice," which reflected the end of the government's commitment to actively redistribute land while being consistent with an individualist conception of the legal right of peasants to land as a form of private property. The imagery used in such publications was still, however, reminiscent of classical revolutionary nationalist peasant symbolism. One pamphlet, for example, presented a case study of the incorporation of a Morelos ejido into Procede amongst historical photographs and text of the life of Zapata and the agrarian reform he was credited with inspiring. The symbolic importance of connecting Zapata to the reform was further underlined by the government's push to make his home state of Morelos the first to incorporate all ejidos into Procede.[25] Agrarian reform, whatever form it took, thus still needed to be explained by way of reference to the ideals of Zapata into the 1990s.

In April 1992 President Salinas gave the official speech at Zapata commemorations in Cuautla, Morelos, and made various statements during the day aimed at promoting a link between Zapata and the reform of Article 27. In one, the president described the reform as a new formula for rural land tenure and justice that he termed "social private property." The president presented the goal of the reform of Article 27 as "the only way to remain faithful to the Zapatista principles" by removing paternalistic and bureaucratic restraints on the autonomy of peasants and, in the process, ensuring that "the great Mexican agrarian social movement that arose in this land [Morelos] remains alive, tying together past and present."[26] In this way, President Salinas portrayed his agrarian reforms as strengthening rather than reversing Zapata's struggle in the present.

The reaction of ejiditarios to the reforms to Article 27 was not uniform, reflecting the diversity of conditions faced by peasants in different parts of Mexico and the heterogeneity of the ejido sector in terms of culture and organization.[27] For example, independent peasants of a radical reformist persuasion such as those involved in the National "Plan de Ayala" Coordinating Committee protested the reform of Article 27 in tune with their broader opposition to the globalizing neoliberal reforms of the de la Madrid and Salinas administrations.[28] However, there appeared to be a cautious general acceptance of the reform to Article 27 by many other peasant communities.

As sociologist Monique Nuitjen argued, while the Procede discourse of "liberating" peasants corresponded to a long-held view within the state bureaucracy that peasants were ignorant and disempowered, her research in the La Canoa ejido in Jalisco showed that over the decades peasants had developed their own informal frameworks for regulating ejidos, often contrary to official policies.[29] In communities such as La Canoa, the division of ejidos into individual plots and selling or, more commonly, renting plots was already an established, if illegal, practice. In this context, the legal certification of ejido lands under Procede was often treated with some suspicion as involving *more* state interference in local affairs. However, it was also viewed as a potentially positive move toward establishing greater certainty for existing systems of managing ejido property.[30] Peasants in this way had already displayed significant flexibility in adapting revolutionary land rights to their needs, particularly in the face of rising emigration from rural communities to cities and the United States for work. Procede was similarly often adapted to local needs through selective appropriations of the various forms of certification available.[31]

Moreover, many independent peasant movements now identified a lack of credit and price supports rather than lack of land as the main challenge for peasants facing the prospect of an influx of cheaper imports under NAFTA.[32] The El Barzón movement formed in 1993 to support rural producers struggling with debt repayments and defaults was particularly prominent in this respect. This movement also drew on Mexican Revolutionary symbolism and was indeed named after a revolutionary song. However, the historical comparison it drew upon most was between the treatment of contemporary rural workers by bankers and the treatment of peasants by hacendados during the Porfiriato.[33] The administration capitalized on such differences among peasants to disarticulate and disperse independent movements as they competed for public resources through the new channels of Procede and Procampo.[34] According to the logic of concertación, the Salinas administration also invited—with some success—independent peasant organizations to participate in direct negotiations with the administration through the Permanent Agrarian Congress (CAP) formed in 1989.[35]

In some parts of Mexico, however, the end of land redistribution was greeted with alarm and sparked significant protest that was often framed as a defense of the gains of the Revolution. This was particularly true where conflicts over land remained a central concern of peasants and where the prospect of the end to land redistribution under Article 27 made a desperate situation appear hopeless. The state that perhaps best exemplified this situation was Chiapas, where 43.7 percent of the population lived on ejidos and thousands were awaiting the resolution of petitions for land to establish or expand ejidos, particularly in the migrant communities of the Lacandón jungle.[36] Chiapas was also the state where the highest percentage of the population identified as indigenous, and it was in this context that debates over land and citizenship rights converged with a movement in defense of the right to cultural and political autonomy for Mexico's indigenous peoples.

The Challenge to *México Mestizo*

In addition to the decades-long decline in the peasant economy, the emergence of the mainly indigenous EZLN rebels from a predominantly indigenous region fed into ongoing debates about the mythology of a homogenous mestizo Mexican race and culture. For example, Octavio Paz pondered in the EZLN uprising's immediate aftermath how the culture of Chiapas's indigenous population could be translated into "modernity."[37] Paz felt that in this respect the economic, social, juridical, and political demands of the indigenous communities would be easy to address as they were inscribed "within the . . . demands of modern Mexico, a nation that has made its own a great part of the cultural and historical inheritance of the West."[38] When it came to indigenous culture and traditions, however, it was difficult for Paz to accept the viability of mediating between European and indigenous cultural traditions other than via liberal democracy, adding a political to the cultural project of mestizaje.

This perspective had deep roots in Mexico's nineteenth-century liberal intellectual traditions and was nurtured during the postrevolutionary era both by official nationalism and Mexican national anthropology.[39] By the 1970s, however, the concept of a homogenous national ethnic and cultural identity was being increasingly questioned and the ineffectiveness of state social policy to address peasant needs further eroded the limited legitimacy of state institutions such as the National Indigenous Institute that promoted integration through mestizaje in indigenous communities.[40] From within the state's anthropological infrastructure, a new generation of scholars who studied and taught at the National School of Anthropology also emerged who challenged the close relationship between anthropologists and the postrevolutionary state.

The anthropologists, who became known as "los Siete Magníficos" (the Magnificent Seven), published their manifesto in the 1970 book *De eso que llaman antropología mexicana* (On So-Called Mexican Anthropology), which argued that Mexican anthropology during the postrevolutionary era had abdicated its critical and moral vocations by siding with the state rather than popular classes. According to this critique, indigenista policies had drifted away from the popular ideals of the Revolution toward the aim of incorporating indigenous people into a dominant "national," "modern" system, which the anthropologists labeled "capitalist" and "dependent." The anthropologists thus described indigenismo's goal of creating a homogenous national society as a form of internal colonialism.[41]

The topic of the ambiguous relationship between Mexican nationalism and the country's indigenous population continued to be a subject of significant scholarly debate during the 1980s. One of the Magníficos, Guillermo Bonfil Batalla, developed perhaps the most influential post-indigenista critique of the association between anthropology, indigenismo, and nationalism in his 1987 book *México profundo* (Deep Mexico). According to Bonfil, mestizo nationalism was in reality an attempt to de-Indianize and dominate the majority indigenous culture by a ruling elite that, whether under liberal, conservative, or revolutionary banners, sought to achieve essentially the same ends as a Western civilizing project of progress, development, and modernization that invalidated the beliefs and practices of Mexico's indigenous civilizations.[42]

Anthropologist Natividad Gutiérrez's interviews conducted during the late 1990s with indigenous intellectuals, students, and professionals revealed a rejection by many indigenous people themselves of the mythology of mestizaje. Gutiérrez's informants described mestizo mythology as implying indigenous cultural inferiority, which instead of promoting a cross-cultural dialogue simply appropriated indigenous culture and knowledge for a nonindigenous audience.[43] A separate study of the reaction by Mexican high school students to ethnographic exhibits at the National Museum of Anthropology in Mexico City during the same period further revealed the students' largely negative view of Mexico's contemporary indigenous population, whom they felt the government should be helping to "civilize."[44] Gutiérrez thus concluded that postrevolutionary indigenista programs aimed at mestizaje had not integrated native ethnicities into a national culture so much as created among indigenous peoples a pervasive sense of cultural and racial inferiority combined with sentiments of exclusion and cultural appropriation by dominant groups.[45]

While ethnicity had not traditionally formed a pole for political organization in Mexico, from the 1970s onward social movements independent from the state began to emerge that based their claim to legitimacy on invoking indigenous identity.[46] As anthropologist Guillermo de la Peña notes, there have been many structural explanations offered for the rise of such movements ranging from the effects of transnational capitalism to social change, the erosion of class identities, and continued racial exclusion.[47] Also contributing to this process was the spread of literacy and education into indigenous communities that, rather than leading to the full acculturation of indigenous people into the dominant national culture, created new leaders who could fight for demands such as linguistic recognition and community rights in the language of the state.[48] Contrary to its aims, the integrationist orientation of state policy toward Mexico's indigenous population had thus also provided indigenous groups with the intellectual tools of the dominant elite, which these groups could use to defend their cultural autonomy.

Similar to the urban social movements that were appearing at roughly the same time, indigenous movements emerged first at the local level and later developed national organizations such as the semi-official National Coordinating Committee of Indigenous People (CNPI).[49] The defense of indigenous rights was in turn incorporated into the demands of independent peasant movements with whom indigenous organizations developed links.[50] Institutions such as the Supreme Indian Councils created during the Echeverría administration to control unrest in the countryside provided another state-created space subsequently used by communities such as the Tojolabals in the Lacandón jungle to organize in opposition to the government.[51]

Neoliberal ideology that envisioned a minimal role for the state in organizing social relations and supported ideas of freedom and diversity also influenced indigenous activism and relations with the state. In particular, ideas of multiculturalism and the extension of universal human rights to indigenous populations had become a major focus of action for nongovernmental organizations and multinational governmental bodies during the 1980s. For example, in 1982 the United Nations began to draft documents dealing with universal concepts of indigenous rights.[52] For the Salinas administration, such an international context was potentially favorable for its reform project as recognizing the cultural rights of indigenous groups in rural Mexico as part of a broader embrace of pluralism. This concept of citizenship rights was not nearly as prescriptive in policy terms as collectivist revolutionary nationalist ideas of the peasant associated with the institution of the ejido.

The Salinas administration thus abandoned historical indigenista discourses of assimilation in favor of describing Mexico as a multicultural country in which cultural diversity was not just permissible but preferable.[53] In 1990 the administration ratified the International Labor Organization (ILO) Convention 169 on Indigenous and Tribal People in Independent Countries that outlined rights for indigenous peoples and responsibilities of states toward them.[54] In 1992 the president further modified Article 4 of the constitution to include a new description of the nation as "pluricultural." Finally, the appointment of Arturo Warman, the most high-profile of the Magnífico critics of mestizo nationalism and state paternalism toward rural communities, first as head of the National Indigenous Institute and then as secretary of agrarian reform, was another sign of the administration's determination to reframe the state's relationship with Mexico's indigenous populations.

For indigenous activists, the adoption of a liberal framework of democracy, multiculturalism, and human rights became increasingly effective relative to the adoption of a revolutionary peasant identity when negotiating their demands with a state that located itself within the transnational currents of neoliberal modernity of the 1990s.[55] Taken as a whole, the emergence of indigenous movements therefore represents a unification of indigenous cultural identity with new codes of modernity in defense of interests previously regarded as premodern and illegitimate under revolutionary nationalism's indigenismo.[56] This also signified an important shift in the template of "Mexicanness" promoted by the state away from class-based, collectivist identities toward the encouragement of pluralism.

A rising assertiveness of indigenous movements invoking distinct, nonmestizo cultural identities was not aimed at secession from the Mexican state, but rather at renegotiating the place of indigenous groups within it.[57] However, indigenous groups did demand significant autonomy from state institutions and differentiated forms of citizenship that corresponded to the geographies of indigenous communities as discrete political and cultural entities. In this way, the indigenous movement challenged not only the notion of the ethnocultural homogeneity of the nation, but also the notion of a homogenous form of citizenship regime that corresponded to the national state's administrative bound-aries.[58] While demands for the symbolic recognition of cultural plural-ism were largely accepted by the state under Salinas, however, such demands for a pluralism of citizenship regimes were not. This included rejecting demands by communities such as the Tojolabals in the Lacandón jungle of Chiapas that spending through programs such as Pronasol be directed toward reinforcing democratic institutions at the local level, thus strengthening local political autonomy.[59]

Situating Chiapas within the Mexican Nation

The environment in which the EZLN's neo-Zapatismo was forged in rural Chiapas highlighted how the uneven presence and sometimes almost total absence of the national state shaped local experiences in different ways throughout Mexico during the postrevolutionary era. These historical differences in turn impacted how certain regions expe-rienced the post-1982 period of crisis and reform. As in other parts of Mexico, the revolutionary nationalist framework was promoted in Chi-apas primarily through the education system, official peasant and labor organizations, and bureaucrats from state institutions such as the sec-retariat of agrarian reform. Even within the state of Chiapas, however, there was significant variation in how successful the penetration of post-revolutionary state institutions and, accordingly, revolutionary nation-alism had been.

Historian Catherine Nolan-Ferrel's research on the coffee-growing Soconusco region of southwest Chiapas demonstrated how Cardenista state-builders exploited the relative weakness of established power net-works to expand state institutions during the 1930s, in the process lim-iting the power of local elites and allowing for (some) agrarian reform.[60] Anthropologist Rosalva Aída Hernández Castillo's research on the indigenous Mam population in the same region of Chiapas near the Guatemalan border similarly showed that some aspects of the popula-tion's relationship with the state was marked by violence, imposition, or exclusion that was intensified by Mexicanization projects on a pop-ulation whose language the state identified as Guatemalan. However, the agrarian reforms of the Cárdenas presidency also strengthened local state-society relations in a positive sense. In particular, the Cardenista land redistribution promoted dialogue with the state through agrarian and corporatist peasant organizations, while the increasing concentration of a previously dispersed population around the ejido further assisted incorporation of Mam communities into state institutional channels.[61]

Where effective, this relationship between state institutions and society established revolutionary nationalism as a mutually acceptable framework of communication between largely indigenous peasant communities and the state. It also granted the PRI some residual legitimacy into at least the 1990s. For example, Nolan-Ferrell quotes the founder of one Soconusco ejido remarking in 1997 that younger ejidatarios lacked respect for the Revolution by failing to support the PRI, which had given peasants their land.[62] In Soconusco, the Zapatista uprising in 1994 also failed to gain significant support.

In eastern Chiapas, however, the effective legitimacy of the postrevolutionary national state was far weaker. During the Cardenista period, the federal secretary of public education found its attempts to expand education into indigenous highland regions had been effectively limited by hostility from local mestizo elites, often including the state governor, whose power depended on continued control of indigenous labor and consumption.[63] While the PRI and corporatist sectoral organizations such as the National Peasant Confederation (CNC) were successfully established in the central highlands, they functioned to largely reinforce existing prerevolutionary elite structures. Even this dynamic of state-society interaction was, however, far less prevalent on the fringes of the highlands and in the eastern Lacandón jungle, where these institutions were mostly absent.[64]

The Lancandón jungle had served as a safety valve for highland conflicts, which from the 1930s into the 1970s pushed several waves of colonists into the jungle. Many of these were escaping harsh working conditions on large estates and coffee plantations in other parts of Chiapas, arriving in the Lacandón jungle in search of freedom and land through state ejido grants. Others were escaping the control of the postrevolutionary Chiapaneco elites, the encroachment of private ranchers on land in highland villages or, particularly from the 1970s, expulsion from highland communities. The Lacandón jungle's population thus grew from an estimated 1,000 colonists in 1950 to an estimated 150,000 in 1990.[65] The pace at which authorities granted land was far too slow to accommodate the rising population, leading to frustration and increasing organization from the 1960s onward in defense of land claims. Communities in the Lacandón jungle had few prospects for survival beyond subsistence farming and coffee growing, and by the time government land redistributions were discontinued in 1992, over 25 percent of Mexico's unresolved land disputes were in Chiapas, the most of any state.[66]

The active role of local Catholic clergy in raising consciousness of class, social justice, and indigenous cultural issues also greatly influenced the political development of the region during this period. While the Mexican Catholic ecclesiastical hierarchy generally adopted a hostile stance toward liberation theology, the Pacífico Sur pastoral region formed by the neighboring states of Chiapas and Oaxaca had a reputation for radical theology, with some exceptions including the diocese of Tapachula, which covered Soconusco.[67] In Chiapas, Samuel Ruiz, bishop of the diocese of San Cristóbal de las Casas from 1960 to 1999, participated in the 1968 Council of Latin American Bishops conference in Medellín, Colombia, where the formative debates over the ideas and implications of liberation theology occurred. The bishop was also one of the defining figures in the political development of the highland and jungle regions of eastern Chiapas covered by his diocese.

Ruiz established schools to educate lay catechists who could teach Catholic doctrine in communities to which Chiapas's small number of ordained clergy were unable to regularly attend. To enhance the relevance of Catholic doctrine, the clergy worked closely with local communities to create a new syncretic form of gospel in indigenous languages that melded Biblical texts with and validated the beliefs and experiences of local communities. This preaching also fused notions of class with cultural identity, while the pastoral education of a lay clergy created new leaders within local communities.[68] The combative stance of delegates at the Indigenous Conference held in San Cristóbal in October 1974 served as the first display of this new dynamic to the outside world.[69]

Through processes of political organization independent from state institutions, the national symbol of Zapata also became a pervasive image in struggles for land and autonomy and thus integrated into local frameworks of identity in the Lacandón jungle. While state efforts to promote revolutionary nationalism had resulted in some prior awareness of Zapata, beginning in the early 1970s external political organizers and growing links between local and national independent peasant organizations led to the reshaping and wider diffusion of the symbol of Zapata locally. Maoist political organizers also arrived in Chiapas from other parts of Mexico during the 1970s and 1980s, and they too claimed Zapata as part of their heritage.[70] The invocation of Zapata and the

Revolution thus became a powerful symbolic weapon used by communities from the Lacandón jungle to legitimate claims for land to the national state that still relied upon revolutionary nationalism for legitimacy but had yet to expand revolutionary nationalist citizenship rights to the region's residents.

One of the main independent organizations that promoted the mythology of Zapata was the Emiliano Zapata Peasant Organization (OCEZ), formed in 1982 by members of the community of Venustiano Carranza, southwest of San Cristóbal. Local peasant organizations such as the OCEZ in turn developed links with national autonomous peasant confederations during the 1980s such as the Independent Confederation of Agricultural Workers and Peasants (CIOAC), the National "Plan de Ayala" Coordinating Committee (CNPA), and, in the early 1990s, the Emiliano Zapata National Independent Peasant Alliance (ANCIEZ).[71] The association between revolutionary nationalist imagery and independent peasant organization grew as land redistribution programs failed and government repression in Chiapas increased during the 1980s.

Chiapaneco peasants were among the scores who marched to Mexico City annually on the anniversary of Zapata's assassination to protest state agrarian policy during the 1980s and 1990s.[72] Independent peasant organizations also played a key role in organizing commemorations and protests on dates of historical importance in the Lacandón jungle. In 1992, for example, the commemoration of Zapata's assassination was a date for mobilization in Chiapas, with groups such as the ANCIEZ using the occasion to protest against NAFTA and the reform of Article 27 in Ocosingo.[73]

In October 1992 the quincentenary of Christopher Columbus's landing in the Americas was commemorated with multiple protests across the state. The most notable of these occurred in San Cristóbal when ten thousand peasants marched from a monument to Bartolomé de las Casas to one controversially erected in 1978 to city founder Diego de Mazariegos—the only monument to a conquistador in Mexico—which was then knocked off its base, dragged to the town hall, and smashed to pieces. During the march, peasants chanted slogans denouncing Salinas's neoliberal reforms and their continued marginalization. It later emerged that some of those present were EZLN leaders and many members of the ANCIEZ had also already or would later join the neo-Zapatista rebellion.[74]

The New Zapatistas and the Politics of Myth

Citing November 17, 1983, as the date of its founding, the EZLN began with a small group of mostly urban, mestizo, and middle-class clandestine political organizers who had formed links with a similarly small group of indigenous political organizers and set up a remote camp in the Lacandón jungle to plan for a coming revolution away from the gaze of the state. The urban group's experiences were shaped by preparation for armed rebellion in clandestine organizations—most significantly the Forces of National Liberation founded in 1969 in Monterrey, Nuevo León—and Marxist-Leninist ideology.[75] One of the postrevolutionary state's strategies to combat the rise of internal revolutionaries had been to adopt a foreign policy of generally supporting leftist revolutionary governments in the region, such as in Cuba and Nicaragua. This proved remarkably successful in stifling international support for Mexican revolutionary movements, and Marcos cited this experience of isolation, if not outright hostility, from international revolutionaries as encouraging the adoption of a focus on *national* liberation over adherence to the doctrine or strategies of international communism.[76]

The EZLN's cause found significant resonance throughout Mexico after the 1994 uprising, in part due to its skillful manipulation of the narratives of Mexican liberal modernity. The Zapatistas identified a critical interpretation of Mexican history as a key political tool for winning support and strategic weapon against the state. Pamphlets such as *El Despertador Mexicano* (The Mexican Awakening), named after *El Despertador Americano* (The American Awakening) issued from 1810 to 1811 by the independence forces led by Miguel Hidalgo, were produced that raised political awareness of contemporary conditions for peasants through reference to a national history of exploitation and the resistance of heroes such as Hidalgo, Guerrero, Zapata, and Villa.[77] As political scientist Neil Harvey identified, the success of the EZLN's discourse at mediating between the local and the universal was thus located "in the convergence of the Zapatistas' critical interpretation of Mexican history and the indigenous people's own stories of humiliation, exploitation, and racism."[78]

The adoption of Zapata as the movement's key symbol and its effectiveness in winning sympathy for the EZLN in other parts of Mexico also revealed the multifaceted nature in which mythology such as revolutionary nationalism works. As Roland Barthes argued, for mythology to be successful, the form it appropriates must maintain the potential to be rooted again in a primordial meaning for its nourishment and to hide its obviousness and popular dismissal as myth. It is therefore through a process of hide-and-seek between a meaning (in this case, of Zapata's biography of revolutionary agrarian struggle) and a concept (the forward progress of the nation under "the Revolution made government") that mythology functions.[79]

Anthropologist Lynn Stephen highlighted how this dynamic functioned in her study of the attitudes of men and women of three ejidos in the central valleys of Oaxaca following the EZLN uprising, which she categorized as "pro-Zapatista and pro-PRI."[80] Stephen found that local histories of productive relationships with the national government and the agrarian bureaucracy as an ally in the communities' struggle to secure land against local elites and rival communities contributed to continuing support for the PRI in the 1990s. Ejidatarios cited Zapata in particular as the individual who initiated this struggle and effectively won for them their rights, which after centuries of marginalization and exploitation were then fulfilled, if often imperfectly, by the PRI state.

Stephen's interviews further revealed that in 1994 many ejidatarios simultaneously drew a direct connection between Emiliano Zapata, the Mexican Revolution, and the EZLN rebellion in a way that increased their sympathy for the EZLN's cause. One respondent, who expressed sympathy for both the PRI and the Zapatistas, explained this connection by stating "when we woke up here [in Oaxaca] and saw what was going on, we took the land away from the large landowners. The government helped us to do that here in our struggle for the ejido. The ejido law never reached Chiapas. Nobody helped them there. Now the PRI has to help them get their land there, or the blood will keep flowing."[81] While this person supported the Salinas administration's agrarian reforms in his own community, he explained them as part of an evolutionary process from which the peasants of Chiapas had so far been excluded. The EZLN's struggle was, in his opinion, therefore also a legitimate one that would allow the peasants of Chiapas to join the forward march of the nation and it was now the PRI state's obligation ensure the fulfillment of their revolutionary citizenship rights.

Taking Emiliano Zapata as its main symbol, the EZLN itself dismantled and reconstructed the Zapata myth in a way that played with notions of time by discarding linear scientific laws of Western history. The resulting construction was local and specific in its incorporation of Tzeltal indigenous religious symbolism largely unknown outside of parts of rural Chiapas, while also being broad and national in its

Figure 5.3. A mural in the EZLN-controlled town of Oventic, Chiapas, shows indigenous imagery, a female soldier holding the EZLN and Mexican flags, and an image of Zapata. Courtesy of Just Coffee Cooperative.

historical sweep through its use of the mythology of Mexican nationalism (fig. 5.3). As Marcos described it, this combination of rural indigenous and urban mestizo elements resulted in "a postmodern language that, paradoxically, is nourished from historical pre-modernity."[82] This playing with time, space, and symbols of repression and resistance was a continuing feature of Zapatista discourse that helped extend its support beyond not just Chiapas, but beyond Mexico.

Perhaps the most imaginative melding of mestizo nationalism and indigenous mythology in EZLN discourse was the Votán Zapata mythology. Votán Zapata in Zapatista communiqués is presented as a spirit that gives form to the formless struggle of the nameless and faceless people of Mexico, materializing through history in the form of Mexico's great heroes, including Emiliano Zapata. Through this symbol, the Zapatistas encapsulated not just the agrarian struggle, but a broader struggle against repression that began with the arrival of Europeans to the Americas.[83] A communiqué released on the anniversary of Zapata's assassination in 1994 in this spirit described Votán Zapata as the "guardian and heart of the people" that directed the

EZLN and "looked out of Miguel [Hidalgo], walked in José María [Morelos], was Vicente [Guerrero], was named in Benito [Juárez] . . . rode in Emiliano [Zapata], cried out in Francisco [Villa]."[84] Now, the communiqué continued, Votán Zapata "took its name in us: Zapatista Army of National Liberation."[85]

The EZLN's blending of historical heroes also played with this tendency in the state's nationalist narrative of progress. Stephen, for example, quoted one ninety-two-year-old ejidatario at El Tule, Oaxaca, who recounted the local history of President Cárdenas's visit and the creation of the ejido in a similar fashion that connected a Christlike Zapata to Cárdenas. According to the ejidatario, "when Cárdenas came here, he said, 'Down with the rich and up with the poor.' He was with Emiliano Zapata. He and Zapata were for the poor people. Zapata was the one who had the idea of taking land away from the hacendados. Zapata suffered for us. He gave his blood so that the campesinos would have some land to work."[86] Both the Zapatistas and the PRI state were now making claims to being the ones who were "with Zapata"; as it turned out, they were competing but not necessarily mutually exclusive.

While the EZLN described its language as postmodern, many of its referents, such as the nation and constitution, were firmly rooted in Mexico's liberal tradition. Indeed, literary theorist Ignacio Sánchez Prado argues that the Zapatistas' adoption of this liberal narrative was symptomatic of a broader weakness of critical debate in postrevolutionary (and post-PRI state) Mexico that could not break free of the "predetermined narrative frame" of liberal modernity.[87] The way in which the Zapatistas used these myths and symbols did, however, also involve critiques of liberal ideals of progress, with the idea of a Zapatista "reenchantment of the world" advanced by sociologist Yvon LeBot and later included in Zapatista discourse further implying a critique of rationalist modernity.[88]

At the time of the Zapatista uprising, the Mexican state was sending out an army of technicians to the countryside to measure rural plots, provide certificates of individual ownership, and open the gates to the rationalizing logic of the global marketplace. The EZLN, in response, criticized neoliberalism as a new barbarity cloaked in ideas of rationalism that attacked and destroyed its victims and then reconstructed and reorganized them to fit within the great jigsaw puzzle of economic globalization.[89] Articulating individual freedom to the achievement of personal dignity through social justice and autonomy, Zapatista discourse directly contested the neoliberal connection of individual freedom to the free market. While its initial proposals and language did not propose a radical reworking of Mexican society as such, the new spaces for debate that the EZLN opened up did provide room for contesting dominant interpretations of nationalism, democracy, citizenship, and modernity in Mexico. In this debate, the EZLN positioned itself, according to Marcos, as "the most beautiful absurdity, the most human madness."[90]

The Legacy of Social Liberalism

Salinas was unwittingly prescient during his fifth informe in September 1993, when he told Mexicans that "in our nation there will always be battles for social justice, so long as the memory and example of Emiliano Zapata remains in Mexicans' hearts."[91] With their cry of "¡Ya basta!" on January 1, 1994, the new Zapatistas dramatically focused attention on those who had been excluded from the state's modernization project for decades but whose plight had become worse as new visions of modernity led to the dismantling of collective rights won by peasants following the Mexican Revolution. Set against the "there is no alternative" globalizing language of neoliberal modernization, the EZLN rebellion caught the imagination of millions of people in Mexico and around the world through a language of resistance that simultaneously harnessed the globalization of communications and political institutions as a space for radical political organizing against the force of the established state and private economic interests. The Zapatistas further rejected the assimilation of local and distinct identities and demands into a hegemonic national state or culture by harnessing myths and symbols that had been crafted, diffused, and nurtured by the state for that very purpose. From the mountains of the Mexican southeast, the EZLN in this manner articulated a vision of democracy different from that guiding the reformists of the Salinas administration and that challenged economic rationalist visions of modernity.

At the same time, other nonstate actors such as independent peasant and indigenous organizations also drew upon symbolic identities embedded within Mexican nationalism to make demands on the state, ranging from direct financial assistance to increased political autonomy. As the institutional and economic framework of the PRI state broke down, those historically excluded from the relatively restricted revolutionary nationalist cultural framework of collective identities found greater opportunity to rework their place within the nation in a symbolic sense. This was evidenced by the increasingly visible struggle of indigenous groups for greater political and cultural recognition during the 1980s and 1990s.

The Salinista project of social liberalism and solidarity, meanwhile, left behind a mixed legacy. The Salinas administration's land reforms were often implemented by communities in a fashion described by Goldring as "having your cake and eating it too," whereby communities combined elements of collective and private property regimes so that they could retain the rights of an ejidatario as well as the benefits of private property through a regime of de facto privatization within the inalienable ejido.[92] Furthermore, official statistics showed that by 1998 only 3.2 percent of ejidos certified under Procede had been completely or partially privatized.[93] In some areas, resistance within the existing bureaucracy of the secretariat of agrarian reform or from Procede officials themselves appears to have undermined the state's attempt to implement its reforms and affect the desired change in attitudes to land use.[94] Procede in this sense did not appear to fundamentally change the cultural value of ejido land as inalienable and communal, at least not in the short to medium term. The states with the lowest levels of ejido certification under Procede by 2006 were those with the highest indigenous peasant populations, namely Chiapas, Oaxaca, and, contrary to Salinas's plans, Zapata's home state of Morelos.[95]

On the issue of indigenous rights, the picture was also mixed. One effect of the modification of the constitutional definition of the nation to "pluricultural" was a shift by indigenous leaders from self-identification as a revolutionary peasant associated with Article 27 to self-identification with indigenous culture associated with Article 4 to establish the legitimacy of their demands in negotiations with state institutions.[96] This evidenced the drift of the state away from seeking legitimacy through its revolutionary social credentials toward seeking legitimacy as pluralistic, liberal, and democratic, signifying a transformation in the way Mexican nationalist discourse articulated identity to citizenship rights. However, while the ideal of mestizaje was no longer official state policy and the indigenista state anthropological apparatus was largely dismantled, assimilation into the Western model of progress critiqued by anthropologists such as Bonfil was still the overriding logic behind state indigenous policies.[97]

The dominant theories of Western policy-making circles during the 1990s had posited a virtuous circle of democracy and development that ran through the capitalist market economy.[98] This logic was implicit in the liberal critiques of neo-Zapatismo and neo-Cardenismo as premodern challenges to the modern reforms of the Salinas administration such as those made by the *Nexos* and *Vuelta* groups. However, the triumphalism of the Salinas project ended in a dramatic return to political and economic crisis during 1994. The next and final sexenio of the twentieth century thus began with the legitimacy of the PRI state at its weakest ebb and ended with the party losing the presidency for the first time in its history. When "change" came, however, it was not in the form of a neo-Zapatista rebel riding out of the mountains of Chiapas. Instead, the PRI handed over the presidency to a conservative Catholic businessman and ex-Coca-Cola executive hailing from Guanajuato, one of the states in which Catholic conservatism had been most vigorous and persistent following the Revolution.

Mexico 2010: Let's Celebrate

After a brief illusion of stability under President Carlos Salinas, during the administration's final year the economic and political future of Mexico was again plunged into a crisis that was to overshadow the term of Salinas's successor, Ernesto Zedillo Ponce de León (1994–2000). On July 2, 2000, over seventy years of unbroken rule by the "revolution made government" came to an end with the election of the PAN's Vicente Fox Quesada to the Mexican presidency. Fox had based his election campaign around the central promise of change, which had undeniable appeal following the period of almost constant crisis that began in 1982. With the PAN and PRI increasingly coinciding on the fundamentals of Mexico's economic model and nationalist mythology, however, the kind of practical change Fox's symbolically important victory over the PRI would bring was unclear.

In 2006 Felipe Calderón was officially elected as the PAN's second president of Mexico by a margin of .56 percent over PRD candidate and former head of the Mexico City government Andrés Manuel López Obrador amid accusations of electoral fraud. The PRI, meanwhile, fell to a distant third place with former Tabasco governor Roberto Madrazo as its candidate.[1] Calderón's victory meant that it would fall to a PAN administration to organize the expected lavish celebrations of the centenary of the Mexican Revolution and bicentenary of Mexican Independence in 2010. With this new PAN administration facing accusations of electoral fraud and preparing to celebrate the myths and symbols of the Mexican Revolution and Insurgente struggle amid a new crisis of drug-related violence sweeping across Mexico, the meaning of July 2, 2000, became even less clear as the first decade of the twenty-first century progressed.

A century earlier, the Porfirio Díaz regime had used the centenary of Hidalgo's grito to celebrate the ideals of peace, progress, and modernity it claimed to have brought to Mexico. The center of Mexico City was draped in electric lights, a flurry of monuments including the Angel of Independence and Juárez Hemiciclo were dedicated, and lavish parades and banquets were held, reaching a crescendo in September 1910.[2] Roughly two months later, however, a revolution began, detonated by Francisco Madero's call for effective suffrage that overturned the Porfirian science of modernity and engulfed Mexico in a wave of violence for much of the next decade. In contrast, the Calderón administration faced doubts about its democratic legitimacy and growing levels of violence and economic uncertainty long before the celebrations began.

During the 2006 campaign, supporters of López Obrador accused President Fox and private business groups such as the CCE of illegally interfering in the election process and alleged media bias against López Obrador.[3] Following the election, López Obrador and his supporters alleged that his narrow defeat was the result of electoral fraud and took to the streets to demand a recount. From the end of July, a protest camp of López Obrador supporters stretched along Mexico City's Paseo de la Reforma through the heart of Mexico City and into the Zócalo, blocking one of Mexico City's central arteries to traffic for almost two months.

With all legal possibilities of a recount exhausted, on Independence Day 2006 López Obrador held a "National Democratic Convention" in the Zócalo, at which supporters determined they would refuse to recognize Calderón as president. Instead, López Obrador would be sworn in as Mexico's "legitimate president" the following November 20, Revolution Day. This legitimate presidency in practice provided the basis for a permanent campaign against and thorn in the side of the Calderón administration. The 2010 celebrations were immediately drawn into this battle, with PRD founder Cuauhtémoc Cárdenas stepping down as president of the committee appointed by Fox to oversee the celebrations following the contested election result.[4]

The movement led by López Obrador was heavily steeped in nationalist historical symbolism. When choosing a coat of arms for his legitimate presidency, López Obrador rejected as "the eagle of conservatives and reactionaries" an updated and streamlined version of Mexico's coat of arms used by the Fox administration. This new coat of arms had replaced the eagle's talons with a slash of red, white, and green and was popularly dubbed the *águila mocha* in a play on the Spanish verb *mochar* (to chop off) and the Mexican slang word *mocho* (Catholic reactionary).[5] López

Figure 6.1. Andrés Manuel López Obrador is sworn in as "Legitimate President" of Mexico on Revolution Day, November 20, 2006, in front of supporters in Mexico City's Zócalo. The backdrop of the stage features the Juarista eagle that the López Obrador movement adopted as its key symbol. Courtesy EPA/Marcos Delgado.

Obrador instead chose an element of Juarista symbolism woven into the daily exchanges of all Mexicans on the twenty-peso note as the symbol of his movement: a nineteenth-century version of the national coat of arms showing an eagle with wings outstretched and associated with liberal resistance to the French intervention. During his Revolution Day inaugural address, López Obrador thus instructed followers to "look to the twenty-peso note, the smallest denomination, because here appears our eagle and the president that we admire, president Benito Juárez García, the greatest in the history of Mexico" (fig. 6.1).[6]

On December 1, Calderón was sworn in as Mexico's constitutional president in the Chamber of Deputies amid pushing, shoving, and shouting PRD deputies, and he became the first Mexican president forced to leave the federal legislature to deliver his inaugural address (fig. 6.2).[7] During his first week as president, Calderón announced that the administration would drop the águila mocha and return to the traditional, twentieth-century form of the Mexican shield for official use.[8] In his first press conference, President Calderón also adopted Juárez as his central referent, repeating phrases of Juárez as well as the exhortation of Insurgente hero José María Morelos to "moderate opulence and indigence" that had been common refrains during López Obrador's presidential campaign.[9] In 2006 the revolutionary

Figure 6.2. The inauguration of President Felipe Calderón (center) in the Chamber of Deputies with outgoing president Vicente Fox to his left. PAN federal deputies took control of the tribunal from deputies allied to López Obrador in order to permit a brief and chaotic inauguration ceremony. Courtesy EPA/ Marcos Delgado.

nationalist framework promoted by the PRI state during the twentieth century thus appeared as central as ever to Mexican political discourse, even though the PRI itself watched this conflict from the sidelines.

In July 2007 the Bank of Mexico announced that it was issuing new twenty-peso notes on which the coat of arms adopted by López Obrador would be replaced with the scales of justice and a book representing the Reform Laws.[10] This new image appeared a direct reference to the Calderón administration's frequent appeals for the respect of state institutions and the rule of law and an answer to López Obrador's retort "to hell with them and their institutions."[11] Despite not winning the presidency, the PRD continued to hold another of Mexico's most high-profile elected offices, with Marcelo Ebrard elected head of the Mexico City government. Using this high-profile bully pulpit, Ebrard described the Bank of Mexico's decision as evidence that the Calderón government "is afraid of the Juarista eagle" and in September that year included the eagle among the traditional illuminated patriotic decorations placed around the Zócalo across the façade of a building directly facing the balcony of the National Palace from which Calderón would give his first Independence Day grito.[12]

Calderón had moved swiftly to ensure the support of the armed forces in the wake of the contested election result. In his inaugural address, the president paid special tribute to the safeguarding of national institutions by the armed forces and during his first week in office announced a pay raise for the military and increased security spending.[13] On December 11, the administration launched what became the defining decision of the Calderón presidency: Operación Conjunta Michoacán (Joint Operation Michoacán). This military campaign called for five thousand troops to be deployed to the state of Michoacán during December 2006 to combat the cultivation and trafficking of illegal drugs as a sign of the new administration's commitment to uphold the rule of law.[14]

What began as a relatively localized operation soon came to resemble a full-scale war involving state security forces and drug cartels that spread across growing areas of Mexico. The violence in the northern state of Chihuahua became so extreme that in March 2008 the administration launched Operación Conjunta Chihuahua and a year later announced the effective militarization of security in the particularly violent border city of Ciudad Juárez.[15] Yet the violence continued to worsen. By April 2010 the war between the Mexican state and organized crime had officially resulted in more than 22,000 deaths and showed no sign of ending.[16] In the two years since the launch of Operación Conjunta Chihuahua, that state alone had witnessed more than 5,000 deaths according to official figures. The Citizen's Council of Public Security and Penal Justice declared Ciudad Juárez the most violent city in the world, with 191 homicides for every 100,000 inhabitants during 2009.[17]

Whether Mexico was at serious risk of becoming—or already was—a failed state became an increasingly common topic of debate in the media and academic circles. A United States Joint Forces Command report made public in January 2009 fed this discussion by naming Mexico alongside Pakistan as one of two major states the Pentagon assessed as facing the possibility of a rapid, sudden collapse.[18] A new period of economic uncertainty caused by the global financial crisis of 2008 further added to the general sense of pessimism about Mexico's present and future, with the Mexican economy contracting by 6.5 percent in 2009.[19] The cover of the first issue of weekly newsmagazine *Proceso* for Mexico's bicentennial year captured this grim situation, showing a bleak arch inscribed with "2010" framed against a gray sky and rising above a cemetery with the headline "Let's celebrate . . ."[20]

Figure 6.3. President Felipe Calderón speaking at the ceremony commemorating the assassination of Emiliano Zapata in Chinameca, Morelos, on April 10, 2010. Courtesy Adolfo Jasso/Gobierno Federal.

During 2010, Calderón personally attended and spoke at a long list of historical commemoration ceremonies. Most notable about the president's speeches was their similarity to those given for decades by representatives of the PRI state. Speaking during that year's Zapata commemoration, Calderón linked Zapata to the institutions of the state through the Constitution of 1917, which, according to Calderón, had "gathered . . . the banners of Zapata and governments emanating from the Revolution, fundamentally that of General Lázaro Cárdenas, gave life to the order to redistribute land, making possible that the land was finally for those who worked it" (fig. 6.3).[21]

In March at the annual Juárez commemoration, the president made explicit reference to the fight against organized crime in a language similar to that used to describe political opposition under the PRI. Presenting Juárez as a defender of the laws and institutions of the state, Calderón stressed that the monopoly of force corresponded to the state. If the enemies of the patria for PRI orators were conservatives and reactionaries, in 2010 Calderón used the phrase to allude to organized crime that "wants to see the country submerged in fear, in violence and hopelessness."[22]

The president further legitimized his administration's fight against organized crime by linking it to past patriotic struggles. Ciudad Juárez was renamed by Porfirio Díaz from Paso del Norte for Benito Juárez in 1888. Referring to the wave of violence that had engulfed it, Calderón argued that federal government in 2010 was fighting for freedoms that had been won with the blood of Mexico's heroes. The president on this basis pledged, "We will [fight] in Ciudad Juárez, that emblematic Northern Pass of [Benito Juárez] and we will [continue to] do so in all of the national territory."[23] Finally, as had PRI orators in past moments of crisis, Calderón reminded his audience that the Mexicans of Juárez's generation had overcome greater obstacles than those of the present and called for unity so that future generations "can grow up in a safe Mexico . . . free from the shadow of violence and terror; in a country of peace that progresses under the protection of laws, in a nation where the respect for law prevails."[24]

On Independence Day, the government staged the year's most lavish celebrations that were broadcast via television into millions of homes across Mexico. The ceremony involved a parade down the Paseo de la Reforma to the Zócalo culminating in a light and laser show. One of the highlights of this spectacle was the assembling of a giant figure called El Coloso (the Colossus) meant to represent the participants of Mexico's war of independence. A new song, "El futuro es milenario" (The Future is Millennial), was also produced for the celebration. However, when it was sung to the crowds in the Zócalo, it was booed and efforts to get the crowd to sing along were met by crowds singing the traditional "Cielito lindo" in unison.[25]

The statue El Coloso sparked a particularly derisive response from observers. While the organizers claimed the appearance of the figure was based on a composite of images of insurgents and revolutionaries, the question of who it most resembled became a topic of speculation in the media and online. The most popular choices included Vicente Fox, assassinated 1994 PRI presidential candidate Luis Donaldo Colosio, Joseph Stalin, fictional local hero Jebediah Springfield from the US animated TV series *The Simpsons*, and patron saint of drug traffickers Jesús Malverde.[26] Indeed, the media reported that during the celebrations users of the social networking site Twitter dubbed it the "NarColoso" to underscore this connection to the ongoing narco violence.[27] Designer Juan Carlos Canfield provoked more controversy when he revealed in an interview that one of his references for the figure was Benjamín Argumedo, a counterrevolutionary who had fought against

Pancho Villa and joined the forces of Victoriano Huerta, who had over-thrown the Madero government.[28]

While by 2010 the López Obrador movement's ability to seriously destabilize the Calderón government had been weakened by factors including infighting within the PRD and the domination of the national agenda by drug-related violence, it continued to constitute an important political force. On the bicentenary of Hidalgo's grito, López Obrador led his followers in a separate "Grito of the Free" at the Plaza de las Tres Culturas in Tlatelolco, Mexico City. Citing the example of the Insurgentes, López Obrador told the crowd, "Today, those gathered here and many others are fighting to defeat in a pacific manner the current oligarchy, the regime of corruption, oppression, and privileges that is destroying the country." Drawing on the 1968 Tlatelolco massacre that took place in the same plaza, López Obrador continued that "from this Plaza de las Tres Culturas, where the students fought for democracy and were sacrificed to the authoritarianism of the PRI, we say that it will not be easy for them to commit a new felony." López Obrador concluded by telling the crowd, "We have history on our side: the patria was not built by the heroes so that it could be sullied by the self-seeking (los ambiciosos)."[29]

The state also channeled debate about the meaning of Mexico's national history during the 2010 commemorations into a television and radio program called Discutamos México (Let's Discuss Mexico) that began in January 2010. Prominent historians gathered in a roundtable format in each episode to discuss different events and themes from Mexican history sequentially from the pre-Columbian period to the present.[30] The episode of the program that best illustrated the democratic teleology that was the major innovation of post-2000 state-promoted nationalism aired on April 30, 2010, and was titled "The Democratic Struggle."[31] Moderated by historian Enrique Krauze, this episode focused on the history of the revolutionary hero with whom the PAN had most clearly identified since the 1980s, Francisco Madero. At the end of the episode, Krauze asked each of the historians on the panel to give their thoughts on the significance of Madero's democratic struggle for the present and to volunteer why they each personally admired Madero. When contrasted with the oppositional language of López Obrador, the reasons these historians gave demonstrated the deep divisions that still existed in Mexico over what the collapse of the PRI system had meant a decade later.

Jean Meyer, an early and important revisionist critic of the state-sanctioned history of the Mexican Revolution, began the concluding remarks by arguing that Madero was most admirable as a president

Figure 6.4. President Calderón leads the inauguration ceremony for a statue of Francisco Madero on Avenida Juárez in Mexico City on the centenary of the Mexican Revolution in November 2010. Courtesy Adolfo Jasso/Gobierno Federal.

who, had he survived, would have saved Mexico eighty years in its transition to democracy. Santiago Portilla, meanwhile, explained that the continued relevance of Madero for Mexicans lay in his role in giving them what a third still did not (presumably erroneously) believe they had: the freedom to express and organize themselves. Javier Lara Bayón refuted suggestions that Mexico's current situation resembled the Porfiriato, instead drawing a comparison between Madero's presidency and contemporary Mexico as that of a fragile democracy in which it was freedom of expression and the press itself that sometimes led to political tension. Krauze solemnly concluded by sentencing, "We are now putting into practice exactly the type of system that Madero, gathering the best liberal and democratic traditions of Mexico, foresaw, for which he fought, and for which he finally died. Remembering freedom is an end in itself, and, like air, it is only appreciated—it is only truly appreciated—when it is lost. Let us hope that we do not have to lose the air of freedom to truly appreciate it."[32]

On Revolution Day, giving one of his final commemorative speeches of the year, Calderón dedicated one of the few significant monuments of 2010: an equestrian statue of Madero located outside the neoclassical Palacio de Bellas Artes in Mexico City (fig. 6.4). Calderón promoted this same historical teleology of democratic transition, speaking of a long and difficult "constructive period" that followed Madero's revolution, the goals of which were not realized until the end of the twentieth century. The president alluded to those who had opposed the PRI state before 2000, stating that "everyone who in the twentieth century fought in our country from diverse trenches for democracy has been, in one way or another, a successor of Madero." According to this narrative, it was only when the PRI was defeated that Mexico reached its democratic end of history and thus, Calderón concluded, "We have begun to live, for the first time and after a long time, in these last decades, the democracy with which the Revolution began."[33]

Despite seeking to draw a clear distinction between itself and the PRI, in 2010 the Calderón administration on such occasions turned to the same rhetorical devices of triumph over adversity and the promotion of national unity as well as the same heroes, myths, and symbols historically employed by the PRI state to legitimize its power. With the support of sympathetic intellectuals, it also promoted a narrative of Mexico having recently arrived at the revolutionary goal of a democracy and freedom that had to be protected from those who did not respect the rule of law. The political party to emerge the most electorally strengthened within this context during the Calderón presidency was also, in fact, the PRI. In the 2009 midterm elections, the PRI won a majority in the federal legislature, and by the end of 2010 the party held nineteen of Mexico's thirty-two state governorships, encompassing roughly 50 percent of the population.[34]

Leaders of the PRI also participated in historical commemorations during 2010 as representatives of other state institutions and embraced the centrality of democracy to the legitimacy of state power. However, they implicitly criticized the PAN's management of the country and the party's efforts to dismiss the legacy of the PRI as inherently authoritarian.[35] During his speech at the official ceremony of the centenary of the Revolution, for example, PRI President of the Senate Manlio Fabio Beltrones celebrated the postrevolutionary state-building project that allowed Mexicans "to construct a state, to transition from caudillismo to a country of institutions, and to consolidate the nation that we are today." On the topic of democracy, Beltrones highlighted popular discontent with the results of the two post-PRI administrations, sentencing that "democracy should be, as we all know, the means and not the end; the means so that governments ensure access to food, health, housing, and education to the entire population."[36]

While postrevolutionary elites had been able to build upon the

Porfirian nationalist narrative to identify the Revolution with progress, the celebrations of 2010 suggested the difficulty contemporary elites had in defining in a practical sense how the change of 2000 had resulted in a political and social model that represented an advance on that which came before. Mexicans were again living through a period of crisis, with even the legitimacy of Mexico's electoral system thrown into doubt once more in 2006. The PRI itself was furthermore still one of the most important political forces in the country. One hundred years after the Mexican Revolution began, and two hundred years since Hidalgo's grito, the great heroes of Mexican nationalism were still very much alive as national myths and symbols. Their relationship to the state and indeed the relationship between Mexican citizens and the state, however, seemed increasingly ambiguous.

CHAPTER SIX

A New Revolution?

Following the triumphalism of the Salinas administration's social liberalism, the final *sexenio* of the PRI system under President Ernesto Zedillo (1994–2000) began with a return to economic crisis followed by further austerity measures, renewed political reform, and increasing recognition of opposition electoral victories. Under Zedillo free market reform deepened and elections became more genuinely competitive than at any time since the PRI's formation. However, the Zedillo administration was characterized not so much by a great historical rupture as by transition. Indeed, the PRI itself remained arguably Mexico's most powerful political party even after it lost the presidency to the PAN's Vicente Fox.

This chapter examines the final stage of the unraveling of the PRI state's hegemonic dominance of Mexican politics and the contested nature of what has been described as Mexico's "transition to democracy." This includes an increasingly unclear relationship between the nation, state, and nationalism during the twelve years of PAN rule. During this period, the historical myths and symbols of revolutionary nationalism not only did not die but also emerged at key political junctures, often frustrating government attempts to further dismantle Mexico's postrevolutionary political, social, and economic order. We will conclude by exploring the return of the PRI to the presidency in 2012 under President Enrique Peña Nieto and the failure of Mexico to convincingly and sustainably emerge from the atmosphere of crisis and uncertainty.

Return to Crisis

As President Ernesto Zedillo took office in December 1994, the illusion of a return to economic prosperity under social liberalism vanished amid a new crisis, dubbed the "peso crisis" or, alluding to a hangover from the recent euphoria surrounding Mexico's apparent economic success, the "tequila crisis."[1] Public debt had ballooned during 1994 as the government sought to encourage economic growth in the lead up to the presidential elections. As doubts grew over the Mexican government's ability to finance these debts, tens of billions of dollars in foreign investment attracted by the opening of Mexico's financial markets began to flow out of the country at the rate of billions of dollars per day by December. Due to the sudden exit of foreign currency, the shell-shocked new administration found itself unable to service foreign debt and Mexico plunged back into a severe crisis in many ways deeper than that of 1982.[2]

In the final week of December, the Zedillo government struggled to deal with the balance of payments crisis through a chaotic devaluation then floating of the peso in a chain of events that became known as the "errors of December."[3] This was followed by the announcement of a series of austerity measures on January 3, 1995, and a more dramatic stabilization plan in March that contained deep budget cuts and a 50 percent rise in the value-added tax paid by consumers.[4] The negative impact on the economy was far more severe than the government anticipated, with the economy contracting by 10.5 and 9.5 percent during the second and third quarters of the year respectively. Moreover, inflation remained a problem and foreign investment failed to return, contributing to the peso's continued fall in value.[5] After having slowly declined during the Salinas presidency, poverty also rose sharply and crime rates soared, particularly in Mexico City.[6]

Mexico's political system by this stage had already entered into crisis. The assassination of the PRI's original presidential candidate, Luis Donaldo Colosio, in a suburb of Tijuana in March 1994 provoked widespread rumors about possible motives that focused on internal rivalries within the PRI. On September 28, during the transition period between administrations, violent rifts within the PRI bubbled to the surface when party secretary José Francisco Ruiz Massieu was gunned down in broad daylight in the center of Mexico City. Rumors again swirled about assassination plots stemming from internal party rivalries and suspicions quickly centered on Raúl Salinas, the outgoing president's brother. Raúl was indeed jailed in February 1995, charged with being the intellectual author of the assassination. His co-accused was a PRI federal deputy from Tamaulipas, Manuel Muñoz Rocha, who fled before he could be arrested.[7] Whereas both the de la Madrid and Salinas administrations oversaw the arrest of high-profile figures in the police force and corporatist workers' organizations early in their terms to prove their commitment to reform, the Zedillo administration struck at the heart of the PRI itself and the family of the former president.

It is difficult to imagine a harder fall from grace for Salinas and his social liberalism project. Salinas had attempted to craft his image as a modernizing president who miraculously restored not only the Mexican political system's legitimacy but brought to fruition the long-held ambitions of Mexico's elite to catapult the country into the club of first-world economies through NAFTA and acceptance into the OECD. Instead, by early 1995 Salinas was a national villain. Popularly likened to the mythical beast chupacabra, which sucks the blood out of livestock, Salinas was portrayed as having tricked Mexicans into believing that prosperity was finally arriving after years of austerity, only to leave millions of people unemployed and in debt with their savings drained from their bank accounts.[8] Accusations flew between Salinas and Zedillo over responsibility for the crisis, representing a break with the established tradition of ex-presidents refraining from criticizing their successors' performance. On March 12, 1995, his brother in prison on murder charges and his reputation in tatters, Salinas flew to New York and into self-imposed exile.[9]

Traditionalists within the PRI who had been bound by party discipline and the apparent success of social liberalism also increasingly made their objections to neoliberal reforms public. Ex-president José López Portillo emerged from his own self-imposed exile to proclaim that de la Madrid and Salinas had sold out Mexico's interests to the United States under the guise of globalization, leaving the country defenseless against the speculative movement of foreign capital. López Portillo, by now established in the popular imagination as the corrupt and frivolous villain of the 1982 debt crisis, described himself as "the last president of the Revolution" and argued that Salinas had plunged Mexico headfirst into neoliberalism while "refusing to call it by its name and with revolutionary shame he called it social liberalism, looking for precedents in [nineteenth-century liberal] Ignacio Ramírez and [twentieth-century intellectual] Jesús Reyes Heroles."[10] The discipline at the highest levels of the revolutionary family was clearly unraveling.

Democratic Revolution

Upon taking office, Zedillo promised a different style of rule than that of his predecessors based on maintaining a "healthy distance" between the executive and the PRI as well as the democratization of Mexico's political system through electoral reforms.[11] In this regard, Zedillo hoped to signal a move away from Mexico's postrevolutionary political model of collectivist institutions connected to the state through a hegemonic state party toward a model in which the PRI would be one among several parties competing for power. During the official 1996 Revolution Day speech, government orator and secretary of the interior Emilio Chuayffet thus spoke not of revolutionary majorities and reactionary minorities but called on Mexicans to celebrate pluralism. Chuayffet now argued that the Revolution was "not a uniform movement, but an amalgam of different visions, demands, grievances, hopes, and leaderships."[12] While this change in state discourse began under de la Madrid, during the Zedillo administration there was a more definitive shift toward celebrating pluralism rather than the will of the majority. The new argument was that, in the words of Chuayffet, the plurality of visions expressed in the Revolutionary struggle "cannot be permanently expressed through unanimity."[13]

One of the most significant political developments of the Zedillo presidency was a perceptible decline in power of the executive branch of government. The executive had traditionally sat atop the pyramidal organization of Mexico's political system and had been strengthened under Salinas. Deference to presidential authority even within the PRI was now more frequently disputed at a local level. The Salinas administration's concertación model of resolving local electoral conflicts through negotiation now proved untenable in situations such as the controversial 1994 Tabasco gubernatorial elections, when Zedillo retreated from indications he would annul the electoral result despite significant evidence of corruption when faced with a rebellious local PRI.[14]

After years of the state's retreat from the economy and their selective weakening under Salinas's neoliberal populism, the corporatist sectoral organizations also now had an increasingly uncertain position within Mexico's political order. The death in June 1997 of Fidel Velázquez, leader of the Mexican Workers' Confederation (CTM) and one of Mexico's most powerful figures since 1941, symbolized not just the death of one of the greatest constants in postrevolutionary Mexican politics, but also a general exhaustion of the formal and informal arrangements that historically underpinned the corporatist institutions of the PRI state as the old guard retired or died. Then-PRD party president López Obrador thus described Velázquez's death as "the beginning of the end of Priísmo."[15]

In this context, the Mexican electoral landscape became significantly more plural. The PRD and PAN negotiated a series of substantial electoral reforms with the Zedillo administration during 1996, including the establishment of a Federal Electoral Institute independent from the executive, a more reliable system of voter accreditation, and new mechanisms for solving electoral disputes. Also significant was that the position of the head of the Mexico City government was now opened to popular election rather than being appointed by the executive.[16]

In the 1997 midterm elections, the PRI for the first time lost its majority in the legislature while the PRD emerged as the largest opposition party in the Chamber of Deputies, closely followed by the PAN.[17] Cuauhtémoc Cárdenas and the PRD also won the elections for head of the Mexico City government, a position which immediately established him as one of the country's most high-profile elected officials. Indeed, one of the most notable extensions of political pluralism under Zedillo was the recognition of PRD electoral victories, including the state governorships in Zacatecas, Baja California Sur, and Tlaxcala. This was a significant development as, while PAN victories to the level of state governor had begun to be recognized under Salinas, the PRD continued to face often violent repression.[18]

Mexico's media landscape also became somewhat more pluralistic during the 1990s. The independent press saw particular growth as stalwarts such as *Novedades* and *Excélsior* lost ground to newer, more critical newspapers such as *Reforma* and *La Jornada*, to which Mexicans increasingly turned for news during the post-1994 crises.[19] Mexico's television landscape also underwent change, though it remained highly concentrated. The Salinas administration sold the Imevisión public broadcasting network to Ricardo Salinas Pliego, who in 1993 launched TV Azteca. Now Mexican broadcast television was effectively a duopoly rather than a monopoly, with Televisa and TV Azteca capturing 98 percent of Mexican television viewers by 1995.[20] The death of Televisa president Emilio Azcárraga Milmo in 1997 and the appointment of his son, Emilio Azcárraga Jean, combined with the November 1997 announcement that after twenty-six years Jacobo Zabludovsky would be replaced as anchor of Televisa's main news program *24 Horas*, increased the sense of perhaps not dramatic change but some renewal.[21]

A continued breakdown of collectivist and state-centered models of political identity and organization during the 1990s further led the Mexican government to increasingly look toward nongovernmental organizations (NGOs) to help formulate and deliver programs targeted at specific groups such as indigenous communities, women, and sexual minorities. On the positive side, sociologist María Luisa Tarrés argued that the drift away from state-centered solutions for social welfare provided spaces in which traditionally marginalized groups could organize and formulate policy in the continuing absence of and intermediary step toward representative, effective, and impartial state institutions.[22] Political scientist Sonia Alvarez, however, critiqued what she called an "NGOization" of political activism associated with neoliberal reform that encouraged a less critical political activism involving cooperation with the state in designing Pronasol-style self-help initiatives to incorporate the masses into the neoliberal market. Alvarez and other critics further queried whether the neoliberal state's recognition of individual over collective rights served to obscure and reinforce systematic inequalities that conditioned access to political or economic power.[23]

There were definite limits to the pluralism pursued and achieved by the Zedillo administration. After 1982, the PRI state displayed urgency in implementing economic reform, political reform was, in contrast, incremental and strategic.[24] While opening spaces within the state to electoral competition, the post-1982 PRI governments also increased the autonomy of economic decision-making from democratic pressures.[25] For example, the Salinas administration granted autonomy to Mexico's central bank in April 1994. Similarly, the privatization of publically held companies and consequent decrease of the state's role in the economy strengthened the relative influence and autonomy of private economic actors. Political scientist Pamela Starr judged that Zedillo's reforms obeyed a logic of not so much creating a truly democratic opening of Mexico's political system as buying the political space needed to carry out desired economic reforms.[26]

Furthermore, incidents of state violence and repression continued to occur during the Zedillo administration. Most notably, in March 1996 seventeen peasants were massacred by state police in Guerrero near the town of Aguas Blancas. There were also serious allegations of PRI complicity in the December 1997 massacre of forty-five Tzotzil members of an organization sympathetic to the EZLN in the Chiapas town of Acteal.[27] The national narrative of democratic transition supported by institutional and legislative change was in such instances powerfully challenged by the persistence of violent methods of political control at the local level in different parts of Mexico.

In the final analysis, the most significant outcome of the policies of the Zedillo administration was a swift advance in the deinstitutionalization of power that began with the 1982 debt crisis. The spectacular collapse of the Salinas social liberalism project was followed under Zedillo by the opening of spaces within the state to an increasing plurality of actors. In the process, the state may have become increasingly plural, but it also became less powerful relative to nonstate actors. Furthermore, the lack of the executive's power in many parts of Mexico became obvious in local outbreaks of violence or political conflict.

The Fight Continues between Revolutionaries, Liberals, and Conservatives

The rituals and language of patriotic commemorations appeared increasingly tired and mechanical as the Zedillo administration wore on with little hint of the Salinas administration's zeal for adapting and reforming revolutionary nationalism. Even Zedillo's first grito ceremony was described by the press as particularly low key, with the number of vivas kept to a small list of Hidalgo, "the heroes that gave us the patria," "our freedom," and Mexico.[28] Zedillo's second grito was similarly brief, and the president responded to reporters' questions about this brevity by joking that "the trick of the grito is not to *gritar* [cry out] too much."[29]

With the war against the EZLN continuing to simmer and flare throughout his presidency, Zedillo did, however, continue his predecessor's tradition of personally attending Zapata commemorations in Morelos.[30] The tone and content of Zedillo's speeches on these occasions also suggested continuity with Salinas's agrarian reform agenda. Indeed, the Zedillo administration largely maintained the institutions and policies of the previous administration, including the titling of ejido lands through Procede.[31]

Some of those within the PRI who felt uncomfortable with the openly neoliberal direction of the party continued to drift toward the PRD. One high-profile example of this movement is former PRI regent of Mexico City and President Salinas's peace negotiator with the EZLN in 1994, Manuel Camacho Solís. In 1996 Camacho Solís signaled his alienation from the PRI by attending a ceremony commemorating the anniversary of Lázaro Cárdenas's birth organized by Cuauhtémoc Cárdenas and attended mostly by PRD sympathizers.[32] Camacho subsequently became a member of the PRD and in 2003 was elected a federal deputy for the party.[33]

Ecclesiastic authorities also became more assertive in Mexico's public life with a lessening of formal and informal restrictions on their political activities during the de la Madrid, Salinas, and Zedillo presidencies. At the plenary assembly of the Mexican Episcopal Conference (CEM) in 1997, the CEM's president Sergio Obeso Rivera declared that the church was one of the few institutions that could "reconstruct someday the confidence and hope of Mexico" in the current climate of crisis.[34] Obeso further implicitly referred to the liberal Reform when acknowledging that priests were among the losers of the "hegemonic redistribution of the nineteenth century" and, in reference to the postrevolutionary period, mentioning that "many times the free expression and teaching of the faith has been restricted and the Catholic vision of the world scorned." However, he also argued that the church had historically played the protagonist in creating the mestizo culture during the colonial period and that effort should be applied to creating a national catechism to help Mexico through the current crisis.[35]

During the late 1990s, those opposed to the increasing role of the Catholic Church in Mexican public life continued to invoke the symbol of Benito Juárez to legitimize their cause. For example, evangelicals gathered at the Juárez Hemiciclo monument on the anniversary of Juárez's birth in 1996 to denounce the state's increasingly friendly relationship with the Catholic Church as betraying the principles of Juárez.[36] The Juárez Hemiciclo was also nicknamed the "Homociclo" by gay activists, as it became the main meeting place for gay-rights gatherings in Mexico City, with monuments to Juárez remaining common meeting places for demonstrations in support of sexual diversity across Mexico into the twenty-first century.[37] Politicians from the PRD, PRI, and other parties that approved legislation recognizing same-sex marriage in Mexico City and Coahuila during 2006 and 2007, respectively, also appealed to Juárez's example when faced with the objections of the church.[38] While such legislative changes were most strongly justified through appeals to liberal citizenship notions of diversity and human rights well established in international political discourse by the late twentieth century, the continued recourse to Juarista symbolism in Mexico demonstrated how transnational discourses of liberal modernity continued to be filtered and translated through established national symbolic frameworks.

During the 1990s, a rift expressed through the figure of Benito Juárez between the PRI and PRD on one hand, and the PAN on the other, emerged that went beyond simple electoral rivalries and centered on identity rather than ideology. While the PRI and PRD adopted mostly opposing positions to neoliberal reform, both parties identified with Mexico's liberal and revolutionary traditions. Furthermore, while the PAN largely agreed with the PRI on neoliberal reform, many of the party's members primarily identified with Mexican Catholic conservative traditions. This division was most notably revealed through the naming of streets and construction (and destruction) of historical monuments by local PAN administrations as they began to win power at a local level.[39]

In March 1997 the national press reported that conservative Catholic Panista mayor of Aguascalientes, Alfredo Reyes Velázquez, had renamed four of the state capital's streets after himself, the date he won the state elections, the date he took office, and PAN founder Manuel Gómez Morin. The fact that the street renamed for the mayor had previously borne the name of Juárez heightened the controversy. Occurring in a region with a deep Catholic tradition including conflict between Catholic militants and the postrevolutionary government during the 1920s and 1930s, critics interpreted this move as evidence of the PAN's lingering hostility to the principle of the secular state symbolized by Juárez. The PRI's Roque Villanueva drew attention to the PAN's efforts to rename streets during his Juárez commemoration speech in March 1997 and further connected it to issues of class and race, stating that he understood that "the humble origin of Juárez annoys those who were born in perfumed elites; the indigenous origin of Juárez annoys those who don't want to pass by indigenous people on their way."[40]

As the controversy in Aguascalientes swirled, representatives of the PRI and PAN also came into conflict over the naming of streets in Ciudad Juárez, Chihuahua. The PAN mayor approved the rebaptism of one after former PAN mayor Francisco Villarreal while ignoring the local PRI leader's proposal to rename another street in honor of assassinated 1994 PRI candidate Luis Donaldo Colosio.[41] Controversy also arose in Monterrey, Nuevo León, where the mayor renamed a street previously named for the constitution after a PAN federal deputy elected in 1946 and renamed another section of a road that bore the name of Reform hero Melchor Ocampo after a local priest.[42] The PAN municipal government in Naucalpan, State of Mexico, also held a referendum that was eventually defeated to rename avenues that bore the names of Luis Donaldo Colosio and ex-president Adolfo López Mateos.[43]

As historian Krystyna Von Hennenberg has argued, public spaces and monuments represent the most visible statements of official intent to construct a collective memory. However, as the most obvious signposts of this official intent, they are also the most vulnerable to change or reinterpretation.[44] Countries such as Russia, Italy, and Spain, where the state underwent significant and often rapid ideological and structural transformation during the twentieth century, thus saw mass changes in the nomenclature of public spaces.[45] However, as such changes rarely involve a wholesale renaming of public spaces, street names also often reveal much about different sediments left behind through processes of historical change.

In Mexico, the naming and renaming of streets and other public spaces had long been central to the symbolic construction of power. Prior to the 1990s, the names of conservative heroes and conservative nationalist symbols had been largely excluded from Mexico's urban landscape. This nomenclature was instead restricted by successive governments to the commemoration of a relatively small number of heroes, myths, and symbols. While significant local heroes also featured, the names of a select group such as Juárez, Zapata, or Cárdenas as well as key dates such as November 20 and documents connecting the state to citizenship rights such as the Constitution of 1917 were repeated in the public spaces of almost every major regional center across the national territory, from the sprawling Ciudad Juárez on the US border with Chihuahua to the small town of Benito Juárez near the southern border between Guatemala and Chiapas.

The PAN had since the 1980s mostly concentrated its political strategy on moving within rather than overtly challenging the revolutionary nationalist framework through identification with heroes such as Madero. The party at a national level thus responded to the controversy in Aguascalientes by distancing itself from the practice of renaming streets and calling on its members to desist from doing so.[46] However, the national party organization struggled to contain the ensuing debate over the true history of Mexico and especially of Juárez, revealing the persistence of counter-hegemonic conservative nationalisms. The president of the PAN in the State of Mexico, Noe Aguilar Tinajero, for example, provoked outraged responses from PRI and PRD leaders by arguing that streets bearing Juárez's name should be renamed, as Juárez was "a traitor to the patria."[47] Fellow PAN leaders and deputies from the State of Mexico further argued that Mexico's true history had been manipulated by the PRI government and called for a positive revalorization of historical figures such as Agustín de Iturbide, nineteenth-century conservative politician and historian Lucas Alamán, and Porfirio Díaz, as well as greater recognition of the PAN's heroes, such as founder Manuel Gómez Morin and 1988 presidential candidate Manuel Clouthier.[48]

Again, the national leadership of the PAN judged that such a close identification with traditional conservatism would hurt the party's chances in the approaching July 1997 federal legislative and Mexico City elections. The party's national president, Felipe Calderón, thus issued a statement describing Mexican history as a common history that included flawed but notable individuals and rejected opening up a debate about Juárez as serving no purpose other than to stir up old stigmas and divisions.[49] Aguilar Tinajero subsequently issued a statement denying that Juárez was a traitor to Mexico. However, in comments to an interviewer after issuing this retraction, he continued to suggest that there was valid historical evidence to at least question Juárez's nationalism.[50]

Representatives of the PRI used the Aguascalientes incident to reinforce historical critiques of the PAN as a party of the church and the "reaction."[51] The National Executive Committee of the PRI thus responded to Aguilar Tinajero's comments with a statement describing them as evidence that the PAN wanted to undermine Mexico's popular national project and, emphasizing Juárez's Zapotec ethnic identity to accuse the PAN of being anti-indigenous. To this end, the statement specifically called on Mexico's indigenous people as well as Juaristas more generally to mobilize in support of patriotic values and symbols.[52] A Day of Juarista Vindication was held on April 4 at the Juárez Hemiciclo in Mexico City as PRI supporters from the State of Mexico pledged to defend streets and plazas named after Juárez and used speeches and banners to accuse the PAN of being sympathetic to Emperor Maximilian.[53] Another gathering of 2,500 priístas was held on the same day in the municipality of Atizapán, State of Mexico, to denounce the PAN's attacks on national heroes.[54]

The PAN candidate for the head of the Mexico City government in 1997 and party veteran Carlos Castillo Peraza was thus forced to deny during the campaign that the PAN was a confessional party and to reiterate that the party believed in freedom of religion.[55] On the same day that priístas gathered at the Juárez Hemiciclo to denounce the PAN as antinationalist, Castillo began his day's campaigning with a guard of honor at a statue of Insurgente hero José María Morelos declaring the PAN's desire to show respect and admiration for one of the fundamental figures of the national history. However, the candidate also found himself confronted at this campaign event with questions about Juárez and the revival of historical conflicts between liberals and conservatives, which he refused to answer. When one reporter specifically asked Castillo whether he considered himself a liberal or conservative, Castillo responded, "Mexican."[56]

The notion of a reemergence of the historical conflict between liberals and conservatives accompanied the PAN's rise during the late 1990s. The national party sometimes reinforced this notion when, for example, in 1996 PAN national president Calderón offered gritos to Agustín de Iturbide and the Virgin of Guadalupe at the party's Independence Day celebrations in Mexico City.[57] As the PAN won more local and state governments, news also appeared in the national press of moralizing reforms undertaken by these governments.[58] When speaking to students at Mexico City's Iberoamericana University, Castillo in fact faced his most hostile questions not in relation to the mayor of Aguascalientes's renaming of streets, but regarding that mayor's censorship of a photographic exhibition on the grounds of public morality.[59] As the PRI state retreated, references to historical battles between liberals and conservatives in this way began to pervade Mexican politics and exposed a tension between the PAN's discourse of freedom and democracy and a strong push by many within the party to enforce conservative Catholic moral values from government.[60]

Ideological conflict waged through historical referents also became increasingly common between the PRD and PAN. For the PRD, the gradual erasing of nationalist symbols from the urban landscape provided a symbolic counterpart to the dismantling of economic nationalist and social spending programs it associated with the Cardenista roots of revolutionary nationalism. At his 1996 Revolution Day speech in the populous State of Mexico municipality of Nezahualcóyotl, PRD national president López Obrador thus reminded the crowd that not only was the PRI now "principal enemy of the program of Madero, Zapata, Villa, and Lázaro Cárdenas" but that the PAN had been formed in opposition to Lázaro Cárdenas and argued it was still motivated by the same aims of protecting privileges and selling out the country.[61] Castillo as the PAN's candidate for head of the Mexico City government, meanwhile, characterized the PRD not as a "decaying PRI" but rather "the PRI that left the PRI in '88."[62] Castillo further drew parallels between the PRD and the Echeverría and López Portillo administrations of the 1970s to imply that a PRD electoral victory in Mexico City represented a greater risk than that of the PRI, which had at least progressed from its pre-1982 statist development policies.[63]

What is most notable about this debate concerning the myths and symbols of revolutionary nationalism is the reticence of the PAN as an institution to publically endorse a reexamination of revolutionary nationalist mythology and the extent to which these conflicts concerned identity more than policy. While some local leaders may have enthusiastically entered into the debate, even the Aguascalientes mayor first attempted to deny that his name had replaced that of Juárez to the national press as pictures of the street signs and electoral credentials of the street's residents bearing the mayor's name were printed alongside such denials.[64] The PAN in this way strongly signaled that it did not want Mexicans to see a PAN electoral victory as representing a great rupture in Mexican history in the sense of a wholesale overthrowing of values associated in the popular imagination with the Mexican Revolution and nineteenth-century liberals.[65]

Calls to refrain from directly engaging in debate about Juárez's legacy in particular indicated the party's preferred tactic of tweaking rather than rewriting the established hegemonic nationalism. Some PRD politicians such as López Obrador did draw direct connections in their speeches between specific heroes and aspects of the post-revolutionary state in order to signal policy differences with other parties. However, by the Zedillo administration the PRI and PAN largely shared an ideological perspective in favor of further free market reform and the institutional left represented by the PRD had largely abandoned socialism. In this sense, belying the increasing competitiveness of electoral contests and debates over symbols such as Juárez, the 1990s were also a time of significant ideological convergence between Mexico's major political parties.

During the 1994 election campaign, there was even widely reported speculation that PAN candidate Diego Fernández de Cevallos refrained from campaigning when he started gaining on Zedillo in opinion polls to allow the PRI another period in office to complete the economic reform process against the backdrop of the EZLN uprising and implementation of NAFTA.[66] By the end of the Zedillo presidency NAFTA was in place and the military conflict with the EZLN had been confined to Chiapas. Furthermore, the dramatic austerity measures adopted in the wake of the 1994–1995 crisis had also largely secured the neoliberal economic model.

¡El cambio ya!

As part of his democratic reform agenda, Zedillo introduced reforms within the PRI such as presidential primaries that replaced the traditional ritual of the *dedazo*, whereby the president choose the PRI's candidate and thus his successor.[67] Beyond the openly bitter nature of the contest between candidates and their supporters, most notable about the PRI primary elections in 1999 was the eagerness of candidates to portray themselves as representing a break from the party's past. This continued into the 2000 presidential elections when the PRI sought to project a message of change, but one based on pragmatism and experience summed up in a PRI candidate Francisco Labastida campaign slogan as "change with purpose."[68]

PRD veteran Cuauhtémoc Cárdenas competed as the party's candidate once more, beginning his campaign in Morelia, Michoacán, by paying homage to the victims of the Tlatelolco massacre. While this underlined a theme of democratic transition that had been present in PRD campaigns since its formation, in 2000 the PRD fell back on the more nationalistic appeal of an "alliance for Mexico."[69] Having struggled to recapture the momentum of 1988 during the 1994 electoral campaign, Cárdenas's electoral prospects in his third campaign soon proved relatively slim. Ironically, Cárdenas's historic victory in the Mexico City elections three years earlier hurt his popularity by linking him to the city's sharp rise in crime and poverty after 1994.[70]

Television was a particularly important actor in the 2000 elections. A 1999 survey by the Federal Electoral Institute (IFE) found that two-thirds of Mexicans learned about politics from television and political actors increasingly tailored their campaigns to use television as a way of transmitting clear, simple messages into millions of Mexican homes.[71] The importance of television was confirmed by a poll that found 79 percent of voters cited television news programs as the source from which they received a lot or some of their political information.[72] This gave television, and particularly the Televisa and TV Azteca consortiums, an enormous and growing amount of influence over Mexican politics.

The candidate who attracted the most interest in the lead-up to the 2000 elections and who more generally appeared best suited to this new era of campaigning was the PAN's Vicente Fox. Fox ticked a number of boxes for Mexican conservatism in the late twentieth century through his public professions of Catholic faith and private business experience as a former Coca-Cola executive with a family background in agribusiness. However, Fox's broader appeal was based on the cultivation of a pragmatic popular image. Putting himself forward as a candidate almost three years prior to the elections, Fox demonstrated a flair for self-promotion. In speeches and interviews peppered with colloquialisms, Fox adopted an informal personal style reflected in campaign attire such as cowboy hats, leather boots, and jeans.[73]

Figure 6.5. PAN presidential candidate Vicente Fox is presented with a portrait of Benito Juárez on a visit to Oaxaca during the 2000 presidential campaign. Courtesy Henry Romero/Reuters.

Debates about historical divisions between liberals and conservatives did continue to emerge during the campaign (fig. 6.5). The most notable example of this was when in September 1999 Fox reenacted Hidalgo's grito holding a standard of the Virgin of Guadalupe presented to him by his sons on the campaign trail. This earned Fox a rebuke from the interior ministry and a fine from the Federal Electoral Institute for contravening the ban on using religious imagery in electoral campaigns.[74] Fox also, however, frequently employed nationalist symbolism, particularly that of the Insurgente independence struggle. The notion of the PRI's defeat as a new independence for Mexico was a recurrent motif of the Fox campaign, and in November 1999 Fox rang the bell of the church in Dolores in another reenactment of Hidalgo's grito to, in his words, "wake up the people of Mexico."[75] Hidalgo thus served as Fox's principal historical reference point, while Fox also cited Madero as an historical figure he particularly admired.[76]

The central theme of the Fox campaign was, however, change. Slogans that ranged from the one-word "Now!" and "Today!" to others such as "The change that works for you" and "Every day there are more of us who want a change" were repeated throughout the campaign to great effect.[77] After eighteen years of almost continual crisis, the promise of change proved more attractive to voters in 2000 than during the 1980s. This promise did lack specifics, however. For example, Fox's economic proposals never moved far beyond general promises to make the economy grow by 7 percent a year, create a million jobs annually, and combat corruption.[78]

During his presidential campaign, Fox did make some symbolically important promises that suggested a post-PRI state would be more open to dialogue and finally support universal citizenship rights guaranteed by the rule of law. Fox committed to investigating the events of October 2, 1968, thus ending decades of impunity and cover-ups characteristic of the Mexican legal system's close relationship with the PRI.[79] Fox also offered to solve the conflict in Chiapas within "fifteen minutes" of becoming president by withdrawing the army and establishing dialogue with the EZLN and other relevant actors.[80] These promises reinforced the idea that the PRI's defeat would mean an end to the authoritarianism, impunity, and the informal rules according to which power worked in Mexico and the beginning of a new, democratic era involving the impartial rule of law and respect for human rights.

Toward the end of the campaign, Fox used polling numbers in his advertising to promote the idea of the useful vote to encourage those planning to vote for Cárdenas—who would surely lose—to cast that vote for Fox as the leading opposition candidate who could realistically end PRI rule.[81] In this way, Fox employed a tactic characteristic of PAN election campaigns since the 1980s that sought to transcend ideology and even policy by making elections a referendum on democracy that required the PRI's defeat to bring about democracy through alternation in power.

Change, Juárez, and Tlatelolco

Fox's election strategy proved a success, with the PAN presidential candidate receiving 42.5 percent of the vote to the PRI's 36 and PRD's 16.6 percent.[82] In his inaugural address, Fox invoked Francisco Madero to establish the historical importance of this victory, proclaiming, "Today, at the close an historical era marked by authoritarianism, the figure [of Madero] rises again as a post which marks the route that never should have been abandoned."[83] However, PRI legislators also used the

speech to suggest the victory of Fox and the PAN represented conservative, reactionary change. When the new president began to talk about
Mexico's education system, the legislators responded by chanting
"Juárez, Juárez, Juárez!" to signify their defense of secular education.[84]
Fox administration officials to some extent encouraged such suspicions
by quickly removing a portrait of Juárez hanging in the presidential
office of Los Pinos and replacing it with one of Madero.[85] Prior to his
inauguration, Fox also visited and prayed at the Basilica of the Virgin
of Guadalupe, a presidential display of religious devotion that would
have been unthinkable under the PRI.[86]

The incoming administration did not appear interested, however, in
fomenting iconoclasm against established national heroes. The portrait
of Juárez thus moved from Los Pinos to the offices of the interior minister and the presidency's spokesperson emphasized to reporters that the
incoming administration respected Juárez as a national hero.[87] Indeed,
Fox spoke at the first official Juárez commemoration of his presidency
held in the National Palace, reassuring Mexicans that "political change
does not require a rupture with our history and those who think so are
wrong."[88] The exchange between PRI legislators and Fox during his
inaugural address and the president's appropriation of revolutionary
hero Madero as a symbol of democracy were instead representative of
a political transition based on subtle adjustments rather than a dramatic
rupture.

The ambiguous relationship between the incoming PAN administration and established nationalist myths based on liberal and revolutionary nationalist traditions did, however, open a rich symbolic space that
could be used by political opponents. Most notably, ex-president of the
PRD López Obrador was also elected head of the Mexico City government on July 2, 2000, and frequently communicated his opposition to
Fox through the symbol of Juárez. At the beginning of López Obrador's
inaugural address four days after that of Fox, a PRD local deputy presented him with a portrait of Juárez and, with the new president in
attendance, López Obrador especially praised Juárez's contribution to
national history during his speech. Press reports the next day noted that
these were some of the few statements that President Fox and Mexico
City cardinal Norberto Rivera, also in attendance, did not applaud.[89]

More than ruptures with Mexico's history, it was the sense of a lack
of change that fed growing popular disappointment with Mexico's post-
2000 political system. The investigation into the Tlatelolco massacre
that over the 1980s and 1990s came to symbolize Mexico's struggle for

democracy was emblematic of the Fox administration's failure to live up to campaign promises of change. Upon taking office, Fox quickly set up a special prosecutor's office to investigate the Tlatelolco massacre and dirty war of the 1960s and 1970s. As had PRI presidents before him, however, Fox faced intense opposition to the investigation from within the state and particularly from the armed forces. Those assigned by the administration to investigate government repression of student protestors thus soon found their work becoming more difficult as the administration retreated from its initially supportive attitude and access to information became increasingly limited. On July 22, 2005, legal definitions so improbable that they appeared designed to fail were finally used to lay the charge of genocide against ex-president Luis Echeverría over the murder of twenty-five students in 1971. A judge predictably dismissed this charge four days later. In the end, Fox's special prosecutor failed to either successfully convict the perpetrators of any crimes or clarify the events themselves.[90]

In 2001 Fox had also promised to help clear up a contemporary example of legal impunity that had gained national and international attention beginning in the early 1990s: the murder of young women in Ciudad Juárez, Chihuahua. Again, the new administration appeared unable or unwilling to effectively apply the legal system to solving this epidemic of murders that became known as a "feminicide."[91] An apparent lack of commitment to seriously tackling the issue caused controversy when in May 2005 Fox complained about the media "reheating" the story and not seeing the continuing murders of young women "in their proper dimension." Fox argued that the issue had already been resolved through prior arrests despite well-publicized allegations of police torture being used to elicit confessions and the fact that the murders continued.[92] The idea of the transition in 2000 as the start of a new era of equality under the rule of law therefore seemed less and less credible as the term of the first post-PRI president progressed.

The defeat of the PRI in 2000 was also not followed by significant economic growth. While between 1941 and 1982 GDP growth never fell below 3 percent, during the Fox presidency it averaged 1 percent. Only 3 million formal jobs were created for the 8 million new entrants to the Mexican labor market during the first decade of the twenty-first century and there was a spike in informal and precarious employment as well as unemployment and migration. In the latter respect, the money sent home by the average 600,000 Mexicans who annually migrated informally to the United States became one of Mexico's principal sources of foreign currency, with yearly remittances to Mexico reaching a record US$26 billion in 2007.[93] On a material level, then, the change promised by Fox also failed to bring about a demonstrable improvement in the lives of most Mexicans.

Even the democratic legitimacy of Mexico's political system was soon thrown into doubt by the Fox administration's response to the rising popularity of López Obrador, a politician who openly criticized the neoliberal model. By early 2004 polls showed López Obrador as the leader in voter preferences for the 2006 presidential elections by a wide margin over potential opponents.[94] In May 2004 the federal Attorney General's Department (PGR) cited legal technicalities involving the construction of a road to a hospital by the Mexico City government to request that the federal Chamber of Deputies vote to remove López Obrador's legal immunity. This proceeding, known as the *desafuero*, would mean that López Obrador would be forced to step down as head of the Mexico City government and almost certainly be prohibited from competing in the 2006 presidential elections.[95]

On the day of the vote, April 7, 2005, López Obrador addressed the Chamber of Deputies and in a nationally televised speech criticized President Fox for "these dishonorable proceedings for our incipient democracy," the Supreme Court "for subordinating the high principles of justice and the Constitution to purely political instructions ordered by the powerful interest groups of the moment," and a general context in which "in the country of impunity . . . they are going to try to disenfranchise me for trying to build a road to a hospital." López Obrador further attempted to discredit the legal action against him as anti-democratic by drawing parallels with the Porfirian regime's exclusion of Madero from the 1910 elections. Indeed, he noted in his speech that the great-grandfather of the Fox government's interior minister, Santiago Creel, had been a minister in Porfirio Díaz's government while Creel's grandfather had participated in the coup in which Madero was overthrown and assassinated. Finally, López Obrador attacked Fox's promise of change, accusing those who promised change of lying and lamenting that "the 'useful vote' has become a 'useless vote,' time has sadly been wasted with the so-called government of change, and nothing has been achieved, absolutely nothing, while there are so many national demands unsatisfied."[96]

The legal situation regarding the case soon deteriorated into a farce that drew state institutions into further disrepute, and Fox found himself shadowed by protestors as he traveled around the country.[97] On

Figure 6.6. Vicente Fox announces a review of the case against López Obrador in a televised address from the presidential residence of Los Pinos in front of a portrait of Francisco Madero. Courtesy Gustavo Benítez/Presidencia/AFP.

April 27, 2005, three days after an estimated 1 million people marched down Mexico City's Paseo de la Reforma to the Zócalo to protest the desafuero, Fox delivered a televised address to the nation in front of a portrait of Madero in which he announced the replacement of the attorney general, a review of the case against López Obrador, and an assurance that "my government will not prevent anyone from participating in the next federal election" (fig. 6.6).[98] It was a humiliating retreat in a battle that cast significant doubt on the democratic vocation of the Fox administration and the credibility of the institutions of the Mexican state more broadly in the post-PRI state era.[99]

Soon after this backdown, in July 2005 Fox unsuccessfully proposed that the anniversary of his election be celebrated as Democracy Day.[100] In May 2006 the government then renamed the publically funded National Institute for Historical Studies of the Mexican Revolution (INEHRM) to the National Institute for Historical Studies of the Mexican Revolutions—a pluralizing of "Revolution"—in order to broaden the institution's remit to include research into the political transition in 2000 as well as the independence struggle.[101] While deemphasizing the central importance of the Mexican Revolution to Mexico's national epic, the government thus also sought to promote Mexico's democratic transition as a new turning point in Mexican history. However, the revolutionary significance of 2000 in terms of practical improvements to the impartial rule of law, the satisfaction of material needs, or even the democratic ability of Mexicans to elect their own leaders remained unclear as Fox prepared to leave office.

The Theology of Oil

As detailed in snapshot 6, the second PAN presidency of Mexico under Felipe Calderón proved more troubled than the first. In contrast to the democratic triumphalism of Fox's victory, the turbulent Calderón administration began amid protest marches and allegations of electoral fraud by López Obrador supporters. The administration ended with Mexico plunged into its most violent period since the Revolution. Under President Calderón the credibility and power of the Mexican state visibly weakened, most vividly through the apparent loss of control by Mexican law enforcement over significant parts of the country to organized crime. Many of the PRI state's remaining rituals of presidential power, such as the inaugural address and annual informe, were also modified in response to the disruptions caused by protesting supporters of López Obrador inside and outside state political institutions. In both cases, the Calderón administration modified the rituals so that the president was no longer required to speak in front of the unpredictable Chamber of Deputies and would instead address the nation on television in front of an invited audience.

The weakness of the executive was also evident when Calderón attempted to reform Mexico's energy sector in 2008 to allow increased private investment in state oil company Pemex, created following Lázaro Cárdenas's oil expropriation in 1938. The symbolic importance of Pemex and the power of the Pemex workers' union had effectively insulated the company from the mass privatization of state-owned assets following the 1982 debt crisis. Fox had, however, proposed and ultimately failed to increase private investment in Pemex operations.[102] In the same way that Salinas and Zedillo paid particular personal attention to commemorating the legacy of Zapata while pursuing contentious agrarian reforms, Fox and Calderón showed great care to personally attend oil-expropriation commemorations. Both presidents attempted to use such occasions to reaffirm that Pemex would not be privatized while at the same time portraying the actions of Lázaro Cárdenas in 1938 as driven by a patriotic desire not so much for public ownership of oil as the maximizing of benefits that Mexicans could derive from the nation's oil reserves.[103]

Calderón made energy reform an early and totemic issue of his presidency and, less than a month after the seventieth anniversary of the oil expropriation, on April 8, 2008, the Calderón administration sent its energy reform proposal to the Chamber of Deputies. The reform sought to increase the independence of the company from the state and Pemex's ability to form strategic alliances with private enterprise in the exploitation, refining, and marketing of Mexico's energy reserves. The administration further proposed the creation of *bonos ciudadanos* (citizen bonds), which could only be purchased by Mexican citizens. This initiative promoted an individualized and direct relationship between Mexicans and Pemex as quasi-shareholders without the state as an intermediary.[104] Explaining the reforms in a nationally televised address, the president once more invoked the example of Lázaro Cárdenas, calling on Mexicans of this generation to act with "true patriotism" to better take advantage of Mexico's natural resources while reiterating that, as oil was "an emblem of national sovereignty," Pemex would not be privatized.[105]

Despite Calderón's attempts to reframe the discussion, the ensuing debate focused precisely on the issue of privatization. Particularly prominent among opponents was López Obrador, who formed a National Movement in Defense of Oil. López Obrador presented the Calderón administration's reforms as illustrative of the contrast between contemporary political and economic elites colluding to divide up national assets for their personal benefit and the patriotic Cárdenas, who had secured Mexico's oil reserves and used the revenues for the good of all the Mexican people (fig. 6.7).[106] In a more concrete sense, opponents of the reform argued that Pemex's undoubted problems resulted from a deliberate and dishonest strategy of underinvestment and overexploitation by the Fox and Calderón administrations designed to create a pretext to privatize Pemex "through the backdoor."[107]

Supporters of the reforms argued that fossilized nationalist mythology was clouding rational debate about how best to develop Mexico's oil resources. A September 2008 issue of the journal *Letras Libres*, which had evolved from *Vuelta* in 1998, that featured extensive analysis of Calderón's reforms by intellectuals and scientists framed this

Figure 6.7. A banner at a López Obrador rally in June 2008 against proposed reforms allowing greater private investment in state oil company Pemex. The text reads "Now it is up to you to defend what is ours" and depicts (left to right) Miguel Hidalgo, Francisco Villa, Lázaro Cárdenas, López Obrador, Emiliano Zapata, and Benito Juárez. Photo by author.

discussion by titling the issue "The Theology of Oil" and featured a cover showing cherubic angels perched on a cloud at the base of an oil barrel emblazoned with the Pemex logo as beams of heavenly light streamed out from behind.[108] In the pages of *El Universal* sociologist Roger Bartra also described the nationalistic vision of oil as "overpowering any scientific, economic, or technical consideration" and historian Héctor Aguilar Camin sentenced that "nationalist mythology" was one of the calamities of Pemex.[109] A common culprit cited by many of these critics were school history textbooks, and *El Universal* published large pictures of the school texts relating to the oil expropriation alongside the comments of intellectuals.[110]

The Calderón administration itself largely avoided such a direct confrontation with revolutionary nationalist mythology. Instead, administration officials continued with a broadly similar argument to that which had underwritten the revolutionary realism of the 1980s and agrarian reform of the 1990s. This argument was that the nationalist course of action that most honored the intent of the heroes of the past was to modernize Pemex rather than preserve the status quo.

Despite treading a well-worn path in this respect, Calderón and the supporters of the reforms ultimately lost the argument. In a practical sense, this was because after having remained largely on the sidelines of the debate, the PRI made a political judgment not to provide the necessary legislative votes to support reforms on the grounds they risked Mexico's sovereignty over its oil reserves.[111] The legislation ultimately negotiated between the PAN and members of the PRI and passed in October 2008 proposed relatively minor reforms and omitted the question of private investment.[112]

The responses to an *El Universal* poll in February 2008 on the reforms provide some clues as to why the Calderón administration failed to win the public debate and secure its signature legislative reform. This poll found that when people were asked who they thought would most benefit from the energy reform, 68 percent nominated "the government" and "businesspeople." When polled on who would least benefit, the most popular responses were "people like you" and "all Mexicans" with 32 and 31 percent respectively choosing each option.[113] This suggests, as Claudio Lomnitz has argued, that in the post-PRI state era "the pyramidal imagery that was typical of revolutionary nationalism has been replaced by various images of the political elite as a free-floating crust of predators."[114] Regardless of what people thought of the merits of the proposed reforms themselves—and opinion for and against was fairly evenly divided—it seemed few were convinced that the Mexican political class and private sector would act in the interests of the Mexican people.

A New Institutional Revolution?

By the end of Calderón's term there was a pervasive sense in public political discussion that Mexico's economic and social model was worn out and needed to be profoundly reformed.[115] During that year's election campaign each candidate again promised change. Despite now-tense relations with the PRD, López Obrador competed once more as the party's candidate in coalition with smaller left-wing parties and argued for a rebirth of the republic that would signify a fourth transformation following on from Independence, the liberal Reform, and the Mexican Revolution.[116] PAN candidate Josefina Vázquez Mota, meanwhile, struggled with the legacy of the previous two PAN administrations while campaigning under the somewhat cryptic slogan "Josefina, Different."[117]

It was, however, the PRI that won back the presidency in 2012. The PRI candidate was Enrique Peña Nieto, an ex-governor (2005–2011) of Mexico's most populous state, the State of Mexico that adjoins Mexico City. Youthful, handsome, and, following the death of his first wife in 2007, married to a former telenovela actress, Peña Nieto was well suited to politics in the television era. Indeed, critics claimed early in the Calderón administration that the Televisa consortium—whose independent political power massively grew as that of the state declined post-2000—was deliberately positioning Peña Nieto as Mexico's next president through frequent and favorable national television coverage.[118] Peña Nieto and the PRI did not promise Mexicans a return to revolutionary nationalism in 2012. The PRI candidate instead proudly professed a lack of ideology and promised voters a pragmatic, practical, and effective government following the turbulence and legislative deadlock of the Calderón and Fox administrations.[119]

While national television coverage and favorable opinion poll ratings leading up to the campaign suggested an easy electoral victory, Peña Nieto faced a bruising campaign. The Internet emerged in 2012 as a particularly important space in which a new generation of politically engaged Mexicans who did not trust either the political class or the private media could disseminate information and organize. Social media sites such as YouTube, Twitter, and Facebook were used to organize protest marches that adopted a nonpartisan but strongly anti–Peña Nieto and antisystem stance through the final months of the campaign.[120] These movements arose following a confrontation between student protesters and the PRI candidate at Mexico City's Iberoamericana University in May 2012 and united under the name #YoSoy132 (#IAm132), the Twitter hashtag used to express solidarity with the students of the Iberoamericana.[121]

Alongside broader critiques of Mexico's political and economic model, a main focus of #YoSoy132 quickly became the concentration of media ownership in Mexico and particularly the power and alleged political bias of the Televisa consortium. The release during the campaign of a series of articles in the UK newspaper the *Guardian* based on allegedly leaked internal documents from Televisa and an associated promotional company fed these protests. The documents outlined hidden sums paid by the Fox administration for promotional campaigns, a concerted strategy of negative coverage on news and entertainment programs to ensure López Obrador did not win the 2006 presidential elections, and payments made from an undisclosed source to promote Peña Nieto's image while governor of the State of Mexico.[122] While Televisa was no longer a "soldier of the PRI," as its then-owner had declared in 1988, such allegations painted the picture of the company involved with political elites in shadowy dealings involving the trafficking of influence and money aimed at shaping electoral outcomes through the control and manipulation of information. Ex-president Fox reinforced this picture of elite collusion obscured by electoral competition when he called on Mexicans in 2012 to cast a useful vote for the PRI to ensure that López Obrador as the candidate who most challenged Mexico's economic model did not win.[123]

On election day, July 1, 2012, Peña Nieto won by a significant margin with 39 percent of votes cast to López Obrador's 32 percent and Vázquez Mota's 26 percent. However, as in 2006, the 2012 presidential elections ended amid doubts over the truly democratic nature of Mexico's political system. In addition to controversy over relations between Peña Nieto and Televisa, PAN and PRD officials made serious allegations of vote buying reinforced by newspaper reports in the days following the elections, illustrated with photographs of customers overwhelming outlets of the supermarket chain Soriana holding cards charged with store credit, which the shoppers claimed to have been given by members of the PRI in exchange for their vote.[124]

A democratic mythology with either 1968 or 2000 as its great rupture directing Mexico toward a democratic present with impartial institutions and free and fair elections thus continued to lack credibility. This lack of credibility became shockingly evident almost two years into the Peña Nieto administration following the disappearance and murder of forty-three students studying at a rural teachers' college in Ayotzinapa, Guerrero. The crime stunned Mexicans due to the brutal nature of the rounding up, executing, and incineration of the bodies of students apparently traveling to a protest march against government teacher-hiring practices. The students had also planned on raising funds to travel to Mexico City to participate in marches commemorating the 1968 Tlatelolco massacre of student protesters.

Behind this crime was a murky web of complicities that appeared to involve the municipal government of Iguala—led by the PRD mayor José Luis Abarca Velázquez—the local police force, and organized criminal syndicates, while rumors also swirled of the Mexican Armed Forces' involvement. Such a dynamic vividly displayed how citizens in many parts of Mexico were left not just unprotected by the state but were at times brutally victimized by state institutions that cooperated with criminal organizations.[125] This crisis affected the legitimacy of the entire Mexican political and justice system.

One result of this crisis of legitimacy was the decomposition of the PRD. While the party during the Calderón administration had become consumed with internal conflicts, these became particularly heated once the dominant faction signed on along with PAN leaders to cooperate with Peña Nieto's reform agenda, titled the Pact for Mexico, soon after the 2012 elections. This led López Obrador to leave the PRD and form a new party called Morena. Following the Ayotzinapa scandal, Cuauhtémoc Cárdenas also resigned after he publically accused the party of becoming too close to the PRI and PAN and losing popular credibility.[126] This fracturing of Mexico's most established left-wing party amid recriminations from its most prominent historical leaders of moral decay reinforced a sense of decay and cynicism pervading Mexico's political, social, and economic life.

As well as the democratic nature of Mexico's political system, the PRI's return to the presidential residency of Los Pinos did not significantly clarify the ambiguous relationship between established nationalist historical myths and symbols and the Mexican state. Where Calderón had failed, the PRI led by Peña Nieto succeeded in passing legislation supported by the PAN to allow private investment in Pemex. Peña Nieto indeed announced these proposals to the nation in a televised address standing in front of a portrait of Lázaro Cárdenas in the very room of Los Pinos where Cárdenas had announced the oil expropriation seventy-five years earlier.[127]

The physical and symbolic topography of monuments, heroes, and myths developed to assist state-building following the Revolution had survived the end of the PRI state and the return of the PRI to the presidency, and they continued to serve as a space for antistate activism. On Revolution Day 2014 tens of thousands of protesters took to the streets to demand justice for the students of Ayotzinapa. Three main contingents departed from the Angel of Independence, Monument to the Revolution, and Plaza de las Tres Culturas in Tlatelolco to converge on the Zócalo. Felipe de la Cruz, the father of one of the disappeared students and spokesman for the other parents, likened the government of Peña Nieto to that of 1968 and told the crowd gathered in the Zócalo that "today, November 20, we do not celebrate the 104th anniversary of the Mexican Revolution. If we are standing here, it is because our government has mutilated our Constitution for its own benefit and to justify its acts."[128]

On December 6, 2014, the centenary of the taking of Mexico City by the troops of Francisco Villa and Emiliano Zapata, protest organizers arranged a symbolic taking of Mexico City for the students of Ayotzinapa. In a march mixing protesters and people on horseback and in historical costume reenacting the entry of Villa and Zapata into Mexico City, participants walked or rode from the Angel of Independence to the Monument to the Revolution. There, Villa's great grandson told the crowd that the revolutionary hero would have been saddened by the execution of the students and called for an end to the violence, disappearances, and chaos that had overtaken Mexico. De la Cruz, meanwhile, referring the identification of the remains of one of the students, Alexander Mora Valencia, told those assembled in front of the monument containing the remains of Villa, Cárdenas, Madero, Carranza, and Calles that those who thought they would sit and cry were wrong. Instead, de la Cruz continued, "We will not cry for Alexander, but hope that his death will be a seed that makes the revolution grow."[129]

The Post-PRI Nation-State

By the time Fox was elected president Mexico's postrevolutionary political and economic model had largely taken the shape that it was to retain post-2000 through a process involving the retreat of the state and a deinstitutionalization of power that took place in fits and starts following the 1982 debt crisis. If the appearance of the PRI state's hegemonic rule was far sturdier than the reality, following the Calderón administration's launching of military operations against drug cartels in December 2006 the appearance of the Mexican state as a "swiss cheese" state whose power was shot full of holes was all too apparent as a seemingly uncontainable wave of violence spread across large parts of Mexico.[130] Since the spectacular collapse of the Salinas administration's social liberalism project in 1994, a defining feature of Mexican public life indeed became a not entirely new but more obvious distance, if not antagonism, between the Mexican state and society and an unclear relationship between local and national authorities.

Revolutionary nationalism gained legitimacy precisely due to its effectiveness as a multidirectional language of communication between elite and popular classes reinforced by the extension of citizenship rights. A similar process did not occur to accompany the dismantling of the PRI state and, in this context, it was unlikely that a new nationalist narrative that posited either October 2, 1968, or July 2, 2000, as a rupture that propelled the Mexican nation toward the present as a superior democratic stage in the nation's history would be convincing. Instead, symbols shaped in the context of the postrevolutionary state- and nation-building project retained popular legitimacy post-2000 but continued to sit uneasily with the neoliberal development model and its attendant mechanisms for popular inclusion within the state such as the election process.

As the institutional and cognitive political framework of legitimate class-based political identities of postrevolutionary corporatism weakened, new identities based on race, culture, gender, or sexuality were increasingly recognized as legitimate by the state as manifestations of modern democratic pluralism. However, confidence in the state's ability to protect citizenship rights old or new did not follow. The two highest-grossing locally produced documentaries in Mexican history were released in cinemas during the Calderón presidency and they reflect this reality. The first was *Fraude: México 2006*, a documentary released in November 2007 detailing the López Obrador movement's claims of electoral fraud by the PAN government in alliance with elements of the PRI and private interests such as Televisa.[131] The second was *Presunto culpable* (Presumed Guilty), a documentary detailing the torturous experience of a twenty-year-old man convicted of murder by a Mexican justice system that appeared designed less to prosecute criminals than to fulfill bureaucratic requirements to record convictions regardless of the evidence.[132]

These films symbolized a deep sense of disillusionment with the fulfillment of the universal liberal democratic citizenship rights such as political pluralism and equality before the law promised by proponents of democratic change pre-2000. This disillusionment included serious questioning about what democracy and the rule of law really meant in regard to how power relations functioned in contemporary Mexico. One of the key languages through which such questions were debated, however, remained revolutionary nationalism and the legacy of its great heroes such as Juárez, Zapata, and Madero.

In October 2007 the PAN mayor of Boca del Río, Veracruz, announced plans to unveil a monument to Vicente Fox along one of the city's main beachfront roads. Running between one named for the independence struggle and one named for PRI president Miguel Alemán (1946–1952), the road alongside which the statue was to be erected had already been renamed the Boulevard Vicente Fox in October 2006, sparking protests from local members of the PRI.[1] The PRI governor of Veracruz, Fidel Herrera, described the decision to build a statue of Fox as a provocation and the day before the planned October 14 unveiling, a group of local members of the PRI gathered at the statue for a protest. In a scene recalling the toppling of the statue of Iraqi dictator Saddam Hussein in Baghdad following the 2003 US invasion, the group pulled the statue to the ground. When it fell, the hand of the statue, which was held aloft as if waving, snapped off and the protestors joked that they'd cut off his hand for being a thief.[2] Municipal authorities were then permitted by the crowd to carry the statue away, patch it up, and re-erect it two months later. At the time of writing, it continues to stand on the Boulevard Vicente Fox with its back to the beach and arm frozen aloft in a wave toward a somewhat desolate area of Boca del Río.

Merely being incorporated into the urban landscape as a statue or street name does not imply that Fox will inevitably be considered a national hero or that July 2, 2000, will be popularly remembered as a significant step forward in the Mexican nation's journey through history. Nor does the toppling of his statue necessarily mean he will be considered a villain. At the end of twelve years of PAN presidencies, people still flew into an airport bearing the name of President Gustavo Díaz Ordaz in Acapulco and lived in a Mexico City neighborhood named for President José López Portillo. That statues, roads, and airports carry the names or images of ex-presidents or public officials does not shape how these figures are remembered, with neither Díaz Ordaz nor López Portillo having overcome negative associations with the 1968 Tlatelolco massacre or the 1982 debt crisis respectively. If history is any guide, how Fox, the "change" of 2000, the challenge of Andrés Manuel López Obrador, or the return of the PRI with Enrique Peña Nieto are remembered will depend on how or if they weave themselves as myths and symbols into the way in which Mexicans perceive the connections between their identities and interests, rather than whether Vicente Fox, López Obrador, or Peña Nieto Boulevards become common features of Mexico's cities and towns.

Revolutionary Nation-Building

The reason for the enduring popular legitimacy of the myths and symbols of revolutionary nationalism is best understood by considering how this nationalist framework represented a progression from Porfirian liberal nationalism. Postrevolutionary elites did not simply add a new revolutionary end of history with associated myths and symbols to the Porfirian liberal synthesis. They instead attempted to move beyond the late Porfiriato's top-down style of nationalist instruction by developing revolutionary nationalism as a framework that permitted—within certain limits—the ongoing and reasonably flexible construction of hegemony through dialogue and negotiation between elite and popular groups. Revolutionary nationalism therefore provided far greater scope than had Porfirian nationalism to serve as a durable idiom in which a broad range of actors across Mexico could communicate.

Heroes such as Emiliano Zapata, Benito Juárez, and Lázaro Cárdenas became part of a shared framework of national myths and symbols through the promotion and repetition of their image using the public education system, state bureaucracy, state-sponsored "invented traditions," and the patriotic remapping of the urban landscape. They came to have popular meaning and legitimacy, however, due to the way such symbols were articulated through revolutionary nationalism to the reasonable promise, if not always practical fulfillment, of gains for Mexicans. These gains included land for peasants, some labor rights for workers, and rising prosperity for the urban middle class. According to this historical narrative, Zapata had fought so that peasants could own the land they worked and Juárez strived to build a modern and secular state as well as to defend the nation against foreign invaders. As the last of revolutionary nationalism's great heroes, Cárdenas translated the cause of the Revolution into reality by nationalizing Mexico's oil reserves and implementing Zapata's dream through mass land redistribution.

How and to what extent revolutionary nationalism became integrated into cognitive frameworks differed widely across Mexico. Even within a single state such as Chiapas, postrevolutionary reforms, if they arrived at all, were often filtered through established power networks that survived the Revolution. The state's rhetoric of social justice was also very often not or only partially supported by material gains. By the late 1950s rising economic inequality and repression of dissident labor movements particularly belied revolutionary appeals for legitimacy. However, revolutionary nationalism at least represented a starting point as a language of negotiation through which popular and elite actors symbolically recognized the legitimacy of one another and could communicate, sometimes with beneficial outcomes for popular classes.

By the 1940s the symbolic framework of revolutionary nationalism was loosely reinforced by the institutional framework of the PRI state. This framework involved a conception of power flowing upward from corporatist peasant, worker, and popular sectoral organizations that integrated the masses into the PRI as a hegemonic state party. The PRI linked these sectoral organizations to an executive, which sat at the top of a political model structured in a way that resembled a pyramid. Again, this national state may have been more jalopy than juggernaut in that it was often unable to impose its will where it faced sustained resistance, as in case of the survival of prerevolutionary power structures in Chiapas and the resistance of Catholicism to the secularization and anticlerical measures of the 1920s and 1930s. It was precisely this weakness, however, that made negotiating its reform agenda an essential part of the construction of the PRI state's hegemonic rule.

During the post-1968 period, the nation and the state were established facts of daily life for most Mexicans. Heroes such as Zapata, Juárez, and Cárdenas may have often arrived in communities as part of a broader template of national identity promoted by the national state. People may have also learned to invoke terms such as "the Revolution" or the names of national heroes when dealing with state officials as a practical concession in return for material benefits. By accepting and adopting the same revolutionary nationalist language throughout Mexico's postrevolutionary twentieth century, however, a diverse array of elite and popular actors contributed to the process of reinforcing and renewing revolutionary nationalism's legitimacy. The fact that both state and nonstate actors often challenged one another using the same revolutionary nationalist myths and symbols demonstrates how it functioned as a symbolic framework for organizing Mexican society that incorporated both state and popular claims to power and legitimacy and as a language of negotiation.

Revolutionary Nationalism in the Neoliberal Era

In the preceding chapters, we have seen how revolutionary nationalist myths and symbols were invoked during the post-1968 period of economic, social, and political transition. A particularly novel aspect of the period following the 1982 debt crisis, when compared to the Cardenista period of state-building of the 1930s, is that the Mexican state drew upon the symbolic power it gained during earlier periods of state-building to legitimize its retreat from rather than expansion into an ever-greater sphere of public life. Such a reordering of Mexico's economic, political, and social model required a relatively strong state and successive PRI administrations from 1982 to 2000 drew on revolutionary nationalism to legitimize their continued rule as they oversaw this process based on their self-presentation as heir to the popular struggles and material advances of the postrevolutionary period.

Officials in the Miguel de la Madrid administration told Mexicans that, while government austerity measures may have been causing pain for millions of Mexicans, state officials were applying these measures to make the Revolution realistic by adapting it to changed realities. The Carlos Salinas administration (1988–1994) next attempted the only reworking of state-society relations for the neoliberal era similar in ambition to 1930s Cardenismo. The administration created think tanks and engaged prominent historians to help it reshape the national narrative according to a framework of social liberalism that emphasized the importance of the nineteenth-century liberal Reform that could be more easily connected to the administration's policies than could revolutionary mythology. In an institutional sense, a framework was created through the National Solidarity Program that distributed state patronage directly from the executive according to a neoliberal populist style of rule. When this project collapsed during the political violence and economic crisis of 1994, the following administration turned strongly toward democratic reform as legitimizing state power. However, the

Ernesto Zedillo administration (1994–2000) still communicated its reform agenda through reference to established nationalist myths and symbols.

Popular actors at the same time invoked revolutionary nationalist myths and symbols to contest the legitimacy of or to pressure the state to address demands that ranged from housing and services in the popular barrios of Mexico City to political autonomy in the jungles of Chiapas. The use of national heroes such as Cárdenas and Zapata to challenge and demand the fulfillment of citizenship rights from the PRI state was not new. Nor were the civil society movements of the 1980s and 1990s an entirely novel phenomenon that signified an awakening of a dormant Mexican civil society. There was already a long tradition of grassroots organizing designed to pressure the state for access to resources.

What was particularly novel about the politics of nationalism in the neoliberal era was the loosening of the symbolic connection between the PRI, the state, and revolutionary nationalism encouraged by neoliberal reform and the retreat of the state. Revolutionary nationalist discourses also increasingly combined with transnational liberal discourses of pluralism that encouraged the breakdown of a limited series of collective identities with associated citizenship rights in favor of an increasing invocation of diversity, for example in terms of cultural or sexual identity, to claim citizenship rights understood as residing in the individual. However, these rights were still often communicated in Mexico through reference to shared revolutionary nationalist symbolism.

Indigenous movements such as those in Chiapas or Juchitán, Oaxaca, drew upon a shared concept of mestizo national identity to pressure the state for greater political and cultural autonomy. In particular, they evoked the valorization of selective elements of indigenous culture in the hegemonic nationalism as providing the primordial roots of the nation to claim legitimacy for demands made on the basis of their indigenous identity. Heroes like Benito Juárez also at times emerged as guardians of individual rights, and indeed Juárez's famous phrase "Respect for the rights of others is peace" was used by gay-rights activists as far afield as Colombia and the Dominican Republic.[3]

Amid the economic crisis of the 1980s, the PAN also found support for an increasingly aggressive strategy of confrontation with the PRI state from private enterprise and the Catholic Church. This conservative opposition to the PRI employed transnational discourses of freedom and democracy associated with a neoliberal third wave of democratic transitions during the 1980s in Latin America and, later, the ex-communist states of Eastern Europe. Defining democracy as electoral pluralism—encapsulated by the recurrent PAN electoral slogan of "change"—and portraying the interventionist state as detrimental to personal freedom, this opposition movement successfully turned electoral contests during the 1980s into referendums on democracy. In these referendums the PRI could not win without democracy losing.

The themes of liberal democracy and revolutionary nationalism combined perhaps most naturally in the discourse of a new institutional left independent from the PRI that arose in the late 1980s. In the 1988 presidential elections Cuauhtémoc Cárdenas, the son of postrevolutionary state-builder and revolutionary nationalist hero Lázaro Cárdenas, seriously challenged the PRI's continued hold on power at the head of a coalition of left-wing parties and ex-members of the PRI. This movement drew upon the symbolic capital of Cardenismo to build popular support, particularly among workers and peasants who had gained the most from Lázaro Cárdenas's land redistribution and economic nationalist policies according to both the revolutionary nationalist narrative and local historical memories. After previously struggling to unite over issues such as whether to adopt international communist or nationalist symbolism, this neocardenista coalition led to the formation of a united party of the Mexican left that invoked both democratic and revolutionary nationalist legitimacy for its political platform and electoral campaigns as the Party of the Democratic Revolution (PRD).

While the neocardenista coalition significantly challenged the post-1982 technocrat-dominated PRI state, the final decades of PRI rule are remarkable for the general stability of Mexico's political model amid an atmosphere of almost perpetual crisis. This stability allowed a new generation of technocratic elites to dismantle the state's corporatist infrastructure in a gradual fashion over the course of almost twenty years. Patriotic appeals to the heroes of the past by PRI officials during this period were often ridiculed in the press and protest movements frequently wielded figures such as Cárdenas and Zapata to combat the state's reform agenda. However, the way in which revolutionary nationalism continued to serve as a discourse of negotiation and Mexico's remarkable political stability reinforces a postrevisionist vision of Mexico's postrevolutionary history that understands the durability of Mexico's postrevolutionary political system as having its roots in a process of negotiated hegemony rather than a straightforward authoritarian imposition of rule.

Contesting Revolution and Democracy

Revolutionary nationalism ultimately proved a double-edged sword for the Mexican state in the neoliberal era. While it could still be effectively used to legitimize state power, it also proved effective in challenging this legitimacy. Specific national heroes now became at times more closely associated with opposition to the state's modernization projects and appeared to restrict the ability of the state to execute certain proposals, such as the Calderón administration's attempts to increase private investment in Pemex. Those who invoked and reinforced Zapatista or Cardenista mythology in opposition political movements during the late twentieth and early twenty-first century in these contexts did not do so purely as a product of state instruction through schoolbooks or because they had traveled every day along streets that bore the names of Zapata or Cárdenas. Instead, they sought to contest reforms aimed at dramatically restructuring Mexico's economy and society that threatened practical citizenship rights they associated with both these mythologies.

As shown in the controversies over the Salinas administration's attempts to alter school history textbooks and signs of PAN hostility to Juárez, when revolutionary nationalist myths and symbols were challenged, many Mexicans saw their own interests and identities also being symbolically attacked. Most efforts to reshape Mexican nationalism for the neoliberal era therefore involved attempts to redefine the meaning of revolutionary nationalist myths and symbols and, in the process, legitimize new national values. Historians such as those associated with the *Nexos* and *Vuelta* journals were during the 1980s and 1990s drafted into the project of democratizing Mexico's present through a reinterpretation of its past.

The new, democratic nationalist narrative crafted during this period had as its central event the Tlatelolco massacre of October 2, 1968. However, this narrative largely retained the main myths and symbols of revolutionary nationalism with subtle reinterpretations. Democracy was promoted by historians such as Enrique Krauze as a new end of history for Mexico, reinforced by the elevation of Francisco Madero and the fight for democracy against authoritarianism to the status of central hero and cause of the Mexican Revolution. As Porfirio Díaz became a deviation from the ideals of the liberal Reform personified by Juárez in the revolutionary nationalist historical narrative, the authoritarian PRI state that enacted the repression of 1968 now became a deviation from the ideals of the Revolution personified by Madero. When the PRI returned to office in 2012, President Enrique Peña Nieto thus presented himself as heir to a struggle for democracy in which the Revolution of 1910 was an early stage and the student movement of 1968 was its major turning point.[4]

The fact that the most significant opposition movements to the PRI during the final decades of its rule either emerged from or sought to locate themselves within the revolutionary nationalist tradition indicates that it had been largely successful in setting cognitive boundaries that broadly contained political action in Mexico. Those who supported Cuauhtémoc Cárdenas in 1988 or Andrés Manuel López Obrador during the 2000s looked backward toward the revolutionary nationalist past for a way forward. The EZLN similarly communicated its Marxist ideology in a language "more practical than theoretical," using the template of revolutionary nationalism to reassure Mexicans that their movement was not antinationalist nor too radical.[5] Those historians who attempted to rewrite Mexico's history for the neoliberal age also did so through a reinterpretation of the same great ruptures and same heroes that structured the revolutionary nationalist narrative to make it less revolutionary and more democratic according to their definitions of the terms.

The politics of nationalism in post-1968 Mexico has been tightly interwoven with political battles over material questions of citizenship rights and access to resources. This reality suggests the need to move beyond both economic and cultural determinist forms of historical analyses as well as modernist, state-focused understandings of nationalism. The continued use of revolutionary nationalist discourse in battles to contest and shape power relations in Mexico since 1968 suggest that its sociological role is less top-down and more complex than modernist theories of nationalism would suggest. This is not to say that a top-down legitimization of power structures was not an element of this dynamic. The failure of any actors, with the possible—and partial—exception of the EZLN, to radically challenge the structure of power in Mexico despite ongoing crises suggests the effectiveness of revolutionary nationalism in broadly reinforcing established power structures. However, people in Mexico during the period covered in this book do not appear to have been entirely blinded to their interests by a revolutionary "false consciousness."

While peasants and workers may not have challenged the entire system, they did continue to seek to better their situation through methods such as resistance to or selective implementation of the Salinas land reforms, allying with independent organizations and political parties, or taking part in the informal or illegal economy. This in turn limited the extent to which the elite neoliberal reform project could be implemented, as not only did a president such as Salinas find it difficult to change the presentation of Zapata in school history textbooks, but his administration could not force people to accept its new formulas for land ownership or the economic reorganization of society more generally. As a broad cognitive framework that connected identity to notions of collective rights, revolutionary nationalism in this way also limited the political options available to elites.

Imagining Mexico beyond the Institutional Revolution

This book began with a journey down the Paseo de la Reforma in Mexico City, describing the monuments that surround Mexico City's central boulevard and the historical movements they represented. Monuments such as the Angel of Independence and the Juárez Hemiciclo were constructed during the first decade of the twentieth century, which was also the last of the Porfiriato. The Monument to the Revolution was built upon foundations laid down during the late Porfiriato and completed during the 1930s, a period of intense postrevolutionary state- and nation-building. In 2009 the Felipe Calderón administration announced a competition to design a new monument that would join those commemorating independence, the Reform, and the Revolution to symbolize Mexico's national identity on the bicentenary of its independence, the centenary of the Mexican Revolution, and a decade after the historic defeat of the PRI in the 2000 presidential elections.

The competition for the 2010 monument asked architects to build a Bicentennial Arch that would stand at the Bosque de Chapultepec end of the central monument-lined stretch of the Paseo de la Reforma. However, the winning design was a 104-meter tower composed of two thin sheets of translucent quartz panels around a steel frame. This caused some controversy, with one architect describing the exercise as akin to holding a competition to design a stadium and then awarding the prize to plans for a hospital.[6] Called the Estela de Luz (Trail of Light), the monument was quickly surrounded by further controversy, allegations of corruption, and delays.

The Estela de Luz finally opened on the evening of January 7, 2012, long after the bicentenary had passed. The president in his remarks at the dedication ceremony paid tribute to the Insurgentes, those who defended Mexico during the foreign interventions of the nineteenth century, as well as the heroes of the Revolution. He also dedicated a sizeable portion of his speech to detailing the technical challenges faced during the monument's construction and acknowledging that it was a controversial project. Nevertheless, Calderón compared it to the great patriotic landmarks that surrounded it such as the Angel of Independence and Museum of Anthropology. Concluding his speech, the president intoned "let the Estela de Luz monument be the emblem of a new era for Mexico . . . upon contemplating this monument and the historical monuments that surround it, [let] us Mexicans feel pride in our country and its history, and to have faith, always have faith, in being the only masters of our own destiny."[7] The architect who designed the monument, César Pérez Becerril, was not invited to the dedication and provided an alternative interpretation. When interviewed about how he felt the monument would be remembered, Pérez Becerril remarked, "It is a good reflection of what is happening in the country: everything poorly executed [and] grubby."[8]

Mexico has never completely moved on from the final chaotic decades of the PRI state to a prolonged post-crisis period. The sheer, featureless design of the Estela de Luz and the controversy that surrounded its construction reflect the ambiguous legacy of the political transition of 2000. Following the Revolution, a new generation of state- and nation-builders had sought to compliment the Porfirian vision of the enlightened state with the institutional and symbolic popular inclusiveness of corporatist collectivist institutions and revolutionary nationalism. On the Monument to the Revolution, they cast in stone representations of class-based peasant and worker identities as well as the liberal Reform and revolutionary laws that at least symbolically extended certain citizenship rights to all Mexicans as part of a national community (fig. C.1). As Mexico's economic and political models were profoundly transformed after 1982, successive administrations failed to translate abstract discourses of democracy, freedom, and change into a similarly compelling image of a post-PRI state Mexico that is a progression from that which came before. It was therefore fitting that the patriotic monument commissioned by the Calderón administration to represent the nation in 2010 was modern and shiny but ultimately blank, allowing people to project onto it whatever interpretations they wished (fig. C.2).

The delays in the construction of the Estela de Luz, the bitterness of its architect, and allegations of corruption surrounding the project were

Figure C.1. Figures on the side of the Monument to the Revolution representing postrevolutionary labor laws. Photo by author.

Figure C.2. The Estela de Luz monument inaugurated by President Felipe Calderón in January 2012 to commemorate the 2010 bicentenary of Mexican independence. Photo by author.

further emblematic of the persistence of many of the negative features of the PRI state after 2000. Following the PRI's defeat, Mexico's justice system proved no more capable of prosecuting those responsible for the Tlatelolco massacre of October 2,1968. Nor was it able to stop the epidemic of young women being murdered in Ciudad Juárez. The military assault on drug cartels launched by the Calderón administration unleashed the greatest wave of violence on Mexico since the Revolution. However, unlike the Revolution, this violence did not center on material or ideological conflicts connected to popular demands, nor did the ultimate goals or strategies of its main protagonists—the federal government and drug cartels—seem clear. President Peña Nieto, in his 2012 inaugural speech, evoked the legacy of the student movement of 1968 to legitimize the Mexican political system and his own rule as democratic. Almost two years later, the Peña Nieto administration was plunged into a crisis of legitimacy as rural teaching students planning to attend a 1968 commemoration were massacred in the state of Guerrero.

There have been brief moments of national triumph since 1968, such as illusions of a sudden catapulting into modernity under the López Portillo and Salinas administrations or the change promised by Fox's election in 2000. However, these triumphs subsequently fell into crises that left their central claims of modernity or democracy severely challenged or discredited. The promise of economic prosperity under a neoliberal economic model has also yet to be fulfilled.

The appearances and disappearances of heroes such as Zapata and Madero and their cries of "land and liberty" and "effective suffrage, no reelection" from street signs, protest marches, and government speeches as the postrevolutionary state was dismantled were not simply the death throes of a fossilized nationalist mythology implanted in the minds of Mexicans by state-building elites. Instead, they functioned as a negotiated framework of myths and symbols that shaped how many people understood and communicated relations of power during a turbulent period of crisis and transition.

Juárez, Zapata, Cárdenas, the Revolution, the Insurgentes, and the liberal Reform have all played a significant role in shaping how Mexicans have experienced and responded to transnational currents of democracy and economic reform since 1968. As elements of a language of rule and resistance, they have sketched the outlines of the paths taken by millions of Mexicans who have fought to survive, repress, and rebel in the neoliberal era. The ways in which the statue of Fox in Boca del Río, the Estela de Luz, or the return of the PRI in 2012 are viewed by future generations of Mexicans will depend on how the country exits from an era of perpetual crisis into a new period of relative stability and consensus. In the meantime, the great heroes of revolutionary nationalism will no doubt continue to be called upon to fight in the never-ending battle to define, defend, and redefine Mexico and the multiple internal frontiers of identity, interests, and values that lie within its national borders.

Introduction

1. Blanche Petrich, "El PAN 'guardó la compostura' unas horas; luego, el triunfalismo," *La Jornada*, July 3, 2000, 1.

2. Dan LaBotz, *Democracy in Mexico: Peasant Rebellion and Political Reform* (Boston, MA: South End Press, 1995), 56–57; Claudio Lomnitz, *Deep Mexico, Silent Mexico: An Anthropology of Nationalism* (Minneapolis: University of Minnesota Press, 2001), 120–21; Horacio Mackinlay and Gerardo Otero, "State Corporatism and Peasant Organizations: Towards New Institutional Arrangements," in *Mexico in Transition: Neoliberal Globalism, the State and Civil Society*, ed. Gerardo Otero (New York: Zed Books, 2004), 72–88.

3. See Verónica Zárate Toscano, "El papel de la escultura conmemorativa en el proceso de construcción nacional y su reflejo en la ciudad de México en el siglo XIX," *Historia Mexicana* 53, no. 2 (October–December 2003): 417–46.

4. James Young, "Memory and Counter-Memory: Toward a Social Aesthetics of Holocaust Memorials," in *The Holocaust's Ghost: Writings on Art, Politics, Law, and Education*, ed. F. C. DeCoste et al. (Edmonton: University of Alberta Press, 2000), 167.

5. Enrique Peña Nieto, "Mensaje a la Nación del Presidente de los Estados Unidos Mexicanos," Presidencia de la República, accessed March 7, 2013, http://www.presidencia.gob.mx/articulos-prensa/mensaje-a-la-nacion-del-presidente-de-los-estados-unidos-mexicanos/.

6. Roberto Garduño, "Gordillo pactó ser titular de la SEP si gana el PRI: AMLO," *La Jornada*, May 13, 2013, 7.

7. Roland Barthes, *Mythologies* (London: Jonathan Cape, 1974), 109–10.

8. Patrice Elizabeth Olsen, *Artifacts of Revolution: Architecture, Society, and Politics in Mexico City, 1920–1940* (Lanham, MD: Rowman & Littlefield, 2008), 77–79.

9. Jocelyn Olcott, *Revolutionary Women in Postrevolutionary Mexico* (Durham, NC: Duke University Press, 2005), 4.

10. As Howard Wiarda, Claudio Lomnitz, and others have noted, corporatism has deep roots in Iberian and colonial Latin American political traditions. Lomnitz, *Deep Mexico, Silent Mexico*, 10; Philippe C. Schmitter, "Still the Century of Corporatism?," in *Trends Toward Corporatist Intermediation*, ed. Philippe C. Schmitter and Gerhard Lehmbruch (Beverly Hills, CA: Sage Publications, 1979), 13; Howard J. Wiarda, "Toward a Framework for the Study of Political Change in the Iberic-Latin Tradition: The Corporative Model," *World Politics*, 25, no. 2 (January 1973): 206–35; Peter J. Williamson, *Varieties of Corporatism: A Conceptual Discussion* (London: Cambridge University Press, 1985), 10.

11. Jeffrey Rubin, *Decentering the Regime: Ethnicity, Radicalism, and Democracy in Juchitán, Mexico* (Durham, NC: Duke University Press, 1997), 244–64; James G. Samstad, "Corporatism and Democratic Transition: State and Labor During the Salinas and Zedillo Administrations," *Latin American Politics and Society* 44, no. 4 (December 2002): 2–5.

12. In terms of sectoral identity, JoAnn Martin found in her study of Tepoztlán, Morelos, during the 1980s and 1990s that not only did state control over regulation of land, labor, education, and social services make it difficult for the community to avoid contact with the state but that self-identification as peasants and the rights gained through the postrevolutionary agrarian reform laws made it difficult to conceptually separate the community from the Mexican state. JoAnn Martin, *Tepoztlán and the Transformation of the Mexican State* (Tucson: University of Arizona Press, 2005), 94–95.

13. A representative figure of the early generation is US commentator and advisor to the Lázaro Cárdenas administration (1934–1940) Frank Tannenbaum. Daniel Cosío Villegas was a particularly influential figure for a later generation of Mexican historians embracing this view, publishing from the 1950s to 1970s. See Daniel Cosío Villegas, *Historia Moderna de Mexico*, vols. 1–7 (Mexico City: Editorial Hermes, 1956–1972); Frank Tannenbaum, *The Mexican Agrarian Revolution* (New York: Macmillan, 1929); Frank Tannenbaum, *Peace by Revolution: Mexico after 1910* (New York: Columbia University Press, 1966).

14. See Octavio Paz, *El ogro filantrópico: Historia y política, 1971–1978* (Mexico City: Editorial Seix Barral, 1979).

15. Alan Knight, "Revisionism and Revolution: Mexico Compared to England and France," *Past and Present* 134, no. 1 (Feb. 1992): 160–99; Allen Wells, "Oaxatepec Revisited: The Politics of Mexican Historiography, 1968–1988," *Mexican Studies/Estudios Mexicanos* 7, no. 2 (Summer 1991): 331–45.

16. Soledad Loaeza, "Desigualdad y democracia," *Nexos* 123, no. 11 (March 1988): 33.

17. See Antonio Gramsci, *Prison Notebooks*, vols. 1–3 (New York: Columbia University Press, 1991); John Schwarzmantle, "Gramsci in His Time and Ours," in *Gramsci and Global Politics: Hegemony and Resistance*, eds. Mark McNally and John Schwarzmantle (Oxon: Routledge, 2009), 2–10.

18.   Stephen E. Lewis, *The Ambivalent Revolution: Forging State and Nation in Chiapas, 1910–1945* (Albuquerque: University of New Mexico Press, 2005); Catherine Nolan-Ferrell, "Agrarian Reform and Revolutionary Justice in Soconusco, Chiapas: Campesinos and the Mexican State, 1934–1940," *Journal of Latin American Studies* 42, no. 3 (August 2010): 551–85; Mary Kay Vaughan, *Cultural Politics in Revolution: Teachers, Peasants, and Schools in Mexico, 1930–1940* (Tucson: University of Arizona Press, 1997).

19.   A collection of essays titled *Everyday Forms of State Formation* that came out of a 1991 conference in California organized to respond to European theories such as that of Corrigan and Sayer pioneered an ongoing dialogue between Mexicanists and scholars of state formation in non-Latin American contexts. Gilbert Joseph and Daniel Nugent, eds., *Everyday Forms of State Formation: Revolution and the Negotiation of Rule in Modern Mexico* (Durham, NC: Duke University Press, 1994).

20.   Phillip Corrigan and Derek Sayer, *The Great Arch: English State Formation as Cultural Revolution* (Oxford: Basic Blackwell, 1985).

21.   Ibid., 4.

22.   Mara Loveman, "The Modern State and the Primitive Accumulation of Symbolic Power," *American Journal of Sociology* 110, no. 6 (May 2005): 1652; Hannu Ruonavaara, "Moral Regulation: A Reformulation," *Sociological Theory* 15, no. 3 (November 1997): 280.

23.   Rick López, *Crafting Mexico: Intellectuals, Artisans, and the State after the Revolution* (Durham, NC: Duke University Press, 2010), 13.

24.   See O'Malley.

25.   See Alan Knight, "Cardenismo: Juggernaut or Jalopy?" *Journal of Latin American Studies* 26, no. 1 (Feb. 1994): 73–107.

26.   See Kevin Middlebrook, *The Paradox of Revolution: Labor, the State, and Authoritarianism in Mexico* (Baltimore, MD: Johns Hopkins University Press, 1995).

27.   See Jeffrey Rubin, *Decentering the Regime: Ethnicity, Radicalism and Democracy in Juchitán, Mexico* (Durham, NC: Duke University Press, 1997).

28.   Jeffrey Rubin, "Popular Mobilization and the Myth of State Corporatism," in *Popular Movements and Political Change in Mexico*, eds. Joe Fowraker and Ann Craig (Boulder, CO: Lynne Rienner Publishers, 1990), 247–67.

29.   Alan Knight, "Weapons and Arches in the Mexican Revolutionary Landscape," in Joseph and Nugent, 54.

30.   David Harvey, "Neoliberalism as Creative Destruction," *Annals of the American Academy of Political and Social Science* 610 (March 2007): 22–44.

31.   Ignacio M. Sánchez Prado, "Claiming Liberalism: Enrique Krauze, *Vuelta*, *Letras Libres*, and the Reconfigurations of the Mexican Intellectual Class," *Mexican Studies/Estudios Mexicanos* 26, no. 1 (Winter 2010): 75–76.

32. Ernesto Zedillo, "Versión estenográfica del mensaje del presidente Ernesto Zedillo, después de las elecciones, desde la residencia oficial de Los Pinos," accessed January 19, 2012, http://zedillo.presidencia.gob.mx/pages/salaprensa4a.html.

33. Eric Van Young, *The Other Rebellion: Popular Violence, Ideology, and the Mexican Struggle for Independence, 1810–1821* (Stanford, CA: Stanford University Press, 2001), 14.

34. See Samuel P. Huntington, *The Third Wave: Democratization in the Late Twentieth Century* (Norman: University of Oklahoma Press, 1991).

35. Van Young, *The Other Rebellion*, 14.

36. Eric Van Young, "Conclusion: The State as Vampire—Hegemonic Projects, Public Ritual and Popular Culture in Mexico, 1600–1990," in *Rituals of Rule, Rituals of Resistance: Public Celebrations and Popular Culture in Mexico*, eds. William H. Beezley, Cheryl E. Martin, and William E. French (Wilmington, DE: Scholarly Resources, 1994), 348–50.

37. Eric Hobsbawm, "Inventing Traditions," in *The Invention of Tradition*, eds. Eric Hobsbawm and Terence Ranger (Cambridge: Cambridge University Press, 2003), 4.

38. See ibid., 1–13.

39. Benjamin, *La Revolución*, 99–103; John R. Gillis, "Memory and Identity: The History of a Relationship," in *Commemorations: The Politics of National Identity*, ed. John R. Gillis (Princeton, NJ: Princeton University Press, 1994), 9.

40. Barthes, 142–45.

41. Benedict Anderson, *Imagined Communities* (London: Verso, 2006), 6.

42. Ernst Renan, "What is a Nation?," in *The Writings of Theorists and Practitioners, Classical and Modern*, ed. Arend Lijphart (Boston, MA: Allyn and Bacon, 1971), 90.

43. Smith *Nationalism*, 45–61.

44. Mauricio Tenorio Trillo, "Essaying the History of National Images," in *After Spanish Rule: Postcolonial Predicaments of the Americas*, eds. Mark Thurner and Andrés Guerrero (Durham, NC: Duke University Press, 2003), 62.

45. This was first published as Claudio Lomnitz, "Nationalism as a Practical System: Benedict Anderson's Theory of Nationalism from the Vantage Point of Spanish America," in *The Other Mirror: Grand Theory through the Lens of Latin America*, eds. Miguel Ángel Centeno and Fernando López-Alves (Princeton, NJ: Princeton University Press, 2001), 329–59. It was subsequently expanded in *Deep Mexico, Silent Mexico*.

46. Lomnitz, *Deep Mexico, Silent Mexico*, 48–49.

47. Ibid., 33.

48. Thomas Benjamin, *La Revolución: Mexico's Great Revolution as Memory, Myth and History* (Austin: University of Texas Press, 2000); Ilene V. O'Malley, *The Myth of the Revolution: Hero Cults and the*

Institutionalization of the Mexican State, 1920–1940 (Westport, CT: Greenwood Press, 1986).

49.   Samuel Brunk, *The Posthumous Career of Emiliano Zapata: Myth, Memory, and Mexico's Twentieth Century* (Austin: University of Texas Press, 2008).

50.   Lynn Stephen, *Zapata Lives! Histories and Cultural Politics in Southern Mexico* (Berkeley: University of California Press, 2002).

51.   Thomas Benjamin, "A Time of Reconquest: History, the Maya Revival, and the Zapatista Rebellion in Chiapas," *The American Historical Review* 105, no. 2 (April 2000): 417–50; Brunk, *Posthumous Career of Emiliano Zapata*; Dennis Gilbert, "Emiliano Zapata: Textbook Hero," *Mexican Studies/Estudios Mexicanos* 19, no. 1 (Winter 2003): 127–59; John Holloway and Eloina Peláez, eds., *Zapatista! Reinventing Revolution in Mexico* (Sterling, VA: Pluto Press, 1998); James H. McDonald, "Whose History? Whose Voice? Myth and Resistance in the Rise of the New Left in Mexico," *Cultural Anthropology* 8, no. 1 (1993): 96–116; Stephen, *Zapata Lives!*.

52.   Consulta Mitofsky, *Los orgullos de los mexicanos: Encuesta nacional en viviendas*, April 2011.

53.   "Benito Juárez, el héroe más buscado en Google," *El Universal*, March 24, 2011, online version.

54.   Charles Weeks, *The Juárez Myth in Mexico* (Tuscaloosa: University of Alabama Press, 1987).

55.   Mauricio Tenorio Trillo, *Mexico at the World's Fairs: Crafting a Modern Nation* (Berkeley: University of California Press, 1996), xi.

56.   "Adios al PRI," *La Jornada*, July 3, 2000, online version.

57.   Mario Vargas Llosa, "De la dictadura perfecta . . . a la democracia difícil," *Reforma*, July 3, 2000, 1.

58.   *Proceso* 1235, July 1, 2000.

Snapshot One

1.   See Eric Zolov, "Showcasing the Land of Tomorrow: Mexico and the 1968 Olympics," *The Americas* 61, no. 2 (2004): 159–88; Celeste González de Bustamante, "1968 Olympic Dreams and Tlatelolco Nightmares: Imagining and Imaging Modernity on Television," *Mexican Studies/Estudios Mexicanos* 26, no. 1 (Winter 2010): 1–30.

2.   Following the IPN intervention, students from this college and the National Autonomous University (UNAM) joined together on July 26, the anniversary of the Cuban Revolution, to march into the Mexico City Zócalo to protest the state's violation of the IPN's autonomy. The students again met with violence as scores of riot police descended on the marchers with battens, leaving hundreds injured. Marches continued during the following weeks, with the largest taking place on August 27, when an unprecedented 400,000 people gathered in the Zócalo to protest state repression. In response to the

growth of the protest movement, in September the army seized control of the campuses of the UNAM and IPN, which only heightened tensions. Barry Carr, *Marxism and Communism in Twentieth-Century Mexico* (Lincoln: University of Nebraska Press, 1992), 258–64; Gilberto Guevara Niebla, *1968: Largo camino a la democracia* (Mexico City: Cal y Arena, 2008), 49–51; Donald Hodges and Ross Gandy, *Mexico Under Siege: Popular Resistance to Presidential Despotism* (London: Zed Books, 2002), 93–96; Enrique Semo (ed.), *México un pueblo en la historia*, vol. 4 (Mexico City: Editorial Nueva Imagen, 1982), 125–26.

3.   Christopher Harris, "Remembering 1968 in Mexico: Elena Poniatowska's *La noche de Tlatelolco* as Documentary Narrative," *Bulletin of Latin American Research* 24, no. 4 (2005): 483.

4.   Elena Poniatowska, *La Noche de Tlatelolco* (Mexico City: Era, 2007), 21.

5.   González de Bustamante, 13.

6.   Ibid., 15–19.

7.   The final government figure was 30 deaths, while in 1969, the student movement's National Strike Council (CNH) put the figure at 150 deaths. In response to Freedom of Information requests, in 2003 the US National Security Archive at George Washington University released embassy cables related to the massacre that were printed in *Proceso*. In these cables embassy officials estimated between 150 and 200 deaths. Eugenia Allier Montaño, "Presentes-pasados del 68 mexicano. Una historización de las memorias públicas del movimiento estudiantil, 1968–2007," *Revista Mexicana de Sociología* 71, no. 2 (April–June 2009): 293; Kate Doyle, "El 68: Desconcierto de Washington," *Proceso* 1405, October 5, 2003, 28–37.

8.   This account of the student movement and October 2 massacre is drawn from the following among a broad range of sources dealing with the events of 1968: Sérgio Aguayo, *1968: Los archivos de la violencia* (Mexico City: Grijalbo, 1998); Raúl Álvarez Garín, *La estela de Tlatelolco: Una reconstrucción histórica del Movimiento Estudiantil* (Mexico City: Grijalbo, 1998); Carlos Monsiváis, Marcelino García Barragán, and Julio Scherer García, *Parte de Guerra: Tlatelolco 68* (Mexico City: Aguilar, 1999); Carlos Monsiváis, *Días de guardar* (Mexico City: Ediciones Era, 1988); Hodges and Gandy, 93–106; Raúl Jardón, *1968: El fuego de la esperanza* (Mexico City: Siglo XXI, 1998); Poniatowska, *La Noche de Tlatelolco*; Ramón Ramírez, *El movimiento estudiantil de México: Julio–diciembre de 1968* (Mexico City: Era, 1998).

9.   The 1968 student movement was preceded by a series of conflicts that had begun to build between the PRI state and various middle and working class groups, which has given rise to the idea of a "long 1968," a decade-long process leading up to the student movement. At their core, these conflicts were a result of the social and economic dislocation caused by the massification of higher education, organization of new sectors among Mexican peasants and Mexico's accelerating industrialization and urbanization in the post–World War II period. In the context of the weakening

influence of traditional social and political bonds, by the late 1950s the PRI responded in an increasingly authoritarian manner to independent worker and peasant opposition movements. Notable among these was the repression of striking railway workers in 1958–1959. The government also responded violently to a doctors' strike in 1964–1965, providing perhaps the closest antecedent of government repression of an urban, largely middle class movement. Adriana Borjas Benavente, *Partido de la Revolución Democrática: Estructura, organización interna y desempeño público, 1989–2003* (Mexico City: Gernika, 2003), 130; Carr, *Marxism and Communism*, 187–224; Gilberto Guevara Niebla, *Democracia en la calle: Crónica del movimiento estudiantil mexicano* (Mexico City: Siglo XXI, 1988), 19–38; Guevara Niebla, *Largo camino a la democracia*, 30–33.

10.   Guevara Niebla, *Largo camino a la democracia*, 24.

11.   Poniatowska, *La Noche de Tlatelolco*.

12.   See Paz, *El ogro filantrópico*.

13.   Allier Montaño, 295–96.

14.   Borjas Benavente, 130–31.

15.   Allier Montaño, 297; Carr, *Marxism and Communism*, 307–19.

16.   José Vilchis and Carlos Velázquez, "Conmemoran el 2 de octubre con dos marchas y un mitin en el Zócalo," *Unomásuno*, October 2, 1984, 5.

17.   Armando Bartra, "The Seduction of the Innocents: The First Tumultuous Moments of Mass Literacy in Postrevolutionary Mexico," in *Everyday Forms of State Formation: Revolution and the Negotiation of Rule in Modern Mexico*, eds. Gilbert M. Joseph and Daniel Nugent (Durham, NC: Duke University Press, 1994), 321; Daniel Chávez, "The Eagle and the Serpent on the Screen: The State as Spectacle in Mexican Cinema," *Latin American Research Review*, 43, no. 3 (2010): 124.

18.   Roberto Villarreal M., "Marcha como protesta y grito como clamor a los caídos," *Excélsior*, October 3, 1984, 5; José Vilchis and Carlos Velázquez, "Conmemoraron el 2 de octubre con dos marchas y un mitin en el Zócalo," *Unomásuno*, October 10, 1984, 5.

19.   Earlier that year, approximately forty homosexual activists from the Homosexual Revolutionary Action Front of a largely communist and anarchist male membership joined a protest march on July 26, 1978, on the anniversary of the Cuban Revolution. However, October 2, 1978, is more broadly understood as the public emergence of a gay and lesbian political movement in Mexico due to the increased diversity and visibility of the participation of groups of men and women. Rafael de la Dehesa, *Queering the Public Sphere in Mexico and Brazil: Sexual Rights Movements in Emerging Democracies* (Durham, NC: Duke University Press, 2010), 16–17; Jordi Diez, "La trayectoria política del movimiento Lésbico-Gay en México," *Estudios Sociológicos* 29, no. 86 (May–August 2011): 695–96; Héctor Domínguez-Ruvalcaba, "From Fags to Gays: Political Adaptations and Cultural Translations in the Mexican Gay Liberation Movement," in *Mexico Reading the United States*, eds. Linda Egan and Mary K. Long (Nashville, TN: Vanderbilt University

Press, 2009), 120; Porfirio Miguel Hernández Cabrera, *La cobertura periodística de las marchas del orgullo lésbico, gay, bisexual y transgenérico de la Ciudad de México*, paper prepared for Meeting of the Latin American Studies Association, Washington D.C., September 6–8, 2001: 3–4; Antonio Media, "30 años de movilizaciones por la libertad sexual," *Letra S* 143, June 5, 2008, accessed January 5, 2015, http://www.jornada.unam.mx/2008/06/05/ls-entrevista2.html.

20.   Carlos Monsiváis, "Ortodoxia y heterodoxia en las alcobas. Hacia una crónica de costumbres y creencias sexuales de México," *Debate Feminista* (April 1995): 196–97.

21.   Allier Montaño, 298–99.

22.   Editorial, "Que nadie olvide," *Unomásuno*, October 2, 1983, 3.

23.   Newspaper coverage was not always sympathetic. For example, in 1989 the generally progovernment newspaper *Excélsior* highlighted a poor turnout at the march and the following year focused on the disruption to traffic and vandalism caused by those commemorating the massacre. Roberto Villarreal M. "Despertó el movimiento popular de 1968 la conciencia cívica de México," *Excélsior*, October 3, 1984, 5. Also see Mario Peralta and Eduardo Rivadeneyra, "Ausencia de líderes del 68 en el XXII aniversario del 2 de Octubre," *Excélsior*, October 3, 1990, 4; "Desquiciamiento del tránsito debido a la marcha por el aniversario del 68," *Excélsior*, October 3, 1990, 4.

24.   See Hermann Bellinghausen and Hugo Hiriart (eds.), *Pensar el 68* (Mexico City: Cal y Arena, 2008); Elaine Carey, *Plaza of Sacrifices: Gender, Power, and Terror in 1968 Mexico* (Albuquerque: University of New Mexico Press, 2005); Ignacio Corona Gutiérrez, *Después de Tlatelolco: las narrativas políticas en México 1976–1990* (Guadalajara: Universidad de Guadalajara, 2001); Guevara Niebla, *Largo camino a la democracia*, 42–46.

25.   Chávez, 134.

26.   "PSUM: con el movimiento de 68 se abrieron espacios democráticos," *Unomásuno*, October 3, 1984, 4.

27.   "Se debe evitar que haya otro Tlatelolco: diputación de AN," *Unomásuno*, October 3, 1984, 4.

28.   Patricia Cerda, "El 68 planteó serio problema de apertura al Estado: el Clero," *Excélsior*, October 3, 1990, 4; Jesús Aranda, "Quedan muchas dudas tras 25 años, dice Talamás," *La Jornada*, October 3, 1993, 6.

29.   "Se debe evitar que haya otro Tlatelolco," 4.

30.   Editorial, "El 2 de octubre y la democracia," *La Jornada*, October 2, 1986, 3.

31.   Not everyone accepted the PRI's attempts at reconciling itself with the events of October 1968. Its motions to hold a minute of silence in the Chamber of Deputies in 1986 and 1987, for example, were greeted with an angry rejection from left-wing opposition parties. In 1986 this was partly due to the PRI representative proposing a minute of silence to remember all the fallen, including soldiers. This occasioned a rebuke from the PSUM and led

other parties of the left—the PRT, PMT and PPS—to abandon the chamber. The following year, another proposed motion by the PRI in the Chamber of Deputies for a minute of silence was ultimately abandoned after a similar threat by parties of the left to leave the chamber. Miguel Ángel Rivera, "Memoria distinta de grupos parlamentarios," *La Jornada*, October 3, 1986, 32; Ricardo Alemán Alemán, "'Parteaguas' nacional, el 2 de octubre, coinciden los partidos," *La Jornada*, October 2, 1987, 32, 6.

32.   Allier Montaño, 302.

33.   Jorge Munguía Espitia, "1968, tema del 98," *Proceso* 1158, January 9, 1999, online version.

34.   Carlos Monsiváis, "Presencia del 68 en 98," *Proceso* 1143, September 26, 1998, online version.

35.   Antonio Jáquez, "México Siglo XX, su serie que comienza con Díaz Ordaz," *Proceso* 1121, April 25, 1998, online version.

36.   Ibid.

37.   Salvador Corro, "De los gobiernos priístas, Emilio Azcárraga ha recibido todos los favores y, como priísta confieso, sabe ser agradecido," *Proceso* 922, July 2, 1994, online version. On Emilio Azcárraga, see Claudia Fernández and Andrew Paxman, *El Tigre: Emilio Azcárraga y su imperio Televisa* (Grijalbo: Mexico City, 2001).

38.   Jáquez, *Proceso* 1121.

39.   Cirio Gómez Leyva, "Entre Díaz Ordaz, Chenalhó y el Padre Maciel," *Milenio Semanal* 37, no. 1, May 11, 1998, 44.

Chapter One

1.   Eric Van Young, *The Other Rebellion: Popular Violence, Ideology and the Mexican Struggle for Independence, 1810–1821* (Stanford, CA: Stanford University Press, 2001), 32–33.

2.   Enrique Florescano, *La bandera mexicana* (Mexico City: Taurus, 1998), 116–17; Enrique Florescano, *Historia de las historias de la nación mexicana* (Mexico City: Taurus, 2002), 282–89.

3.   Timothy Anna, "Agustín de Iturbide and the Process of Consensus," in *The Birth of Modern Mexico, 1780–1824*, ed. Christon I. Archer (Wilmington, DE: Scholarly Resources, 2003), 188–89.

4.   Hugh Hamil, "An 'Absurd Insurrection'? Creole Insecurity, Pro-Spanish Propaganda, and the Hidalgo Revolt," in Archer, ed., 63; Alan Knight, *Mexico: The Colonial Era* (Cambridge: Cambridge University Press, 2002), 329; Van Young, *The Other Rebellion*, 33–34.

5.   Anna, "Agustín de Iturbide," 188–89.

6.   Alan Knight, "Peasants into Patriots: Thoughts on the Making of the Mexican Nation," *Mexican Studies/Estudios Mexicanos* 10, no. 1 (Winter 1994): 143.

7.   These groups have also been respectively dubbed federalists and centralists. Anna, "Agustín de Iturbide," 187–204; Manuel Chust and Ivana Frasquet, "Orígenes federales del republicanismo en México, 1810–1824," *Mexican Studies/Estudios Mexicanos* 24, no. 2 (Summer 2008): 371.

8.   Moisés González Navarro, *El pensamiento político de Lucas Alamán* (Mexico City: Fondo de Cultura Económica, 1952), 63; Enrique Florescano, *Historia de las historias*, 338; Editors of *El Tiempo*, "A Conservative Profession of Faith," in *The Mexico Reader: History, Culture, Politics*, eds. Gilbert M. Joseph, and Daniel Nugent (Durham, NC: Duke University Press, 2002), 221–25.

9.   Two major strands of liberalism existed by the mid-nineteenth century: The *moderado* (moderate) strand championed by provincial elites traced its heritage back to the federalist constitution of 1824 and the Bourbon Reforms, seeking to establish the state's authority over the church, curtail corporate privileges, and free economic activity from administrative barriers. The radical (or popular) *puro* liberalism was championed by intellectuals, villages, and municipalities and centered on demands for municipal autonomy and popular sovereignty. Brian R. Hamnett, "Liberalism Divided: Regional Politics and the National Project During the Mexican Restored Republic, 1867–1876," *Hispanic American Historical Review* 76, no. 4 (November 1996): 660–63; Guy P. C. Thompson, *Patriotism, Politics, and Popular Liberalism in Nineteenth-Century Mexico: Juan Francisco Lucas and the Puebla Sierra* (Wilmington, DE: Scholarly Resources, 1999), 273.

10.   Florescano, *Historia de las historias*, 29; Enrique Florescano, *Imágenes de la patria a través de los siglos* (Mexico City: Taurus, 2005), 103–5.

11.   Javier Rodríguez Piña, "Conservatives Contest the Meaning of Independence, 1846–1855," in *Viva Mexico! Viva la Independencia! Celebrations of September 16*, eds. William H. Beezley and David E. Lorey (Wilmington, DE: SR Books, 2001), 101–29.

12.   Brian F. Connaughton, "El difícil juego de 'tres dados: la ley, la opinión y las armas' en la construcción del Estado mexicano," in *Poder y legitimidad en México en el siglo XIX*, ed. Brian F. Connaughton (Iztapalapa: UAM, 2003), 339–43.

13.   Ibid., 363–66.

14.   Hamnett, "Liberalism Divided," 661–68.

15.   Jennie Purnell, "With All Due Respect: Popular Resistance to the Privatization of Communal Lands in Nineteenth-Century Michoacán," *Latin American Research Review* 34, no. 1 (1999): 85–86; Richard Weiner, *Race, Nation, and Market: Economic Culture in Porfirian Mexico* (Tucson: University of Arizona Press, 2004), 12–13.

16.   Mara Loveman, "The Modern State and the Primitive Accumulation of Symbolic Power," *American Journal of Sociology* 110, no. 6 (May 2005): 1657–58.

17.   When the Reform Laws were incorporated into the constitution in 1873, they included provisions for religious toleration, civil marriage contracts, prohibition of the acquisition of landed property or mortgages by religious institutions, removal of the oath on the crucifix, the invalidation of monastic vows and the prohibition of the foundation of new orders. Brian R. Hamnett, "Liberalism Divided," 665; Knight, *The Colonial Era*, 262–64.

18.   Guillermo de la Peña, "Social and Cultural Policies toward Indigenous Peoples: Perspectives from Latin America," *Annual Review of Anthropology* 34 (2005): 721.

19.   Purnell, 88–92.

20.   Peter F. Guardino, *Peasants, Politics, and the Formation of Mexico's National State: Guerrero, 1800–1857* (Stanford, CA: Stanford University Press, 1996), 8–10; Van Young, *The Other Rebellion*, 28–29.

21.   Florencia Mallon, *Peasant and Nation: The Making of Postcolonial Mexico and Peru* (Berkeley: University of California Press, 1995), 92–96; Alan Knight, "The Peculiarities of Mexican History: Mexico Compared to Latin America, 1821–1992," *Journal of Latin American Studies* 24, Quincentenary Supplement (1992): 118–25.

22.   Patrick J. McNamara, *Sons of the Sierra: Juárez, Díaz, and the people of Ixtlán, Oaxaca, 1855–1920* (Chapel Hill: University of North Carolina Press, 2007), 28–49; Mallon, *Peasant and Nation*, 84–85; Guy P. Thompson, "Bulwarks of Patriotic Liberalism: The National Guard, Philharmonic Corps and Patriotic Juntas in Mexico, 1847–88," *Journal of Latin American Studies* 22, no. 1–2 (March 1990): 33–36; Guy P. Thompson, "Popular Aspects of Liberalism in Mexico," *Bulletin of Latin American Research* 10, no. 3 (1991): 279–87.

23.   Romana Falcón, "Force and the Search for Consent: The Role of the *Jefaturas Políticas* of Coahuila in National State Formation," in eds. Joseph and Nugent, 113–14; McNamara, *Sons of the Sierra*, 3; Mallon, *Peasant and Nation*, 24–32; Thompson, "Popular Aspects of Liberalism," 273–86.

24.   McNamara, *Sons of the Sierra*, 19; Thompson, "Popular Aspects of Liberalism," 268–72; John Tutino, *From Insurrection to Revolution in Mexico: Social Bases of Agrarian Violence, 1750–1940* (Princeton, NJ: Princeton University Press, 1986), 496–98.

25.   Mallon, *Peasant and Nation*, 6–7.

26.   Hamnett, "Liberalism Divided," 666; Mallon, *Peasant and Nation*, 247–75.

27.   McNamara, *Sons of the Sierra*, 12; Mallon, *Peasant and Nation*, 61; Knight, "Peculiarities of Mexican History," 118–26; Thompson, "Popular Aspects of Liberalism," 286–87.

28.   McNamara, *Sons of the Sierra*, 57–58; Michael Costeloe, "The Junta Patriótica and the Celebration of Independence in Mexico City, 1825–1855," *Mexican Studies/Estudios Mexicanos* 13, no. 1 (Winter 1997): 23–24; Robert H. Duncan, "Embracing a Suitable Past: Independence Celebrations

under Mexico's Second Empire, 1864–6," *Journal of Latin American Studies* 30, no. 2 (May 1998): 249–77.

29. Charles Hale, *Justo Sierra: Un liberal del Porfiriato* (Mexico City: Fondo de Cultura Económica, 1997), 90.

30. Florescano, *Historia de las historias*, 353–59.

31. The masterwork of this historiography was the five-volume *México a través de los siglos* (Mexico Through the Centuries, 1887–1889) overseen by Vicente Riva Palacio and other prominent intellectuals. This work structured Mexican history into a progress through five epochs: ancient Mexican civilizations, colonial New Spain, the Insurgency, independent Mexico, and the Reform. Thomas Benjamin, *La Revolución: Mexico's Great Revolution as Memory, Myth, and History* (Austin: University of Texas Press, 2000), 18; Florescano, *Historia de las historias*, 353–59.

32. Florescano, *Historia de las historias*, 375–78.

33. Ibid., 191–93.

34. Ibid., 379–80.

35. During the fifteen years following Juárez's death, a resolution was passed in the national congress to have his name inscribed in gold letters in the building's session chamber, the name "Avenida Juárez" adorned part of the route by which Juárez's troops entered Mexico city in 1867 following victory over the French, and biographies began to appear connecting Juárez to the liberal cause and, through this, to the Porfirian state. Charles A. Weeks, *The Juárez Myth in Mexico* (Tuscaloosa: University of Alabama Press, 1987), 30–36.

36. For example, historian Matthew Esposito notes many scathing critics of official honors extended to liberal caudillo Jesús González Ortega upon his death with a complete absence of mention in the press of his conflicts with Juárez. Matthew Esposito, "The Politics of Death: State Funerals as Rites of Reconciliation in Porfirian Mexico, 1876–1889," *The Americas* 62, no. 1 (July 2005): 85.

37. Mauricio Tenorio Trillo, *Mexico at the World's Fairs: Crafting a Modern Nation* (Berkeley: University of California Press, 1996), 66.

38. Weeks, 26–48.

39. Esposito has described how the funeral train that transported the body of ex-president Sebastian Lerdo de Tejada along the nearly two-thousand-kilometer route from the US border to his burial in Mexico City was used as an occasion to strengthen national consciousness through the repetition of patriotic ceremonies at each stop along the way. Esposito, 88–89.

40. Falcón, 116.

41. Isabel Fernández Tejado and Carmen Nava Nava, "Images of Independence in the Nineteenth Century: The Grito de Dolores, History, and Myth," in eds. Beezley and Lorey, 33–34.

42. Duncan, 276.

43.　Tenorio Trillo, "1910 Mexico City," 170.

44.　Alan Knight, "Mexico's Three Fin de Siècle Crises," in *Cycles of Conflict, Centuries of Change: Crisis, Reform and Revolution in Mexico*, eds. Elisa Servín, Leticia Reina, and John Tutino (Durham, NC: Duke University Press, 2007), 167; McNamara, *Sons of the Sierra*, 122–87; Mark Wasserman, "You Can Teach an Old Revolutionary History New Tricks: Regions, Popular Movements, Culture and Gender in Mexico, 1820–1940," *Latin American Research Review* 43, no. 2 (2008): 260–71.

45.　Mallon, *Peasant and Nation*, 23; Weiner, 8–9.

46.　Weiner, 16, 25–33.

47.　McNamara, *Sons of the Sierra*, 102–3.

48.　Weiner, 26.

49.　Quoted in Brian R. Hamnett, "Liberalism Divided," 677.

50.　Falcón, 133; McNamara, *Sons of the Sierra*, 97–100; Thompson, *Juan Francisco Lucas*, 258–60.

51.　For example, see Esposito, 65–94.

52.　Mauricio Tenorio Trillo, "1910 Mexico City: Space and Nation in the City of the Centenario," in eds. Beezley and Lorey, 167.

53.　Claudio Lomnitz, *Deep Mexico, Silent Mexico: An Anthropology of Nationalism* (Minneapolis: University of Minnesota Press, 2001), 13–14.

54.　Weeks notes, for example, that workers' movements such as the Gran Círculo de Obreros de México (Great Circle of Mexican Workers) used the commemoration of Juárez's death from as early as 1876 as an occasion to praise Juárez for guaranteeing their right to association through the Constitution of 1857, symbolically asserting their rights as both workers in a class sense and as Mexican citizens. Weeks, 33.

55.　McNamara, *Sons of the Sierra*, 123–68.

56.　Friedrich Katz, *The Life and Times of Pancho Villa* (Stanford, CA: Stanford University Press, 1998), 799.

57.　Ibid.

58.　Katz, 798.

59.　Timothy Henderson, *The Worm in the Wheat: Rosalie Evans and the Agrarian Struggle in the Puebla-Tlaxcala Valley of Mexico, 1906–1927* (Durham, NC: Duke University Press, 1998), 40–41.

60.　There was increasing labor unrest from 1906 onward, particularly from textile and mine workers, as workers organized in movements that were critical of capitalism and influenced by discourses such as social liberalism, social Catholicism, and anarchism as factory and mine owners retrenched and further squeezed their workers to remain profitable. Meanwhile, state and federal governments raised taxes as revenue declined, provoking widespread dissatisfaction in states such as Chihuahua that crossed class barriers. Rodney D. Anderson, *Outcasts in Their Own Land: Mexican Industrial Workers, 1960–1911* (DeKalb: Northern Illinois University Press, 1976),

99–135; Barry Carr, *El movimiento obrero y la política en México, 1910–1929* (Mexico City: SEP, 1976), 36–46; Katz, 797–98; McNamara, *Sons of the Sierra*, 175–76; Weiner, 18.

61. Knight and Mallon have somewhat differently mapped the causes of popular uprising. While Knight in his mapping of Revolution separates the *agrarista* movement that demanded land from the large haciendas and the *serrano* movement that organized around political autonomy, Mallon has argued that both evolved in constant historical interaction and formed the discursive cores around political programs that had been debated since at least the Reform period. In Morelos, where expanding sugar haciendas had been able to ameliorate peasant unrest after displacing them from their lands with the offer of some material security through employment, the collapse in demand for sugar led to displaced peasants now finding themselves unemployed, which provided the catalyst for revolution. Katz, 797; Knight, "Mexico's Three Fin de Siècle Crises," 159; Mallon, *Peasant and Nation*, 320–21; Purnell, 99–101.

62. Enrique Ochoa, *Feeding Mexico: The Political Uses of Food Since 1910* (Wilmington, DE: Scholarly Resources, 2000), 25–26.

63. Henderson, 41–43; Alan Knight, *The Mexican Revolution*, vol. 1 (Cambridge: Cambridge University Press, 1990), 261–64.

64. Purnell, 93; John Womack, Jr., *Zapata and the Mexican Revolution* (London: Thames and Hudson, 1969), 400–404.

65. Henderson, 41.

66. Ibid., 43.

67. Benjamin, *La Revolución*, 42–45; John Womack, *Zapata and the Mexican Revolution*, 400–404.

68. Ilene O'Malley, *The Myth of the Revolution: Hero Cults and the Institutionalization of the Mexican State, 1920–1940* (Westport, CT: Greenwood Press, 1986), 21.

69. Adolfo Gilly, *The Mexican Revolution* (New York: New Press, 2005), 185–93; Katz, 795.

70. Gilly, *The Mexican Revolution*, 190–93.

71. See Barry Carr, "The Casa del Obrero Mundial, Constitutionalism and the Pact of February 1915," in *El trabajo y los trabajadores en la historia de México/Labor and Laborers through Mexican History*, eds. Elsa Cecilia Frost, Michael C. Meyer and Josefina Zoraida Vázquez (Tucson and Mexico City: University of Arizona Press/Colegio de México, 1979), 603–31; Barry Carr, "The Mexican Economic Debacle and the Labor Movement: A New Era or More of the Same?," in *Modern Mexico: State, Economy, and Social Conflict*, eds. Nora Hamilton and Timothy F. Harding (Beverly Hills, CA: Sage Publications, 1986), 205–31.

72. Katz, 767.

73. Mary Kay Vaughan, *Cultural Politics in Revolution: Teachers,*

Peasants, and Schools in Mexico, 1930–1940 (Tucson: University of Arizona Press, 1997), 35.

74. Falcón, 108.

75. Phillip Corrigan and Derek Sayer, *The Great Arch: English State Formation as Cultural Revolution* (Oxford: Basic Blackwell, 1985), 4.

76. For example, the Obregón government initially conceded to Oaxaqueños the right to continue swearing allegiance to the Constitution of 1857 connected to the local support for the *juarista* cause. In Yucatán state, which was relatively untouched by the revolutionary war, General Salvador Alvarado from the northern state of Sonora oversaw a government after 1915 that implemented a series of important changes such as abolishing debt peonage and redistributing land from the large henequen estates that profoundly changed the Yucatecan economy and society. However, such reform was only undertaken after careful studies of local conditions had been conducted and cross-class support networks had been built, and was further supported by comprehensive educational reforms focused on literacy and citizenship. Gilbert M. Joseph, *Revolution from Without: Yucatán, Mexico, and the United States, 1880–1924* (Durham, NC: Duke University Press, 1988), 93–121; McNamara, *Sons of the Sierra*, 156–157.

77. Vaughan, *Cultural Politics in Revolution*, 4.

78. See Wendy Waters, "Remapping Identities: Road Construction and Nation Building in Postrevolutionary Mexico," in *The Eagle and the Virgin: Nation and Cultural Revolution in Mexico, 1920–1940*, eds. Mary Kay Vaughan and Stephen E. Lewis (Durham, NC: Duke University Press, 2006), 221–42.

79. Ibid., 235–39.

80. See Jean Meyer, *La cristiada* (Mexico City: Siglo XXI, 1974).

81. Adriana Borjas Benavente, *Partido de la Revolución Democrática: Estructura, organización interna y desempeño público, 1989–2003*, vol. 1 (Mexico City: Ediciones Gernika, 2003), 42–49; Luis Garrido, *El Partido de la Revolución Institucionalizada: La formación del nuevo estado en México, 1928–1945* (Mexico City: Siglo XXI, 2005), 177–238; Dan La Botz, *Democracy in Mexico: Peasant Rebellion and Political Reform* (Boston, MA: South End Press, 1995), 56–57; and Horacio Mackinlay and Gerardo Otero, "State Corporatism and Peasant Organizations: Towards New Institutional Arrangements," in *Mexico in Transition: Neoliberal Globalism, the State, and Civil Society*, ed. Gerardo Otero (New York: Zed Books, 2004), 72–88.

82. Francisco J. Paoli Bolio, *Estado y sociedad en México, 1917–1984* (Mexico City: Oceano, 1985), 34; Eric Zolov, *Refried Elvis: The Rise of the Mexican Counterculture* (Berkeley: University of California Press, 1999), 4.

83. Purnell, 117–18; Vaughan, *Cultural Politics in Revolution*, 30–31.

84. Jocelyn Olcott, *Revolutionary Women in Postrevolutionary Mexico* (Durham, NC: Duke University Press, 2005), 12.

85. Barry Carr, "The Fate of the Vanguard under a Revolutionary State:

Marxism's Contribution to the Construction of the Great Arch," in eds. Joseph and Nugent, 346; Ronald Loewe, *Maya or Mestizo? Nationalism, Modernity, and its Discontents* (Ontario: University of Toronto Press, 2010), 26–27.

86.   Waters, 225.

87.   Stephen R. Niblo, *Mexico in the 1940s: Modernity, Politics, and Corruption* (Wilmington, DE: SR Books, 1999), 81–86.

88.   Ben R. Schneider, "Why Is Mexican Business So Organized?" *Latin American Research Review* 37, no. 1 (2002): 78–80.

89.   Lomnitz, *Deep Mexico, Silent Mexico*, 74.

90.   This was done by weakening the independence of internal party blocs in selecting candidates for popular election, strengthening the more urban middle-class popular sector over previously powerful peasant and labor sectors, and establishing greater state control over the leaders of the corporate sectors, the most emblematic of whom was Fidel Velázquez, who served as head of the Confederation of Mexican Workers (CTM) in 1941 until his death in 1997. Ruth Berins Collier and David Collier, *Shaping the Political Arenas: Critical Junctures, the Labor Movement, and Regime Dynamics in Latin America* (Notre Dame, IN: University of Notre Dame Press, 2002), 416–20.

91.   Soledad Loaeza, *El Partido Acción Nacional: la larga marcha, 1939–1994. Oposición leal y partido de protesta* (Mexico City: Fondo de Cultura Económica, 1999), 55–56; Soledad Loaeza, "Entre el pluralismo y la fragmentación," *Nexos* 160, no. 14 (April 1991): 27–29.

92.   Loaeza, *El Partido Acción Nacional*, 68.

93.   For example, presidential candidates to emerge from the revolutionary tradition often faced electoral fraud and violence, including José Vasconcelos (1929), Juan Andrew Almazán (1940), Ezequiel Padilla (1946), Miguel Henríquez Guzmán (1952) and Cuauhtémoc Cárdenas (1988). Loaeza, *El Partido Acción Nacional*, 69.

94.   Enrique González Pedrero, "Jesús Reyes Héroles: El político humanista," *Nueva Época* 59 (January 2009): 2–3.

95.   Philip S. Gorski, *The Disciplinary Revolution: Calvinism and the Rise of the State in Early Modern Europe* (Chicago, IL: University of Chicago Press, 2003), 167–68.

96.   By way of contrast, sociologist Matthias Vom Hau found that an already infrastructurally powerful state in 1930s Argentina supported within its cultural machinery sufficient resistance to limit Peronist attempts at transforming nationalist discourse. Matthias Vom Hau, "State Infrastructural Power and Nationalism: Comparative Lessons from Mexico and Argentina," *Studies in Comparative International Development* 43, nos. 3–4, (December 2008): 334–54.

97.   Vaughan, *Cultural Politics in Revolution*, 25–42.

98.   See Dennis Gilbert, "Rewriting History: Salinas, Zedillo, and the

1992 Textbook Controversy," *Mexican Studies/Estudios Mexicanos* 13, no. 2 (Summer 1997): 271–97.

99. Catherine Nolan-Ferrell, "Agrarian Reform and Revolutionary Justice in Soconusco, Chiapas: Campesinos and the Mexican State, 1934–1940," *Journal of Latin American Studies* 42, no. 3 (August 2010): 556–57.

100. Waters, 228.

101. Vaughan, *Cultural Politics in Revolution*, 47–76.

102. Olcott, 14; Ibid., 7.

103. Jeffrey Rubin, *Decentering the Regime: Ethnicity, Radicalism, and Democracy in Juchitán, Mexico* (Durham, NC: Duke University Press, 1997), 11–15.

104. See José Vasconcelos, *La raza cósmica: Misión de la raza ibero-americana* (Madrid: Agencia Mundial de Librería, 1920).

105. Manuel Gamio, *Forjando Patria: Pro-Nacionalismo* (Boulder, CO: University Press of Colorado, 2010).

106. Claudio Lomnitz, "Bordering on Anthropology: The Dialectics of a National Tradition in Mexico," *Revue de Synthèse* 4, nos. 3–4 (July–December 2000): 349.

107. Consuelo Sánchez, *Los Pueblos Indígenas: Del indigenismo a la autonomía* (Mexico City: Siglo XXI, 1999), 41.

108. Consuelo Sánchez, 43; Guillermo de la Peña, "Social Citizenship, Ethnic Minority Demands, Human Rights, and Neoliberal Paradoxes: A Case Study in Western Mexico," in *Multiculturalism in Latin America: Indigenous Rights, Diversity, and Democracy*, ed. Rachel Sieder (Houndmills: Palgrave Macmillan, 2002), 131; de la Peña, "Social and Cultural Policies," 728–29; Sánchez, 43–50.

109. While its budget and legitimacy was often limited, according to anthropologist Guillermo de la Peña, the INI did achieve some legitimacy in the context of a rollout of land redistribution and state social policies into the countryside. De la Peña, "Social Citizenship," 131.

110. O'Malley, 22–23.

111. Benjamin, *La Revolución*, 69–70.

112. Armando Bartra, "The Seduction of the Innocents: The First Tumultuous Moments of Mass Literacy in Postrevolutionary Mexico," in eds. Joseph and Nugent, 307–8; Benjamin, *La Revolución*, 73–77.

113. Benjamin, *La Revolución*, 20–21.

114. Ibid., 73.

115. Waters, 229.

116. Chief among the programs compulsorily broadcast was *La Hora Nacional* (The National Hour), a one-hour weekly program beginning in 1937 containing cultural and government programming that had to be carried by all stations in the country. See Joy Elizabeth Hayes, *Radio Nation:*

Communication, Popular Culture and Nationalism in Mexico, 1920–1950 (Tucson: University of Arizona Press, 2000).

117. Much of this control was implied rather than overt, encouraging self-censorship over direct government intervention. For example, the state maintained a monopoly over the production and importation of paper that could be used to maintain an overriding if unarticulated authority over the printed press alongside the strategic use of public funds for advertising upon which most publications' survival depended. Hayes, 244–47; John Mraz, "Today, Tomorrow, and Always: The Golden Age of Illustrated Magazines in Mexico, 1937–1960," in *Fragments of a Golden Age: The Politics of Culture in Mexico Since 1940*, eds. Gilbert Joseph, Anne Rubenstein, and Eric Zolov, (Durham, NC: Duke University Press, 2001), 121–23.

118. Daniel Chávez, 121–24.

119. Seth Fein, "Myths of Cultural Imperialism and Nationalism in Golden Age Mexican Cinema," in eds. Joseph et al., 181; Niblo, 94–95.

120. Vaughan, *Cultural Politics in Revolution*, 8; Stanley Ross, *Is the Mexican Revolution Dead?* (New York: Alfred Knopf, 1966); Alan Wells, "Oaxtepec Revisited: The Politics of Mexican Historiography, 1968–1988," *Mexican Studies/Estudios Mexicanos* 7, no. 2 (Summer 1991): 333–34; Zolov, *Refried Elvis*, 7–8.

Snapshot Two

1. Francisco González Gómez and Marco Antonio González Gómez, *Del porfirismo al neoliberalismo* (Mexico City: Ediciones Quinto Sol, 2007), 191.

2. David Harvey, *A Brief History of Neoliberalism* (Oxford: Oxford University Press, 2005), 86.

3. Judith Adler Hellman, *Mexico in Crisis*, 2nd ed. (New York: Holmes & Meier, 1988), 217–18.

4. The most significant social spending initiatives of this presidency were the General Coordination of the National Plan for Disadvantaged Zones and Marginalized Groups (COPLAMAR), begun in 1977 and designed to coordinate development projects and government funding directed at disadvantaged groups and regions, and the National Food System (SAM), begun in 1980 and designed to promote both the distribution and production of basic foodstuffs. Rosa María Mirón and Germán Pérez, *López Portillo: Auge y crisis de un sexenio* (Mexico City: Plaza y Valdés, 1988), 58–85.

5. Matthew Gutman, *The Romance of Democracy: Compliant Defiance in Contemporary Mexico* (Berkeley: University of California Press, 2002), 88.

6. Nora Lustig, *Mexico: The Remaking of an Economy* (Washington, DC: Brookings Institute, 1998), 20–24.

7. Mirón and Pérez, 118.

8.   See Siamack Shojai and Bernard Katz, eds., *The Oil Market in the 1980s: A Decade of Collapse* (New York: Praeger, 1992).

9.   Mirón and Pérez, 118.

10.   Ibid., 116–23.

11.   González Gómez and González Gómez, 193–94.

12.   On February 17, 1982, the government devalued the peso against the US dollar by almost 70 percent. On March 9 a Program of Economic Policy Adjustment was announced, which included reductions in public spending and the reinforcing of price controls. On August 6 a double exchange rate was established between the US dollar and the peso, with a preferential valuation determined by the Bank of Mexico applying to the importation of basic goods alongside a free exchange rate set by supply and demand. Announcing what would come to be known as "*mexdólares*," on August 12 the government introduced a controversial new measure for stabilizing the peso that meant that all withdrawals from bank accounts denominated in US dollars would now be paid in pesos. Mirón and Pérez, 134–53.

13.   Fernando Ortega, "Ante el presidente, que se dice devaluado, los empresarios ofrecen sacrificarse, por tres meses," *Proceso* 281, March 22, 1982, 10.

14.   For example, Editorial, "VI informe: Las expectativas," *Unomásuno*, September 1, 1982, 3; Mario Alberto Reyes, "Propone CTM nacionalizar empresas de bienes básicos," *Unomásuno*, September 1, 1982, 3.

15.   Roberto González Pérez, "Será el interés general el que mande en mis decisiones," *Excélsior*, September 1, 1982, 1.

16.   José López Portillo, "VI Informe de Gobierno del Presidente Constitucional de los Estados Unidos Mexicanos José López Portillo 1° de septiembre de 1982," in *Informes Presidenciales*, José López Portillo (Mexico City: Servicio de Documentación, Investigación y Análisis del Congreso de la Unión, 2006), 299.

17.   Ibid., 302.

18.   Ibid., 303.

19.   Ibid., 304.

20.   Ibid., 338.

21.   Claudio Lomnitz, "Narrating the Neoliberal Moment: History, Journalism, Historicity," *Public Culture* 20, no. 1 (Winter 2008): 39–40.

22.   "El inicio de otra batalla histórica," *Unomásuno*, September 2, 1982, 1, 4.

23.   Óscar González López, "1859–1938–1982: Años decisivos," *Excélsior*, September 3, 1982, 7–8.

24.   Heberto Castillo, "Un gran paso adelante," *Proceso* 305, September 6, 1982, 35; Enrique Maza, "Y pasó a la historia," *Proceso* 305, September 6, 1982, 38–40.

25. Nidia Marín and Mario Ruiz Redondo, "Apoyo total de la izquierda," *Excélsior,* September 2, 1982, 8.

26. Héctor Águila Camín, "Memorias de una expropiación," *Nexos* 58, no. 5 (1982): 22.

27. Enrique Krauze, "El Timón y la tormenta," *Vuelta* 71, no. 6 (1982): 22.

28. Luis Gutiérrez R., "500 mil personas en la manifestación de apoyo," *Unomásuno,* September 4, 1982, 1.

29. Aurora Berdejo Arvizu, "Otra vez la Revolución marcha y bifurca caminos: JLP," *Excélsior,* September 4, 1982, 1.

30. Ibid.

31. Editorial, "Apoyo entusiasta," *Excélsior,* September 4, 1982, 6.

32. Eduardo Arvizu, "Izó JLP la bandera mexicana en la central Banamex," *El Universal,* September 7, 1982, 1.

33. López Portillo, "VI Informe," 341.

Chapter Two

1. Roderic Ai Camp, *Mexico's Mandarins: Crafting a Power Elite for the Twenty-First Century* (Berkeley: University of California Press, 2002), 152–204; Miguel Ángel Centeno, *Democracy Within Reason: Technocratic Revolution in Mexico* (University Park: Pennsylvania State University Press, 1997), 101–44.

2. For example, Harvey, *A Brief History of Neoliberalism* (Oxford: Oxford University Press, 2005); Richard L. Harris and Melinda J. Seid, "Introduction," in *Critical Perspectives on Globalization and Neoliberalism in the Developing Countries,* eds. Richard L. Harris and Melinda J. Seid (Leiden: Brill, 2000); and Gérard Duménil and Dominique Lévy, "The Neoliberal (Counter-)Revolution," in *Neoliberalism: A Critical Reader,* eds. Alfredo Saad-Filho and Deborah Johnston (London: Pluto Press, 2005), 9–19.

3. Marion Fourcade-Gourinchas and Sarah L. Babb, "The Rebirth of the Liberal Creed: Paths to Neoliberalism in Four Countries," *American Journal of Sociology* 108, no. 3 (November 2002): 534–35.

4. Camp, *Mexico's Mandarins,* 128–30.

5. An earlier example of this principle in action is the harsh conditions placed on the bankrupt New York City government in 1975, which "established the principle that in the event of a conflict between the integrity of financial institutions and bondholders' returns, on the one hand, and the well-being of citizens on the other, the former was to be privileged." Harvey, *A Brief History of Neoliberalism,* 48.

6. Fourcade-Gourinchas and Babb, 562

7. Centeno, *Democracy Within Reason,* 26.

8. Sarah Babb, *Managing Mexico: Economists from Nationalism to*

Neoliberalism (Princeton, NJ: Princeton University Press, 2004), 176–77; Daniel C. Levy and Kathleen Bruhn, *Mexico: The Struggle for Democratic Development* (Berkeley: University of California Press, 2006), 163–64.

9.   Camp, *Mexico's Mandarins*, 154.

10.   Judith Adler Hellman, *Mexico in Crisis*, 2nd ed. (New York: Holmes & Meier, 1988), 187–88.

11.   Centeno, *Democracy Within Reason*, 150–52; Peter H. Smith, *Labyrinths of Power: Political Recruitment in Twentieth-Century Mexico* (Princeton, NJ: Princeton University Press, 1979), 165.

12.   Centeno, *Democracy Within Reason*, 88–90.

13.   Harvard, Yale, Massachusetts Institute of Technology (MIT), and Stanford were the preferred destinations of these students. Yale, through its International and Foreign Economic Administration, for example, drew in such prominent architects of neoliberalism in Mexico as Mancera Aguayo, Petricioli Iturbide, Jesús Silva Herzog (treasury secretary, 1982–1986), Jaime Serra Puche (secretary of commerce and development, 1988–1994) and Ernesto Zedillo (budgeting and programming secretary, 1986–1988; president, 1994–2000). In Mexico the private university most important in educating this new technocratic elite was Mexico City's Autonomous Technological Institute of Mexico (ITAM). Camp, *Mexico's Mandarins*, 134–74; Centeno, *Democracy Within Reason*, 118–20; Daniel C. Levy, "The Political Consequences of Changing Socialization Patterns," in *Mexico's Political Stability: The Next Five Years*, ed. Roderic Ai Camp (Boulder, CO: Westview Press, 1986), 23–25.

14.   Oliver Schöller and Olaf Groh-Samberg, "The Education of Neoliberalism," in *Neoliberal Hegemony: A Global Critique*, eds. Dieter Plehwe, Bernhard Walpen, and Gisela Neunhöffer (Oxon: Routledge, 2006), 172–73.

15.   Dieter Plehwe and Bernhard Walpen, "Between Network and Complex Organization: The Making of Neoliberal Knowledge and Hegemony," in eds. Dieter Plehwe et al., 31–39.

16.   Camp, *Mexico's Mandarins*, 187; Fernando Ortega, "Los empresarios exhiben su voracidad y el PRI pretende callarlos," *Proceso* 332, January 31, 1983, 27.

17.   Héctor Águilar Camín, "A través del túnel," *Nexos* 60, no. 5 (December 1982): 14.

18.   While neoliberal reform became closely associated with a process of democratic transition during the 1980s in Latin America, its initial expressions in the authoritarian regimes of Chile and Argentina during the 1970s were based on a similar divorce between policy and politics. The justifications of authoritarian rule in Chile provide a particularly explicit example of this divide, with a 1977 editorial in the influential Chilean daily newspaper *El Mercurio* citing as a benefit of military rule that "it can enforce a model conceived by experts, without yielding nor attending to . . . the social reactions produced by its implementation." See Juan Gabriel Valdéz, *Pinochet's*

Economists: The Chicago School in Chile (Cambridge: Cambridge University Press, 1995); Bertha Lerner de Shiebaum, "1983: La ruptura frente al populismo, el compromiso con la austeridad y la renovación moral," *Revista Mexicana de Sociología* 45, no. 2 (April–June 1983): 545–74; Kurt Weyland, "Clarifying a Contested Concept: Populism in the Study of Latin American Politics," *Comparative Politics* 34, no. 1 (October 2001): 8.

19. Miguel de la Madrid Hurtado, "Discurso de Toma de Posesión de Miguel de la Madrid Hurtado como Presidente Constitucional de los Estados Unidos Mexicanos," accessed February 2, 2010, http://www.biblioteca.tv/artman2/publish/1982_73/Discurso_de_Toma_de_Posesi_n_de_Miguel_de_la_Madri_69.shtml.

20. Jose Fernández Santillán, "Estado y neoliberalismo en México," *Nexos* 7, no. 74 (February 1984): 37–41.

21. Centeno, *Democracy Within Reason*, 192.

22. Babb, *Managing Mexico*, 247–50.

23. Federico Reyes Heroles, "Regreso a diciembre," *Nexos* 66, no. 6 (June 1983): 52.

24. Centeno, *Democracy Within Reason*, 193–94.

25. Rolando Cordera and Raúl Trejo Delarbre, "Señales de diciembre (Notas sobre la Crisis, la Cámara, la Izquierda y el Nuevo Gobierno)," *Nexos* 63, no. 6 (March 1983): 27–28.

26. Carlos Acosta, "El gobierno sigue el programa del PAN: Meyer," *Proceso* 363, October 10, 1983, 29.

27. Camp, *Mexico's Mandarins*, 204–5.

28. Centeno, *Democracy Within Reason*, 194–96.

29. Carlos A. Medina, "Fallaron las predicciones de desintegración," *Excélsior*, September 17, 1983, 14.

30. Roberto Vizcaíno, "Nada cambiará la política exterior de México en Centroamérica, dice Lugo Gil," *Unomásuno*, November 21, 1984, 3.

31. Víctor Avilés, "México no replegará su política en Centroamérica," *Unomásuno*, March 22, 1983, 1, 4.

32. A. Ortiz Reza, "Ya no caben violencia ni demagogia: García Sainz," *Excélsior*, May 22, 1983, 1, 8; Gerardo Reyes, "La rectoría económica de la nación no se negocia: RAV," *Excélsior*, May 22, 1983, 29.

33. Reyes, *Excélsior*, May 22, 1983.

34. For a good general description of this phenomenon in a general sense, see John R. Gillis, "Memory and Identity: The History of a Relationship," in *Commemorations: The Politics of National Identity*, ed. John R. Gillis (Princeton, NJ: Princeton University Press, 1994), 19–20.

35. Benjamin, *La Revolución*, 42.

36. Víctor Áviles, "El pensamiento de Juárez, vigente: García Ramírez," *La Jornada*, March 22, 1985, 3.

37.   "La división artificial, inadmisible: Dávila Narro," *Unomásuno*, March 22, 1983, 2.

38.   Víctor Avilés, "En política, ni extranjeros ni clero: Lugo Gil," *Unomásuno*, March 22, 1984, 6.

39.   Vizcaíno, *Unomásuno*, November 21, 1984, 3.

40.   José Ureña, "Rechazo total a la 'intervención extranjera': Mendoza Berrueto," *La Jornada*, March 22, 1986, 6.

41.   Miguel Ángel Rivera, "Campaña deslegitimadora de la reacción en México: Lugo Verduzco," *La Jornada*, March 22, 1986, 1, 6.

42.   Pablo Hiriart, "Inconclusa, la Revolución, reconoce Bartlett," *La Jornada*, November 21, 1985, 6.

43.   Ibid.

44.   See Francis Fukuyama, *The End of History and the Last Man* (Toronto: Macmillan, 1992).

45.   Bruce Michael Bagley, "Interdependencia y política estadounidense hacia México en los años ochenta," in *México y los Estados Unidos: El manejo de la relación*, ed. Riordan Roett (Mexico City: Siglo XXI, 1989), 300–304.

46.   Richard J. Mieslen, "Killings in Mexico Bring U.S. Anger into the Open," *New York Times*, March 10, 1985, A5.

47.   Joel Brinkley, "Mexico City Depicted as a Soviet Spies' Haven," *New York Times*, June 23, 1985, A1.

48.   Bagley, 304–5; William Stockton, "Mexico's Bad Image in the U.S. and Vice Versa," *New York Times*, June 1, 1986, A2.

49.   C. Velasco Molina, "Límite intolerable de intervención en la era reaganiana," *Excélsior*, May 22, 1986, 1, 10.

50.   Manuel Robles, "Programa con episodios de elecciones pasadas, enfocado al futuro," *Proceso* 493, April 12, 1985, online version.

51.   Elías Chávez, "Defensa en abstracto: Indigna a la Cámara el reportaje de 'Newsweek' y no cita lo que dice," *Proceso* 490, March 22, 1985, online version.

52.   Despite the PAN's refusal, suspicions of the party's motives deepened following the approaches made in August 1986 to leaders of the PAN by a private fundraiser for Colonel Oliver North's support of the Nicaraguan Contras, who offered the party American support in return for financially assisting the Contra. Bagely, 306.

53.   "Nunca lograrán políticos extranjeros desprestigiar al país: Rodríguez y R.," *Excélsior*, May 22, 1986, 1, 18.

54.   José Ureña, "Rechazo total a 'la intervención extranjera': Mendoza Berrueto," *La Jornada*, March 22, 1986, 6.

55.   Pascual Salanueva Camargo, "Serios riesgos corren identidad e independencia nacionales," *La Jornada*, September 17, 1986, 6, 32.

56. Ibid., 32.

57. Wayne A. Cornelius, *The Political Economy of Mexico under De la Madrid: The Crisis Deepens, 1985–1986* (San Diego, CA: Center for U.S.-Mexican Studies, 1986), 4–7.

58. Ibid., 11.

59. Ibid., 13–16.

60. Centeno, *Democracy Within Reason*, 191.

61. Carlos A. Medina, "Fallaron las predicciones de desintegración," *Excélsior*, September 17, 1983, 14.

62. Nidia Marin, "No nos socavarán las calumnias: Del Marzo," *Excélsior*, May 22, 1986, 32.

63. Aurelio Ramos M., "'La crisis no ha sido superada, pero está controlada,'" *Excélsior*, November 21, 1983, 1.

64. Ibid., 42.

65. "Declara Ruiz Massieu que es necesario 'cambiar mucho,'" *La Jornada*, May 22, 1985, 3.

66. Ibid.

67. Mario García Sordo, "SRA: no hay tierras afectables; en Morelos, 580 latifundios: CNC," *Unomásuno*, April 11, 1983, 5.

68. These groups were organized under the National Coordinator of the Plan de Ayala (CNPA) in association with the Independent Center of Agricultural Workers and Peasants (CIOAC), and the General Union of Workers and Peasants of Mexico (UGOCM-Roja) and the Emiliano Zapata Union of Villagers in association with the Revolutionary Peasant Alliance. "Denuncias y peticiones en las concentraciones de campesinos," *Unomásuno*, April 11, 1984, 1, 6.

69. "Denuncias y peticiones," 1, 6.

70. Gonzalo Álvarez de Villar, "Zapata, símbolo de una lucha no concluida: Othón Salazar," *Unomásuno*, April 10, 1984, 4.

71. Guillermo Correa, "Traiciones, piratería y zancadillas, entre las centrales agrarias," *Proceso* 440, April 6, 1985, online version.

72. Rosa Rojas and Hermenegildo Castro, "Califica de inauténtica la SRA a la marcha campesina," *La Jornada*, April 11, 1985, 10.

73. Guillermo Correa, "30,000 campesinos, aquí; actos en 22 estados para impugnar la SRA," *Proceso* 441, April 13, 1985, online version.

74. Bolívar Hernández, "Tierras, créditos y cese de la represión, sus demandas," *La Jornada*, April 11, 1985, 1.

75. Rosa Rojas and Hermenegildo Castro, "Califica de inauténtica," 10.

76. Hermenegildo Castro, "Llamó la SRA a campesinos a luchar al lado del régimen," *La Jornada*, April 11, 1987, 7.

77. Correspondents, "Con plantones y demandas los campesinos recordaron a Zapata," *La Jornada*, April 11, 1987, 7.

78.   Rosa Rojas, "Tres marchas campesinas en el DF; demandan tierra, libertad y justicia," *La Jornada*, April 11, 1987, 28.

79.   Samuel Brunk, "Remembering Emiliano Zapata: Three Moments in the Posthumous Career of the Martyr of Chinameca," *Hispanic American Historical Review* 78, no. 3 (August 1998): 463.

80.   Eric Van Young, "Conclusion: The State as Vampire—Hegemonic Projects, Public Ritual and Popular Culture in Mexico, 1600–1990," in *Rituals of Rule, Rituals of Resistance: Public Celebrations and Popular Culture in Mexico*, eds. William H. Beezley, Cheryl E. Martin, and William E. French (Wilmington, DE: Scholarly Resources, 1994), 345.

Snapshot Three

1.   Alberto Aziz Nassif, "Chihuahua y los límites de la democracia electoral," *Revista Mexicana de Sociología* 49, no. 4 (1987): 166–71.

2.   With candidates in just 34 of the state's 67 municipalities, the PAN's voting total in 1983 was only 3,598 below that of the PRI. In the 1985 legislative elections the PAN officially won three of the state's ten federal deputations by district while claiming fraud prevented the recognition of a genuine total of five deputations won. José Fuentes Mares, "En el verano chihuahuense pesarán más los factores anexos que los candidatos," *Proceso* 484, February 8, 1986, online version; Yemile Mizrahi, "Las Elecciones en Chihuahua," in *Elecciones y partidos políticos en México*, eds. Manuel Larrosa and Leonardo Valdés (Mexico City: UAM-Iztapalapa, 1994), 133.

3.   Carlos Alba Vega and Hélène Rivière d'Arc, "Empresarios locales: ¿actores del cambio político?," in *Desarrollo y política en la frontera norte*, eds. Carlos Alba Vega and Alberto Aziz Nassif (Tlalpan: CIESAS, 2000), 23–24; Paul Cooney, "The Mexican Crisis and the Maquiladora Boom: A Paradox of Development or the Logic of Neoliberalism?," *Latin American Perspectives* 28, no. 3 (2001): 60–62; Deborah Cohen, *Braceros: Migrant Citizens and Transnational Subjects in the Postwar United States and Mexico* (Chapel Hill: University of North Carolina Press, 2011), 240; Robert B. South, "Transnational 'Maquiladora' Location," *Annals of the Association of American Geographers* 80, no. 4 (1990): 550–54.

4.   Julia Preston and Samuel Dillon, *Opening Mexico: The Making of a Democracy* (New York: Farrar, Straus and Giroux, 2004), 124; Francisco Reveles Vázquez, *El PAN en la oposición: Historia Básica* (Mexico City: Gernika, 2003), 142.

5.   Alba Vega and Rivière d'Arc, 29.

6.   Mark Wasserman, *Persistent Oligarchs: Elites and Politics in Chihuahua, Mexico, 1910–1940* (Durham, NC: Duke University Press, 1993), 117.

7.   Ibid., 74–83.

8.   Alberto Aziz Nassif, *Chihuahua: Historia de una alternativa*

(Mexico City: La Jornada Ediciones, 1994), 75–77; Kathleen Staudt and Carlota Aguilar, "Political Parties, Women Activists' Agendas and Household Relations: Elections on Mexico's Northern Frontier," *Mexican Studies/ Estudios Mexicanos* 8, no. 1 (Winter 1992): 96; Francisco Ortiz Pinchetti, "El candidato priísta en Juárez, un magnate, define: PRI y PAN persigue iguales objetos, por diferentes caminos," *Proceso* 496, May 3, 1986, online version.

9. Soledad Loaeza, *El Partido Acción Nacional: la larga marcha, 1939–1994. Oposición leal y partido de protesta* (Mexico City: Fondo de Cultura Económica, 1999), 391; Francisco Ortiz Pinchetti, "El PAN, sólo pretexto para expresar su voluntad," *Proceso* 496, May 3, 1986, online version.

10. Wasserman, *Persistent Oligarchs*, 138–41.

11. Francisco Ortiz Pinchetti, "El PRI ha trabajado para ganar mientras la oposición habla de fraude, dice Gurría," *Proceso* 504, June 28, 1986, online version.

12. The Instituto de Seguridad y Servicios Sociales de Trabajadores del Estado (ISSTE) and the Instituto Mexicano del Seguro Social (IMSS) provide social security and health services to state and private workers respectively.

13. Carlos Monsiváis, "Crónica de Chihuahua: ¿en qué parte del camino perdimos la revolución?," *Proceso* 479, January 4, 1986, online version.

14. Ortiz Pinchetti, *Proceso* 496, May 3, 1986.

15. Through 1985 and into 1986, the Chihuahua government was in conflict with organized labor, particularly steel workers, who protested against the government and existing corporatist organizations while supporting non-PRI affiliated organizations. Peasants in Chihuahua had also successfully fought against PRI-allied peasant official organizations the CNC and the League of Agrarian Communities to gain higher prices for their crops from the government, in 1985 forming the Democratic Peasant Movement (MDC) as an independent peasant organization and taking actions such as occupying and sacking state-run Conasupo supermarkets. In 1988 the MDC changed its name to the Democratic Peasant Front (FDC). Aziz Nassif, *Historia de una alternativa*, 79; Raúl Trejo Delarbre, *Crónica del sindicalismo en México, 1976–1988* (Mexico City: Siglo XXI, 1990), 184–85.

16. Aziz Nassif, *Historia de una alternativa*, 83.

17. Ibid., 79.

18. Ibid., 77–80.

19. Francisco Ortiz Pinchetti, "El movimiento democrático electoral, dispuesto a paralizar Chihuahua," *Proceso* 503, June 21, 1986, online version; Caroline Beer, "Measuring the Impact of Popular Organization: The Frente Democrático Campesino in Chihuahua, Mexico" (Paper prepared for Meeting of the Latin American Studies Association, Guadalajara, 1997), 9.

20. Aziz Nassif, *Historia de una alternativa*, 71–83; Francisco Ortiz

Pinchetti, "El padrón electoral y las casillas, clave del fraude," *Proceso* 503, June 21, 1986, online version; Ortiz Pinchetti, *Proceso* 496, May 3, 1986.

21.   Aziz Nassif, *Historia de una alternativa*, 90–91; Loaeza, *El Partido Acción Nacional*, 389; Ortiz Pinchetti, *Proceso* 503, June 21, 1986.

22.   Roderic Ai Camp, *Crossing Swords: Politics and Religion in Mexico* (New York: Oxford University Press, 1997), 63.

23.   Aziz Nassif, *Historia de una alternativa*, 85.

24.   Francisco Ortiz Pinchetti, "Decisión de paralizar la entidad si hay fraude," *Proceso* 504, June 28, 1986, online version.

25.   Ortiz Pinchetti, *Proceso* 496, May 3, 1986.

26.   Enrique Maza, "En descomposición, la clase política de Chihuahua," *Proceso* 499, May 24, 1986, online version.

27.   Francisco Ortiz Pinchetti, "La homilía del hermano Baeza," *Proceso* 505, July 5, 1986, online version.

28.   Manuel Robles, "Programa con episodios de elecciones pasadas, enfocado al futuro," *Proceso* 493, April 12, 1986, online version.

29.   Enrique Maza, "El PRI contrata una agencia para que dé a conocer a Baeza en Estados Unidos y contrarraestar al PAN," *Proceso* 499, May 24, 1985, online version.

30.   Francisco Ortiz Pinchetti, "Antes que se conocieran las cifras oficiales, de la Madrid proclamó el triunfo del PRI," *Proceso* 506, July 12, 1986, online version.

31.   Aziz Nassif, *Historia de una alternativa*, 93–94.

32.   Aziz Nassif, *Historia de una alternativa*, 94; Francisco Ortiz Pinchetti, "Tras el fraude, el manipuleo informativo," *Proceso* 506, July 12, 1986, online version.

33.   Robles, *Proceso* 493, April 12, 1986.

34.   The only opposition victories recognized were of the PAN in the municipality of Nuevo Casas Grandes and the Popular Socialist Party (PPS) in Gómez Farías. Francisco Ortiz Pinchetti, "Chihuahua: De la ira a la cerrazón, del fraude al menosprecio oficial," *Proceso* 507, July 19, 1986, online version.

35.   Despite this initial response, the PRI had been largely successful in dividing the local business community and calls for protest actions from private sector organizations met with little success. Aziz Nassif, *Historia de una alternativa*, 106; Loaeza, *El Partido Acción Nacional*, 393; Francisco Ortiz Pinchetti, "Tras el fraude."

36.   The civil disobedience measures included boycotts against newspapers and radio stations judged to be biased toward the PRI and blocking the state's highways if the victory of the usurpers was upheld by electoral authorities. Aziz Nassif, *Historia de una alternativa*, 95–96; Preston and Dillon, 135–36.

37.   Camp, *Crossing Swords*, 64; Francisco Ortiz Pinchetti, "Campaña

orquestrada, las críticas a la suspensión de misas: el Arzobispo Almeida," *Proceso* 507, July 19, 1986, online version.

38. Following direct lobbying from federal interior minister Manuel Bartlett, the Vatican intervened and the suspension of mass was ultimately rescinded. Camp, *Crossing Swords*, 64–66.

39. Francisco Ortiz Pinchetti, "Luis H. Álvarez, tres semanas en huelga de hambre: 'Quiero vivir, pero como hombre libre,'" *Proceso* 507, July 19, 1986, online version.

40. Aziz Nassif, *Historia de una alternativa*, 99; Loaeza, *El Partido Acción Nacional*, 394–95.

41. Francisco Ortiz Pinchetti, "Todo concluye en Chihuahua: Se modificó un código, se tomaron palacios y hay nuevos alcaldes," *Proceso* 519, September 11, 1986, online version.

42. Ortiz Pinchetti, "Decisión de paralizar"; Soledad Loaeza, "Julio de 86: La cuña y el palo," *Nexos* 103, no. 9 (1986): 19.

Chapter Three

1. Jesús J. Silva-Herzog Márquez, "Memorias del ornitorrinco," *Nexos* 17, no. 194 (February 1994): 29–39.

2. Soledad Loaeza, *El Partido Acción Nacional: la larga marcha, 1939–1994. Oposición leal y partido de protesta* (Mexico City: Fondo de Cultura Económica, 1999), 27; Soledad Loaeza, "El llamado de las urnas," *Nexos* 8, no. 90 (June 1985): 16.

3. Incentives for participation included granting registration to formally outlawed parties, lowering the voter support needed for conserving registration from 3 to 1.5 percent, granting temporary registration to new parties, permitting greater representation for minor parties in the federal Chamber of Deputies and gesturing toward greater electoral transparency. As a disincentive for nonparticipation, parties that did not participate in a federal election would now automatically lose their registration. Todd A. Eisenstadt, *Courting Democracy in Mexico: Party Strategies and Electoral Institutions* (Cambridge: Cambridge University Press, 2004), 39.

4. Miguel de la Madrid Hurtado, "Discurso de Toma de Posesión de Miguel de la Madrid Hurtado como Presidente Constitucional de los Estados Unidos Mexicanos," accessed February 2, 2010, http://www.biblioteca.tv/artman2/publish/1982_73/Discurso_de_Toma_de_Posesi_n_de_Miguel_de_la_Madri_69.shtml.

5. Secretaría de Programación y Presupuesto, *Plan Nacional de Desarrollo, 1983–1988* (Mexico City: Secretaría de Programación y Presupuesto, 1983), 576.

6. José López Portillo, Demetrio Sodi, and Infante Fernando Díaz, *Quetzalcóatl* (Mexico City: Sahop, 1977); Alan Riding, *Distant Neighbors: A Portrait of the Mexicans* (New York: Vintage Books, 2000), 15.

7.   Eisenstadt, *Courting Democracy*, 41; Soledad Loaeza, "Entre el pluralismo y la fragmentación," *Nexos* 14, no. 160 (April 1991): 27–29; Loaeza, *El Partido Acción Nacional*, 218; Victoria E. Rodríguez, "The Politics of Decentralisation in Mexico: From Municipio Libre to Solidaridad," *Bulletin of Latin American Research*, 12, no. 2 (May 1993): 133–37.

8.   Miguel de la Madrid Hurtado, "I Informe de Gobierno del Presidente Constitucional de los Estados Unidos Mexicanos Miguel de la Madrid Hurtado 1° de septiembre de 1983," in Miguel de la Madrid Hurtado, *Informes Presidenciales* (Mexico City: Servicio de Documentación, Investigación y Análisis del Congreso de la Unión, 2006), 5.

9.   While in 1960 Mexico officially became a predominantly urban country, the percentage of the population living in urban areas had risen from 50.7 percent in that year to 66.3 percent in 1980 and the percentage of the workforce in agriculture dropped from 57 percent to 26 percent. Héctor Aguilar Camín, "El canto del futuro," *Nexos* 100, no. 9 (April 1986): 15.

10.   Lilia Venegas, "Women in the Border: The Panista Militants of Tijuana and Ciudad Juárez," in *Women's Participation in Mexican Political Life*, ed. Victoria E. Rodríguez (Boulder, CO: Westview Press, 1998), 209–10.

11.   The PAN did face opposition from another historical Catholic opposition movement from the Sinarquista millenarian tradition in the electoral process post-1977 for the first time since the 1940s in the form of the Mexican Democratic Party (PDM). The PDM's platform in 1982 differed from the PAN's in its radical opposition to capitalist as well as socialist forms of political, economic, and social organization. PDM support was particularly concentrated in the states of San Luis Potosí, Guanajuato, Michoacán, Tlaxcala, and Jalisco. There was also strong electoral support in regions with a strong Sinarquista tradition in the 1930s and 1940s, including Chilapa, Guerrero, where the party managed to win control of municipal government as it also did in the city of Guanajuato. Nationally, however, the PDM ended up as the fourth-placed opposition party in 1982 and polled behind both the PAN and left-wing PSUM in both chambers of Congress and for president. See Silvia Gómez Tagle, "El Partido Demócrata Mexicano y su presencia en la sociedad," *Revista Mexicana de Sociología* 46, no. 2 (April–June 1984), 75–110; Roderic Ai Camp, *Crossing Swords: Politics and Religion in Mexico* (New York: Oxford University Press, 1997), 6.

12.   Camp, *Crossing Swords*, 4–7.

13.   This was manifested in the replacement of several bishops considered sympathetic to liberation theology with traditionalists during the 1980s, including the high-profile bishop of Cuernavaca, Morelos, Sergio Méndez Arceo, whose replacement in March 1983 was greeted enthusiastically by anticommunist youth organizations and whose immediate successor replaced twenty-five priests in two months as part of an effort to reverse the impact of Méndez Arceo's preaching. Carlos Fazio, "La Iglesia anticomunista empieza a desplazar a la de los pobres," *Proceso* 333, March 21, 1983, 18–23; Camp, *Crossing* Swords, 85–99.

14.   Joseph M. Palacios, *The Catholic Social Imagination: Activism and the Just Society in Mexico and the United States* (Chicago, IL: University of Chicago Press, 2007), 19.

15.   Camp, *Crossing Swords*, 7; Soledad Loaeza, "La rebelión de la Iglesia," *Nexos* 78, no. 7 (June 1984): 14–15.

16.   Ben Ross Schneider, "Why Is Mexican Business So Organized?," *Latin American Research Review* 37, no. 1 (2002): 87.

17.   Bartra, "Viaje al centro de la derecha," 15.

18.   David Harvey, *A Brief History of Neoliberalism* (Oxford: Oxford University Press, 2005), 43.

19.   David Harvey, "Neoliberalism as Creative Destruction," *Annals of the American Academy of Political and Social Science* 610, no. 21 (2007): 25–26.

20.   Harvey, *A Brief History of Neoliberalism*, 21.

21.   This discourse was further promoted by think tanks associated with organizations such as the CCE and publications aimed at the business community, including the magazines *Expansión, Negocios y Bancos, Decisión, USEM,* and the bulletin *Acción.* Miguel Abruch Linder, "La cruzada empresarial," *Nexos* 64, no. 6 (April 1983): 25; Fernando Ortega, "Los empresarios exhiben su voracidad y el PRI pretende callarlos," *Proceso* 326, January 31, 1983, 26–27; Ricardo Tirado and Matilde Luna, "El Consejo Coordinador Empresarial de México: De la unidad contra el reformismo a la unidad para el TLC (1975–1993)," *Revista Mexicana de Sociología* 57, no. 4 (October–December 1995): 27–59.

22.   "Sólo el Presidente puede limitar el poder presidencial: Krauze," *Proceso* 313, November 1, 1982, 27.

23.   Francisco Ortiz Pinchetti, "No hubo paro, mas sí ataques al presidente y loas al gobernador," *Proceso* 306, September 13, 1982, 17–18.

24.   Consejo Coordinador Empresarial, "Aclaraciones Necesarias (advertisement)," *Excélsior,* September 3, 1982, 3.

25.   Herminio Rebollo, "Se opondrán los comerciantes organizados a la renuncia de la libertad: Goicoechea Luna," *El Universal,* September 6, 1982, 9.

26.   Abelardo Martín y Víctor Manuel Juárez, "Censuran las medidas gubernamentales los dirigentes del sector privado," *Unomásuno,* September 2, 1982, 9.

27.   Particularly notable is *Negocios y Bancos* columnists and first chief of the Traditional Falangists of Mexico, Celerino Salmerón, who only used the Hispanicized spelling "Méjico" in his columns and attacked the "official history" of revolutionary nationalism. Celerino Salmerón, "Socialismo y comunismo marxistas, condenados por materialistas y anticristianos," *Negocios y Bancos* 609, July 7, 1982, 12–14; Celerino Salmerón, "La Historia Oficial no es Científica, sino Artificial Arma de Partido," *Negocios y Bancos* 616, October 31, 1982, 18.

28.   Jean-François Prud'homme, "Interest Representation and the Party System in Mexico," in *What Kind of Democracy? What Kind of Market? Latin America in the Age of Neoliberalism,* eds. Philip D. Oxhorn and Graciela Ducatenzeiler (University Park: University of Pennsylvania Press, 1998), 177. Francisco Valdés Ugalde, *Autonomía y Legitimidad: Los empresarios, la política y el estado en México* (Mexico City: Siglo Veintiuno, 1997), 219.

29.   Valdés Ugalde, *Autonomía y legitimidad,* 208–9.

30.   For example, during the Atalaya 82 (Watchtower 82) conference organized by the CCE in response to the economic crisis, guests included not only economic advisors to the government of UK Prime Minister Margaret Thatcher, but French Catholic philosopher Gustave Thibon. Coparmex also historically cited Catholic social doctrine as a source of ideological guidance. In some rare cases there were also direct institutional links between business and church institutions, such as that between Catholic organization Opus Dei and the Pan-American Institute of Advanced Business Training (IPADE), an influential business school run by the Iberoamericana University in Mexico City. Arce Alferez, "Asalto Total a Occidente: Se pulverizan todos sus valores en beneficio del bolchevismo," *Negocios y Bancos* 609, July 15, 1982, 7–10; Oscar Hinojosa, "El Opus Dei avanza en la conquista del poder en México," *Proceso* 343, May 30, 1983, 11–15; Loaeza, *El Partido Acción Nacional,* 358; Carlos Ramírez, "Meta de la gran empresa: regular la economía, con inspiración religiosa," *Proceso* 273, January 25, 1982, 11–13.

31.   Aziz Nassif, "Chihuahua y los límites," 163.

32.   Francisco Reveles Vázquez, "Las fracciones del Partido Acción Nacional: Una interpretación," *Revista Mexicana de Sociología* 60, no. 3 (July–September 1998): 53–54; Laborde, 162.

33.   Joseph L. Klesner, "Electoral Competition and the New Party System in Mexico," *Latin American Politics and Society* 47, no. 2 (Summer 2005): 104–5; Reveles Vázquez, *El PAN en la oposición,* 100–110; Reveles Vázquez, "Las fracciones del Partido Acción Nacional," 53–54; Tania Hernández Vicencia, "Paradojas, acuerdos y contradicciones: El Partido Acción Nacional," in *Los Partidos Políticos en México: ¿Crisis, adaptación o transformación?,* ed. Francisco Reveles Vázquez (Mexico City: Gernika, 2005), 167.

34.   René Delgado, "Oposición de PAN y PDM a medidas gubernamentales," *Unomásuno,* September 3, 1982, 2.

35.   Loaeza, *El Partido Acción Nacional,* 362–68; Carlos Arriola, *Ensayos sobre el PAN* (Mexico City: Miguel Ángel Porrua, 1994), 47.

36.   The entry of agrobusiness figures into the party following the agrarian reforms of the Echeverría period and into the 1980s made the states of Sinaloa and Sonora, where it previously had little presence, into two of the PAN's major centers of support. In northern states such as Coahuila, Chihuahua, and Nuevo León, local business networks also often had stronger links with private enterprise in the United States than with the traditional

centers of the Mexican business and politics in Mexico City and Guadalajara. In a broader sense the PAN's center of support thus increasingly drifted northward from traditional southern strongholds such as Mexico City, Yucatán, and Oaxaca. Alba Vega and Rivière d'Arc, 355–58.

37.   Loaeza, *El Partido Acción Nacional*, 367–68; Francisco Reveles Vázquez, *El PAN en la Oposición*, 140.

38.   Arnaldo Córdova, "El PAN, partido gobernante," *Revista Mexicana de Sociología* 54, no. 3 (July–September 1992): 225; Eisenstadt, *Courting Democracy*, 1–2.

39.   Elías Chávez, "Los priístas hablan de democracia y no la practican: Al país sólo le falta un buen gobierno: Pablo Emilio Madero," *Proceso* 295, June 28, 1982, 12–15.

40.   Loaeza, *El Partido Acción Nacional*, 362–63; Reveles Vázquez, *El PAN en la oposición*, 125.

41.   Arnaldo Córdova, "Nocturno de la democracia mexicana, 1917–1984," *Nexos* 98, no. 9 (February 1986): 24; Loaeza, *El Partido Acción Nacional*, 367.

42.   José María Alanís, "En Monterrey, mil panistas se incrustaron en el desfile," *La Jornada*, November 21, 1985, 3.

43.   Laborde, 171–72.

44.   Salvador Corro, "No son los priístas los que rinden homenaje a los héroes," *Proceso* 449, June 8, 1985, online version.

45.   Octavio Paz, "Hora Cumplida (1929–1985)," *Vuelta* 9, no. 103 (June 1985): 10.

46.   Barry Carr, *Marxism and Communism in Twentieth-Century Mexico* (Lincoln: University of Nebraska Press, 1992), 266–78.

47.   Ibid., 302–3.

48.   Barry Carr, "The Fate of the Vanguard under a Revolutionary State: Marxism's Contribution to the Construction of the Great Arch," in *Everyday Forms of State Formation: Revolution and the Negotiation of Rule in Modern Mexico*, eds. Gilbert M. Joseph and Daniel Nugent (Durham, NC: Duke University Press, 1994), 331–33.

49.   Ibid., 328.

50.   For example, Lombardismo and the independent unionism of the electricians' union SUTERM during the early to mid 1970s. In the 1980s the PMT and the MAP (which dissolved into the PSUM in 1981) also closely identified with revolutionary nationalism. Carr, *Marxism and Communism*, 282–84; Christopher Domínguez Michael, "Quién es quién en la izquierda mexicana," *Nexos* 54, no. 5 (June 1982): 29.

51.   Adriana Borjas Benavente, *Partido de la Revolución Democrática: Estructura, organización interna y desempeño público, 1989–2003* (Mexico City: Gernika, 2003), 135.

52.   The groups that formed the PSUM included the Corriente Izquierda

(CI), Movimiento de Acción Política (MAP), and some members of the 68 and guerrilla movements. The other major party of the left in the 1980s was the Trotskyite Revolutionary Workers' Party (PRT). Borjas Benavente, 138.

53.   Carr, *Marxism and Communism,* 280–90; Arnaldo Córdova, "La cuestión nacional y la campaña electoral," *Proceso* 276, February 15, 1982, 33; Arnaldo Córdova, "Nación y nacionalismo en México," *Nexos* 83, no. 7 (November 1984): 30.

54.   Carr, "Mexican Communism," 218; Roberto Rock, "Advierte Jorge Alcocer sobre las reacciones de la derecha ante las medidas de López Portillo," *El Universal,* September 6, 1982, 1.

55.   Jorge Áviles, "De la Madrid, declarado Presidente electo; sólo el PAN votó en contra," *El Universal,* September 10, 1982, 1; Gerardo Galarza, "En la Cámara, sólo el PAN se alza en contra el daño moral: 'Soga al cuello de los informadores,'" *Proceso* 320, December 20, 1982, 16–17.

56.   Enrique Krauze, "Por una democracia sin adjetivos," *Vuelta* 8, no. 86 (January 1984): 12; Enrique Krauze, "El gobierno, la izquierda y la democracia," *Vuelta* 8, no. 91 (June 1984): 42; Octavio Paz, "Hora Cumplida (1929–1985)," *Vuelta* 9, no. 103 (June 1985): 10–11. Also see Ignacio M. Sánchez Prado, "Claiming Liberalism: Enrique Krauze, *Vuelta, Letras Libres,* and the Reconfigurations of the Mexican Intellectual Class," *Mexican Studies/Estudios Mexicanos* 26, no. 1 (Winter 2010): 47–78.

57.   Oscar Hinojosa, "En el II Congreso Nacional el PSUM mostró su inmadurez y cayó en contradicciones," *Proceso* 355, August 22, 1983, 16–21.

58.   Borjas Benavente, *Partido de la Revolución Democrática,* 135–37; Carr, "Mexican Communism," 220; Adolfo Gilly, "Las tres opciones de izquierda," *Proceso* 452, June 29, 1985, online version.

59.   Following the 1977 electoral reforms, the independent left as a whole saw its vote grow between 1982 and 1979 by 30 percent, while results in local elections doubled between 1980 and 1983. By way of contrast, the right-wing parties of the PAN and Mexican Democratic Party (PDM) saw their vote grow by 120 percent between 1979 and 1982, and in local elections between 1980 and 1983 that growth was 176 percent. Enrique Semo, "1985: La opción socialista," *Proceso* 429, January 19, 1985, online version.

60.   Judith Adler Hellman has questioned the extent to which the characteristics or tactics of these movements could be considered "new" social movements as they were generally described by political scientists according to the favored term for independent popular political organizations in Latin America more broadly during the 1970s and 1980s. Hellman argues that both their form and tactics are largely analogous to well-established tactics of popular protest in postrevolutionary Mexico. Judith Adler Hellman, "Mexican Popular Movements, Clientelism, and the Process of Democratization," *Latin American Perspectives* 21, no. 2 (Spring 1994): 124–42.

61.   Fabio Barbosa, "Las Utopías Cambiantes," *Nexos* 68, no. 6 (August 1983): 35–47; Paul L. Haber, "The Art and Implications of Political

Restructuring in Mexico: The Case of Urban Popular Movements," in *The Politics of Economic Restructuring: State-Society Relations and Regime Change in Mexico*, eds. Maria L. Cook, Kevin J. Middlebrook, and Juan Molinar Horcasitas (La Jolla, CA: Center for U.S.-Mexican Studies, 1994), 279–80; Judith Adler Hellman, "Mexican Popular Movements, Clientelism, and the Process of Democratization," *Latin American Perspectives* 21, no. 2 (Spring 1994): 127–30.

62. Vivienne Bennett, "Orígenes del Movimiento Urbano Popular Mexicano: pensamiento político y organizaciones políticas clandestinas, 1960–1980," *Revista Mexicana de Sociología* 55, no. 3 (July–September 1993): 89–102; Vivienne Bennett, "Everyday Struggles: Women in Urban Popular Movements and Territorially Based Protests in Mexico," in *Women's Participation in Mexican Political Life*, ed. Victoria E. Rodríguez (Boulder, CO: Westview Press, 1998), 120–21.

63. Independent organizations also began to combine through *coordinadoras* (sectoral coordinating bodies), such as the National "Plan de Ayala" Coordinating Committee and the National Coordinating Committee of the Urban Popular Movement (CONAMUP) that resembled broad social movements. Furthermore, during the early 1980s three multisectoral fronts were formed according to political currents: the Revolutionary Left Organization–Mass Line (OIR-LM), Revolutionary National Civic Association (ACNR), and Socialist Current (CS). Barry Carr, "The Mexican Left, the Popular Movements, and the Politics of Austerity, 1982–1985," in *The Mexican Left, the Popular Movements, and the Politics of Austerity*, eds. Barry Carr and Ricardo Anzaldúa Montoya (San Diego, CA: Center for U.S.-Mexican Studies, 1986), 16; Haber, 282; Juan José Rojas Herrera and Eduardo Moyano Estrada, "Acción colectiva y representación de intereses en la agricultura Mexicana: el caso del sector ejidal," *Agricultura y Sociedad* 82 (January–April 1997): 51–54.

64. During the postrevolutionary period, in their efforts to curb what were identified as traditional male vices such as alcoholism, violence, and sexual promiscuity as well as the influence of Catholic traditionalism, the state provided some spaces for the selective empowerment of women as domestic promoters of the health and education of the family. Institutions of the expanding state also provided greater opportunities for women who entered the public service through the expanding education system as nurses, hygienists, juvenile justice and social workers, and gymnasts and athletic directors promoting physical discipline. However, while new, the opportunities opened to women also tended to reinforce patriarchal ideas about women's rights and roles in society. Specific women's demands such as the extension of voting rights to women—not granted until 1953—were also subordinated to the revolutionary nationalist class-based framework of identities and rights. Jocelyn Olcott, "The Center Cannot Hold: Women on Mexico's Popular Front," in *Sex in Revolution: Gender, Politics, and Power in Modern Mexico*, eds. Jocelyn Olcott, Mary Kay Vaughan, and Gabriela Cano (Durham, NC: Duke University Press, 2006), 234; Carmen Ramos Escandón, "Women and Power

in Mexico: The Forgotten Heritage, 1880–1954," in ed. Rodríguez, 98–99; Mary Kay Vaughan, "Pancho Villa, the Daughters of Mary, and the Modern Woman: Gender in the Long Mexican Revolution," in eds. Olcott et al., 28.

65. Bennett, "Everyday Struggles," 118.

66. See Jocelyn Olcott, *Revolutionary Women in Postrevolutionary Mexico* (Durham, NC: Duke University Press, 2005); Vaughan, "Pancho Villa," 21–32.

67. Lynn Stephen, "Rural Women's Grassroots Activism, 1980–2000," in eds. Olcott et al., 248–50.

68. Carr, "The Mexican Left," 9; Venegas, 209–10.

69. One partial exception to this formal distance is the case of the Coalition of Workers, Peasants and Students of the Isthmus (COCEI), centered in Juchitán, Oaxaca, which did form an alliance with the Mexican Communist Party and subsequently the PSUM to compete electorally for local government to become the first and only municipality under a left-wing government in 1981. However, the COCEI's alliance with the PCM/PSUM was largely a tactical and temporary decision to win local power on the basis of an existing party's registration. Jeffrey W. Rubin, *Decentering the Regime: Ethnicity, Radicalism, and Democracy in Juchitán, Mexico* (Durham, NC: Duke University Press, 1997), 161–205; Jeffrey W. Rubin, "State Politics, Leftist Oppositions, and Municipal Elections," in *Electoral Patterns and Perspectives in Mexico*, ed. Arturo Alvarado (La Jolla, CA: Center for U.S.-Mexican Studies, 1986), 127–60; Ernesto Reyes, "Los priístas decretan la desaparición de poderes en Juchitán y el cabildo pide amparo," *Proceso* 353, August 8, 1983, 6–7.

70. Jeffrey W. Rubin, "COCEI in Juchitán: Grassroots Radicalism and Regional History," *Journal of Latin American Studies* 26, no. 1 (February 1994): 122.

71. Preston and Dillon, 108.

72. Lynn Stephen, "Rural Women's Grassroots Activism," 252.

73. In the wake of the 1985 Mexico City earthquake, several new loosely allied women's organizations were formed, including the Network Against Violence Toward Women, the Feminist Peasant Network, and the Network of Popular Educators, who employed a discourse dubbed *feminismo popular* (popular feminism), which united immediate material concerns of women to strategic gender activism. Bennett, "Everyday Struggles," 123; Stephen, "Rural Women's Grassroots Activism," 251.

74. These chronicles, which appeared in publications *Proceso*, *Cuadernos Políticos* and *El Cotidiano*, were republished in Carlos Monsiváis, *Entrada Libre: Crónicas de la sociedad que se organiza* (Mexico City: Ediciones Era, 1987).

75. Monsiváis, *Entrada Libre*; also see Elena Poniatowska, *Nada, nadie. Las voces del temblor* (Mexico City: Era, 1988).

76. Carlos Monsiváis, "Muerte y resurrección del nacionalismo mexicano," *Nexos* 109, no. 10 (January 1987): 13–22.

77. Jorge Cadena-Roa, "Strategic Framing, Emotions, and Superbarrio—Mexico City's Masked Crusader," in *Frames of Protest: Social Movements and the Framing Perspective*, eds. Hank Johnston and John A. Noakes (Oxford: Rowman & Littlefield, 2005), 73–74.

78. Angélica Cuéllar Vázquez, *La noche es de ustedes, el amanecer es nuestro* (Mexico City: UNAM, 1993), 77.

79. Quoted in Jorge Cadena-Roa, 78.

80. Hector Tobar, "Who Was That Masked Man? Ask the INS," *Los Angeles Times*, February 25, 1989; Frank del Olmo, "A 'Viva Super Barrio' in L.A. Is Not Exactly the Message Official Mexico Likes to Hear," *Los Angeles Times*, March 20, 1989.

81. See Devra Weber, "Historical Perspectives on Transnational Mexican Workers in California," in *Border Crossings: Mexican and Mexican-American Workers*, ed. John Mason Hart (Wilmington, DE: Scholarly Resources, 1998), 209–33.

82. See Angélica Cuéllar Vázquez, "Superbarrio y Asamblea de Barrios: un proyecto cultural y una moral alternativa en la Ciudad de México," in *Cultura, sociedad civil y proyectos culturales en México*, ed. Héctor Rosales (Mexico City: Dirección General de Culturas Populares/Centro Regional de Investigaciones Multidisciplinarias, 1994), 169–78; Cadena-Roa, 69–88.

83. Haber, 281–82.

84. Jorge Laso de la Vega, *La Corriente Democrática: Hablan los protagonistas* (Mexico City: Editorial Posada, 1987), 257–58.

85. A 1993 novella and subsequent play by Ignacio Solares under this title examined the contemporary crisis of authority in Mexico as the postrevolutionary social and political order crumbled. Ignacio Solares, *El gran elector* (Mexico City: Joaquín Mortiz, 1993).

86. Borjas Benavente, 165–66; Luis Javier Garrido, *La Ruptura: La Corriente Democrática del PRI*, Mexico City, Grijalbo, 1993, 113.

87. Borjas Benavente, 168; Garrido, 63–76.

88. García Calderón and Figueiras Calderón, 37.

89. Borjas Benavente, 183.

90. Garrido, 161–69.

91. Borjas Benavente, 189.

92. Reflecting this colloquial style, his nickname *Maquío* was often used for campaign material and he undertook an often unconventional campaign, for example appearing on the beach in Veracruz dressed in a bathing suit in order to "demystify" the presidency. Loaeza, *El Partido Acción Nacional*, 441–442; Guillermo Zamora, "La dirigencia panista ve en Clouthier la llegada de un nuevo estilo, 'lo que necesitamos,'" *Proceso* 578, November 28, 1987, electronic version; Ricardo Alemán Alemán, "Mítin de

Clouthier en traje de baño para desmitificar la Presidencia," *La Jornada*, Mach 28, 1988, 12, 32.

93. Elías Chávez, "De la Madrid se dice único responsable de la política económica y, ante el rumor, Salinas se proclama ya presidente," *Proceso* 584, January 9, 1988, online version.

94. Oscar Hinojosa, "Otro accidente a acarreados del PRI; el candidato, se dedica a oir quejas," *Proceso* 587, January 30, 1988, online version.

95. Raúl Rodríguez Castañeda, "El priísta Emilio Azcárraga y su esposa fueron en su yate a ver la nobleza europea y salvar a Venecia," *Proceso* 587, January 30, 1988, online version.

96. García Calderón and Figueiras Calderón, 48.

97. Teresa Gurza, "La empresa, el mejor invento del ser humano: Clouthier," *La Jornada*, January 9, 1988, 8, 38.

98. Ricardo Alemán Alemán, "Clouthier: gobierno y PRI desobedientes inciviles," *La Jornada*, February 24, 1988, 40.

99. Ricardo Alemán Alemán, "Menos gobierno, el programa," *La Jornada*, February 3, 1988, 40, 16.

100. Ricardo Alemán Alemán, "¡Filipinas! Llamado de Clouthier a desobedecer," *La Jornada*, March 16, 1988, 40; Ricardo Alemán Alemán, "Postulados de la Revolución 'siguen en el debe del PRI,'" *La Jornada*, March 24, 1988, 16.

101. Rafael Bermúdez, "*Maquío* echado de la Autónoma Benito Juárez de Oaxaca," *La Jornada*, March 18, 1988, 36.

102. Ricardo Alemán Alemán, "Recibimiento masivo a Manuel Clouthier," *La Jornada*, June 24, 1988, 8.

103. Miguel Ángel Rivera, "Energía en la defensa del interés nacional: Salinas en la frontera," *La Jornada*, March 22, 1988, 10; Enrique Garay, "Poco respuesta a Cárdenas," *La Jornada*, March 22, 1988, 32.

104. Ricardo Alemán Alemán, "¡Auxilio! gritan los panistas en la línea divisoria de cara a EU," *La Jornada*, March 22, 1988, 12, 32.

105. Ibid.

106. Ricardo Alemán Alemán, "En Mérida, jornada exitosa para el candidato del PAN," *La Jornada*, March 1, 1988, 8.

107. Ricardo Alemán and Felipe Cobián, "En Autlán, el mitin más desairado de Clouthier," *La Jornada*, February 8, 35.

108. Alemán Alemán, "¡Filipinas!," 40.

109. Kwanok Kim, "Contradictory Aspects of Democratization and Neoliberal Economic Reform: The Philippines and Korea in Comparative Perspective," *Korea Observer* 32, no. 1 (April 2001): 140–42.

110. Enrique Garay, "Condena de MMH a quienes pretenden la confrontación belicosa entre mexicanos," *La Jornada*, March 22, 1988, 1, 6.

111. Cristina Martin, "Insiste Clouthier en que debe seguirse el modelo de Filipinas," *La Jornada*, April 7, 1988, 32.

112. Hermenegildo Castro and Javier Villegas, "Cárdenas llama de nuevo a defender el voto," *La Jornada*, April 15, 1988, 16.

113. García Calderón and Figueiras Calderón, 50–51.

114. Alejandro Caballero and Víctor Ballinas, "Crítica priísta al medro con Lázaro Cárdenas," *La Jornada*, February 9, 1988, 10; Salvador Corro and Oscar Hinojosa, "Salinas enteró de qué es La Laguna," *Proceso*, 589, February 13, 1988, online version.

115. Adolfo Gilly, "El general no volvió; vino su hijo . . . contra el gobierno," *La Jornada*, February 12, 1988, 11.

116. Corro and Hinojosa, *Proceso*, 589.

117. Ernesto Reyes, "En la Mixteca también esperan la vuelta de Lázaro Cárdenas," *Proceso* 590, February 20, 1988, online version.

118. Guillermo Correa, "Mimado en la Mixteca, Cárdenas invita a acudir al Zócalo el día 18," *Proceso* 591, February 27, 1988, online version; Hermenegildo Castro, "Llama Cárdenas a la convergencia de las distintas fuerzas democráticas," *La Jornada*, February 22, 1988, 14, 40.

119. Hermenegildo Castro, "El acarreo es humillante: Cárdenas," *La Jornada*, February 23, 1988, 16.

120. Ibid.

121. Carlos Monsiváis, "En La Laguna, Cuauhtémoc cosechó el fruto de la ignorancia del PRI sobre Lázaro Cárdenas," *Proceso* 589, February 13, 1988, online version.

122. Claudio Lomnitz, "Narrating the Neoliberal Moment: History, Journalism, Historicity," *Public Culture*, 20, no. 1 (Winter 2008): 39–40.

123. Adolfo Gilly, ed., *Cartas a Cuauhtémoc Cárdenas* (Mexico City: Era, 1989).

124. JoAnn Martin, *Tepoztlán and the Transformation of the Mexican State* (Tucson: University of Arizona Press, 2005), 118–19.

125. Ibid., 20–24.

126. Caballero and Ballinas, "Crítica priísta al medro."

127. Miguel de la Madrid, "No volveremos a incurrir en la tentación populista," *La Jornada*, May 7, 1988, 15.

128. Miguel Ángel de Rivera, "Llama Salinas a los campesinos a impulsar una nueva reforma agraria," *La Jornada*, April 11, 1988, 14.

129. Hermenegildo Castro, "Acuerdan en Xochimilco crear una central campesina," *La Jornada*, April 11, 1988, 11, 40.

130. Rubén Álvarez, "Recuerdan petroleros a Cárdenas, sin precisar el nombre de pila," *La Jornada*, March 19, 1988, 14.

131. Hermenegildo Castro, "Conmemoró el FDN en el Zócalo la nacionalización," *La Jornada*, March 19, 1988, 1, 23.

132. Carlos Acosta et al., "Dos zócalos en el cincuentenario petrolero," *Proceso* 594, March 19, 1988, online version.

133. Miguel Ángel Granados Chapa, "Plaza Pública," *La Jornada*, March 25, 1988, 1, 4.

134. Carlos Marín, "Cardenismo hoy, ni en telenovela," *Proceso* 614, June 8, 1988, online version.

135. Ricardo Alemán Alemán, "Mitin de 30 mil panistas en Hermosillo," *La Jornada*, June 25, 1988, 36.

136. Borjas Benavente, 204–5.

137. The PMS was formed in 1987 from a merger of the PSUM and PMT during a new attempt at unity by the various parties of the parliamentary left following poor results in the 1985 federal legislative elections. The new party further attempted to address the left's weaknesses by adapting socialism to national traditions, which included insisting on a link between democracy and pluralism, supporting a mixed (public/private) economy, and identifying the party with the social justice ideals of Zapata, Villa, and Cárdenas. Borjas Benavente, 146–47.

138. René Delgado, "En abril, el voto favorecía a Salinas," *La Jornada*, May 23, 1988, 1.

139. Alejandro Caballero, "Heberto Castillo: en Cuauhtémoc, el espíritu de Lázaro Cárdenas," *La Jornada*, June 5, 1988, 12.

140. Borjas Benavente, 204–5.

141. Cuauhtémoc Cárdenas, "Tarea inaplazable, reconstruir la nación," *La Jornada*, June 26, 1988, 1.

142. Carlos Salinas de Gortari, "Defenderé independencia y soberanía: Salinas de Gortari," *La Jornada*, July 3, 1988, 9.

143. Azucena Valderrábano, "Clouthier exigió respeto al voto; la disyuntiva, 'democracia o autoriarismo,'" *La Jornada*, July 3, 1988, 11, 32.

144. Elías Chávez, "'Se cayó el sistema' afloran las dudas," *Proceso* 610, July 9, 1988, online version.

145. Martha Anaya, *1988: El año en que calló el sistema* (Mexico City: Debolsillo, 2009), 13–21; Elías Chávez, *Proceso* 610; Preston and Dillon, 163–64.

146. Oscar Hinojosa, "Trampas, componendas, presiones, manipulación," *Proceso* 610, July 9, 1988, online version.

147. Borjas Benavente, 216.

148. The states in which the FDN won the greatest percentage of the vote were Michoacán (63.8 percent), Morelos (57.7 percent), Estado de México (51.6 percent), DF (49.2 percent), and Baja California (37.2 percent). Iván Zavala, "El nuevo régimen," *Cuaderno de Nexos* 11, no. 128 (August 1988): v.

149. Carlos Monsiváis, "La confianza, en lucha con la desconfianza, une

a oposicionistas; cambia el domicilio del temor," *Proceso* 610, July 9, 1988, online version.

150. Gilly, *Cartas a Cuauhtémoc Cárdenas*, 23–26.

Snapshot Four

1. Fernando Serrano Migallón, *El Grito de Independencia: Historia de una pasión nacional* (Mexico City: Miguel Ángel Porrúa, 1981), 10.

2. Isabel Fernández Tejado and Carmen Nava Nava, "Images of Independence in the Nineteenth Century: The Grito de Dolores, History and Myth," in *¡Viva México! ¡Viva la Independencia!: Celebrations of September 16*, eds. William Beezley and David Lorey (Wilmington, DE: Scholarly Resources, 2001), 3.

3. For example, a newspaper report listed as the *saldo rojo* (negative balance) of the night of September 15, 1984, "fifteen deaths, 122 injured, robberies worth a total of around 35 million pesos, 64 people taken to the Public Prosecutor for having committed various infractions, multiple burnings of tires in public roads and losses of approximately 30 million pesos." "Presidió DLM la ceremonia del grito y el desfile militar," *Unomásuno*, September 17, 1984, 5.

4. Carlos Acosta et al., "El fraude electoral técnicamente un golpe de Estado, dijo Cárdenas en el Zócalo," *Proceso* 611, July 16, 1988, online version.

5. *Judas* are large figures made out of papier-mâché that traditionally take the form of a human or colorful devil figures that represent evil. They are burned using fire and pyrotechnics during Easter Sunday or New Year festivities in town squares, particularly in rural Mexico. William Beezley, *Judas at the Jockey Club and Other Episodes of Porfirian Mexico* (Lincoln: University of Nebraska Press, 2004), 89–124.

6. Acosta et al., *Proceso* 611.

7. Oscar Hinojosa, "Cárdenas dispuesto a la conciliación, si se respeta la voluntad popular," *Proceso* 611, July 23, 1988, online version.

8. Silvia González Marín, ed., *La prensa partidista en las elecciones de 1988* (Mexico City: UNAM, 1992), 241–42.

9. Elías Chávez, "Ante la calificación final," *Proceso* 615, August 13, 1988, online version.

10. Gerardo Galarza, "En gritos gasten los presuntos el poco tiempo que tienen," *Proceso* 616, August 20, 1988, online version; Pascal Beltrán del Río, Homero Campa, and Gerardo Galarza, "El PRI cierra ojos y oidos y aprueba hasta ilícitos; se encona el Colegio Electoral," *Proceso* 617, August 27, 1988, online version; González Marín, 245–46.

11. Raúl Monge, "Con acarreados y amenazados Salazar Toledano 'gana la calle,'" *Proceso* 617, August 27, 1988, online version.

12. Elías Chávez, Gerardo Galarza, and Oscar Hinojosa, "Estrenó el

Congreso el rudo lenguaje de la democracia," *Proceso* 618, March 7, 1988, online version.

13.   Ibid.

14.   Julia Preston and Samuel Dillon, *Opening Mexico: The Making of a Democracy* (New York: Farrar, Straus and Giroux, 2004), 177.

15.   Cuauhtémoc Cárdenas, "El FDN obtuvo la votación más alta en la elección presidencial," *La Jornada*, September 18, 1988, 12.

16.   Ibid.

17.   Ricardo Alemán Alemán, "En acto paralelo, los panistas dieron su grito en El Ángel," *La Jornada*, September 17, 1988, 9.

18.   The precise phrase associated with the "Grito de Dolores" is generally "Abajo el mal gobierno!" (Down with bad government!). Pascal Beltrán del Río, "'No me voy: Me tendrán que aguantar para rato': Y Maquío dio El Grito," *Proceso* 620, September 17, 1988, online version. Alemán Alemán, "En acto paralelo," 9.

19.   Beltrán del Río, online version.

20.   "Unión, Religión, Independencia" was the motto of the First Mexican Empire and was featured on the country's flag during this period. Ibid.

21.   Alejandro Caballero and Roberto Zamarripa, "Protestas en el Zócalo en la ceremonia de El Grito," *La Jornada*, September 17, 1988, 6.

22.   It was returned roughly thirty minutes later to a *La Jornada* reporter. Ibid.

23.   Carlos Acosta, Raúl Monge, Miguel Cabildo, and Manuel Robles, "Un politizado 15 de septiembre," *Proceso* 620, September 17, 1988, online version; Caballero and Zamarripa, "Protestas en el Zócalo," 6.

24.   Caballero and Zamarripa, "Protestas en el Zócalo," 6.

25.   Acosta, Monge, Cabildo, and Robles, "Un politizado 15 de septiembre"; Caballero and Zamarripa, "Protestas en el Zócalo," 6.

26.   Roberto Fuentes Vivar, "37 mil personas desfilaron del Zócalo a Chapultepec," *La Jornada*, September 17, 1987, 7.

27.   Ibid.

Chapter Four

1.   It has also been described as a historical/sociological phenomenon arising through multiclass coalitions during the periods of industrialization in Latin America, particularly in the 1930s and 1940s. However, the persistence of populism has led to this perspective being largely abandoned. Kenneth M. Roberts, "Neoliberalism and the Transformation of Populism in Latin America: The Peruvian Case," *World Politics* 48, no. 1 (October 1995): 85.

2.   Alan Knight, "Populism and Neo-Populism in Latin America,

Especially Mexico," *Journal of Latin American Studies* 30, no. 2 (May 1998): 231–32.

3.   Rogelio Hernández Rodríguez, "Inestabilidad política y presidencialismo en México," *Mexican Studies/Estudios Mexicanos* 10, no. 1 (Winter 1994): 190–91.

4.   See Jolle Demmers, Alex E. Fernández Jilberto, and Barbara Hogenboom, "The Transformation of Latin American Populism: Regional and Global Dimensions," in *Miraculous Metamorphoses: The Neoliberalization of Latin American Populism*, eds. Jolle Demmers, Jilberto, Fernández, and Barbara Hogenboom (London: Zed Books, 2001), 1–21; Rudiger Dornbusch and Sebastian Edwards, "The Macroeconomics of Populism," in *The Macroeconomics of Populism in Latin America*, eds. Rudiger Dornbusch and Sebastian Edwards (Chicago, IL: University of Chicago Press, 1991), 7–13; Robert Kaufman and Barbara Stallings, "The Political Economy of Populism," in eds. Dornbusch and Edwards, 15–43; Jeffrey Sachs, *Social Conflict and Populist Policies in Latin America* (Cambridge: NBER Working Paper no. 2897, 1989).

5.   See Carlos Bazdresch and Santiago Levy, "Populism and Economic Policy in Mexico: 1970-1982," in eds. Dornbusch and Edwards, 223–62.

6.   One example was Enrique Krauze, who argued that many on the left in Mexico continued to hold on to outdated statist ideas inspired by socialism. Such people in the media, academia, and politics were, according to Krauze, not just pathetic and boring but "dangerous." Enrique Krauze, "Falsos profetas," *Vuelta* 15, no. 171 (February 1991), 52–53.

7.   Roberts, 83–87.

8.   Kurt Weyland, "Neopopulism and Neoliberalism in Latin America: How Much Affinity?," *Third World Quarterly* 24, no. 6 (2003): 1097–98. Also, Roberts, 84–85, gives a good summary of the previously dominant analytical approaches to populism.

9.   Roberts, 89.

10.   See Knight, "Populism and Neo-Populism," 223–48; Roberts, 82–116; Weyland, 1095–115.

11.   Weyland, "Neopopulism and Neoliberalism," 1097.

12.   David Harvey, *A Brief History of Neoliberalism* (Oxford: Oxford University Press, 2007), 64–67; Weyland, "Neopopulism and Neoliberalism," 1098.

13.   Francisco González, *Dual Transitions from Authoritarian Rule: Institutionalized Regimes in Chile and Mexico, 1970-2000* (Baltimore, MD: Johns Hopkins University Press, 2008), 31.

14.   Weyland, "Neopopulism and Neoliberalism," 1099.

15.   Roberts, 90.

16.   Paul Haber, "The Art and Implications of Political Restructuring in Mexico: The Case of Urban Popular Movements," in *The Politics of Economic Restructuring: State-Society Relations and Regime Change in*

Mexico, eds. Maria L. Cook, Kevin J. Middlebrook, and Juan Molinar Horcasitas (San Diego, CA: Center for U.S.-Mexican Studies, 1994), 277–303.

17.   Carlos Salinas de Gortari, "Discurso de Toma de Posesión de Carlos Salinas de Gortari como Presidente Constitucional de los Estados Unidos Mexicanos," accessed August 3, 2010, http://cronica.diputados.gob.mx/DDebates/54/1er/Ord/19881201.html.

18.   According to Hutchinson, moral innovators are reformist nationalists who promote a vision of the nation in which "the golden age was used to transform the accepted meanings of tradition and modernity so that they were one and the same, and thereby persuade their adherents to ally in the national project." John Hutchinson, "Myth Against Myth: The Nation as Ethnic Overlay," in *History and National Destiny: Ethnosymbolism and Its Critics*, eds. Montserrat Guibernau and John Hutchinson (Oxford: Blackwell, 2004), 117.

19.   Dan LaBotz, *Mask of Democracy: Labor Suppression in Mexico Today* (Boston, MA: South End Press, 1992), 103–5.

20.   Enrique Masa, "Tres presidentes le rindieron pleitesía," *Proceso* 637, January 14, 1989, online version.

21.   It was later alleged that these were munitions belonging to the armed forces. La Botz, *Mask of Democracy*, 105–6; Julia Preston and Samuel Dillon, *Opening Mexico: The Making of a Democracy* (New York: Farrar, Straus and Giroux, 2004), 193.

22.   Preston and Dillon, 193.

23.   Carlos Salinas de Gortari, "I Informe de Gobierno del Presidente Constitucional de los Estados Unidos Mexicanos Carlos Salinas de Gortari 1° de noviembre de 1989," in Carlos Salinas de Gortari, *Informes Presidenciales* (Mexico City: Servicio de Documentación, Investigación y Análisis del Congreso de la Unión, 2006), 27–28.

24.   Robert R. Kaufman and Guillermo Trejo, "Regime Transformation and PRONASOL: The Politics of the National Solidarity Programme in Four Mexican States," *Journal of Latin American Studies* 29, no. 3 (1997), 719.

25.   The three streams of action identified were "Solidarity for Social Wellbeing," focusing on health, nutrition, education, housing, basic services, and regularization of land ownership; "Solidarity for Production," creating opportunities for employment and development by supporting farming, agro-industrial, piscatorial, forestry, mining, and micro-industrial activities; and "Solidarity for Regional Development," involving the construction of infrastructure and regional development projects. Julián F. Bertranou, "Programa Nacional de Solidaridad ¿un nuevo o un viejo modelo de política pública?" *Revista Mexicana de Sociología* 55, no. 3 (July–September 1993), 228; Coordinación de Comunicación del Programa de Solidaridad, *La Solidaridad en el Desarrollo Nacional* (Mexico City: SEDESOL, 1993), 10–11.

26.   Ibid., 15–17.

27.   Denise Dresser, *Neopopulist Solutions to Neoliberal Problems: Mexico's National Solidarity Program* (San Diego, CA: Center for U.S.-Mexican Studies, 1991); Demmers, "Neoliberal Reforms," 170; Knight, "Salinas and Social Liberalism," in *Dismantling the Mexican State?*, eds. Rob Aitken, Nikki Craske, Gareth A. Jones, and David E. Stansfield (London: Macmillan, 1996), 1–23; Rob Aitken, "Neoliberalism and Identity: Redefining State and Society in Mexico," in eds. Aitken et al., 24–38; Gerardo Manuel Ordónez Barba, "Programas de combate de la pobreza," in *Los retos de la política social en la frontera norte de México*, eds. Gerardo Manuel Ordónez Barba and Marcos Sergio Reyes Santos (Tijuana: El Colegio de la Frontera Norte, 2006), 246–48; Juan Molinar Horcasitas and Jeffrey Weldon, "Electoral Determinants and Consequences of National Solidarity," in *Transforming State-Society Relations in Mexico: The National Solidarity Strategy*, eds. Wayne Cornelius, Ann Craig, and Johnathan Fox (San Diego, CA: Center for U.S.-Mexican Studies, 1994), 139; Ann Varley, "Delivering the Goods: Solidarity, Land Regularisation, and Urban Services," in eds. Aitken et al., 204–5.

28.   Bertranou, 241; Haber, "The Art and Implications of Political Restructuring," 292.

29.   Miguel Armando López Leyva, *La encrucijada: Entre la protesta social y la participación electoral 1988* (Mexico City: Flacso, 2007), 60–64; Lilia Venegas, "Women in the Border: The Panista Militants of Tijuana and Ciudad Juárez," in *Women's Participation in Mexican Political Life*, ed. Victoria E. Rodríguez (Boulder, CO: Westview Press, 1998), 209–10.

30.   JoAnn Martin, *Tepoztlán and the Transformation of the Mexican State* (Tucson: University of Arizona Press, 2005), 197; Jeffrey Rubin, *Decentering the Regime: Ethnicity, Radicalism, and Democracy in Juchitán, Mexico* (Durham, NC: Duke University Press, 1997), 190–92.

31.   Haber, "The Art and Implications," 293–94; Rubin, *Decentering the Regime*, 190–91.

32.   Haber, "The Art and Implications," 296–301.

33.   Varley, 208–210.

34.   Haber, "The Art and Implications," 280–81.

35.   Clyde Haberman, "Pope, Amid Mexico's Poor, Laments," *New York Times*, May 8, 1990; Varley, 215–24.

36.   Carlos Salinas de Gortari, "II Informe de Gobierno del Presidente Constitucional de los Estados Unidos Mexicanos Carlos Salinas de Gortari 1° de noviembre de 1990," in Salinas de Gortari, *Informes Presidenciales*, 117.

37.   Ibid., 242.

38.   In 1988 Salinas received one in four votes in Chalco while the PRI won this district and 121 out of 123 municipalities in the State of Mexico in 1991, compared to only forty-one municipal victories in the State of Mexico three years earlier. Ibid., 216–23.

39.   This support extended to the formation in 1990 of a new labor

federation called the Federation of Goods and Services Union (FESBES) under the STRM's leadership as a counterweight to the powerful CTM. Demmers, "Neoliberal Reforms," 170.

40. See Toledo, 195–218.

41. Hernández Rodríguez, 211.

42. See James G. Samstad, "Corporatism and Democratic Transition: State and Labor during the Salinas and Zedillo Administrations," *Latin American Politics and Society* 44, no. 4 (Winter 2002): 1–28.

43. Oscar Hinojosa, "La malquerencia entre Salinas y La Quina surgió a la luz pública en 1984 y fue creciendo," *Proceso* 637, January 14, 1989, online version; La Botz, *Mask of Democracy*, 105–6; Kevin Middlebrook, *The Paradox of Revolution: Labor, the State, and Authoritarianism in Mexico* (Baltimore, MD: Johns Hopkins University Press, 1995), 293–94; James Samstad and Ruth Collier, "Mexican Labor and Structural Reform Under Salinas: New Unionism or Old Stalemate?," in *The Challenge of Institutional Reform in Mexico*, ed. Riordan Roett (Boulder, CO: Lynn Rienner Publishers, 1995), 26.

44. Ilán Bizberg, "Modernization and Corporatism in Government-Labour Relations," in *Mexico: Dilemmas of Transition*, ed. Neil Harvey (London: British Academic Press, 1993), 305–6; Maria L. Cook, *Organizing Dissent: Unions, the State, and the Democratic Teachers' Movement in Mexico* (University Park: Pennsylvania State University Press, 1996), 267–68.

45. La Botz, *Mask of Democracy*, 108–12; Samstad and Collier, 26.

46. Salinas de Gortari, "I Informe," 25–26.

47. Carlos Salinas de Gortari, "IV Informe de Gobierno del Presidente Constitucional de los Estados Unidos Mexicanos Carlos Salinas de Gortari 1° de noviembre de 1992," in Salinas de Gortari, *Informes Presidenciales*, 255.

48. Toby Miller and George Yúdice, *Cultural Policy* (London: Sage, 2002), 131–32.

49. See Elodie Marie Bordat, "Institutionalization and Change in Cultural Policy: CONACULTA and Cultural Policy in Mexico (1988–2006)," *International Journal of Cultural Policy* 19, no. 2 (March 2013): 222–48.

50. Gavin O'Toole, "A New Nationalism for a New Era: The Political Ideology of Mexican Neoliberalism," *Bulletin of Latin American Research* 22, no. 3 (2003): 275.

51. See Cambio XXI, *El Liberalismo Social I* (Mexico City: Cambio XXI Fundación Mexicana, 1992); Coordinación de Comunicación del Programa de Solidaridad, 3.

52. Knight, "Salinas and Social Liberalism," 7.

53. Dennis Gilbert, "Rewriting History: Salinas, Zedillo and the 1992 Textbook Controversy," *Mexican Studies/Estudios Mexicanos* 13, no. 2 (Summer 1997): 275–76.

54. René Villareal, "Economía del Liberalismo Social mexicano: ideología y práctica," in Cambio XXI, 64–65.

55. Ibid., 66–67.

56. Carlos Salinas de Gortari, "El Liberalismo Social: nuestro camino," in Cambio XXI, 18–27.

57. See Peter Taylor-Gooby, *Reframing Social Citizenship* (Oxford: Oxford University Press, 2008).

58. See Erhard Berner and Benedict Phillips, "Left to Their Own Devices? Community Self-Help between Alternative Development and Neoliberalism," *Community Development Journal* 40, no. 1 (January 2005): 17–29; Bob Jessep, "Liberalism, Neoliberalism, and Urban Governance: A State–Theoretical Perspective," *Antipode* 34, no. 3 (December 2002): 452–72.

59. The idea for NAFTA is generally credited to Salinas as a bilateral free-trade agreement proposed by Mexico to the United States that was designed to make Mexico more attractive to foreign investors following the president's dispiriting experience of investor skepticism at the February 1990 World Economic Forum in Davos, Switzerland. The following June, Salinas and US president George H. W. Bush announced the negotiation of a bilateral free-trade agreement and when formal negotiations began the following year, Canada had joined what was now a "North American" free-trade agreement. Maxwell Cameron and Brian Tomlin, *The Making of NAFTA: How the Deal Was Done* (Ithaca, NY: Cornell University Press, 2000), 1–3.

60. Stephen Morris, *Gringolandia: Mexican Identity and Perceptions of the United States* (Oxford: Rowman & Littlefield, 2005), 43–44.

61. Stephen Morris, "Reforming the Nation: Mexican Nationalism in Context," *Journal of Latin American Studies* 31, no. 2 (May 1999): 371.

62. Morris, *Gringolandia*, 16–17.

63. Charles L. Davis and Horace A. Bartilow, "Cognitive Images and Support for International Economic Agreements with the United States Among Mexican Citizens," *Latin American Politics and Society*, 49, no. 2 (Summer 2007): 133–35; Stephen Morris and John Passé-Smith, "What a Difference a Crisis Makes: NAFTA, Mexico, and the United States," *Latin American Perspectives* 28, no. 3 (May 2001): 137–39; Pamela Starr, "The Two 'Politics of NAFTA' in Mexico," *Law and Business Review of the Americas* 16, no. 4 (Fall 2010): 840.

64. Morris and Passé-Smith, 139.

65. Morris, *Gringolandia*, 75.

66. Carlos Salinas de Gortari, "V Informe de Gobierno del Presidente Constitucional de los Estados Unidos Mexicanos Carlos Salinas de Gortari 1° de noviembre de 1993," in Salinas de Gortari, *Informes Presidenciales*, 341.

67. Carlos Salinas de Gortari, "III Informe de Gobierno del Presidente Constitucional de los Estados Unidos Mexicanos Carlos Salinas de Gortari 1° de noviembre de 1991," in Salinas de Gortari, *Informes Presidenciales*, 155.

68. Ángel Soriano, "No Habrá Marcha Atrás en Nuestra Posición Sobre

el Sector Energético, en el TLC: Lozoya Thalmann," *Excélsior*, May 22, 1993, 5; Salinas de Gortari, "IV Informe de Gobierno," 236.

69. Salinas de Gortari, "V Informe de Gobierno," 343–44.

70. Judith Adler Hellman, "Mexican Perceptions of Free Trade: Support and Opposition to NAFTA," in *The Political Economy of the North American Free Trade Agreement*, eds. Ricardo Grinspun and Maxwell Cameron (New York: St. Martin's Press, 1993), 93.

71. Correspondents, "Marchas en varios estados por el 2 de octubre," *La Jornada*, October 3, 1993, 5.

72. Cuauhtémoc Cárdenas, "TLC: Una propuesta alternativa," *Nexos* 162, no. 14 (June 1991): 51–55.

73. Ángel Soriano, "Referéndum Sobre el TLC, Pide Cuauhtémoc," *Excélsior*, January 21, 1993, 58.

74. Morris, *Gringolandia*, 60–62.

75. For a collection of essays detailing Castañeda's perspectivas on US-Mexican relations in the context of the NAFTA negotiations, see Jorge Castañeda, *La casa por la ventana: México y América después de la Guerra Fría*, (Mexico City: Cal y Arena, 1993).

76. Morris, *Gringolandia*, 16.

77. Cecilia Imaz Bayona, *La nación mexicana transfronteras: Impactos sociopolíticos en México de la emigración a Estados Unidos* (Mexico City: UNAM, 2008), 142–43; Morris, *Gringolandia*, 74.

78. Imaz Bayona, 1–13.

79. Davis and Bartilow, 133; Imaz Bayona, 41.

80. F. Fernández Ponte, "Mantendremos Firmeza de Acción," *Excélsior*, September 17, 1983, 1, 16.

81. Imaz Bayona, 28.

82. Héctor Aguilar Camín, "La invención de México," *Nexos*, 187, no. 16 (July 1993): 49–61.

83. Héctor Aguilar Camín and Lorenzo Meyer, *A la sombra de la Revolución Mexicana* (Mexico City: Cal y Arena, 1989), viii.

84. Tania Carreño King and Angélica Vázquez del Mercado, "La hija de la invención: Una entrevista con Edmundo O'Gorman," *Nexos* 190, no. 16 (October 1993): 45; Tania Carreño King and Angélica Vázquez del Mercado, "La disputa por la historia: Una entrevista con Lorenzo Meyer," *Nexos* 191, no. 16 (November 1993): 41.

85. The first round of history texts were produced during the 1960s under López Mateos and his successor Gustavo Díaz Ordaz, with new texts being issued during the 1970s under President Luis Echeverría and remaining in schools until the revisions of the Salinas presidency. The first round of history texts in the 1960s had been produced by separate authors whose works were selected by juried competition. The second round of the Echeverría presidency was coordinated by historian Josefina Zoraida Vázquez from the

Colegio de México and examined history within a broader social sciences framework. This approach was ideologically in tune with that of the Echeverría administration's economic development and foreign policies as foreign economic relations were discussed from the perspective of dependency theory. Gilbert, "Rewriting History," 271–97.

86. Ibid., 276–77.

87. Ibid.

88. Salvador Martínez and Roberto Vizcaino, "Recursos Crecientes para la Federalización Educativa," *Excélsior*, May 19, 1992, 10.

89. Miguel Ángel Granados Chapa, "Plaza Pública," *La Jornada*, August 20, 1992, 1, 4.

90. Gilbert, "Rewriting History," 273.

91. Granados Chapa, "Plaza Pública," 4.

92. Ibid., 1.

93. Elvira Vargas, *La Jornada*, August 26, 1992; Patricia Vega, "Grabadora en mano, el enviado de la SEP constató el inesperado repunte del interés por la historia," *La Jornada*, August 26, 1992, 6.

94. Matilde Pérez U., "Falsa imagen del indígena en textos de historia para primaria," *La Jornada*, August 29, 1992, 12.

95. Bordat, "Institutionalization and Change," 233; Claudio Lomnitz, "An Intellectual's Stock in the Factory of Mexico's Ruins," *American Journal of Sociology* 103, no. 4 (January 1998): 1057–58.

96. Granados Chapa, "Plaza Pública," 1, 4.

97. Bordat, "Institutionalization and Change," 233; Enrique Krauze, "La prueba de los niños (la primera de dos partes)," *La Jornada*, September 8, 1992, 1, 16.

98. Héctor Aguilar Camín, "El contexto de los textos," *Nexos* 15, no. 178 (October 1992): 33–37.

99. Manuel Enríquez Osorio, "Exigirán maestros y PRD modificar los libros de texto," *La Jornada*, August 23, 1992, 15.

100. Ibid., 15.

101. Rosa Elvira Vargas, "En la plaza de Santo Domingo, lección pública para 'recuperar el pasado,'" *La Jornada*, September 9, 1992, 1, 18.

102. Oscar Camacho Guzmán, "'Los Niños Héroes sí están,' responde Idolina Moguel a críticas," *La Jornada*, August 27, 1992, 1; Patricia Vega, "Grabadora en mano," 6.

103. Camacho Guzmán, 18.

104. Roberto Zamarripa, "Presionó EU en 1989 para cambiar el libro de historia," *La Jornada*, September 9, 1992, 19.

105. Paul Garner, *Porfirio Díaz: Profiles in Power* (Oxon: Routledge, 2010), 12–15; Enrique Krauze, *Porfirio Díaz: Místico de la Autoridad* (Mexico City: Fondo de la Cultura Económica, 1987); Carlos Monsivaís, *Las*

herencias ocultas de la reforma liberal del siglo XIX (Mexico City: Random House Mondadori, 2006).

106. Gilbert, "Rewriting History," 275–77.

107. Enríquez Osorio, 15.

108. Cook, 270–72.

109. Rosa Elvira Vargas, "Nuevo Sindicalismo censura a los libros de primaria por dogmáticos," *La Jornada*, August 21, 1992, 15.

110. Gordillo became leader of the SNTE following mass teacher protests in 1989. In this instance, the government directly intervened to request the demission of long-time leader Carlos Jonguitud Barrios and SNTE secretary general Refugio Araujo del Ángel. Gordillo, a recognized political ally of Salinas and the PRI's Mexico City Regent Manuel Camacho, was then named as the union's new secretary general following negotiations between the interior minister with local secretary generals of the union. The teacher's union, Mexico's largest, had an important power base in Cárdenas stronghold Mexico City, and the Salinas administration placed significant priority on close relations with Gordillo and the SNTE. Maria Lorena Cook, *Organizing Dissent: Unions, the State and the Democratic Teachers' Movement in Mexico* (University Park: Pennsylvania State University Press, 1996), 270–72; Rosa Elvira Vargas, "Los libros de historia para primaria debe tener carácter experimental, considera Nuevo Sindicalismo," *La Jornada*, August 28, 1992, 17.

111. Rosa Elvira Vargas, "Pedirá el SNTE que se revisen los textos de historia," *La Jornada*, August 29, 1992, 13.

112. Rosa Elvira Vargas, "Revisarán SEP y SNTE los libros de historia," *La Jornada*, September 6, 1992, 1, 16.

113. Roberto Zamarripa, "Analizarán comisiones de Educación del Congreso los libros de historia," *La Jornada*, September 3, 1992, 3.

114. Néstor Martínez, "El PRI se manifestó por modificar los libros de texto para primaria," *La Jornada*, September 22, 1992, 15.

115. Zamarripa, "Analizarán comisiones," 3.

116. Daniel Cazés, "Ayer, 2 de octubre: la historia oficial," *La Jornada*, October 3, 1992, 9.

117. See Matthias Vom Hau, "State Infrastructural Power and Nationalism: Comparative Lessons from Mexico and Argentina," *Studies in Comparative International Development* 43, nos. 3–4 (2008), 334–54.

118. Gilbert, "Rewriting History," 288–89.

119. José Antonio Román, "Es sano que un pueblo conozca su 'verdadera historia,'" *La Jornada*, August 27, 1992, 18; René Alberto López, "Fortalecen la conciencia nacional los nuevos libros de texto: Conalte," *La Jornada*, August 27, 1992, 18.

120. José Antonio Román, "CEM: los libros de texto, inicio de reconciliación con la historia," *La Jornada*, September 12, 1992, 15.

121. Néstor Martínez, "Pide la UNPF a maestros no secundar el boicot a los nuevos textos de historia," *La Jornada*, September 2, 1992, 19.

122. Zamarripa, "Analizarán comisiones," 3.

123. Roberto Zamarripa, "El PAN apoya la tendencia de los textos de historia: Castillo Peraza," *La Jornada*, September 4, 1992, 14.

124. Rosa Elvira Vargas, "Un avance, los nuevos textos," *La Jornada*, September 23, 1992, 19.

125. Pascual García Alba Iduñate, "Precisiones sobre los nuevos libros de texto," *La Jornada*, August 21, 1992, 1, 18; Manuel Enríquez Osorio, "Exigirán maestros y PRD modificar los libros de texto," *La Jornada*, August 23, 1992, 15.

126. Lourdes Galaz, "CSG: Niños Héroes, parte histórica esencial," *La Jornada*, September 14, 1992, 25.

127. Salvador Guerrero Chiprés, "Reivindica Salinas a los Niños Héroes y a Juárez en el grito," *La Jornada*, September 17, 1992, 25.

128. Lourdes Galaz, "Legalidad y Soberanía, Bases del Estado Mexicano Actual," *La Jornada*, September 17, 1992, 15.

129. Roberto Zamarripa, "Los nuevos libros sólo serán para este ciclo escolar: Zedillo," *La Jornada*, September 5, 1992, 15; Rosa Elvira Vargas, "No se corregirán los libros de historia; la reforma integral, en 1993: Zedillo," *La Jornada*, September 9, 1992, 1, 20.

130. Rosa Elvira Vargas and David Carrizales, "En diciembre, las correcciones a libros de historia," *La Jornada*, September 25, 1992, 17; Rocio Ortega, "Entregarán en 2 meses 'fe de erratas' de libros," *El Norte*, September 25, 1992, 1.

131. Gilbert, "Rewriting History," 272.

132. Ibid.

133. Aguilar Camín, "El contexto de los textos," 33–37.

Snapshot Five

1. Genoveva Flores, *La seducción de Marcos a la prensa: Versiones sobre el levantamiento zapatista* (Mexico City: Miguel Ángel Porrúa, 2004), 14–15; Carlos Salinas de Gortari, "II Informe de Gobierno del Presidente Constitucional de los Estados Unidos Mexicanos Carlos Salinas de Gortari 1° de noviembre de 1990," in Carlos Salinas de Gortari, *Informes Presidenciales* (Mexico City: Servicio de Documentación, Investigación y Análisis del Congreso de la Unión, 2006), 89–90.

2. EZLN, "First Declaration from the Lacandón Jungle," in Subcomandante Marcos, *¡Ya Basta! Ten Years of the Zapatista Uprising* (Oakland, CA: AKA Press, 2004), 643.

3. Ibid.

4. Ibid.

5.   Ibid., 644–45.

6.   Chris Gilbreth and Gerardo Otero, "Democratization in Mexico: The Zapatista Uprising and Civil Society," *Latin American Perspectives* 28, no. 4 (July 2001): 11.

7.   Gloria Muñoz Ramírez, *The Fire and the Word: A History of the Zapatista Movement* (San Francisco, CA: City Lights Books, 2008), 107.

8.   Salvador Guerrero Chiprés and Alonso Urrutia, "AN: provoca violencia 'la nefasta' labor de los gobiernos caciquiles," *La Jornada*, January 4, 1994, 16.

9.   José Antonio Román and Oscar Camacho, "Condenan obispos de Chiapas la manipulación de indígenas," *La Jornada*, January 4, 1994, 21.

10.   Rosa Icela Rodríguez, "Debate en el PRD en torno al conflicto armado en Chiapas," *La Jornada*, January 16, 1994, 22.

11.   Editorial, "Contra la violencia," *Cuaderno de Nexos* 68 (February 1994): iii–iv.

12.   Hector Águilar Camín, "Compuerta," *Cuaderno de Nexos* 68 (February 1994): ix.

13.   Ibid., xiv.

14.   Enrique Krauze, "Procurando entender," *Vuelta Suplemento Extraordinario* (February 1994): J–L; Octavio Paz, "Chiapas, ¿nudo ciego o tabla de salvación?" *Vuelta Suplemento Extraordinario* (February 1994): C–D.

15.   Elena Gallegos and Emilio Lomas, "Seguimos dispuestos al diálogo: CSG," *La Jornada*, January 7, 1994, 1.

16.   Ibid.

17.   Brock Pitawanakwat, "The Mirror of Dignity: Zapatista Communications and Indigenous Resistance" (master's thesis, University of Regina, 2000), 70–71.

18.   Muñoz Ramírez, 110–11.

19.   Carlos Puig, "Cartas, audiencias en el Congreso, comisiones oficiales y privadas a Chiapas," *Proceso* 898 January 15, 1994, online version.

20.   B. Johnston, S. Morales, and C. Puig, "'Estamos en guerra, los derechos no son prioridad,'" *Proceso* 898, January 15, 1994, online version.

21.   EZLN, *EZLN: Documentos y comunicados*, vol. 1 (Mexico City: Era, 2003), 4.

22.   Kathleen Bruhn, "Antonio Gramsci and the *Palabra Verdadera*: The Political Discourse of Mexico's Guerrilla Forces," *Journal of Interamerican Studies and World Affairs* 41, no. 2 (Summer 1999): 30–41.

23.   Yvon LeBot, *Subcomandante Marcos: El sueño Zapatista* (Barcelona: Plaza y Janés, 1997), 127–28.

24.   Ibid.

25. Subcomandante Marcos, *Conversations with Durito: Stories of the Zapatistas and Neoliberalism* (Brooklyn, NY: Autonomedia, 2005).

26. Bruhn, "Antonio Gramsci," 46.

27. Carlos Acosta Córdova, "El levantamiento Zapatista pone en aprietos al sistema," *Proceso* 899, January 22, 1994, online version.

28. Subcomandante Marcos, "Who Must Ask for Pardon and Who Can Grant It?" in Subcomandante Marcos, *Shadows of Tender Fury: The Letters and Communiqués of Subcomandante Marcos and the Zapatista Army of National Liberation* (New York: Monthly Review Press, 1995), 80.

29. Samuel Brunk, *The Posthumous Career of Emiliano Zapata: Myth, Memory, and Mexico's Twentieth Century* (Austin: University of Texas Press, 2008), 230.

30. LeBot, 240–41.

31. Gilbreth and Otero, 20.

32. Ibid.

33. Muñoz Ramírez, 117–18.

34. Ibid., 118.

35. John Womack, *Rebellion in Chiapas: An Historical Reader* (New York: New Press, 1999), 280.

36. CCRI-CG of the EZLN, "Second Declaration of the Lacandón," in Subcomandante Marcos, *Shadows of Tender Fury*, 251.

Chapter Five

1. Ana María Alonso, "Conforming Disconformity: Mestizaje, Hybridity, and the Aesthetics of Mexican Nationalism," *Cultural Anthropology* 19, no. 4 (November 2004): 469.

2. Jeffrey Rubin, "Popular Mobilization and the Myth of State Corporatism," in *Popular Movements and Political Change in Mexico*, eds. Joe Fowraker and Ann Craig (Boulder, CO: Lynne Rienner Publishers, 1990), 247–67.

3. Sergio Zendejas and Gail Mummert, "Beyond the Agrarian Question: The Cultural Politics of Ejido Natural Resources," in *The Transformation of Rural Mexico: Reforming the Ejido Sector*, eds. Wayne A. Cornelius and David Myhre (La Jolla, CA: Center for U.S.-Mexican Studies, 1998), 177.

4. Jessa Lewis, "Agrarian Change and Privatization of Ejido Land in Northern Mexico," *Journal of Agrarian Change* 2, no. 3 (July 2002): 404; María Teresa Vázquez Castillo, *Land Privatization in Mexico: Urbanization, Formation of Regions, and Globalization in Ejidos* (New York: Routledge, 2004), 2–3.

5. Monique Nuijten, "Family Property and the Limits of Intervention:

The Article 27 Reforms and the PROCEDE Programme in Mexico," *Development and Change* 34, no. 3 (June 2003): 482.

6.   Graciela Flores Lúa, Luisa Paré, and Sergio Sarmiento Silva, *Las voces del campo: Movimiento campesino y política agrarian, 1976–1984* (Mexico City: Siglo XXI, 1988), 36–44.

7.   José López Portillo, "IV Informe de Gobierno del Presidente Constitucional de los Estados Unidos Mexicanos José López Portillo y Pacheco 1º de septiembre de 1980," in José López Portillo, *Informes Presidenciales* (Mexico City: Servicio de Documentación, Investigación y Análisis del Congreso de la Unión, 2006), 185–86.

8.   The López Portillo program was first underpinned by the Mexican Food System (SAM) established in 1977, while the Ley de Fomento Agrario introduced in 1980 legalized increased commercialization of ejido land. Graciela Flores Lúa, Luisa Paré, and Sergio Sarmiento Silva. *Las voces del campo: Movimiento campesino y política agrarian, 1976–1984*. (Mexico City: Siglo XXI, 1988), 43–51.

9.   Ibid., 53.

10.   Kirsten Appendini, 'La transformación de la vida económica del campo mexicano,' in *El impacto social de las políticas de ajuste en el campo mexicano*, ed. Jean François Prud'Homme (Mexico City: Plaza y Valdes, 1995), 35–38; Neil Harvey, *The Chiapas Rebellion: The Struggle for Land and Democracy* (Durham, NC: Duke University Press, 1999) 178–83.

11.   Appendini, 31–32; Lewis, 405; Miguel Meza Castillo, *La Reforma del Sistema Financiero Rural* (Washington, DC: Woodrow Wilson International Center for Scholars, 2011).

12.   Appendini, 33–34; Wayne A. Cornelius and David Myhre, "Introduction," in eds. Cornelius and Myhre, 9; Blanca Rubio, "Las organizaciones independientes en México: Semblanza de las opciones campesinos ante el proyecto neoliberal," in *Neoliberalismo y organización social en el campo mexicano*, ed. Hubert C. Grammont (Mexico City: Plaza y Valdés, 2002), 119–23; Flores Lúa et al., 49–50.

13.   Hubert Cartón de Grammont, "El campo hacia el fin del milenio," *Nexos* 169, no. 15, (January 1992): 49–53; Vázquez Castillo, 38–39.

14.   Neil Harvey, 187–88.

15.   Juan José Rojas Herrera and Eduardo Moyano Estrada, "Acción colectiva y representación de intereses en la agricultura Mexicana: el caso del sector ejidal," *Agricultura y Sociedad* 82 (January–April 1997): 60–61.

16.   Cornelius and Myhre, 9; Lewis, 406; Nuijten, "Family Property," 476; Vázquez Castillo, 40–41.

17.   Luin Goldring, "Having Your Cake and Eating It Too: Selective Appropriation of Ejido Reform in Michoacán," in eds. Cornelius and Myhre, 145.

18.   Rojas Herrera and Moyano Estrada, 46.

19. Guillermo Correa, "La 'contrarreforma agraria,' en marcha," *Proceso* 784, November 9, 1991, online version.

20. Ibid.

21. Guillermo Correa, "Artículo 27: Estrategia verbal para llegar a los cambios," *Proceso* 785, November 16, 1991, online version.

22. Rodrigo Vera, "En Michoacán, el primer acto de apoyo a la iniciativa de Salinas," *Proceso* 784, January 9, 1991, online version.

23. Nuijten, 229.

24. Stephen, *Zapata Lives!*, 65–66.

25. Ibid., 67–70.

26. Renato Dávalos, "Se Titularán Todas las Parcelas Este Sexenio: Salinas," *Excélsior*, April 11, 1992, 1.

27. Rojas Herrera and Moyano noted that this diversity included "highly modernised ejidos, communities and cooperatives clearly oriented toward the market and run according to business logic, to marginal, barely capitalised ejidos and oriented to family consumption run according to a logic closer to that of traditional peasants." Rojas Herrera and Moyano Estrada, 46.

28. Ibid., 70–72.

29. Nuijten, "Organizing the Peasants," 229.

30. Lewis, 402–20; Nuijten, "Family Property," 489–93.

31. Under Procede, ejidatarios were offered three possible titles: *solares* (house plots), *parcelas* (farm plots), and a percentage of common goods including common lands. Ejidatarios could also choose to have the outlines of the ejido and/or individual plots measured and certified. Examinations by Haenn and Perramond in Campeche, Guanajuato, and Sonora found different combinations of these measuring and titling arrangements being adopted depending on local ecological, economic, and social circumstances. Nora Haenn, "The Changing and Enduring Ejido: A State and Regional Examination of Mexico's Land Tenure Counter-Reforms," *Land Use Policy* 23, no. 2 (April 2006): 138–41; Eric P. Perramond, "The Rise, Fall, and Reconfiguration of the Mexican Ejido," *Geographical Review* 98, no. 3 (April 2010): 367–68.

32. For example, the Democratic Peasants' Front (FDC) in Chihuahua. See Laura B. Pozos, "La formación y acciones promovidas por el Frente Democrático Campesino de Chihuahua, para mejorar las condiciones de vida y equidad," *Revista Futuros* 3, no. 1 (2003): online version; Rojas Herrera and Moyano Estrada, 47.

33. See Guadalupe Rodríguez and Gabriel Torres, "Los agroproductores frente a las políticas neoliberals: El Barzón y COMAGRO," *Espiral* 1, no. 1 (September–December, 1994): 129–76.

34. Rojas Herrera and Moyano Estrada, 57–58.

35. The Congreso Agrario Permanente grouped both PRI affiliated

peasant organizations (CNC, CCI, CAM, UGOCM, MN400P) and indepen-
dent organizations (UNORCA, CIOAC, CODUC, UGOCP, CCC,
ALCANO, UNTA). Hubert C. Grammont and Horacio Mackinlay,
"Campesino and Indigenous Social Organizations Facing Democratic
Transition in Mexico, 1938–2006," *Latin American Perspectives* 36, no. 4
(July 2009): 27–28.

36. Stephen, *Zapata Lives!*, 63.

37. Octavio Paz, "Chiapas, ¿nudo ciego o tabla de salvación?," *Vuelta
Suplemento Extraordinario* (February 1994): E.

38. Ibid., F.

39. Lomnitz defined "national anthropology" as an anthropological tradition fostered by educational and cultural institution for the development of
studies of their own nation. The difference between "national anthropolo-
gies" in peripheral nations with early dates of independence such as most of
Latin America and anthropological traditions in the great metropolitan centers of Europe and the United States is that the latter was situated within a
civilizing horizon conceived of as being abroad. Claudio Lomnitz, "Bordering
on Anthropology: The Dialectics of a National Tradition in Mexico," *Revue
de Synthèse* 4, no. 3–4 (July–December 2000): 347.

40. Guillermo de la Peña, "Social Citizenship, Ethnic Minority
Demands, Human Rights, and Neoliberal Paradoxes: A Case Study in
Western Mexico," in *Multiculturalism in Latin America: Indigenous Rights,
Diversity, and Democracy*, ed. Rachel Sieder (Houndmills: Palgrave
Macmillan, 2002), 131.

41. Arturo Warman, Margarita Nolasco, Guillermo Bonfil, Mercedes
Olivera, and Enrique Valencia, *De eso que llaman antropología mexicana*
(Mexico City: Editorial Nuestro Tiempo, 1970).

42. Guillermo Bonfil Batalla, *Mexico Profundo: Reclaiming a
Civilization* (Austin: University of Texas Press, 1996).

43. See Natividad Gutiérrez, "What Indians Say about Mestizos: A
Critical View of the Archetype of Mexican Nationalism," *Bulletin of Latin
American Research* 17, no. 3 (September 1998): 285–301.

44. Alonso, 478–79.

45. Gutiérrez, "What Indians Say," 298.

46. Sergio Sarmiento Silva, "El Consejo Nacional de Pueblos Indígenas
y la política indigenista," *Revista Mexicana de Sociología*, 47, no. 3 (July–
September 1985): 200–202.

47. Guillermo de la Peña, "Social and Cultural Policies toward
Indigenous Peoples: Perspectives from Latin America," *Annual Review of
Anthropology* 34 (2005): 731–32.

48. Ibid, 731; Gabbert, 158–59; Natividad Gutiérrez, "Indigenous
Political Organizations and the Nation-State: Bolivia, Ecuador, Mexico,"
Alternatives: Global, Local, Political 35, no. 3 (July–September 2010): 263.

49. Grammont and Mackinlay, 27.

50. Rojas Herrera and Moyano Estrada, 70.

51. During the Echeverría administration, state indigenous policy had been directed toward increasing the organization of the indigenous population and increasing land redistribution to indigenous communities. Such institutions created and supported under Echeverría soon became hostile to the López Portillo administration as it returned to a more traditional *indigenista* stance that subsumed indigenous questions under general rural development plans through initiatives such as Coplamar. Sarmiento Silva, 203–10; Shannan L. Mattiace, "Regional Renegotiations of Space: Tojolabal Ethnic Identity in Las Margaritas, Chiapas," *Latin American Perspectives* 28, no. 2 (March 2001): 78.

52. During the 1990s the UN further proclaimed an International Year of the World's Indigenous Populations in 1993, an International Decade of the World's Indigenous Population in December 1994, and an International Day of the World's Indigenous Populations to be celebrated every August 9. The awarding of the Nobel Peace Prize to indigenous Guatemalan activist Rigoberta Menchú in 1992 also reinforced a global focus on indigenous identity connected with ideas of human rights. Julian Burger, "Pueblos indígenas: Sus derechos y la acción internacional," in *Pueblos indígenas, derechos humanos e interdependencia global*, ed. Patricia Morales (Mexico City, Siglo Veintiuno, 2002), 13–15; De la Peña, "Social and Cultural Policies," 732.

53. De la Peña, "Social Citizenship, Ethnic Minority Demands," 129; Sarmiento Silva, 211–14.

54. Neil Harvey, 201–2; Deborah J. Yashar, "Democracy, Indigenous Movements, and the Postliberal Challenge in Latin America," *World Politics* 52, no. 1 (October 1999), 90.

55. De la Peña, "Social Citizenship," 132–45.

56. Natividad Gutiérrez, "La autonomía y la resolución de conflictos étnicos: Los Acuerdos de San Andrés Larráinzar," *Revista Nueva Antropología* 19, no. 63 (October 2003): 19–20.

57. Gutiérrez, "What Indians Say about Mestizos," 287–88; Yashar, 77.

58. Yashar defines "citizenship regimes" as the combination of citizenship rights and modes of interest representation under a particular political system. Yashar, 92–93.

59. Tojolobal activist and Mexican Socialist Party federal deputy Margarito Ruiz Hernández from the Chiapas Lacandón Jungle emerged as a leading postindigenista critic of the Salinas administration's gestures in this respect. Ruiz Hernández specifically criticized the administration's failure to extend reforms of Article 4 to an entire chapter of constitutional indigenous rights nor support the creation of democratically based regional development plans with the funding provided to indigenous communities through Pronasol. David Harvey, 202–3.

60. Catherine Nolan-Ferrell, "Agrarian Reform and Revolutionary Justice in Soconusco, Chiapas: Campesinos and the Mexican State, 1934–1940," *Journal of Latin American Studies* 42, no. 3 (August 2010): 572–73.

61.   Rosalva Aída Hernández Castillo, "Entre la resistencia civil y el rechazo silencioso: Distintas respuestas de los campesinos mames a la rebelión zapatista," in *Tierra, libertad y autonomía: impactos regionales del zapatismo en Chiapas*, eds. Shannan L. Mattiace, Rosalva Aída Hernández, and Jan Rus (Mexico City: Ciesas, 2002), 128–32.

62.   Ibid., 584.

63.   In Chiapas, the term *ladino* is more commonly used to describe a person of nonindigenous descent in a similar sense to *mestizo* in the rest of Mexico. This is also true of Guatemala, of which Chiapas formed part of the colonial jurisdiction and then independent nation before joining Mexico in 1824. More recently, ladino has also come to refer to indigenous people who adopted an urban, nontraditional lifestyle in a fashion similar to the word *cholo* in Andean South America. Stephen, *Zapata Lives!*, 84–85.

64.   Neil Harvey, 54–58; Stephen, *Zapata Lives!*, 57–61.

65.   The dominant immigrant groups were Tzeltal and Chol indigenous groups from eastern and northern highlands, while smaller numbers of Tojolobal and Tzotzil indigenous groups from the southeast and central highlands respectively also immigrated. Neil Harvey, 61–62; Stephen, *Zapata Lives!*, 102.

66.   Stephen, *Zapata Lives!*, 102.

67.   Hernández Castillo, 133; Kristin Norget, "The Politics of Liberation: The Popular Church, Indigenous Theology, and Grassroots Mobilization in Oaxaca, Mexico," *Latin American Perspectives* 24, no. 5 (September 1997): 96–127; Rubin, "State Politics, Leftist Oppositions," 127–60; Rubin, "COCEI in Juchitán: Grassroots Radicalism and Regional History," *Journal of Latin American Studies* 26, no. 1 (February 1994): 109–36.

68.   The most notable example of this syncretism was the merging of the Exodus story with the experience of colonization following its translation into Tzeltal in 1972 by brothers working in the Lacandón's largest municipality of Ocosingo. See Norget, 96–127; Stephen, *Zapata Lives!*, 111–12; Womack, *Rebellion in Chiapas*, 128–47.

69.   Neil Harvey, 76–79; Sarmiento Silva, 204–5; Stephen, *Zapata Lives!*, 111–12; Womack, *Rebellion in Chiapas*, 148–61.

70.   Neil Harvey, 79–90; Stephen, *Zapata Lives!*, 119–20.

71.   Neil Harvey, 108–9.

72.   Ibid., 148–60.

73.   Thomas Benjamin, "A Time of Reconquest: History, the Maya Revival, and the Zapatista Rebellion in Chiapas," *American Historical Review* 105, no. 2 (April 2000): 442–43.

74.   Ibid., 442.

75.   Neil Harvey, 164–65.

76.   LeBot, 125–28.

77.   Jorge Fuentes Morúa, "De El Despertador Mexicano 1993 a

Rebeldía 2003," *Casa del Tiempo* 1, no. 8 (June 2008), 8–9; LeBot, 123–26; Stephen, *Zapata Lives!*, 133–36.

78. Neil Harvey, 166.

79. Roland Barthes, *Mythologies* (London: Jonathan Cape, 1974), 121–27.

80. Lynn Stephen, "Pro-Zapatista and Pro-PRI: Resolving Contradictions of Zapatismo in Rural Oaxaca," *Latin American Research Review* 32, no. 2 (1997): 41–70.

81. Ibid., 65.

82. LeBot, 348.

83. Neil Harvey, 165.

84. CCRI-CG of the EZLN, "Votán Zapata," in ed. Ross, 196–97.

85. Ibid., 197.

86. Stephen, "Pro-Zapatista and Pro-PRI," 48.

87. Ignacio M. Sánchez Prado, "Claiming Liberalism: Enrique Krauze, *Vuelta*, *Letras Libres*, and the Reconfigurations of the Mexican Intellectual Class," *Mexican Studies/Estudios Mexicanos* 26, no. 1 (Winter 2010): 76.

88. This phrasing recalled the characterization of the Enlightenment by philosophers Max Horkheimer and Theodor Adorno as leading to a disenchantment of the world that discarded myth and meaning for science and objectivity. See Max Horkheimer and Theodor Adorno, *Dialectic of Enlightenment* (London: Allen Lane, 1972).

89. Subcomandante Marcos, "Siete piezas sueltas del rompecabezas mundial," in *EZLN: Documentos y comunicados*, vol. 4, EZLN (Mexico City: Ediciones Era, 2003), 48–72.

90. Subcomandante Marcos, "Inauguración de la reunión preparatoria Americana del encuentro intercontinental por la humanidad y contra el neoliberalismo," in *EZLN: Documentos y comunicados*, 213.

91. Carlos Salinas de Gortari, "V Informe de Gobierno del Presidente Constitucional de los Estados Unidos Mexicanos Carlos Salinas de Gortari 1° de noviembre de 1993," in Salinas de Gortari, *Informes Presidenciales*, 343.

92. Goldring, 145–72; Haenne, 144.

93. Cornelius and Myhre, 11–13; Nuijten, "Family Property," 475–95.

94. Haenne, 143; Nuijten, "Organizing the Peasants," 230.

95. The percentage of land certified was: Oaxaca, 50 percent; Chiapas, 60 percent; Morelos 69 percent. Perramond, 364. For more ejido case studies, see eds. Cornelius and Myhre.

96. Ibid., 144–45.

97. De la Peña, "Social Citizenship," 129–51.

98. Pamela K. Starr, "Monetary Mismanagement and Inadvertent Democratization in Technocratic Mexico," *Studies in Comparative International Development* 33, no. 4 (Winter 1999), 35–65.

Snapshot Six

1.   See Óscar Camacho and Alejandro Almazán, *La victoria que no fue: López Obrador: Entre la guerra sucia y la soberbia* (Mexico City: Grijalbo, 2006); Andrés Manuel López Obrador, *La mafia nos robó la presidencia* (Mexico City: Grijalbo, 2007).

2.   See Michael Gonzalez, "Imagining Mexico in 1910: Visions of the *Patria* in the Centennial Celebration in Mexico City," *Journal of Latin American Studies* 39, no. 3 (July 2007): 495–533; Mauricio Tenorio Trillo, "1910 Mexico City: Space and Nation in the City of the *Centenario*," *Journal of Latin American Studies* 28, no. 1 (Feb. 1996): 75–104.

3.   Pablo Cabañas Díaz, "El financiamiento de los partidos y el poder de los medios," in *Campañas, partidos y candidatos: Elección 2006*, ed. Carola García Calderón (Mexico City: Plaza y Valdes, 2007), 306–15; Camacho and Almazán, 60–68.

4.   Francisco Reséndiz, "Cuauhtémoc Cárdenas deja Comisión del Bicentenario," *El Universal*, November 16, 2006, online version.

5.   Andrés Manuel López Obrador, "Aquí está la muestra de lo que somos y de lo que seremos capaces de llevar a cabo: AMLO," *La Jornada*, November 21, 2006, online version.

6.   Ibid.

7.   Jesús Aranda, "Primer Presidente sin homenaje en Palacio," *La Jornada*, December 2, 2006, online version.

8.   Felipe Calderón, "Palabras del Presidente de los Estados Unidos Mexicanos, Lic. Felipe Calderón Hinojosa, en la presentación de la Imagen de la Presidencia," accessed June 18, 2011, http://www.presidencia.gob. mx/2006/12/palabras-del-presidente-de-los-estados-unidos-mexicanos-lic-felipe-calderon—hinojosa-en-la-presentacion-de-la-imagen-de-la-presidencia/.

9.   Emiliano Ruiz, "Adopta Calderón discurso juarista," *Reforma*, December 4, 2006, 6.

10.   Juan Antonio Zuñiga, "El Banco de México emitirá un nuevo billete de 20 pesos en los próximos días," *La Jornada*, July 6, 2007, online version.

11.   Emiliano Ruiz Parra and Érika Hernández, "Desdeña AMLO a instituciones," *Reforma*, September 2, 2006, 6.

12.   Silvia Arellano, "'Le tienen miedo al águila juarista': Marcelo Ebrard," *Milenio*, November 16, 2008, online version; Alberto Cuevas, "No quitarán 'águila republicana' del zócalo," *El Universal*, August 30, 2007, online version.

13.   Claudia Herrera and Roberto González, "Seguridad y gasto social, las prioridades en el presupuesto," *La Jornada*, December 6, 2006, online version.

14.   "Anuncio sobre la Operación Conjunta Michoacán," accessed June

18, 2011, http://www.presidencia.gob.mx/2006/12/anuncio-sobre-la-operacion-conjunta-michoacan/.

15.   The administration announced that more than five thousand federal troops and 1,800 federal police officers would be sent to Ciudad Juárez in an attempt to restore order in the city. Marcela Turati, "La toma de Ciudad Juárez," *Proceso* 1688 (March 8, 2008): 6–10.

16.   Silvia Otero, "No investigan 95% de muertes en 'guerra,'" *El Universal*, June 21, 2010, online version.

17.   Rubén Villalpando, "Falló el Operativo Conjunto Chihuahua, coinciden diversos sectores sociales," *La Jornada*, March 28, 2010, 7; Redacción, "Juárez es la ciudad más violenta del mundo," *El Universal*, January 11, 2010, online version.

18.   Bernd Debusmann, "Among top U.S. fears: A failed Mexican state," *New York Times*, January 9, 2009; Jesús Silva-Herzog Márquez, "¿Estado fallido?," *Reforma*, February 2, 2009, 10.

19.   Alma Saavedra, "Economía mexicana se contrae 6.5% en el 2009," *El Economista*, February 23, 2010, online version.

20.   Rogelio Naranjo, "Continuidad," *Proceso* 1731 (January 3, 2010).

21.   Felipe Calderón, "El Presidente Calderón en la Ceremonia Cívica Conmemorativa al XCI Aniversario de la Muerte del Gral. Emiliano Zapata Salazar," accessed April 20, 2011, http://www.presidencia.gob.mx/2010/04/el-presidente-calderon-en-la-ceremonia-civica-conmemorativa-al-xci-aniversario-de-la-muerte-del-gral-emiliano-zapata-salazar/.

22.   Felipe Calderón, "El Presidente Calderón, durante la Ceremonia del CCIV Aniversario del Natalicio del Licenciado Benito Juárez García," accessed June 18, 2011, http://www.presidencia.gob.mx/2010/03/el-presidente-calderon-durante-la-ceremonia-del-cciv-aniversario-del-natalicio-del-licenciado-benito-juarez-garcia/.

23.   Ibid.

24.   Ibid.

25.   Rafael Montes, "Sabotean canción del Bicentenario en Zócalo," *El Universal*, September 15, 2010, online version.

26.   Nurit Martínez Carballo, "'Barroco e inútil' discutir por 'El coloso': Lujambio," *El Universal*, September 22, 2010, online version.

27.   Julio Hernández López, "Astilleros," *La Jornada*, September 17, 2010, online version.

28.   Ariane Díaz, "*El Coloso* no retrata ningún personaje en particular: SEP," *La Jornada*, September 20, 2010, 15.

29.   Jaime Avilés, "La arenga en el Grito de los Libres fue 'por los de abajo,'" *La Jornada*, September 17, 2010, online version.

30.   This program comprising one hundred and fifty episodes began on January 25, 2010, and was shown on Channel 11 and rebroadcast through state radio, television and Internet outlets. Felipe Calderón, "El Presidente

Calderón en la presentación del programa Discutamos México." January 2010, *Presidencia de la República,* accessed June 18, 2011, http://www. presidencia.gob.mx/2010/01/el-presidente-calderon-en-la-presentacion-del-programa-discutamos-mexico/.

31. See Claudio Lomnitz, "An Intellectual's Stock in the Factory of Mexico's Ruins," *American Journal of Sociology* 103, no. 4 (1998): 1052–65; Ignacio M. Sánchez Prado, "Claiming Liberalism: Enrique Krauze, *Vuelta, Letras Libres,* and the Reconfigurations of the Mexican Intellectual Class," *Mexican Studies/Estudios Mexicanos* 26, no. 1 (Winter 2010): 47–78.

32. SEP and Canal 11 TV México, "La Lucha Democrática," *Discutamos México,* episode 30, aired April 30, 2010.

33. Felipe Calderón, "El Presidente Calderón en la ceremonia del inicio de la Revolución Mexicana y homenaje a Don Francisco I. Madero," accessed June 18, 2010, http://www.presidencia.gob.mx/2010/11/el-presidente-calderon-en-la-ceremonia-del-centenario-del-inicio-de-la-revolucion-mexicana-y-homenaje-a-don-francisco-i-madero/.

34. Despite their conflict over the legitimacy of Calderón's election, by early 2010 the PAN and PRD were forming ad hoc coalitions in state elections to combat the PRI's rise. Such coalitions placed political pragmatism above ideological considerations and recent hostilities, with critics drawing on the terminology of the bitter rivalry between Calderón and López Obrador to characterize the coalitions as alliances of "espurios y legítimos" (fake ones and legitimate). By the end of 2010, the PAN and PRD each held five governorships on their own and three in coalition. "Elecciones 2010: Las alianzas PAN-PRD arrebataron tres estados," *Milenio,* December 27, 2010, online version; Horacio Jiménez, "Habrá nuevo mapa político para 2011," *El Universal,* December 30, 2010, online version.

35. Alonso Urrutía, "Dirigentes priístas reprochan a Calderón la conducción del país," *La Jornada,* September 17, 2010, online version.

36. "Diversas intervenciones en la ceremonia del centenario del inicio de la Revolución Mexicana y homenaje a Don Francisco I. Madero," accessed June 18, 2011, http://www.presidencia.gob.mx/2010/11/diversas-intervenciones-en-la-ceremonia-del-centenario-del-inicio-de-la-revolucion-mexicana-y-homenaje-a-don-francisco-i-madero/.

Chapter Six

1. "Mexico still feels tequila crisis hangover," *Financial Times,* December 19, 2004, 1.

2. Much of this debt was hidden as it was raised through dollar-denominated government bonds called *tesobonos* that were omitted from official budget figures. Julia Preston and Samuel Dillon, *Opening Mexico: The Making of a Democracy* (New York: Farrar, Straus and Giroux, 2004), 246–48.

3. Enrique Quintan, "Los errores de diciembre," *Reforma*, December 20, 1995, 24.

4. Pamela K. Starr, "Monetary Mismanagement and Inadvertent Democratization in Technocratic Mexico," *Studies in Comparative International Development* 33, no. 4 (Winter 1999): 40–44.

5. Ibid., 45–48.

6. Alicia Puyana and José Romero, *México: De la crisis de la deuda al estancamiento económica* (Mexico City: Colegio de México, 2009), 265.

7. Preston and Dillon, 250–53.

8. Artist Vicente Razo compiled a collection of the ubiquitous Salinas caricatures, many of which featured the ex-president as *chupacabras*, that was published as Vicente Razo, *The Official Museo Salinas Catalogue* (Santa Monica, CA: Smart Art Press, 2002).

9. Preston and Dillon, *Opening Mexico*, 253.

10. Elías Chávez, "López Portillo juzga," *Proceso* 960, March 27, 1995, online version.

11. Carlos García Calderón and Leonardo Figueiras Tapia, *Medios de comunicación y campañas electorales, 1988–2000* (Mexico City: Plaza y Valdés, 2006), 178.

12. Guadalupe Irizar, "La democracia es una inversion," *Reforma*, November 21, 1996, 1.

13. Irizar, 1.

14. Blanca Gómez, *¿Y quién es? Historia de un hombre enigmático* (Mexico City: Planeta, 2005), 147; George Grayson, *Mesías mexicano: Biografía crítica de Andrés Manuel López Obrador* (Mexico City: Grijalbo, 2006), 117.

15. García Calderón and Figueiras Tapia, 188.

16. Leonardo Curzio, *Gobernabilidad, democracia y videopolítica en Tabasco, 1994–1999* (Mexico City: Plaza y Valdés, 2000), 83.

17. The PRI further lost six local elections to the PAN (Jalisco, Baja California, Guanajuato, Nuevo León, Querétaro, and Aguascalientes) and four to the PRD (Mexico City/DF, Zacatecas, Tlaxcala, and Baja California Sur) during 1997. In addition to the PRD's gains, the PAN also spectacularly increased its territorial representation. Ibid., 68.

18. The PRD estimated that around three hundred party members were killed for their political affiliation during the Salinas administration. Adriana Borjas Benavente, *Partido de la Revolución Democrática: Estructura, organización interna y desempeño público, 1989–2003* (Mexico City: Gernika, 2003), 523.

19. Chappell H. Lawson, *Building the Fourth Estate: Democratization and the Rise of a Free Press in Mexico* (Berkeley: University of California, 2002), 61–92.

20. Juan Enrique Huerta-Wong and Rodrigo Gómez García, "Concentración y diversidad de los medios de comunicación y las

telecomunicaciones en México," *Comunicación y Sociedad* 19 (January–June, 2013): 123.

21.   García Calderón and Figueiras Tapia, 194–95.

22.   Anthropologist Lynn Stephen also argued that the NGOs of the 1990s provided spaces for a freer exchange of political ideas. For example, self-defined feminists in gender-focused NGOs came into direct contact with women across a wide range of social movements, such as rural and indigenous women. Such a shift in policy formulation and in political discourse toward individual human rights as central to modern liberal democracy also helped reinvigorate the gay and lesbian movement during the second half of the 1990s. Rafael de la Dehesa, *Queering the Public Sphere in Mexico and Brazil: Sexual Rights Movements in Emerging Democracies* (Durham, NC: Duke University Press, 2010), 3–20; Jordi Diez, "La trayectoria política del movimiento Lésbico-Gay en México," *Estudios Sociológicos* 29, no. 86 (May–August 2011): 704–7; Jordi Diez, "Explaining Policy Outcomes: The Adoption of Same-Sex Unions in Buenos Aires and Mexico City," *Comparative Political Studies* 46, no. 2 (February 2013): 222; María Luisa Tarrés, "The Role of Women's Nongovernmental Organizations in Mexican Public Life," in *Women's Participation in Mexican Political Life*, ed. Victoria E. Rodríguez (Boulder, CO: Westview Press, 1998), 132–44; Lynn Stephen, "Rural Women's Grassroots Activism, 1980–2000," in *Sex in Revolution: Gender, Politics, and Power in Modern Mexico*, eds. Jocelyn Olcott, Mary Kay Vaughan, and Gabriela Cano (Durham, NC: Duke University Press, 2006), 253.

23.   Sonia E. Alvarez, "Advocating Feminism: The Latin American Feminist NGO 'Boom,'" *International Feminist Journal of Politics* 1, no. 2 (September 1999): 191–92; Elena Beltrán Pedreira, "Público y privado. (Sobre feministas y liberales: argumentos en un debate acerca de los límites de lo político)," *Debate Feminista* 9, no. 18 (October 1998): 14–32; De la Dehesa, 10–12.

24.   Miguel Ángel Centeno, *Democracy Within Reason: Technocratic Revolution in Mexico* (University Park: Pennsylvania State University Press, 1999), 20.

25.   Bertha Lerner de Shiebaum, "1983: La ruptura frente al populismo, el compromiso con la austeridad y la renovación moral," *Revista Mexicana de Sociología* 45, no. 2 (April–June 1983): 573–74; Kurt Weyland, "Clarifying a Contested Concept: Populism in the Study of Latin American Politics," *Comparative Politics* 34, no. 1 (October 2001): 8.

26.   Starr, 37.

27.   García Calderón and Figueiras Tapia, 193.

28.   Juan Arvizu, "Emotiva arenga libertaria, en la noche del 'Grito,'" *El Universal*, September 17, 1995, 1, 22.

29.   Roberto Garduño, "'El chiste del Grito es no gritar mucho,' dice Zedillo a ellos que se sorprendieron por la brevedad," *La Jornada*, September 17, 1996, 1.

30. Samuel Brunk, *The Posthumous Career of Emiliano Zapata: Myth, Memory, and Mexico's Twentieth Century* (Austin: University of Texas Press, 2008), 239.

31. The general orientation and institutions such as the agrarian attorney general's office survived into the 2000s; however, it proceeded at a slower rate than was originally envisioned, with 77 percent of ejidos certified through PROCEDE by the end of 2001. The actual change in land-ownership patterns also did not dramatically change through much of Mexico. However, Jessa Lewis in her study of the Yaqui Valley of Sonora showed how some of the effects of longer-term neoliberal reforms did impact on land use in that region. According to Lewis, the immediate effect of the Salinas reform of Article 27 in this region was a huge jump in the percentage of ejidatarios renting out their land to commercial farmers—the majority by 1999—as a result of the difficulties they faced accessing credit following the retreat of state support mechanisms. Jessa Lewis, "Agrarian Change and Privatization of Ejido Land in Northern Mexico," *Journal of Agrarian Change* 2 no. 3 (July 2002): 402–20; Monique Nuijten, "Family Property and the Limits of Intervention: The Article 27 Reforms and the PROCEDE Programme in Mexico," *Development and Change* 34, no. 3 (June 2003): 491.

32. The PRD won the governorships of Tlaxcala with ex-Priísta Alfonso Sánchez Anaya as part of the Alianza Democrática coalition with three smaller parties and of Zacatecas with ex-mayor of the state capital and then member of Congress Ricardo Monreal in 1997. In 1998 the PRD won the governorship of Baja California Sur with ex-PRI mayor of the state capital La Paz Leonel Cota Montaño supported by a significant group that split with the PRI to support Cota Montaño. Borjas Benavente, 209–21.

33. García Calderón and Figueiras Tapia, 134–37; Raúl Ortego, "Aniversario luctuoso de Lázaro Cárdenas," *La Jornada*, May 22, 1996, 1.

34. Salvador Guerrero, "Obeso: la Iglesia católica, decidida a movilizar al país en forma pacífica," *La Jornada*, April 8, 1997, 1.

35. Ibid.

36. María Elena Medina, "Critican evangélicos al Gobierno," *Reforma*, March 22, 1995, 6.

37. Porfirio Miguel Hernández Cabrera, "La cobertura periodística de las marchas del orgullo lésbico, gay, bisexual y transgenérico de la Ciudad de México," paper prepared for Meeting of the Latin American Studies Association, Washington D.C. (September 6–8, 2001): 5–6; La Redacción, "Desmienten masones que acción de LGBTTTI agraviara a Juárez," *El Heraldo de San Luis Potosí*, July 8, 2014, online version; María Rivera, "Imperó el espíritu laico durante el segundo festival El Amor en los Tiempos del Cambio," *La Jornada*, February 15, 2002, online version.

38. Dirección de Comunicación Social, "A 150 años de la ley sobre libertad de cultos, aún estamos acechados por quienes añoran el poder perdido" (Gobierno de la Ciudad de México, Boletín 2417/10); Lucía Pérez, "Piden a obispo no hacer proselitismo," *El Siglo de Torreón*, April 4, 2014, online

version; Gabriela Romero Sánchez, "Cuestiona Ebrard que el clero aún busque influir en la tarea pública," *La Jornada*, September 27, 2009, 33.

39.   For example, in October 1996 the mayor of Monterrey changed the name of Constitution Boulevard to Antonio L. Rodríguez, a PAN federal deputy elected in 1946. José Gerardo Mejia, "Descalifica dirigencia 'rebautizo' de calles," *Reforma*, March 27, 1997, 2.

40.   Miguel Perez, 2.

41.   Javier Kuramura, "PRI y PAN se disputan las calles," *Reforma*, March 26, 4.

42.   David Carrizales, "Panistas en Nuevo León: cambios de nomenclatura y medidas morales," *La Jornada*, March 29, 1997, online version.

43.   Magdalena Robles, Jorge X. López, and Alejandro Caballero, "Defiende PAN a sus 'heroes,'" *Reforma*, March 27, 1997, 6.

44.   Krystyna von Henneberg, "Monuments, Public Space, and the Memory of Empire in Modern Italy," *History and Memory* 16, no. 1. (Spring 2004): 41.

45.   See J. Carlos González Faraco and Michael Murphy, "Street Names and Political Regimes in an Andalusian Town," *Ethnology* 36, no. 2 (Spring 1997): 123–48; Von Henneberg, 37–85.

46.   Gerardo Mejia, "Descalifica dirigencia," 2.

47.   Guadalupe Loaeza, "A Juárez," *El Norte*, April 6, 1997, 8.

48.   Robles et al., 6.

49.   José Gerardo Mejía and Daniela Pastrana, "Descarta PAN debate sobre Benito Juárez," *Reforma*, April 2, 1997, 6.

50.   Aguilar Tinajero specifically cited as evidence the work of Celerino Salmerón, a Mexican phalange leader and ex-columnist for *Business and Banks* magazine whose historical work was highly critical of Juárez, the Insurgentes, and the Revolution. Ibid.

51.   Miguel Angel Juárez, "Desacuerdo en San Lázaro," *Reforma*, April 2, 1997, 6.

52.   Patricia Sotelo, "Anuncian movilización," *Reforma*, April 2, 1997, 6.

53.   Daniel Lizarraga, "Arrementen contra el PAN; reivindica el PRI a Juárez," *Reforma*, April 5, 1997, 6.

54.   Daniel Millán and Alfredo Rodríguez, "Protestan priístas el agravio a héroes," *Reforma*, April 5, 1997, 7.

55.   Daniela Pastrana, "Rechaza Castillo afectar libertades," *Reforma*, April 5, 1997, 6.

56.   Ibid.

57.   David Vicenteno et al., "Vive la capital noche tranquila," *Reforma*, September 16, 1996, 1.

58.   In a reaction to criticisms of the PAN governor of Jalisco's banning of the use by government secretaries of miniskirts, Manuel Arciniega Portilla

proposed a PAN miniskirt pageant for members and supporters of the party. Miguel Ángel Juárez, "Ensenará PAN 'chamorros,'" *Reforma*, January 24, 1997, 2.

59. Alejandro Caballero, "Pide Castillo juzgar a AN por sus exitos," *Reforma*, April 9, 1997, 5.

60. See Alejandro Brito, "Auge y (relativa) caída de la intolerancia crónica del PAN en el poder," *Debate Feminista* 6, no. 12 (October 1995): 321–36.

61. Alejandro Guidiño and Rosa Icela Rodríguez, "Convoca López Obrador lucho por mejores empleos y salarios," *La Jornada*, November 21, 1996, 1.

62. ' Alejandro Caballero, "Entrevista: Carlos Castillo Peraza, 'Mi lucha es contra el PRD,'" *Reforma*, April 8, 1997, 5; Daniela Pastrana, "Cuestiona PAN fortunas de Cárdenas y Del Mazo," *Reforma*, April 7, 1997, 1.

63. Caballero, 5.

64. Carlos Antonio Gutiérrez, "Pruebas en Aguascalientes," *La Jornada*, March 26, 1997, online version.

65. González Faraco and Murphy, 125–26.

66. García Calderón and Figueiras Tapia, 169.

67. In 1999 the internal contest between the candidate clearly identified with Zedillo, Francisco Labastida, and Tabasco governor Roberto Madrazo, supported by traditionalist sectors of the party, soon turned bitter. Madrazo's supporters complained of unequal treatment in the media and presidential interference in favor of Labastida, clouding attempts to brand the party as, according to its 2000 election slogan, "the New PRI." Also competing for the nomination was PRI traditionalist Manuel Bartlett. García Calderón and Figueiras Tapia, 215–23.

68. Ibid., 222.

69. Ibid., 214.

70. This became particularly acute following the murder of television host Francisco "Paco" Stanley in June 1999 when leaving a Mexico City restaurant just after midday, which led to a prolonged public war between the Cárdenas government and one of Mexico's two main television networks, TV Azteca, which implicated Cárdenas as responsible for Mexico City's rising crime rate. See Angélica Cuéllar Vázquez, *Análisis sociológico del caso Stanley: La construcción social de las verdades jurídicas* (Mexico City: UNAM, 2004).

71. García Calderón and Figueiras Tapia, 192.

72. Ibid.

73. An example of this construction of the Fox persona were comments made by the then-candidate to a *New York Times* reporter: "Fox is an outsider. He's a citizen worried about his country who gave up his business life to work for change. Very few Mexicans believed you could beat the PRI.

They needed to see an aggressive guy, a rough guy with boots and his sleeves rolled up who wouldn't shrink from a fight from social justice. . . . Really, I'm not that tough guy; I'm human and emotional. But I'm building up that image." Preston and Dillon, 491–92.

74.   Guadalupe Irizar, "Castigan a PRI y PAN con $17 mil," *Reforma*, November 25, 1999, 8.

75.   Eduardo Ruiz-Healy, *En voz de Vicente: Entrevistas a Fox* (Mexico City: Oxford University Press, 2000), 117.

76.   Ibid., 84–85.

77.   García Calderón and Figueiras Tapia, 200.

78.   Ibid., 207.

79.   Sergio Aguayo Quezada, Javier Treviño Rangel, and María Pallais, "Neither Truth nor Justice: Mexico's De Facto Amnesty," *Latin American Perspectives* 33, no. 2 (March 2006): 58.

80.   "Entrevista Vicente Fox: 'Pactaría con Marcos en quince minutos,'" *El Norte*, February 27, 2000, 8.

81.   García Calderón and Figueiras Tapia, 207.

82.   Ibid., 244.

83.   Vicente Fox, "Mensaje de Toma de Posesión," accessed October 2, 2011, http://fox.presidencia.gob.mx/actividades/discursos/?contenido=4.

84.   Ibid.

85.   Roberto Gutiérrez y Alejandro Moreno, "Encuesta: Más guadalu-panos que juaristas," *Reforma*, February 5, 2001, 6.

86.   José Antonio Román, "Oró el guanajuatense ante la imagen de la tilma de Juan Diego," *La Jornada*, December 2, 2000, 2.

87.   Judith Amador, Alvaro Delgado, and Rodolfo Montes, "Quitan Juárez de Los Pinos," *El Norte*, December 17, 2000, 20.

88.   Jesús Aranda and Alonso Urrutia, "Apela Fox 'a la buena fe de la política' para lograr una paz digna en Chiapas," *La Jornada*, March 22, 2001, online version; Ivan Rendon et al., "Reviven las pugnas liberales y la derecha," *Reforma*, March 22, 2001, 12.

89.   Raúl Llanos y Gabriela Romero, "Estado de bienestar en el DF, a partir del 2001: López Obrador," *La Jornada*, December 6, 2000, 1.

90.   See Aguayo Quezada et al., 56–68.

91.   Ileana Rodríguez, *Liberalism at Its Limits: Crime and Terror in the Latin American Cultural Text* (Pittsburgh, PA: University of Pittsburgh Press, 2009), 153–54.

92.   José Luis Ruiz y Liliana Alcántara, "Fox: aclarados, los feminicid-ios; refuta CNDH," *El Universal*, May 31, 2005, online version.

93.   Clara Jusidman, "Desigualdad y política social en México," *Nueva Sociedad* 220 (March–April 2009): 194–95; José Woldenberg, "Jóvenes, tra-bajo, sindicatos," *Reforma*, August 18, 2011, 14.

94. Alejandra Lajous, *AMLO: Entre el temor y la atracción. Una crónica del 2003 al 2005* (Mexico City: Oceano, 2006), 55.

95. The legal foundation of the case involved the expropriation of private land, known as El Encino, by the Mexico City government and the construction of an access road to a hospital in violation of a court order. According to the federal attorney general's case, the owner of the property had received a court injunction to halt work on the road in March 2001. However, it was claimed that the government had continued work after this date, a crime for which there was no corresponding punishment. There was, however, a corresponding legal penalty for the crime of "abuse of authority" and this was the charge presented against López Obrador by the Attorney General. Lajous, 225–26; Alejandro Trelles and Héctor Zagal, *AMLO: Historia política y personal del Jefe de Gobierno del D.F.* (Mexico City: Plaza Janés, 2004), 168–69.

96. Renato Davalos and Andrea Becerril, "Fox actuó con dolo para degradar las instituciones, acusa López Obrador," *La Jornada*, April 8, 2005, online version.

97. On April 20 the Attorney General's department announced that two "citizens" had paid López Obrador's bail despite his insistence against posting bail. It was soon revealed that these citizens were PAN deputies from the Mexico City legislature who claimed they had previously discussed the course of action with ex-party president and eventual 2006 presidential candidate Felipe Calderón. Two days later the judge at the Reclusorio Oriente jail returned the case to the public ministry due to irregularities over this bail posting. Lajous, 237–42.

98. Rosa Elvira Vargas, "'Renuncia' Macedo; revisión total al expediente de López Obrador: Fox," *La Jornada*, April 28, 2005, online version.

99. A poll published in the *Reforma* newspaper in May 2004 found that 70 percent of people surveyed in Mexico City and 65 percent nationally classified the *desafuero* as "a political maneuver" while only 22 percent and 19 percent respectively classified it as "a strictly legal measure." "Ven maniobra política mediante acción apegada a la ley," *Reforma*, May 20, 2004, online version.

100. Alejandro Torres, "Festejo sin sello popular," *El Universal*, July 3, 2005, online version.

101. Victor Fuentes, "Suman a la Historia 'revolución' del 2000," *Reforma*, April 14, 2005, 1.

102. Israel Rodríguez and Rosa Elvira Vargas, "Pemex ofrece proyecto alternativo a sus socios en la construcción de Fénix," *La Jornada*, September 7, 2005, online version.

103. Vicente Fox, "Ceremonia conmemorativa del LXIII Aniversario de la Expropiación Petrolera," accessed February 26, 2013, http://fox.presidencia.gob.mx/actividades/?contenido=730; Vicente Fox, "Ceremonia conmemorativa del LXVIII Aniversario de la Expropiación Petrolera," accessed February 26, 2013, http://fox.presidencia.gob.mx/

actividades/?contenido=24083; Vicente Fox, "Ceremonia conmemorativa del 67 Aniversario de la Expropiación Petrolera," accessed February 26, 2013, http://fox.presidencia.gob.mx/actividades/?contenido=17294.

104. Felipe Calderón, "Mensaje a la Nación del Presidente Felipe Calderón con motivo de la iniciativa entregada al Senado de la República," accessed February 27, 2013, http://calderon.presidencia.gob.mx/2008/04/mensaje-a-la-nacion-del-presidente-felipe-calderon-con-motivo-de-la-iniciativa-entregada-al-senado-de-la-republica/.

105. Ibid.

106. Andrés Manuel López Obrador, *La gran tentación: El petróleo en México* (Mexico City: Random House Mondadori, 2008), 9–10.

107. PRD Distrito Federal, *Julio 27: La Consulta Va* (pamphlet).

108. *Letras Libres* 10, no. 117 (September 2008).

109. Thelma Gómez Durán, "Nacionalismo recobra bríos por debate petrolero," *El Universal*, June 8, 2008, A14–15.

110. Nurit Martínez, "Expropiación se adueña de libros de texto," *El Universal*, June 8, 2008, A14.

111. Leticia Robles de la Rosa, "Lo que el PRI decía en 2008; estatuto atajó privatización," *Excélsior*, August 8, 2013, online version.

112. Xóchitl Álvarez, "Califica Fox de 'pírrica y pequeña' la reforma energética," *El Universal*, October 27, 1998, online version.

113. Jorge Buendía y Javier Márquez, "Ciudadanía está indecisa sobre la reforma a Pemex," *El Universal*, May 12, 2008, online version.

114. Lomnitz, *Deep Mexico, Silent Mexico*, 120.

115. J. Jaime Hernández, "'Agotado, el modelo económico y social,'" *El Universal*, June 20, 2012, 2.

116. Érika Hernández, "El rol de Michoacán," *Reforma*, June 26, 2012, 9; Andrés Manuel López Obrador, "En Ciudad Juárez, Chihuahua, iniciará la restauración de la República, manifiesta López Obrador," accessed June 21, 2012, http://lopezobrador.org.mx/2012/06/20/en-ciudad-juarez-chihuahua-iniciara-la-restauracion-de-la-republica-manifiesta-lopez-obrador/.

117. Horacio Jiménez, "'Invitaré a Molina a gabinete,'" *El Universal*, June 20, 2012, A5.

118. La Redacción, "Al estilo Atlacomulco," *Proceso* 1662, August 7, 2008, online version.

119. Carlos Puig, "Enrique Peña Nieto: La lógica pragmática," *Letras Libres* 163 (June 2012): 17.

120. Diana Guillén, "Mexican Spring? #YoSoy132, the Emergence of an Unexpected Collective Actor in the National Political Arena," *Social Movement Studies* 12, no. 4 (2013): 473–74.

121. On May 11 during an appearance in front of students at Mexico

City's Iberoamericana University, students taunted the PRI candidate for violence against protestors in San Salvador Atenco while he was governor of the State of Mexico. Peña Nieto was then prevented from leaving the university by chanting students and footage emerged on the Internet showing the candidate apparently cornered in a small room at the university surrounded by security agents and appearing agitated. In an attempt to limit the damage of this spectacle to Peña Nieto's image, spokespeople for the campaign claimed the protesters were not real students but PRD supporters. Following the statements of the Peña Nieto campaign official, 131 students posted videos on the website YouTube in which they verified their identity as Iberoamericana students by displaying their student identification cards. "131 alumnos de la Ibero responden," accessed March 2, 2013, http://www.youtube.com/ watch?v=P7XbocXsFkI.

122. Jo Tuckman, "Computer Files Link TV Dirty Tricks to Favourite for Mexico Presidency," *Guardian*, June 7, 2012, online version.

123. Redacción, "PAN: 'Fox es un miserable, miope, cínico, torpe, ingrato, rancio,'" *Reforma*, June 26, 2012, 6.

124. Electoral authorities ultimately ruled that there was insufficient evidence of vote buying or other electoral irregularities to invalidate the election. Leslie Gómez, "Ubica IFE fondeos a tarjetas de Monex," *Reforma*, August 23, 2013, 3; Josefina Quintero, "Compras de pánico en Soriana ante el temor de que el PRI cancelara tarjetas," *La Jornada*, July 3, 2012, 33.

125. Gustavo Castillo García, "PGR: Los 43 habrían sido ejecutados y calcinados," *La Jornada*, November 8, 2014, 2.

126. Alma E. Muñoz and Georgina Saldierna, "Renuncia Cuauhtémoc Cárdenas al partido que fundó hace 25 años," *La Jornada*, November 26, 2014, 16.

127. Francisco Reséndez, "Pemex no se vende, sólo se moderniza, reitera Peña Nieto," *El Universal*, August 12, 2013, online version.

128. Emir Olivares, Fernando Camacho, and Alonso Urrutia, "El gobierno sabe dónde están los 43 normalistas," *La Jornada*, November 21, 2014, 2.

129. Emir Olivares, Patricia Muñoz, and César Arellano, "'Peña, tú no eres Ayotzinapa,' claman en multitudinaria marcha," *La Jornada*, December 2, 2014, 3; Alonso Urrutia, Carolina Gómez, Laura Poy, and Matilde Pérez, "'¡Fuera Peña!,' gritan miles cuando el padre de Alexander confirma la muerte del normalista," *La Jornada*, December 7, 2014, 7.

130. Jeffrey Rubin, "Popular Mobilization and the Myth of State Corporatism," in *Popular Movements and Political Change in Mexico*, eds. Joe Foweraker and Ann Craig (Boulder, CO: Lynne Rienner Publishers, 1990), 247–67.

131. Luis Mandoki (dir.), *Fraude: México 2006* (Mexico: Contra el Viento Films, 2007).

132. Roberto Hernández and Geoffrey Smith (dirs.), *Presunto culpable*

(Mexico: Abogados con Cámara, 2009); Héctor Rosas, "Ya es récord en la taquilla," *El Norte*, May 3, 2011, 15.

Conclusion

1.   Andrés T. Morales, "Rechazan poner el nombre de Fox a bulevar en Boca del Río," *La Jornada*, January 9, 2007, online version.

2.   Andrés T. Morales, "Derriban en Veracruz la estatua de Fox y le cortan la mano 'por rata,'" *La Jornada*, October 14, 2007, online version.

3.   Luis Antonio Rodríguez, "Comunidad gay en santo domingo realiza una caravana para exigir sus derechos," *ElRayaso.com*, July 4, 2011, accessed December 7, 2014, http://elrayaso.blogspot.com/2011/07/comunidad-gay-en-santo-domingo-realiza.html; "Lanzan polémica publicidad de campaña para elecciones a Senado con homosexuales," *El Espectador*, January 15, 2014, online version.

4.   Enrique Peña Nieto, "Mensaje a la Nación del Presidente de los Estados Unidos Mexicanos," accessed May 7, 2013, http://www.presidencia.gob.mx/articulos-prensa/mensaje-a-la-nacion-del-presidente-de-los-estados-unidos-mexicanos/.

5.   Yvon LeBot, *Subcomandante Marcos: El sueño Zapatista* (Barcelona: Plaza y Janés, 1997), 127–28.

6.   "Desaprueban proyecto ganador del Arco del Bicentenario," *El Economista*, April 22, 2009, online version.

7.   Felipe Calderón, "El Presidente Felipe Calderón durante de inauguración de la Estela de Luz," accessed February 2, 2012, http://www.presidencia.gob.mx/2012/01/el-presidente-felipe-calderon-durante-la-inauguracion-de-la-estela-de-luz/.

8.   Jorge Ricardo, "César Pérez Becerril: 'Engañaron al Presidente,'" *Reforma*, January 9, 2012, 68.

Primary Sources

Government Publications and Internet Archives

Cambio XXI. *El Liberalismo Social I*. Mexico City, Cambio XXI: 1992.

Coordinación de Comunicación del Programa de Solidaridad. *La Solidaridad en el Desarrollo Nacional*. Mexico City: SEDESOL, 1993.

De la Madrid Hurtado, Miguel. "Discurso de Toma de Posesión de Miguel de la Madrid Hurtado como Presidente Constitucional de los Estados Unidos Mexicanos." Accessed February 2, 2010. http://www. biblioteca.tv/artman2/publish/1982_73/Discurso_de_Toma_de_ Posesi_n_de_Miguel_de_la_Madri_69.shtml.

———. *Informes Presidenciales*. Mexico City: Servicio de Documentación, Investigación y Análisis del Congreso de la Unión, 2006.

Flores Milán, Dalinda, ed. *La agenda del PRI en el México del siglo XXI: Bases para la plataforma electoral federal 2000*. Mexico City: Fundación Colosio, 1999.

López Portillo, José. *Informes Presidenciales*. Mexico City: Servicio de Documentación, Investigación y Análisis del Congreso de la Unión, 2006.

Presidencia de la República. Ernesto Zedillo Sexenio. http://zedillo. presidencia.gob.mx.

———. Felipe Calderón Sexenio. http://www.presidencia.gob.mx.

———. Vicente Fox Sexenio. http://fox.presidencia.gob.mx.

Salinas de Gortari, Carlos. "Discurso de Toma de Posesión de Carlos Salinas de Gortari como Presidente Constitucional de los Estados Unidos Mexicanos." Accessed August 3, 2010. http://cronica.diputados.gob. mx/DDebates/54/1er/Ord/19881201.html.

———. *Informes Presidenciales*. Mexico City: Servicio de Documentación, Investigación y Análisis del Congreso de la Unión, 2006.

Secretaría de Programación y Presupuesto. *La Constitución Política de los*

Estados Unidos Mexicanos al través de los regímenes revolucionarios, 1917–1990. Mexico City: SPP, 1990.

————. Plan Nacional de Desarrollo, 1983–1988. Mexico City: SPP, 1983.

Periodicals and Electronic News Sources

El Economista, Mexico City
El Espectador, Bogotá
Excélsior, Mexico City
Financial Times, London
Guardian, London
El Heraldo, San Luis Potosí
La Jornada, Mexico City
Letra S, Mexico City
Letras Libres, Mexico City
Milenio, Mexico City
Milenio Semenal, Mexico City
Negocios y Bancos, Mexico City
New York Times, New York
Nexos, Mexico City
El Norte, Monterrey
Proceso, Mexico City
El Rayaso.com, Santo Domingo
Siempre!, Mexico City
El Siglo, Torreón
El Universal, Mexico City
Unomásuno, Mexico City
Vuelta, Mexico City

Film and Television

Gómez, Leopoldo (producer). México: La historia de su democracia. Mexico: Televisa, 2004.

Hernández, Roberto, and Geoffrey Smith (directors). Presunto culpable. Mexico: Abogados con Cámara, 2009.

Mandoki, Luis (director). Fraude: México 2006. Mexico: Contra el Viento Films, 2007.

SEP and Canal 11 TV México. "La Lucha Democrática." Discutamos México, episode 30, aired April 30, 2010.

Books and Pamphlets

Consulta Mitofsky. *Los orgullos de los mexicanos: Encuesta nacional en viviendas.* April 2011.

EZLN. *EZLN: Documentos y comunicados.* 5 vols. Mexico City: Era, 2003.

Gamio, Manuel. *Forjando Patria: Pro-Nacionalismo.* Boulder, CO: University Press of Colorado, 2010.

Gilly, Adolfo, ed. *Cartas a Cuauhtémoc Cárdenas.* Mexico City: Era, 1989.

Hernández y Lazo, Begoña, ed. *Celebración del 20 de noviembre, 1910–1985.* Mexico City: INEHRM, 1985.

Krauze, Enrique. *Porfirio Díaz: Místico de la Autoridad.* Mexico City: Fondo de la Cultura Económica, 1987.

López Obrador, Andrés Manuel. *La gran tentación: El petroleo de México.* Mexico City: Grijalbo, 2008.

———. *La mafia nos robó la presidencia.* Mexico City: Grijalbo, 2007.

López Portillo, José, Demetrio Sodi, and Infante Fernando Díaz. *Quetzalcóatl.* Mexico City: Sahop, 1977.

Monsiváis, Carlos. *Días de Guardar.* Mexico City: Era, 1988.

———. *Entrada Libre: Cronicas de la sociedad que se organiza.* Mexico City: Era, 1987.

Muñoz Ledo, Porfirio. *La ruptura que viene: Crónica de una transición caótica.* Mexico City: Random House Mondadori, 2007.

Poniatowska, Elena. *Nada, nadie: Las voces del temblor.* Mexico City: Era, 1988.

———. *La Noche de Tlatelolco.* Mexico City: Era, 2007.

Ruiz-Healy, Eduardo. *En voz de Vicente: Entrevistas a Fox.* Mexico City: Oxford University Press, 2000.

Subcomandante Marcos. *Conversations with Durito: Stories of the Zapatistas and Neoliberalism.* Brooklyn, NY: Autonomedia, 2005.

———. *Shadows of Tender Fury: The Letters and Communiqués of Subcomandante Marcos and the Zapatista Army of National Liberation.* New York: Monthly Review Press, 1995.

———. *¡Ya Basta! Ten Years of the Zapatista Uprising.* Oakland, CA: AKA Press, 2004.

Vasconcelos, José. *La raza cósmica: Misión de la raza iberoamericana.* Madrid: Agencia Mundial de Librería, 1920.

Secondary Sources

Aguayo Quezada, Sergio. *1968: Los archivos de la violencia.* Mexico City: Grijalbo, 1998.

Aguayo Quezada, Sergio, Javier Treviño Rangel, and María Pallais. "Neither Truth nor Justice: Mexico's De Facto Amnesty." *Latin American Perspectives* 33, no. 2 (March 2006): 56–68.

Aguilar Camín, Héctor, and Lorenzo Meyer. *A la sombra de la Revolución Mexicana.* Mexico City: Cal y Arena, 1989.

Aitken, Rob, Nikki Craske, Gareth A. Jones, and David E. Stansfield, eds. *Dismantling the Mexican State.* London: Macmillan, 1996.

Alba Vega, Carlos, and Alberto Aziz Nassif, eds. *Desarrollo y política en la frontera norte.* Tlalpan: CIESAS, 2000

Allier Montaño, Eugenia. "Presentes-pasados del 68 mexicano. Una historización de las memorias públicas del movimiento estudiantil, 1968–2007." *Revista Mexicana de Sociología* 71, no. 2 (April–June 2009): 287–318.

Alvarado, Arturo, ed. *Electoral Patterns and Perspectives in Mexico.* La Jolla, CA: Center for U.S.-Mexico Studies, 1986.

Alvarez, Sonia E. "Advocating Feminism: The Latin American Feminist NGO 'Boom.'" *International Feminist Journal of Politics* 1, no. 2 (September 1999): 181–209.

Álvarez Carín, Raúl. *La estela de Tlatelolco: Una reconstrucción histórica del Movimiento Estudiantil.* Mexico City: Grijalbo, 1998.

Anaya, Martha. *1988: El año en que calló el sistema.* Mexico City: Debolsillo, 2009.

Anderson, Benedict. *Imagined Communities.* London: Verso, 2006.

Anderson, Rodney D. *Outcasts in their Own Land: Mexican Industrial Workers, 1960–1911.* DeKalb: Northern Illinois University Press, 1976.

Appendini, Kirsten. "La transformación de la vida económica del campo mexicano." In *El impacto social de las políticas de ajuste en el campo mexicano*, edited by Jean François Prud'Homme, 31–104. Mexico City: Plaza y Valdes, 1995,

Archer, Christon I., ed. *The Birth of Modern Mexico, 1780–1824.* Wilmington, DE: Scholarly Resources, 2003.

Arriola, Carlos. *Ensayos sobre el PAN.* Mexico City: Miguel Ángel Porrúa, 1994.

Arvide, Isabel. *Al final del túnel.* Mexico City: Editorial Leega, 1982.

Aziz Nassif, Alberto. *Chihuahua: Historia de una alternativa.* Mexico City: La Jornada Ediciones, 1994.

———. "Chihuahua y los límites de la democracia electoral." *Revista Mexicana de Sociología* 49, no. 4 (October–December 1987): 159–226.

Babb, Sarah. *Managing Mexico: Economists from Nationalism to Neoliberalism.* Princeton, NJ: Princeton University Press, 2004.

Barthes, Roland. *Mythologies.* London: Jonathan Cape, 1974.

Bartra, Roger. *Blood, Ink, and Culture: Miseries and Splendors of the Post-Mexican Condition.* Durham, NC: Duke University Press, 2002.

Basave Benitez, Agustin F. *Mexico mestizo: Análisis del nacionalismo mexicano en torno a la mestizofilia de Andrés Molina Enríquez.* Mexico City: Fondo de Cultura Económica, 1992.

Beer, Caroline. *Measuring the Impact of Popular Organization: The Frente Democrático Campesino in Chihuahua, Mexico.* Paper prepared for Meeting of the Latin American Studies Association, Guadalajara, Mexico, 1997, online version.

Beezley, William H. *Judas at the Jockey Club and Other Episodes of Porfirian Mexico.* Lincoln: University of Nebraska Press, 2004.

Beezley, William H., and David H. Lorey, eds. *¡Viva Mexico! ¡Viva la Independencia!: Celebrations of September 16.* Wilmington, DE: SR Books, 2001.

Beezley, William H., Cheryl E. Martin, and William E. French, eds. *Rituals of Rule, Rituals of Resistance: Public Celebrations and Popular Culture in Mexico.* Wilmington, DE: Scholarly Resources, 1994.

Bellinghausen, Hermann, and Hugo Hiriart, eds. *Pensar el 68.* Mexico City: Cal y Arena, 2008.

Beltrán Pedreira, Elena. "Público y privado. (Sobre feministas y liberales: Argumentos en un debate acerca de los límites de lo político)." *Debate Feminista* 9, no. 18 (October 1998): 14–32.

Benjamin, Thomas. *La Revolución: Mexico's Great Revolution as Memory, Myth, and History.* Austin: University of Texas Press, 2000.

———. "A Time of Reconquest: History, the Maya Revival, and the Zapatista Rebellion in Chiapas." *American Historical Review* 105, no. 2 (April 2000): 417–50.

Bennett, Vivienne. "Orígenes del Movimiento Urbano Popular Mexicano: Pensamiento político y organizaciones políticas clandestinas, 1960–1980." *Revista Mexicana de Sociología* 55, no. 3 (July–September 1993): 89–102.

Berner, Erhard, and Benedict Phillips. "Left to Their Own Devices? Community Self-Help between Alternative Development and Neoliberalism." *Community Development Journal* 40, no. 1 (January 2005): 17–29.

Bertranou, Julián F. "Programa Nacional de Solidaridad ¿un nuevo o un viejo modelo de política pública?" *Revista Mexicana de Sociología* 55, no. 3 (July–September 1993): 225–43.

Bonfil Batalla, Guillermo. *Mexico Profundo: Reclaiming a Civilization.* Austin: University of Texas Press, 1996.

Bordat, Elodie Marie. "Institutionalization and Change in Cultural Policy: CONACULTA and Cultural Policy in Mexico (1988–2006)." *International Journal of Cultural Policy* 19, no. 2 (March 2013): 222–48.

Borjas Benavente, Adriana. *Partido de la Revolución Democrática: Estructura, organización interna y desempeño público, 1989–2003.* Mexico City: Gernika, 2003.

Brito, Alejandro, "Auge y (relativa) caída de la intolerancia crónica del PAN en el poder." *Debate Feminista* 6, no. 12 (October 1995): 321–36.

Bruhn, Kathleen. "Antonio Gramsci and the Palabra Verdadera: The Political Discourse of Mexico's Guerrilla Forces." *Journal of Interamerican Studies and World Affairs* 41, no. 2 (Summer 1999): 29–55.

———. *Taking on Goliath: The Emergence of a New Left Party and the Struggle for Democracy in Mexico.* University Park: Pennsylvania State University Press, 1997.

Brunk, Samuel. *The Posthumous Career of Emiliano Zapata: Myth, Memory, and Mexico's Twentieth Century.* Austin: University of Texas Press, 2008.

———. "Remembering Emiliano Zapata: Three Moments in the Posthumous Career of the Martyr of Chinameca." *Hispanic American Historical Review* 78, no. 3 (August 1998): 457–90.

Camacho, Óscar, and Alejandro Almazán. *La victoria que no fue: López Obrador: Entre la guerra sucia y la soberbia.* Mexico City: Grijalbo, 2006.

Cameron, Maxwell, and Brian Tomlin. *The Making of NAFTA: How the Deal Was Done.* Ithaca, NY: Cornell University Press, 2000.

Camp, Roderic A. *Crossing Swords: Politics and Religion in Mexico.* New York: Oxford University Press, 1997.

———. *Mexico's Mandarins: Crafting a Power Elite for the Twenty-First Century.* Berkeley: University of California Press, 2002.

———, ed. *Mexico's Political Stability: The Next Five Years.* Boulder, CO: Westview Press, 1986.

Canudas Sandoval, Enrique. *Las venas de plata en la historia de México: Síntesis de historia económica siglo XIX.* Vol. 3. Villahermosa: Editorial Utopía, 2005.

Carey, Elaine. *Plaza of Sacrifices: Gender, Power, and Terror in 1968 Mexico.* Albuquerque: University of New Mexico Press, 2005.

Carr, Barry. *Marxism and Communism in Twentieth-Century Mexico.* Lincoln: University of Nebraska Press, 1992.

———. "Mexican Communism 1968–1981: Eurocommunism in the Americas?" *Journal of Latin American Studies* 17, no. 1 (May 1985): 201–28.

———. *El movimiento obrero y la política en México, 1910–1929.* Mexico City: SEP, 1976.

Carr, Barry, and Ricardo Anzaldúa Montoya, eds. *The Mexican Left, the Popular Movements, and the Politics of Austerity.* La Jolla, CA: Center for U.S.-Mexican Studies, 1986.

Castañeda, Jorge. *La casa por la ventana: México y América después de la Guerra Fría.* Mexico City: Cal y Arena, 1993.

Centeno, Miguel A. *Blood and Debt: War and the Nation-State in Latin America.* University Park: University of Pennsylvania Press, 2002.

———. *Democracy Within Reason: Technocratic Revolution in Mexico.* University Park: Pennsylvania State University Press, 1994.

Centeno, Miguel A., and Fernando López-Alves, eds. *The Other Mirror: Grand Theory Through the Lens of Latin America.* Princeton, NJ: Princeton University Press, 2001.

Chand, Vikram. *Mexico's Political Awakening.* Notre Dame, IN: University of Notre Dame Press, 2001.

Chávez, Daniel. "The Eagle and the Serpent on the Screen: The State as Spectacle in Mexican Cinema." *Latin American Research Review* 43, no. 3 (2010): 115–41.

Chorba, Carrie C. *Mexico from Mestizo to Multicultural: National Identity and Recent Representations of the Conquest.* Nashville, TN: Vanderbilt University Press, 2007.

Chust, Manuel, and Ivana Frasquet. "Orígenes federales del republicanismo en México, 1810–1824." *Mexican Studies/Estudios Mexicanos* 24, no. 2 (Summer 2008): 363–98.

Coerver, Don M. *Mexico: An Encyclopedia of Contemporary Culture.* Santa Barbara, CA: ABC-CLIO, 2004.

Cohen, Deborah. *Braceros: Migrant Citizens and Transnational Subjects in the Postwar United States and Mexico.* Chapel Hill: University of North Carolina Press, 2011.

Collier, Ruth Berins, and David Collier. *Shaping the Political Arenas: Critical Junctures, the Labor Movement, and Regime Dynamics in Latin America.* Notre Dame, IN: University of Notre Dame Press, 2002.

Connaughton, Brian F., ed. *Poder y legitimidad en México en el siglo XIX.* Mexico City: UAM-Iztapalapa, 2003.

Cook, Maria L. *Organizing Dissent: Unions, the State and the Democratic*

Teachers' Movement in Mexico. University Park: Pennsylvania State University Press, 1996.

Cook, Maria L., Kevin J. Middlebrook, and Juan Molinar Horcasitas, eds. *The Politics of Economic Restructuring: State-Society Relations and Regime Change in Mexico*. La Jolla, CA: Center for U.S.-Mexican Studies, 1994.

Cooney, Paul. "The Mexican Crisis and the Maquiladora Boom: A Paradox of Development or the Logic of Neoliberalism?" *Latin American Perspectives* 28, no. 3 (May 2001): 55–83.

Córdova, Arnaldo. "El PAN, partido gobernante." *Revista Mexicana de Sociología* 54, no. 3 (July–September 1992): 221–40.

Cornelius, Wayne A. *The Political Economy of Mexico under De la Madrid: The Crisis Deepens, 1985–1986*. La Jolla, CA: Center for U.S.-Mexican Studies, 1986.

Cornelius, Wayne A., Ann L. Craig, and Jonathan Fox. *Transforming State-Society Relations in Mexico: The National Solidarity Strategy*. La Jolla, CA: Center for U.S.-Mexican Studies, 1994.

Cornelius, Wayne A., Todd A. Eisenstadt, and Jane Hindley, eds. *Subnational Politics and Democratization in Mexico*. La Jolla, CA: Center for U.S.-Mexico Studies, 1999.

Cornelius, Wayne A., and David Myhre, eds. *The Transformation of Rural Mexico: Reforming the Ejido Sector*. La Jolla, CA: Center for U.S.-Mexican Studies, 1998.

Corona Gutiérrez, Ignacio. *Después de Tlatelolco: Las narrativas políticas en México (1976–1990)*. Guadalajara: Universidad de Guadalajara, 2001.

Corrigan, Phillip, and Derek Sayer. *The Great Arch: English State Formation as Cultural Revolution*. Oxford: Basic Blackwell, 1985.

Cosío Villegas, Daniel. *Historia Moderna de México*. 7 vols. Mexico City: Editorial Hermes, 1956–1972.

Costeloe, Michael. "The Junta Patriótica and the Celebration of Independence in Mexico City, 1825–1855." *Mexican Studies/Estudios Mexicanos* 13, no. 1 (Winter 1997): 21–53.

Crespo, José A. *Contra la historia oficial: Episodios de la vida nacional desde la Conquista hasta la Revolución*. Mexico City: Debate, 2009.

Cuéllar Vázquez, Angélica. *Análisis sociológico del caso Stanley: La construcción social de las verdades jurídicas*. Mexico City: UNAM, 2004.

———. *La noche es de ustedes, el amanecer es nuestro*. Mexico City: UNAM, 1993.

Curzio, Leonardo. *Gobernabilidad, democracia y videopolítica en Tabasco, 1994–1999*. Mexico City: Plaza y Valdés, 2000.

Davis, Charles L., and Horace A. Bartilow. "Cognitive Images and Support for International Economic Agreements with the United States Among Mexican Citizens." *Latin American Politics and Society* 49, no. 2 (Summer 2007): 123–48.

De la Dehesa, Rafael. *Queering the Public Sphere in Mexico and Brazil: Sexual Rights Movements in Emerging Democracies*. Durham, NC: Duke University Press, 2010.

De la Peña, Guillermo. "Social and Cultural Policies toward Indigenous Peoples: Perspectives from Latin America." *Annual Review of Anthropology* 34 (2005): 717–39.

Demmers, Jolle, Fernández Jilberto, and Barbara Hogenboom, eds. *Miraculous Metamorphoses: The Neoliberalization of Latin American Populism*. London: Zed Books, 2001.

Diez, Jordi. "Explaining Policy Outcomes: The Adoption of Same-Sex Unions in Buenos Aires and Mexico City." *Comparative Political Studies* 46, no. 2 (February 2013): 212–35.

———. "La trayectoria política del movimiento Lésbico-Gay en México." *Estudios Sociológicos* 29, no. 86 (May–August 2011): 687–712.

Dominguez, Jorge I., and James A. McCann. *Democratizing Mexico: Public Opinion and Electoral Choices*. Baltimore, MD: Johns Hopkins University Press, 1996.

Domínguez-Ruvalcaba, Héctor. "From Fags to Gays: Political Adaptations and Cultural Translations in the Mexican Gay Liberation Movement." In *Mexico Reading the United States*, edited by Linda Egan and Mary K. Long, 116–34. Nashville, TN: Vanderbilt University Press, 2009.

Dornbusch, Rudiger, and Sebastian Edwards, eds. *The Macroeconomics of Populism in Latin America*. Chicago, IL: University of Chicago Press, 1991.

Dresser, Denise. *Neopopulist Solutions to Neoliberal Problems: Mexico's National Solidarity Program*. San Diego, CA: Center for U.S.-Mexican Studies, 1991.

Duncan, Robert H. "Embracing a Suitable Past: Independence Celebrations under Mexico's Second Empire, 1864–6." *Journal of Latin American Studies* 30, no. 2 (May 1998): 249–77.

Eisenstadt, Todd A. *Courting Democracy in Mexico: Party Strategies and Electoral Institutions*. Cambridge: Cambridge University Press, 2004.

Esposito, Matthew. "The Politics of Death: State Funerals as Rites of

Reconciliation in Porfirian Mexico, 1876–1889." *Americas* 62, no. 1 (July 2005): 65–94.

Fernández, Claudia, and Andrew Paxman. *El Tigre: Emilio Azcárraga y su imperio Televisa*. Mexico City: Grijalbo, 2001.

Flores, Genoveva. *La seducción de Marcos a la prensa: Versiones sobre el levantamiento zapatista*. Mexico City: Miguel Ángel Porrúa, 2004.

Florescano, Enrique. *La bandera mexicana*. Mexico City: Taurus, 1998.

———. *Historia de las historias de la nación mexicana*. Mexico City: Taurus, 2002.

———. *Imágenes de la patria a través de los siglos*. Mexico City: Taurus, 2005.

Flores Lúa, Graciela, Luisa Paré, and Sergio Sarmiento Silva. *Las voces del campo: Movimiento campesino y política agrarian, 1976–1984*. Mexico City: Siglo XXI, 1988.

Flores Margadant, Guillermo. "Official Mexican Attitudes Toward the Indians: An Historical Essay." *Tulane Law Review* 54, no. 4 (June 1980): 964–86.

Fourcade-Gourinchas, Marion, and Sarah L. Babb. "The Rebirth of the Liberal Creed: Paths to Neoliberalism in Four Countries." *American Journal of Sociology* 108, no. 3 (November 2002): 533–79.

Foweraker, Joe, and Ann Craig, eds. *Popular Movements and Political Change in Mexico*. Boulder, CO: Lynne Rienner Publishers, 1990.

Frost, Elsa Cecilia, Michael C. Meyer, and Josefina Zoraida Vázquez, eds. *El trabajo y los trabajadores en la historia de México/Labor and Laborers through Mexican History*. Tucson and Mexico City: University of Arizona Press/Colegio de México, 1979.

Fuentes Morúa, Jorge. "De El Despertador Mexicano 1993 a Rebeldía 2003." *Casa del Tiempo* 1, no. 8 (June 2008): 8–15.

Fukuyama, Francis. *The End of History and the Last Man*. Toronto: Macmillan, 1992.

Gabbert, Wolfgang. *Becoming Maya: Ethnicity and Social Inequality in Yucatán Since 1500*. Tucson: University of Arizona Press, 2004.

García Calderón, Carlos, and Leonardo Figueiras Tapia. *Medios de comunicación y campañas electorales (1988–2000)*. Mexico City: Plaza y Valdés, 2006.

Garner, Paul. *Porfirio Díaz: Profiles in Power*. Oxon: Routledge, 2010.

Garrido, Luis J. *El Partido de la Revolución Institucionalizada: La formación del nuevo estado en México (1928–1945)*. Mexico City: Siglo XXI, 2005.

————. *La Ruptura: La Corriente Democrática del PRI*. Mexico City: Grijalbo, 1993.

Gellner, Ernest. *Nations and Nationalism*. 2nd ed. Malden: Blackwell, 2006.

Gilbert, Dennis. "Emiliano Zapata: Textbook Hero." *Mexican Studies/Estudios Mexicanos* 19, no. 1 (Winter 2003): 127–59.

————. "Rewriting History: Salinas, Zedillo, and the 1992 Textbook Controversy." *Mexican Studies/Estudios Mexicanos* 13, no. 2 (Summer 1997): 271–97.

Gilbreth, Chris, and Gerardo Otero. "Democratization in Mexico: The Zapatista Uprising and Civil Society." *Latin American Perspectives* 28, no. 4 (July 2001): 7–29.

Gillis, John R., ed. *Commemorations: The Politics of National Identity*. Princeton, NJ: Princeton University Press, 1994.

Gilly, Adolfo. *The Mexican Revolution*. New York: New Press, 2005.

Gómez, Blanca. *¿Y quién es? Historia de un hombre enigmático*. Mexico City: Planeta, 2005.

Gómez Tagle, Silvia. "El Partido Demócrata Mexicano y su presencia en la sociedad." *Revista Mexicana de Sociología* 46, no. 2 (April–June 1984): 75–110.

González, Michael. "Imagining Mexico in 1910: Visions of the *Patria* in the Centennial Celebration in Mexico City." *Journal of Latin American Studies* 39, no. 3 (July 2007): 495–533.

González de Alba, Luis. *Las mentiras de mis maestros*. Mexico City: Cal y Arena, 2002.

González de Bustamante, Celeste. "1968 Olympic Dreams and Tlatelolco Nightmares: Imagining and Imaging Modernity on Television." *Mexican Studies/Estudios Mexicanos* 26, no. 1 (Winter 2010): 1–30.

González Faraco, J. C., and Michael D. Murphy. "Street Names and Political Regimes in an Andalusian Town." *Ethnology* 36, no. 2 (Spring 1997): 123–48.

González Gómez, Francisco, and Marco Antonio González Gómez. *Del porfirismo al neoliberalismo*. Mexico City: Ediciones Quinto Sol, 2007.

González Marín, Silvia, ed. *La prensa partidista en las elecciones de 1988*. Mexico City: UNAM, 1992.

González Navarro, Moisés. *El pensamiento político de Lucas Alamán*. Mexico City: Fondo de Cultura Económica, 1952.

González Pedrero, Enrique. "Jesús Reyes Heroles: El político humanista." *Nueva Época* 59 (January 2009): 2–3.

Gorski, Philip S. *The Disciplinary Revolution: Calvinism and the Rise of the*

State in Early Modern Europe. Chicago, IL: University of Chicago Press, 2003.

Grammont, Hubert C., ed. *Neoliberalismo y organización social en el campo mexicano.* Mexico City: Plaza y Valdés, 2002.

Grammont, Hubert C., and Horacio Mackinlay. "Campesino and Indigenous Social Organizations Facing Democratic Transition in Mexico, 1938–2006." *Latin American Perspectives* 36, no. 4 (July 2009): 21–40.

Gramsci, Antonio. *Prison Notebooks.* 3 vols. New York: Columbia University Press, 1991.

Grayson, George. *Mesías mexicano: Biografía crítica de Andrés Manuel López Obrador.* Mexico City: Grijalbo, 2006.

Grinspun, Ricardo, and Maxwell Cameron, eds. *The Political Economy of the North American Free Trade Agreement.* New York: St. Martin's Press, 1993.

Guardino, Peter F. *Peasants, Politics, and the Formation of Mexico's National State: Guerrero, 1800–1857.* Stanford, CA: Stanford University Press, 1996.

Guevara Niebla, Gilberto. *1968: Largo camino a la democracia.* Mexico City: Cal y Arena, 2008.

———. *Democracia en la calle: Crónica del movimiento estudiantil mexicano.* Mexico City: Siglo XXI, 1988.

Guibernau, Montserrat, and John Hutchinson, eds. *History and National Destiny: Ethnosymbolism and Its Critics.* Oxford: Blackwell, 2004.

Guillén, Diana. "Mexican Spring? #YoSoy132, the Emergence of an Unexpected Collective Actor in the National Political Arena." *Social Movement Studies* 12, no. 4 (2013): 471–76.

Gutiérrez, Natividad. "La autonomía y la resolución de conflictos étnicos: Los Acuerdos de San Andrés Larráinzar." *Revista Nueva Antropología* 19, no. 63 (October 2003): 11–39.

———. "Indigenous Political Organizations and the Nation-State: Bolivia, Ecuador, Mexico." *Alternatives: Global, Local, Political* 35, no. 3 (July–September 2010): 259–68.

———. *Nationalist Myths and Ethnic Identities: Indigenous Intellectuals and the Mexican State.* Lincoln: University of Nebraska Press, 1999.

———. "What Indians Say about Mestizos: A Critical View of the Archetype of Mexican Nationalism." *Bulletin of Latin American Research* 17, no. 3 (September 1998): 285–301.

Gutman, Matthew. *The Romance of Democracy: Compliant Defiance in Contemporary Mexico.* Berkeley: University of California Press, 2002.

Haenn, Nora. "The Changing and Enduring Ejido: A State and Regional

Examination of Mexico's Land Tenure Counter-Reforms." *Land Use Policy* 23, no. 2 (April 2006): 136–46.

Hale, Charles, ed. *Justo Sierra: Un liberal del Porfiriato*. Mexico City: Fondo de Cultura Económica, 1997.

Hamilton, Nora, and Timothy F. Harding, eds. *Modern Mexico: State, Economy, and Social Conflict*. Beverly Hills, CA: Sage Publications, 1986.

Hamnett, Brian R. "Liberalism Divided: Regional Politics and the National Project During the Mexican Restored Republic, 1867–1876." *Hispanic American Historical Review* 76, no. 4 (November 1996): 659–89.

Harris, Christopher. "Remembering 1968 in Mexico: Elena Poniatowska's *La noche de Tlatelolco* as Documentary Narrative." *Bulletin of Latin American Research* 24, no. 4 (2005): 481–95.

Harris, Richard L., and Melinda J. Seid, eds. *Critical Perspectives on Globalization and Neoliberalism in the Developing Countries*. Leiden: Brill, 2000.

Harvey, David. *A Brief History of Neoliberalism*. Oxford: Oxford University Press, 2005.

———. "Neoliberalism as Creative Destruction." *Annals of the American Academy of Political and Social Science* 610 (March 2007): 22–44.

Harvey, Neil. *The Chiapas Rebellion: The Struggle for Land and Democracy*. Durham, NC: Duke University Press, 1999.

———, ed. *Mexico: Dilemmas of Transition*. London: British Academic Press, 1993.

Hayes, Joy E. *Radio Nation: Communication, Popular Culture and Nationalism in Mexico, 1920–1950*. Tucson: University of Arizona Press, 2000.

Hellman, Judith A. "Mexican Popular Movements, Clientelism, and the Process of Democratization." *Latin American Perspectives* 21, no. 2 (Spring 1994): 124–42.

———. *Mexico in Crisis*. 2nd ed. New York: Holmes & Meier, 1988.

Henderson, Timothy. *The Worm in the Wheat: Rosalie Evans and the Agrarian Struggle in the Puebla-Tlaxcala Valley of Mexico, 1906–1927*. Durham, NC: Duke University Press, 1998.

Hernández Cabrera, Porfirio Miguel. *La cobertura periodística de las marchas del orgullo lésbico, gay, bisexual y transgenérico de la Ciudad de México*. Paper prepared for Meeting of the Latin American Studies Association, Washington, DC, September 6–8, 2001.

Hernández Rodríguez, Rogelio. "Inestabilidad política y presidencialismo en

México." *Mexican Studies/Estudios Mexicanos* 10, no. 1 (Winter 1994): 187–216.

Hobsbawm, Eric. "Nationalism and National Identity in Latin America." In *Pour une histoire économique et sociale internationale: mélanges offerts a Paul Bairoch*, edited by Bouda Etemad, Jean Baton, and Thomas David, 313–23. Geneva: Editions Passé Présent, 1995.

———. *Nations and Nationalism Since 1780: Programme, Myth, Reality.* Cambridge: Cambridge University Press, 1992.

Hobsbawm, Eric, and Terence Ranger, eds. *The Invention of Tradition.* Cambridge: Cambridge University Press, 2003.

Hodges, Donald, and Ross Gandy. *Mexico Under Siege: Popular Resistance to Presidential Despotism.* London: Zed Books, 2002.

Holloway, John, and Eloina Peláez, eds. *Zapatista! Reinventing Revolution in Mexico.* Sterling, VA: Pluto Press, 1998.

Holzner, Claudio. *Poverty of Democracy: The Institutional Roots of Political Participation in Mexico.* Pittsburgh, PA: University of Pittsburgh Press, 2010.

Horkheimer, Max, and Theodor Adorno. *Dialectic of Enlightenment.* London: Allen Lane, 1972.

Huerta-Wong, Juan Enrique, and Rodrigo Gómez García. "Concentración y diversidad de los medios de comunicación y las telecomunicaciones en México." *Comunicación y Sociedad* 19 (January–June, 2013): 113–51.

Huntington, Samuel P. *The Third Wave: Democratization in the Late Twentieth Century.* Norman: University of Oklahoma Press, 1991.

Imaz Bayona, Cecilia. *La nación mexicana transfronteras: Impactos sociopolíticos en México de la emigración a Estados Unidos.* Mexico City: UNAM, 2008.

Itzigsohn, José, and Matthias Vom Hau. "Unfinished Imagined Communities: States, Social Movements, and Nationalism in Latin America." *Theory and Society* 35, no. 2 (April 2006): 193–212.

Jardón, Raúl. *1968: El fuego de la esperanza.* Mexico City: Siglo XXI, 1998.

Jessep, Bob. "Liberalism, Neoliberalism, and Urban Governance: A State-Theoretical Perspective." *Antipode* 34, no. 3 (December 2002): 452–72.

Johnston, Hank, and John A. Noakes, eds. *Frames of Protest: Social Movements and the Framing Perspective.* Oxford: Rowman & Littlefield, 2005.

Joseph, Gilbert M. *Revolution from Without: Yucatán, Mexico, and the United States, 1880–1924.* Durham, NC: Duke University Press, 1988.

Joseph, Gilbert M., and Timothy J. Henderson, eds. *The Mexico Reader: History, Culture, Politics*. Durham, NC: Duke University Press, 2002.

Joseph, Gilbert M., and Daniel Nugent, eds. *Everyday Forms of State Formation: Revolution and the Negotiation of Rule in Modern Mexico*. Durham, NC: Duke University Press, 1994.

Jusidman, Clara. "Desigualdad y política social en México." *Nueva Sociedad* 220 (March–April 2009): 190–206.

Katz, Friedrich. *The Life and Times of Pancho Villa*. Stanford, CA: Stanford University Press, 1998.

Kaufman, Robert R., and Guillermo Trejo. "Regime Transformation and PRONASOL: The Politics of the National Solidarity Programme in Four Mexican States." *Journal of Latin American Studies* 29, no. 3 (October 1997): 717–45.

Kim, Kwanok. "Contradictory Aspects of Democratization and Neoliberal Economic Reform: The Philippines and Korea in Comparative Perspective." *Korea Observer* 32, no. 1 (April 2001): 137–61.

Klesner, Joseph L. "Electoral Competition and the New Party System in Mexico." *Latin American Politics and Society* 47, no. 2 (Summer 2005): 103–42.

———. "The Not-So-New Electoral Landscape in Mexico." Paper presented at Mexico's 2003 Mid-Term Election Results: The Implications for the LIX Legislature and Future Party Consolidation Conference, Institute of Latin American Studies, University of Texas at Austin, September 15–16, 2003.

Knight, Alan. "Cardenismo: Juggernaut or Jalopy?" *Journal of Latin American Studies* 26, no. 1 (February 1994): 73–107.

———. *The Mexican Revolution*. Cambridge: Cambridge University Press, 1990.

———. *Mexico: The Colonial Era*. Cambridge: Cambridge University Press, 2002.

———. "Peasants into Patriots: Thoughts on the Making of the Mexican Nation." *Mexican Studies/Estudios Mexicanos*, 10, no. 1 (Winter 1994): 135–61.

———. "The Peculiarities of Mexican History: Mexico Compared to Latin America, 1821–1992." *Journal of Latin American Studies* 24, Quincentenary Supplement (1992): 99–144.

———. "Populism and Neo-Populism in Latin America, Especially Mexico." *Journal of Latin American Studies* 30, no. 2 (May 1998): 223–48.

———. "Revisionism and Revolution: Mexico Compared to England and France." *Past and Present* 134, no. 1 (February 1992): 159–99.

Krauze, Enrique. *Mexico, A Biography of Power: A History of Modern Mexico, 1810–1996.* New York: Harper Collins, 1998.

LaBotz, Dan. *Democracy in Mexico: Peasant Rebellion and Political Reform.* Boston, MA: South End Press, 1995.

———. *Mask of Democracy: Labor Suppression in Mexico Today.* Boston, MA: South End Press, 1992.

Lajous, Alejandra. *AMLO: Entre el temor y la atracción. Una crónica del 2003 al 2005.* Mexico City: Océano, 2006.

Larrosa, Manuel, and Leonardo Valdés, eds. *Elecciones y partidos políticos en México.* Mexico City: UAM-Iztapalapa, 1994.

Laso de la Vega, Jorge. *La Corriente Democrática: Hablan los protagonistas.* Mexico City: Editorial Posada, 1987.

Lawson, Chappell H. *Building the Fourth Estate: Democratization and the Rise of a Free Press in Mexico.* Berkeley: University of California Press, 2002.

LeBot, Yvon. *Subcomandante Marcos: El sueño Zapatista.* Barcelona: Plaza y Janés, 1997.

Lerner de Shiebaum, Bertha. "1983: La ruptura frente al populismo, el compromiso con la austeridad y la renovación moral." *Revista Mexicana de Sociología* 45, no. 2 (April–June 1983): 545–74.

Levy, Daniel C., and Kathleen Bruhn. *Mexico: The Struggle for Democratic Development.* Berkeley: University of California Press, 2006.

Lewis, Jessa. "Agrarian Change and Privatization of Ejido Land in Northern Mexico." *Journal of Agrarian Change* 2, no. 3 (July 2002): 401–19.

Lewis, Stephen E. *The Ambivalent Revolution: Forging State and Nation in Chiapas, 1910–1945.* Albuquerque: University of New Mexico Press, 2005.

Lijphart, Arend, ed. *The Writings of Theorists and Practitioners, Classical and Modern.* Boston, MA: Allyn and Bacon, 1971.

Loaeza, Soledad. *El Partido Acción Nacional: La larga marcha, 1939–1994. Oposición leal y partido de protesta.* Mexico City: Fondo de Cultura Económica, 1999.

Loewe, Ronald. *Maya or Mestizo? Nationalism, Modernity, and Its Discontents.* Ontario: University of Toronto Press, 2010.

Lomnitz, Claudio. "Bordering on Anthropology: The Dialectics of a National Tradition in Mexico." *Revue de Synthèse* 4, no. 3–4 (July–December 2000): 345–79.

———. *Deep Mexico, Silent Mexico: An Anthropology of Nationalism.* Minneapolis: University of Minnesota Press, 2001.

————. "An Intellectual's Stock in the Factory of Mexico's Ruins." *American Journal of Sociology* 103, no. 4 (January 1998): 1052–65.

————. "Narrating the Neoliberal Moment: History, Journalism, Historicity." *Public Culture* 20, no. 1 (Winter 2008): 39–56.

López, Rick. *Crafting Mexico: Intellectuals, Artisans, and the State after the Revolution.* Durham, NC: Duke University Press, 2010.

López Leyva, Miguel Armando. *La encrucijada: Entre la protesta social y la participación electoral (1988).* Mexico City: Flacso, 2007.

Loveman, Mara. "The Modern State and the Primitive Accumulation of Symbolic Power." *American Journal of Sociology* 110, no. 6 (May 2005): 1651–83.

Lustig, Nora. *Mexico: The Remaking of an Economy.* Washington, DC: Brookings Institute, 1998.

Macías-González, Victor, and Anne Rubenstein. "Masculinity and History in Modern Mexico." In *Masculinity and Sexuality in Modern Mexico,* edited by Victor Macías-González and Anne Rubenstein, 1–21. Albuquerque: University of New Mexico Press.

MacLachlan, Colin, and William Beezley. *El Gran Pueblo: A History of Greater Mexico.* Upper Saddle River, NJ: Prentice Hall, 2004.

Mallon, Florencia. *Peasant and Nation: The Making of Postcolonial Mexico and Peru.* Berkeley: University of California Press, 1995.

María Alonso, Ana. "Conforming Disconformity: "Mestizaje, Hybridity, and the Aesthetics of Mexican Nationalism." *Cultural Anthropology* 19, no. 4 (November 2004): 459–90.

Martin, JoAnn. *Tepoztlán and the Transformation of the Mexican State: The Politics of Loose Connections.* Tucson: University of Arizona Press, 2005.

Marván Laborde, María. "La concepción del municipio en el Partido Acción Nacional." *Revista Mexicana de Sociología* 50, no. 2 (April–June 1988): 161–78.

Matthews, Michael. "Railway Culture and the Civilizing Mission in Mexico, 1876–1910." PhD Diss., University of Arizona, 2008.

Mattiace, Shannan L. "Regional Renegotiations of Space: Tojolabal Ethnic Identity in Las Margaritas, Chiapas." *Latin American Perspectives* 28, no. 2 (March 2001): 73–97.

Mattiace, Shannan L., Rosalva Aída Hernández, and Jan Rus, eds. *Tierra, libertad y autonomía: Impactos regionales del zapatismo en Chiapas.* Mexico City: Ciesas, 2002.

McDonald, James H. "Whose History? Whose Voice? Myth and Resistance in the Rise of the New Left in Mexico." *Cultural Anthropology* 8, no. 1 (February 1993): 96–116.

McNally, Mark, and John Schwarzmantle, eds. *Gramsci and Global Politics: Hegemony and Resistance*. Oxon: Routledge, 2009.

McNamara, Patrick. *Sons of the Sierra: Juárez, Díaz, and the People of Ixtlán, Oaxaca, 1855–1920*. Chapel Hill: University of North Carolina Press, 2007.

Meyer, Jean. *La cristiada*. Mexico City: Siglo XXI, 1974.

Meza Castillo, Miguel. *La Reforma del Sistema Financiero Rural*. Washington, DC: Woodrow Wilson International Center for Scholars, 2011.

Middlebrook, Kevin. *The Paradox of Revolution: Labor, the State, and Authoritarianism in Mexico*. Baltimore, MD: Johns Hopkins University Press, 1995.

Miller, Nicola. "The Historiography of Nationalism and National Identity in Latin America." *Nations and Nationalism* 12, no. 2 (April 2006): 201–21.

Miller, Toby, and George Yúdice. *Cultural Policy*. London: Sage, 2002.

Mirón, Rosa M., and Germán Pérez. *López Portillo: Auge y crisis de un sexenio*. Mexico City: Plaza y Valdés, 1988.

Monsiváis, Carlos. *Las herencias ocultas de la reforma liberal del siglo XIX*. Mexico City: Random House Mondadori, 2006.

———. "Ortodoxia y heterodoxia en las alcobas. Hacia una crónica de costumbres y creencias sexuales de México." *Debate Feminista* 6, no. 2 (April 1995): 183–210.

Monsiváis, Carlos, Marcelino García Barragán, and Julio Scherer García, *Parte de Guerra: Tlatelolco 68*. Mexico City: Aguilar, 1999.

Morales, Patricia, ed. *Pueblos indígenas, derechos humanos e interdependencia global*. Mexico City: Siglo Veintiuno, 2002.

Morris, Stephen. *Gringolandia: Mexican Identity and Perceptions of the United States*. Oxford: Rowman & Littlefield, 2005.

———. "Reforming the Nation: Mexican Nationalism in Context." *Journal of Latin American Studies* 31, no. 2 (May 1999): 363–97.

Morris, Stephen, and John Passé-Smith. "What a Difference a Crisis Makes: NAFTA, Mexico, and the United States." *Latin American Perspectives* 28, no. 3 (May 2001): 124–49.

Muñoz Ramírez, Gloria. *The Fire and the Word: A History of the Zapatista Movement*. San Francisco, CA: City Lights Books, 2008.

Niblo, Stephen R. *Mexico in the 1940s: Modernity, Politics, and Corruption*. Wilmington, DE: SR Press, 1999.

Nolan-Ferrell, Catherine. "Agrarian Reform and Revolutionary Justice in Soconusco, Chiapas: Campesinos and the Mexican State,

1934–1940." *Journal of Latin American Studies* 42, no. 3 (August 2010): 551–85.

Norget, Kristin. "The Politics of Liberation: The Popular Church, Indigenous Theology, and Grassroots Mobilization in Oaxaca, Mexico." *Latin American Perspectives* 24, no. 5 (September 1997): 96–127.

Nuijten, Monique. "Family Property and the Limits of Intervention: The Article 27 Reforms and the PROCEDE Programme in Mexico." *Development and Change* 34, no. 3 (June 2003): 475–97.

Ochoa, Enrique. *Feeding Mexico: The Political Uses of Food Since 1910.* Wilmington, DE: Scholarly Resources, 2000.

Olcott, Jocelyn. *Revolutionary Women in Postrevolutionary Mexico.* Durham, NC: Duke University Press, 2005.

Olcott, Jocelyn, Mary Kay Vaughan, and Gabriela Cano, eds. *Sex in Revolution: Gender, Politics, and Power in Modern Mexico.* Durham, NC: Duke University Press, 2006.

Olsen, Patrice Elizabeth. *Artifacts of Revolution: Architecture, Society, and Politics in Mexico City, 1920–1940.* Lanham, MD: Rowman & Littlefield, 2008.

O'Malley, Ilene V. *The Myth of the Revolution: Hero Cults and the Institutionalization of the Mexican State, 1920–1940.* Westport, CT: Greenwood Press, 1986.

Ordóñez Barba, Gerardo Manuel. "Programas de combate de la pobreza." In *Los retos de la política social en la frontera norte de México,* edited by Gerardo Manuel Ordóñez and Marcos Sergio Reyes Santos, 244–82. Tijuana: El Colegio de la Frontera Norte, 2006.

Otero, Gerardo, ed. *Mexico in Transition: Neoliberal Globalism, the State and Civil Society.* New York: Zed Books, 2004.

O'Toole, Gavin. "A New Nationalism for a New Era: The Political Ideology of Mexican Neoliberalism." *Bulletin of Latin American Research* 22, no. 3 (2003): 269–90.

Oxhorn, Philip D., and Graciela Ducatenzeiler, eds. *What Kind of Democracy? What Kind of Market? Latin America in the Age of Neoliberalism.* University Park: University of Pennsylvania Press, 1998.

Palacios, Joseph M. *The Catholic Social Imagination: Activism and the Just Society in Mexico and the United States.* Chicago, IL: University of Chicago Press, 2007.

Paoli Bolio, Francisco J. *Estado y sociedad en México, 1917–1984.* Mexico City: Océano, 1985.

Paz, Marie-José, Adolfo Castañón, and Danubio Torres Fierro, eds. *A treinta* años de Plural (1971–1976): Revista fundada y dirigida por Octavio Paz. Mexico City: Fondo de Cultura Economica, 2001.

Paz, Octavio. El ogro filantrópico: Historia y política, 1971–1978. Mexico City: Editorial Seix Barral, 1979.

Pérez Montfort, Ricardo. Avatares del nacionalismo. Mexico City: CIESAS, 2000.

Perramond, Eric P. "The Rise, Fall, and Reconfiguration of the Mexican Ejido." Geographical Review 98, no. 3 (April 2010): 356–71.

Pitawanakwat, Brock. "The Mirror of Dignity: Zapatista Communications and Indigenous Resistance." Masters thesis, University of Regina, 2002.

Plehwe, Dieter, Bernhard Walpen, and Gisela Neunhöffer, eds. Neoliberal Hegemony: A Global Critique. Oxon: Routledge, 2006.

Pollock, Graham. "Civil Society Theory and Euro-Nationalism." Studies in Social & Political Thought 4 (March 2001): 31–56.

Pozos, Laura B. "La formación y acciones promovidas por el Frente Democrático Campesino de Chihuahua, para mejorar las condiciones de vida y equidad." Revista Futuros 3, no. 1 (2003): online version.

Preston, Julia, and Samuel Dillon. Opening Mexico: The Making of a Democracy. New York: Farrar, Straus and Giroux, 2004.

Purnell, Jennie. "With All Due Respect: Popular Resistance to the Privatization of Communal Lands in Nineteenth-Century Michoacán." Latin American Research Review 34, no. 1 (1999): 85–121.

Puyana, Alicia, and José Romero. México: De la crisis de la deuda al estancamiento económica. Mexico City: Colegio de México, 2009.

Ramírez, Ramón. El movimiento estudiantil de México: Julio–Diciembre de 1968. Mexico City: Era, 1998.

Razo, Vicente. The Official Museo Salinas Catalogue. Santa Monica, CA: Smart Art Press, 2002.

Reveles Vázquez, Francisco. "Las fracciones del Partido Acción Nacional: Una interpretación." Revista Mexicana de Sociología 60, no. 3 (July–September 1998): 43–59.

———. El PAN en la oposición: Historia Básica. Mexico City: Gernika, 2003.

———, ed. Los Partidos Políticos en México: ¿Crisis, adaptación o transformación? Mexico City: Gernika, 2005.

Riding, Alan. Distant Neighbors: A Portrait of the Mexicans. New York: Vintage Books, 2000.

Roberts, Kenneth M. "Neoliberalism and the Transformation of Populism in

Latin America: The Peruvian Case." *World Politics* 48, no. 1 (October 1995): 82–116.

Rodríguez, Guadalupe, and Gabriel Torres. "Los agroproductores frente a las políticas neoliberales: El Barzón y COMAGRO." *Espiral* 1, no. 1 (September–December 1994): 129–76.

Rodríguez, Ileana. *Liberalism at Its Limits: Crime and Terror in the Latin American Cultural Text*. Pittsburgh, PA: University of Pittsburgh Press, 2009.

Rodríguez, Victoria E. "The Politics of Decentralisation in Mexico: From Municipio Libre to Solidaridad." *Bulletin of Latin American Research* 12, no. 2 (May 1993): 133–45.

———, ed. *Women's Participation in Mexican Political Life*. Boulder, CO: Westview Press, 1998.

Roett, Riordan, ed. *The Challenge of Institutional Reform in Mexico*. Boulder, CO: Lynn Rienner Publishers, 1995.

———. *México y los Estados Unidos: El manejo de la relación*. Mexico City: Siglo XXI, 1989.

Rojas, Alejandro. *Mitos de la historia mexicana: De Hidalgo a Zedillo*. Mexico City: Planeta, 2006.

Rojas Herrera, Juan J., and Eduardo Moyano Estrada. "Acción colectiva y representación de intereses en la agricultura Mexicana: El caso del sector ejidal." *Agricultura y Sociedad* 82 (January–April 1997): 45–78.

Rosales, Héctor, ed. *Cultura, sociedad civil y proyectos culturales en México*. Mexico City: Dirección General de Culturas Populares/Centro Regional de Investigaciones Multidisciplinarias, 1994.

Ross, Stanley, ed. *Is the Mexican Revolution Dead?* New York: Alfred Knopf, 1966.

Rubenstein, Anne. *Bad Language, Naked Ladies, and Other Threats to the Nation: A Political History of Comic Books in Mexico*. Durham, NC: Duke University Press, 1998.

Rubenstein, Anne, and Eric Zolov, eds. *Fragments of a Golden Age: The Politics of Culture in Mexico Since 1940*. Durham, NC: Duke University Press, 2001.

Rubin, Jeffrey W. "COCEI in Juchitán: Grassroots Radicalism and Regional History." *Journal of Latin American Studies* 26, no. 1 (February 1994): 109–36.

———. *Decentering the Regime: Ethnicity, Radicalism, and Democracy in Juchitán, Mexico*. Durham, NC: Duke University Press, 1997.

Ruonavaara, Hannu. "Moral Regulation: A Reformulation." *Sociological Theory* 15, no. 3 (November 1997): 277–93.

Saad-Filho, Alfredo, and Deborah Johnston, eds. *Neoliberalism: A Critical Reader*. London: Pluto Press, 2005.

Sachs, Jeffrey. *Social Conflict and Populist Policies in Latin America*. Cambridge: NBER Working Paper no. 2897, 1989.

Salinas de Gortari, Carlos. *El Reto*. Mexico City: Editorial Diana, 1988.

Samstad, James G. "Corporatism and Democratic Transition: State and Labor during the Salinas and Zedillo Administrations." *Latin American Politics and Society* 44, no. 4 (Winter 2002): 1–28.

Sánchez, Consuelo. *Los Pueblos Indígenas: Del indigenismo a la autonomía*. Mexico City: Siglo XXI, 1999.

Sánchez Prado, Ignacio M. "Claiming Liberalism: Enrique Krauze, *Vuelta*, *Letras Libres*, and the Reconfigurations of the Mexican Intellectual Class." *Mexican Studies/Estudios Mexicanos* 26, no. 1 (Winter 2010): 47–78.

Sarmiento Silva, Sergio. "El Consejo Nacional de Pueblos Indígenas y la política indigenista." *Revista Mexicana de Sociología* 47, no. 3 (July–September 1985): 197–215.

Schmitter, Philippe C., and Gerhard Lehmbruch, eds. *Trends Toward Corporatist Intermediation*. Beverly Hills, CA: Sage Publications, 1979.

Schneider, Ben R. "Why Is Mexican Business So Organized?" *Latin American Research Review* 37, no. 1 (2002): 77–118.

Semo, Enrique, ed. *México: Un pueblo en la historia*. Vol. 4. Mexico City: Editorial Nueva Imagen, 1982.

Serrano Migallón, Fernando. *El Grito de Independencia: Historia de una pasión nacional*. Mexico City: Miguel Ángel Porrúa, 1981.

Servín, Elisa, Leticia Reina, and John Tutino, eds. *Cycles of Conflict, Centuries of Change: Crisis, Reform and Revolution in Mexico*. Durham, NC: Duke University Press, 2007.

Sheppard, Randal. "Nationalism, Economic Crisis and 'Realistic Revolution' in 1980s Mexico." *Nations and Nationalism* 17, no. 2 (July 2011): 500–519.

Shirk, David. *Mexico's New Politics: The PAN and Democratic Change*. Boulder, CO: Lynne Rienner, 2005.

Shojai, Siamack, and Bernard Katz, eds. *The Oil Market in the 1980s: A Decade of Collapse*. New York: Praeger, 1992.

Sieder, Rachel, ed. *Multiculturalism in Latin America: Indigenous Rights, Diversity, and Democracy*. Houndmills: Palgrave Macmillan, 2002.

Smith, Anthony D. *Nationalism*. Cambridge: Polity Press, 2005.

Smith, Peter H. *Labyrinths of Power: Political Recruitment in Twentieth-Century Mexico.* Princeton, NJ: Princeton University Press, 1979.

Solares, Ignacio. *El gran elector.* Mexico City: Joaquín Mortiz, 1993.

Soler Durán, Alcira. *La crisis del Corporativismo en México: La CTM en 1987.* Cuernavaca: UNAM, 1993.

South, Robert B. "Transnational 'Maquiladora' Location." *Annals of the Association of American Geographers* 80, no. 4 (December 1990): 549–70.

Starr, Pamela K. "Monetary Mismanagement and Inadvertent Democratization in Technocratic Mexico." *Studies in Comparative International Development* 33, no. 4 (Winter 1999): 35–65.

———. "The Two "Politics of NAFTA" in Mexico." *Law and Business Review of the Americas* 16, no. 4 (Fall 2010): 839–54.

Stephen, Lynn. "Pro-Zapatista and Pro-PRI: Resolving the Contradictions of Zapatismo in Rural Oaxaca." *Latin American Research Review* 32, no. 2 (1997): 41–70.

———. *Zapata Lives! Histories and Cultural Politics in Southern Mexico.* Berkeley: University of California Press, 2002.

Stuadt, Kathleen, and Carlota Aguilar. "Political Parties, Women Activists' Agendas and Household Relations: Elections on Mexico's Northern Frontier." *Mexican Studies/Estudios Mexicanos* 8, no. 1 (Winter 1992): 87–106.

Tannenbaum, Frank. *The Mexican Agrarian Revolution.* New York: Macmillan, 1929.

———. *Peace by Revolution: Mexico after 1910.* New York: Columbia University Press, 1966.

Taylor-Gooby, Peter. *Reframing Social Citizenship.* Oxford: Oxford University Press, 2008.

Tenorio Trillo, Mauricio. "1910 Mexico City: Space and Nation in the City of the *Centenario.*" *Journal of Latin American Studies* 28, no. 1 (February 1996): 75–104.

———. "Essaying the History of National Images." In *After Spanish Rule: Postcolonial Predicaments of the Americas,* edited by Mark Thurner and Andrés Guerrero, 58–86. Durham, NC: Duke University Press, 2003.

———. *Mexico at the World's Fairs: Crafting a Modern Nation.* Berkeley: University of California Press, 1996.

Thompson, Guy P. C. "Bulwarks of Patriotic Liberalism: The National Guard, Philharmonic Corps and Patriotic Juntas in Mexico, 1847–88." *Journal of Latin American Studies* 22, no. 1–2 (March 1990): 31–68.

———. *Patriotism, Politics, and Popular Liberalism in Nineteenth-Century Mexico: Juan Francisco Lucas and the Puebla Sierra.* Wilmington, DE: Scholarly Resources, 1999.

———. "Popular Aspects of Liberalism in Mexico." *Bulletin of Latin American Research* 10, no. 3 (1991): 265–92.

Thurner, Mark. *From Two Republics to One Divided: Contradictions of Postcolonial Nationmaking in Andean Peru.* Durham, NC: Duke University Press, 1997.

Tirado, Ricardo, and Matilde Luna. "El Consejo Coordinador Empresarial de México: De la unidad contra el reformismo a la unidad para el TLC (1975–1993)." *Revista Mexicana de Sociología* 57, no. 4 (October–December 1995): 27–59.

Trejo Delarbre, Raúl. *Crónica del sindicalismo en México (1976–1988).* Mexico City: Siglo XXI, 1990.

Trelles, Alejandro, and Héctor Zagal. *AMLO: Historia política y personal del Jefe de Gobierno del D.F.* Mexico City: Plaza Janés, 2004.

Tutino, John. *From Insurrection to Revolution in Mexico: Social Bases of Agrarian Violence, 1750–1940.* Princeton, NJ: Princeton University Press, 1986.

Valdés Ugalde, Francisco. *Autonomía y Legitimidad: Los empresarios, la política y el estado en México.* Mexico City: Siglo XXI, 1997.

Valdéz, Juan G. *Pinochet's Economists: The Chicago School in Chile.* Cambridge: Cambridge University Press, 1995.

Van Young, Eric. *The Other Rebellion: Popular Violence, Ideology and the Mexican Struggle for Independence, 1810–1821.* Stanford, CA: Stanford University Press, 2001.

Vaughan, Mary K. *Cultural Politics in Revolution: Teachers, Peasants, and Schools in Mexico, 1930–1940.* Tucson: University of Arizona Press, 1997.

Vaughan, Mary K., and Stephen E. Lewis. *The Eagle and the Virgin: Nation and Cultural Revolution in Mexico, 1920–1940.* Durham, NC: Duke University Press, 2007.

Vázquez Castillo, María T. *Land Privatization in Mexico: Urbanization, Formation of Regions, and Globalization in Ejidos.* New York: Routledge, 2004.

Vom Hau, Matthias. "State Infrastructural Power and Nationalism: Comparative Lessons from Mexico and Argentina." *Studies in Comparative International Development* 43, no. 3–4 (December 2008): 334–54.

Von Henneberg, Krystyna. "Monuments, Public Space, and the Memory of

Empire in Modern Italy." *History and Memory* 16, no. 1 (Spring 2004): 37–85.

Warman, Arturo, Margarita Nolasco, Guillermo Bonfil, Mercedes Olivera, and Enrique Valencia. *De eso que llaman antropología mexicana.* Mexico City: Editorial Nuestro Tiempo, 1970.

Wasserman, Mark. *Persistent Oligarchs: Elites and Politics in Chihuahua, Mexico, 1910–1940.* Durham, NC: Duke University Press, 1993.

———. "You Can Teach an Old Revolutionary History New Tricks: Regions, Popular Movements, Culture, and Gender in Mexico, 1820–1940." *Latin American Research Review* 43, no. 2 (2008): 260–71.

Weber, Devra. "Historical Perspectives on Transnational Mexican Workers in California." In *Border Crossings: Mexican and Mexican-American Workers,* edited by John Mason Hart, 209–33. Wilmington, DE: Scholarly Resources, 1998.

Weeks, Charles A. *The Juárez Myth in Mexico.* Tuscaloosa: University of Alabama Press, 1987.

Weiner, Richard. *Race, Nation, and Market: Economic Culture in Porfirian Mexico.* Tucson: University of Arizona Press, 2004.

Wells, Allen. "Oaxatepec Revisited: The Politics of Mexican Historiography, 1968–1988." *Mexican Studies/Estudios Mexicanos* 7, no. 2 (Summer 1991): 331–45.

Weyland, Kurt. "Clarifying a Contested Concept: Populism in the Study of Latin American Politics." *Comparative Politics* 34, no. 1 (October 2001): 1–22.

———. "Neopopulism and Neoliberalism in Latin America: How Much Affinity?" *Third World Quarterly* 24, no. 6 (2003): 1095–115.

Wiarda, Howard J. "Toward a Framework for the Study of Political Change in the Iberic-Latin Tradition: The Corporative Model." *World Politics* 25, no. 2 (January 1973): 206–35.

Williams, Gareth. *The Mexican Exception: Sovereignty, Police, and Democracy.* New York: Palgrave Macmillan, 2011.

Williamson, Peter J. *Varieties of Corporatism: A Conceptual Discussion.* London: Cambridge University Press, 1985.

Womack, John. *Rebellion in Chiapas: An Historical Reader.* New York: New Press, 1999.

———. *Zapata and the Mexican Revolution.* London: Thames and Hudson, 1969.

Yashar, Deborah J. "Democracy, Indigenous Movements, and the Postliberal Challenge in Latin America." *World Politics* 52, no. 1 (October 1999): 76–104.

Young, James. "Memory and Counter-Memory: Toward a Social Aesthetics of Holocaust Memorials." In *The Holocaust's Ghost: Writings on Art, Politics, Law, and Education*, edited by F. C. DeCoste and Bernard Schwartz, 165–78. Edmonton: University of Alberta Press, 2000.

Zárate Toscano, Verónica. "El papel de la escultura conmemorativa en el proceso de construcción nacional y su reflejo en la ciudad de México en el siglo XIX." *Historia Mexicana* 53, no. 2 (October–December 2003): 417–46.

Zolov, Eric. *Refried Elvis: The Rise of the Mexican Counterculture.* Berkeley: University of California Press, 1999.

———. "Showcasing the Land of Tomorrow: Mexico and the 1968 Olympics." *Americas* 61, no. 2 (October 2004): 159–88.